To Elaine and James Hill,
with best wishes.
Harold Van Winkle

Bradenton, Florida, Oct 25, 1995

SPEAKING FREELY

Your Right of Free Speech and Its Legal Limitations

SPEAKING FREELY

Your Right of Free Speech and Its Legal Limitations

Harold Van Winkle

MANCORP PUBLISHING, INC.
Tampa, Florida

Library of Congress Cataloging-in-Publication Data

Van Winkle, Harold, 1906-
    Speaking freely : your right of free speech and its legal limitations / by Harold Van Winkle.
        p.   cm.
    Includes bibliographical references and index.
    ISBN 0-931541-20-4
    1. Freedom of speech--United States.   I. Title.
KF4772.Z9V3   1993
342.73'0853--dc20
[347.302853]   93-9602
                                                                   CIP

ISBN 0-931541-20-4

Acknowledgments

The author is grateful for reviews of all or portions of the manuscript of this book before publication, by:

The Honorable Durand J. Adams, Judge, Twelfth Judicial District of Florida.

Dr. Donna Dickerson, Chair, Department of Mass Communications, University of South Florida, Tampa, Florida.

Mark Goodman, Executive Director, Student Press Law Center, Washington D. C.

Dr. Alan Larson, Professor of Communication, Clarion University of Pennsylvania.

Dr. John P. Mellon, President Emeritus, Western State College of Colorado.

Professor Harold Norris, Detroit College of Law.

John E. Perry, General Manager, WKSU-FM Radio Station, Kent State University.

Dr. Jack Sandler, Consulting Editor, Mancorp Publishing, Inc., Tampa, Florida.

I am also indebted to the publisher, Dr. M. N. Manougian, President, Mancorp Publishing, Inc., for his meticulous review and suggestions.

CONTENTS

❀

PREFACE

❀

No form of speech is totally free. All are limited by social custom and by government. This book attempts to explain clearly and simply the legal limitations that restrict the major forms of communication in the United States. Such an attempt is admittedly audacious because, like the shifting sands of the desert, law is never static. New cases continue to be filed in the courts in astonishing variety, new judges occupy the bench as time goes by, and new laws are enacted while old ones are amended as legislators respond to changing needs and circumstances.

Legal limitations of speech and the press as expressed in the state and federal statutes and city ordinances are entirely too numerous to be listed here. Rather, since laws are what the courts say they are as applied to specific cases, the legal limitations to free speech as presented here are primarily in the form of court decisions in representative cases rather than as statutes.

The U.S. Constitution states in Article II, Section 1: "The judicial Power of the United States, shall be vested in one supreme Court, and in such inferior Courts as the Congress may from time to time ordain and establish," but it says nothing about the power of the Supreme Court to pronounce the final word on the constitutionality of laws. That power was established in the case of *Marbury v. Madison* in 1803 when the Court, with John Marshall as Chief Justice, ruled that Congress had exceeded its power in the enactment of the

Judiciary Act of 1801. He reasoned that when law and constitutional provisions conflict, judges must honor the Constitution. Seven years later in 1810 in the case of *Fletcher v. Peck* the Court assumed the power of voiding acts of state legislatures "by reason of their repugnance to the Federal Constitution."

Some observers contend that the courts, and the federal judiciary in particular, have assumed unwarranted power in prescribing remedies for social and economic problems that properly lie within the province of elective legislative bodies. Be that as it may, the higher courts have made and continue to make momentous decisions that affect the law and the life of the country.

In discussing laws and court cases as they impact on the right to free speech, this book contains nothing original. Everything in it has already been published, in books, magazines, newspapers, law volumes, and court proceedings. Rather, the information reviewed here has been selected from a wide variety of sources and presented in what the author hopes is a logical and readable manner for everyone interested in the rights and limits of free speech.

The aim is to present the major facets of freedom of speech and the legal limitations as they are, factually and without value judgments. What should be, what is desirable and/or undesirable, is left for the reader to decide.

Harold Van Winkle
Bradenton, Florida

CHAPTER

1

❉

FREE SPEECH ISN'T
TOTALLY FREE

CHAPTER ONE

FREE SPEECH ISN'T
TOTALLY FREE

❦

"I can say what I please, can't I?"
"It's a free country, isn't it?"

Those are good questions, but they cannot be answered *Yes* or *No*. Freedom is too complex for simple answers.

The right of free speech and a free press is guaranteed by the U.S. Constitution, as everybody knows. The statement is clear and brief.

First, it would be well to reread the entire First Amendment, which has been called the First Freedom:

■ Congress shall make no law respecting the establishment of religion, or prohibiting the free exercise thereof; or abridging the freedom of speech, or of the press; or the right of the people peaceably to assemble, and to petition the Government for a redress or grievances.

Next, let us examine this portion of the Amendment:

■ Congress shall make no law . . . abridging the freedom of speech, or of the press . . .

and then review that sentence with the emphasis on these two words, *no law*:

■ Congress shall make NO LAW. . .

When it is read that way, the sentence implies that no restrictions *of any kind* on speech or the press are permitted. In other words, anything goes.

Some people, including constitutional authorities, agree with that interpretation. Both Hugo L. Black, a justice of the U.S. Supreme Court for 34 years from 1937 to 1971, and Justice William O. Douglas, who served for 36 years from 1939 to 1975, argued that, where the Constitution says "no law," it means just that, *no law*.

Despite these opinions, freedom of speech and of the press in the United States stops when it injures or threatens to injure another person, persons, or society. Also, it is limited because no one freedom or right can be exercised to the exclusion of other freedoms and rights. Accordingly, legal limitations have been placed on speech and press that:

- ❑ Defame the character or reputation of another
- ❑ Are in contempt of court
- ❑ Invade privacy
- ❑ Assault or threaten someone
- ❑ Attempt to defraud
- ❑ Incite riots and disturb the peace
- ❑ Tend to corrupt morals with obscenity and pornography
- ❑ Infringe on copyright
- ❑ Advocate overthrow of the government by force, or endanger national security.

Laws on those subjects vary from state to state. Also, since no two court cases are alike, the law under which a trial is being conducted must be interpreted as it applies to the facts and circumstances of that particular case. It is therefore impossible to list rules that apply in all cases and in every jurisdiction.

It is government that places legal limitations on speech and provides penalties for going beyond those limits. Such laws essentially remind us that every freedom is accompanied

3

by a corresponding responsibility; that everyone is accountable for his speech and actions.

There are, of course, civil limitations to free speech, but these are not legal codes or enforced by government officials. A person can start a quarrel, lose a friend, or disrupt a social gathering by using unacceptable or offensive speech without breaking the law.

A disclaimer to the harmful impact of a spoken expression offers no protection either legally or socially. A person can say that he did not intend to offend anyone or break the law, but that does not absolve him of the consequences, whether he says it in advance or after the fact.

The press is the only industry and religion the only institution *guaranteed* immunity from government by the U.S. Constitution, and immunity as stated in the First Amendment places no limit on freedom of speech and the press and requires no responsibilities to accompany that freedom. In contrast, such guarantee in many of the state constitutions include a caveat. As an example, the constitution of Michigan reads:

■ Every person may freely speak, write, and publish his views on all subjects, being responsible for the abuse of such right; and no law shall be enacted to restrain or abridge the liberty of speech or of the press.

With no *prior* restraint by government, which the First Amendment has been interpreted to mean, publishers and broadcasters have often been accused and, at times, have been guilty of bias, distortion, sensationalism, poor taste, libel, and invasion of privacy — that is, of being irresponsible. In that regard, Alex de Tocqueville, nineteenth-century historian, once wrote:

■ In order to enjoy the inestimable benefits that liberty of the press insures, it is necessary to submit to the inevitable evils that it creates.

4

Being singled out for immunity from government could be interpreted to mean that freedom of the press is superior to other freedoms, but that would be incorrect. As Anthony Lewis, prize-winning journalist, has stated: "The idea that journalism has a different and superior status in the Constitution is not only an unconvincing but dangerous doctrine."

The fundamental purpose of the First Amendment, as has often been said, is to enlighten the people, enlightenment being necessary for participation in a democracy. The guarantee of freedom of speech and the press was thus granted, not as a boon to printers and publishers, but rather to the people, with the press an agency for enlightenment. Under such broad guarantee of freedom, the publication of unpopular ideas could be expected; but as has been frequently pointed out, unpopular ideas are the only kind that need First Amendment protection. And, as Michael Kinsley stated, "The expression of bad ideas is less dangerous than giving the government the power to sort out the good from the bad."[1]

Although the First Amendment is so frequently thought of as guaranteeing freedom of speech and the press, which it does, and most of this book is devoted to aspects of that freedom, the Amendment actually begins with the "separation of church and state." The first clause reads, "Congress shall make no law respecting the establishment of religion, or prohibiting the free exercise thereof."

The U.S. Supreme Court has handed down a number of decisions regarding the Establishment Clause of the First Amendment, some of which affect freedom of speech as it relates to public prayer. The most widely discussed of these decisions occurred in *Engel v. Vitale* in 1962 in which the Court ruled that state-prescribed prayer in public schools is unconstitutional.[2]

---

1. *Time*, February 22, 1988.
2. Steven I. Engel et al v. William J. Vitale Jr. et al, 82 S.Ct 1261, 370 U.S. 421 (June 25, 1962).

That case arose after the Board of Regents of New York, which has broad powers over the public schools, adopted a prayer for use in the schools. The prayer read:

■ Almighty God, we acknowledge our dependence upon Thee, and we beg Thy blessing upon us, our parents, our teachers, and our country.

The Board of Education of New Hyde Park ordered that the prayer be said aloud by every class at the beginning of every school day. The parents of ten pupils objected by filing suit in court to compel the Board of Education to discontinue the use of an official prayer in the public schools, which they contended was contrary to the beliefs, religions, or religious practices of themselves and their children.

Both the Supreme Court of New York and the Court of Appeals upheld the Board of Education, ruling that the order was permissible so long as no pupils were required to participate if saying the prayer was contrary to their beliefs or that of their parents. The U.S. Supreme Court, however, in an 8-to-1 decision reversed that ruling. Justice Hugo L. Black stated in the majority opinion that New York's program of daily classroom invocation of God's blessings as prescribed in prayer promulgated by its Board of Regents was a "religious activity," and use of the public school system to encourage recitation of such prayer was a practice wholly inconsistent with the Establishment Clause of the Constitution, though pupils were not required to participate over their or their parents' objection.

"The government should refrain from writing official prayers," the Court stated, adding that "that sort of activity should be left to the people or to their ministers."

Thirty years later in 1992 the U.S. Supreme Court handed down a similar decision regarding prayers at public school commencement exercises. The case arose over a policy established several years earlier by the School Committee and the Superintendent of Schools of Providence, Rhode Island, permitting principals to invite members of the clergy to give invocations and benedictions at middle and high school graduations.

Among the graduates of the Nathan Bishop Middle School on June 29, 1989, was Deborah Weisman, a 14-year-old girl whose father, Daniel Weisman, objected to having the prayers at her graduation. Four days before the ceremony, he petitioned the court to issue a temporary restraining order to prohibit school officials from including prayers as part of the program, but the court refused to do so. The principal, Robert E. Lee, then invited Rabbi Leslie Gutterman of Temple Beth El in Providence to give the invocation and the benediction, and he accepted.

Deborah and her parents attended the graduation, but four days later her father asked the court to issue a permanent injunction barring Providence school officials from inviting the clergy to give prayers at public school graduations. In response the District Court enjoined officials from continuing the practice on the ground that it violated the Establishment Clause of the First Amendment, a decision that was affirmed by the Court of Appeals. That was upheld by the U.S. Supreme Court in a 5-to-4 decision in which it ruled that graduation prayer is unconstitutional because the state in effect required participation in a religious exercise.[3]

"The government involvement with religious activity in this case is pervasive to the point of creating a state-sponsored and state-directed religious exercise in a public school," the Court stated.

The decision hinged in large degree on freedom of attendance. School officials defended the policy by arguing that students had the option of attending or not attending grad-

----

3. Robert E. Lee, Individually and as Principal of Nathan Bishop Middle School, et al v. Daniel Weisman etc., 112 Sup. Ct. 2649, 120L.Ed 2d 467 (June 24, 1992).

uation, that they were not coerced. That argument was rejected by the Court. In the majority opinion, Justice Anthony Kennedy stated:

■   In this society, high school graduation is one of life's most significant occasions, and a student is not free to absent herself from the exercises in any real sense of the term "voluntary." Also not dispositive is the contention that prayers are an essential part of these ceremonies because for many persons the occasion would lack meaning without the recognition that human achievements cannot be understood apart from their spiritual essence. This position fails to acknowledge that what for many was a spiritual imperative was for the Weismans religious conformance compelled by the State.

It also gives insufficient recognition to the real conflict of conscience faced by a student who would have to choose whether to miss graduation or conform to the state-sponsored practice, in an environment where the risk of compulsion is especially high.

In making that decision the Court pointed to what it saw as an inherent difference between public school commencement and the opening of a state legislative day. Nine years earlier the Court had ruled that the Nebraska State Legislature's practice of opening each legislative day with a prayer by a chaplain paid by the state was not a violation of the Establishment Clause of the First Amendment.[4]

"The atmosphere of a state legislature's opening, where adults are free to enter and leave with little comment and for any number of reasons, cannot compare with the constraining potential of the one school event most important for the student to attend," the Court stated.

---

4. Frank Marsh, State Treasurer et al v. Ernest Chambers, 463 U.S. 783 (July 5, 1983).

While the decision in that case was pending, another case based on the First Amendment Establishment Clause was awaiting adjudication. It had been brought in 1990 by Lamb's Chapel, an evangelical Christian church, in Center Moriches, Long Island, New York. The Chapel had requested permission to use a room in Center Moriches High School after school hours to show a six-part film series on a "Christian perspective" of family life and child rearing.

School officials refused permission because of a policy based on a state law that had been interpreted as prohibiting the use of public school buildings by any group for religious purposes, although social, civic, and recreational uses of the buildings by community groups were permitted.

In a decision handed down June 7, 1993, the U.S. Supreme Court ruled that religious groups must be treated the same as other groups in regard to the use of school facilities after school hours.[5]

In the opinion, Justice Byron White stated that the school district's refusal to permit the use of the school by Lamb's Chapel was "plainly invalid" because it amounted to discrimination against speech. As family life and child rearing are subjects that the school district permitted other speakers to address, Justice White said, the district could not deny a forum to those wishing to address the subject from a religious viewpoint.

In the decision, the Court reaffirmed a precedent it had set earlier that outlined a three-part test for determining when a government action or program amounts to the unconstitutional establishment of religion.[6] The precedent, enunciated in 1971, states that an action will pass the test as long as it has a secular purpose, it does not advance or inhibit religion as its principal effect, and it does not foster excessive entanglement with religion.

5. Lamb's Chapel v. Center Moriches School District, Docket No. 91-2024 (June 7, 1993).
6. Lemon v. Kurtzman (1971).

A response to the court ban on prayers at commencement ceremonies in public schools was the presentation of prayers by students in a scattering of schools across the country. A ruling by an appellate court in Texas that student-initiated, student-led prayers are permissible paved the way for such prayers at commencement, for example, at Clear Lake High School in Houston on June 29, 1993. The U.S. Supreme Court refused on June 7 to hear an appeal of that appellate court ruling, thus leaving the decision stand.

CHAPTER

2

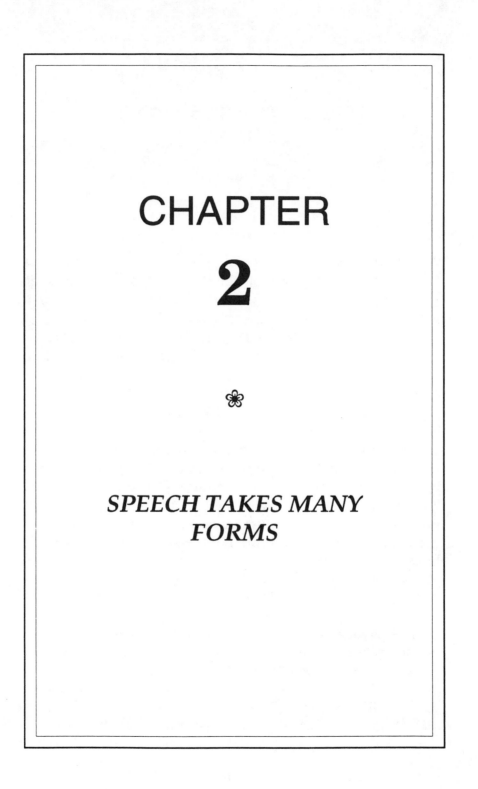

*SPEECH TAKES MANY
FORMS*

SPEECH TAKES MANY FORMS

❃

"Freedom of speech and of the press" as stated in the First Amendment has been interpreted to include all forms of communication. It is a freedom that is not limited to a person's voice or the printed word.

"The First Amendment literally forbids the abridgement only of 'speech,' but we have long recognized that its protection does not end at the spoken or written word," stated Justice William J. Brennan Jr. in the majority opinion of the U.S. Supreme Court on June 21, 1989, in the case of *Texas v. Johnson.*[1]

Carrying a sign, marching in a parade, and taking part in a protest demonstration are some of the ways people express their beliefs and feelings — virtually all recognized by the courts as forms of "speech." Humans have an astonishing number of methods for communicating information and ideas that include but are not limited to the spoken word. Among them:

■ Casual conversation, speeches, sermons, debates, personal and business letters.

■ Body language, including smiles, frowns, grimaces, shrugs, hugs and kisses, handshakes, nod or shake of the head, whistling, spitting, pats on the back or turning away

---

1. Texas v. Gregory Lee Johnson, 491 U.S. 397 (June 21, 1989).

and remaining silent, as well as clothing, costumes, uniforms, hair style, and facial makeup.

■ All printed material, including books, pamphlets, newspapers, magazines, bulletins, newsletters, and direct mail as well as all forms of advertising including billboards, signs and posters, and sky writing.

■ Motion pictures, dramas, songs, stunts, photographs, paintings, effigies, sculpture, graffiti, cartoons, and signs.

■ Electronic communication by radio, ranging from walkie-talkie to a 50,000-watt clear-channel station and from world-wide short wave to citizens' band, television, telephone, telegraph, telex, facsimile, cable, satellite, computer w/ modem, and audio and video tape recordings, and public address systems.

■ Demonstrations, parades, passing out leaflets, using sound trucks, playing phonograph or tape recordings on street corners, and picketing.

Interesting, is it not, that a person does not have to say a word to exercise his right of free speech? While there are many ways of communicating besides speaking, there can be problems in using them, just as a person can get into trouble by talking.

One reason the matter is not simple is that one freedom or right can conflict with another freedom or right. Imagine, for example, a community noted for its production of fine honey, where the beekeepers decide to have a parade through town during the annual Honey Festival. Everyone has freedom to travel on public roads and streets whenever he wishes to do so with a considerable degree of safety and convenience; but a parade may obstruct traffic on some streets, sometimes for hours. In other words, freedom to promote the use of honey with a parade and freedom to travel a particular route at a particular time can result in a conflict.

Another example of such conflict would be that of a person who proselytizes for his own religious belief by playing a tape recorder and distributing leaflets on a busy street corner. Although he would be exercising his right of free speech, he might also be interfering with pedestrian traffic, disturbing the peace with his recorded message or songs, and causing the street to be littered as passersby take the leaflets and then drop them on the pavement.

Business signs along streets and highways are also a form of speech, but they can be in violation of zoning regulations or city ordinances if they are offensive, noisy, or so large or so near the street as to be traffic hazards.

Freedom of speech in any form then is limited or ends when it interferes with the rights and freedoms and safety of others. Both local and state governments have the authority and the power to enact and to enforce ordinances that limit various forms of speech and expression for the common good. One responsibility of city government is protection of residents from annoyance, theft, and violence that might occur if there were no restrictions on uninvited sales persons, solicitors and evangelists canvassing homes or persons posing as such.

The city of Brookfield, Wisconsin, has an ordinance that states that "it is unlawful for any person to engage in picketing before or about the residence or dwelling of any individual in Brookfield." A court case arose over the ordinance when representatives of the Right-to-Life movement picketed the home of Dr. Benjamin M. Victoria, a resident who performed abortions in two nearby communities. Between April 20 and May 20, 1985, a group of about 15 demonstrators stood for an hour or two most days in the street in front of the doctor's home in Black Forest, a subdivision of Brookfield, carrying signs and shouting.

Contending that peaceful, public-issue picketing in a public forum such as a street is a form of speech protected by the First Amendment, the demonstrators filed suit to enjoin enforcement of the municipal ordinance that prohibited their picketing. Although supported by the lower courts, the U.S.

Supreme Court disagreed. In a majority opinion delivered by Justice Sandra Day O'Connor, the Court held that "the ordinance serves a significant government interest in protecting residential privacy, and as it is narrowly tailored, it thus does not violate the First Amendment guarantee of freedom of speech."[2]

Going from house to house, however, or standing on a busy street corner handing out literature, or playing a message on a loudspeaker downtown, or using other such means to express one's views are forms of speech that the courts have often protected. A case arose a number of years ago in Griffin, Georgia, which had an ordinance that prohibited the distribution of circulars, handbills, advertising material, or literature of any kind without written permission from the city manager. A woman named Amy Lovell was arrested for handing out copies of a religious pamphlet titled *The Golden Age* without permission, tried and found guilty, and sentenced to 50 days in jail in default of paying a fine of $50.

The case eventually reached the U.S. Supreme Court, which in 1938 decided without dissent that the ordinance was too broad since it prohibited any kind of literature at any time in any place without permission, rather than restricting the kind of literature that could be distributed, such as material that is pornographic or would tend to incite unlawful conduct.[3]

The next year the Court ruled on four cases involving city ordinances that restricted or prohibited distribution of handbills and pamphlets and found all of them unconstitutional under the Fourteenth Amendment.[4]

---

2. Russell C. Frisby et al v. Sandra C. Schultz and Robert C. Braun, 108 S Ct. 2495, 487 U.S. 474 (June 27, 1988).
3. Lovell v. City of Griffin, 303 U.S. 444 (1938).
4. Schneider v. State of New Jersey (town of Irvington); Young v. People of the State of California; Snyder v. City of Milwaukee; and Nichols v. Commonwealth of Massachusetts, 308 U.S. 147 (1939).

In Los Angeles a man was arrested for handing out handbills "upon a public thoroughfare" announcing a meeting of the "Friends Lincoln Brigade" at which speakers would discuss the Spanish civil war. His conviction was upheld by the California appeals court on the grounds that the police had the power to prevent littering of the streets.

A similar of case arose in Milwaukee, where a man was picketing a meat market and handing out flyers asking passersby not to trade with that market. In Worcester, Massachusetts, a man was arrested for passing out leaflets announcing a meeting to protest actions of the state unemployment administration. In Irvington, New Jersey, a member of the Watch Tower Bible and Tract Society was arrested and convicted for canvassing without a permit.

In its decision reversing the convictions in those four cases, the U.S. Supreme Court stated: "We hold that a municipality cannot . . . require all who wish to disseminate ideas to present them first to police authorities for their consideration and approval, with the discretion in the police to say some ideas may, while others may not, be carried to the homes of citizens; some persons may, while others may not, disseminate information from house to house."

Other cases have followed, with the Supreme Court generally adhering to the principle stated in its decision in those four cases; namely, that while methods other than licensing the distribution of leaflets and books to prevent fraud, trespass, and annoyance may be less efficient, that consideration "does not empower a municipality to abridge freedom of speech and the press."

Americans have not been reluctant to exercise their constitutional right of the people "peaceably to assemble, and to petition the Government for a redress of grievances," as guaranteed in the First Amendment. The latter half of the 20th century especially has seen large-scale and disrupting forms of symbolic speech in the form of marches and demonstrations, with Freedom Riders in the early 1960s marching to end

16

racial segregation in Southern States; demonstrations in opposition to the war in Vietnam in the late 1960s and early1970s; sit-ins and picketing in the conflict over abortion rights in the 1980s.

People have greater freedom to express their feelings and beliefs through demonstrations, marches, speeches, and stunts on public property such as parks and streets than they have on privately-owned property. Anyone who goes on private property without permission of the owner is trespassing, and that is unlawful.

The distinction between public and some private property, however, is of little practical importance to most people, except in a legal sense. For example, a shopping mall is privately owned, either by an individual or a company, and so is an individual shop or store. Yet we walk into them with the same freedom that we enter the city park or the county courthouse or public library. We park our cars on the shopping mall lot with the same freedom that we park on a city street. But what rights of free speech do we have on privately-owned property that is open to the public? The courts have not been entirely consistent in their decisions on that question, in part because no two cases are alike.

A significant decision regarding private property was made by the U.S. Supreme Court in 1946 in the case of *Marsh v. State of Alabama.*[5] The case arose when a woman named Grace Marsh, a Jehovah's Witness, handed leaflets regarding her religion to passersby on the sidewalk near the post office in Chickasaw, Alabama. The town was unusual in that it was totally owned by the Gulf Shipping Corporation, so even the sidewalks and streets were private property.

The Corporation had posted signs in stores and around town that the area was private property and that distribution of literature or solicitation without written permission was

---

5. Marsh v. State of Alabama, 326 U.S. 501 (1946).

prohibited. The Jehovah's Witness was told that she could not hand out leaflets without a permit and that no permit would be issued. Asked to leave, she refused to do so. She was then arrested and later convicted for violating an Alabama law that made it a crime to remain on private property after being warned not to do so.

The case eventually reached the U.S. Supreme Court, which reversed the conviction by a vote of 5 to 3, ruling that when the rights of owners of property are balanced against the free press and the religious freedoms of the people, "the latter occupy a preferred position." The majority opinion reads in part, "The more an owner, for his advantage, opens up his property for use by the public, the more do his rights become circumscribed by the statutory and constitutional rights of those who use it . . . ."

That part of the decision became known as the Marsh Doctrine and was influential in a case involving the Logan Valley Shopping Center near Altoona, Pennsylvania. There the Shopping Center management prohibited picketing in a parking lot adjacent to a supermarket in the Center by union members trying to organize the employees in the supermarket. In a decision handed down in 1968 the Supreme Court ruled in a 6-to-3 vote that the Center could not bar peaceful picketing in the parking lot.[6]

In the majority opinion the Court stated that a shopping center is the equivalent of a company town and that the union could not communicate effectively with the supermarket's customers at any other location. The decision also stated in part: "Since peaceful picketing and leaflet distribution on streets, sidewalks, parks, and other similar places are . . . historically associated with the exercise of the First Amendment rights, no distinction could be made for the same kind of public thoroughfare just because it is privately owned."

---

6. Amalgamated Food Employees Union Local 590 v. Logan Valley Plaza, 391 U.S. 308 (1968).

Four years later in 1972, however, the Supreme Court wasn't so sure that the right to free speech was superior to property rights. Rather than making a decision in a case similar to the Logan Valley case in Pennsylvania, the Court remanded it to a lower court. The case originated in Indianapolis when the Central Hardware Company ordered labor organizers off its two parking lots. The majority opinion in this case held that precedents in other cases did not apply in this one.[7]

In another case in the same year the Supreme Court ruled in a 5 to 4 vote in favor of the property owner rather than five individuals who had been handing out leaflets in 1968 in the Lloyd Shopping Center in Portland, Oregon, in opposition to the war in Vietnam.[8]

The protestors were not causing any disturbance or littering the premises by handing out leaflets to anyone who would take them, but they were warned by security guards that they might be arrested if they continued to distribute the leaflets to passersby in the Center. They then left the Center and handed out leaflets on a public street.

The case was tried in the U.S. District Court in Oregon where Chief Judge Gus J. Solomon found for the protestors. In his decision, he pointed out that the shopping center was open to the general public, that it is of vast size and complexity covering 50 acres with more than a thousand parking spaces for cars and 60 stores, shops, professional offices, sidewalks, and an auditorium. He also pointed out that efforts were made to attract the public by inviting the use of the Center by such organized groups as the Salvation Army for Christmas solicitations, the American Legion for poppy sales, and presidential candidates for political speeches.

The case was then moved to the Court of Appeals, which upheld the District Court decision favoring the protestors and citing decisions of the U.S. Supreme Court in the Marsh and

7. Central Hardware Co. v. NLRB, 407 U.S. 539 (June 22, 1972).
8. Lloyd Corporation, Ltd. v. Tanner, 407 U.S. 551 (June 22, 1972).

the Logan Valley cases as precedents.

The U.S. Supreme Court, however, reversed those decisions and found for the Shopping Center, stating that anti-war activities such as passing out leaflets were not related to the shopping center and could be carried on anywhere else on the streets of Portland, but not on the private property of Lloyd's. In the majority opinion, Justice Lewis F. Powell Jr., said that property doesn't "lose its private character merely because the public is invited to use it for designated purposes."

The freedom to exercise the First Amendment, in its various forms, is still subject to interpretation with conflicting initiatives more prominent at some times than at other times.

Among kinds of speech legally proscribed is sexual harrassment in the workplace. That became a violation of federal law after the enactment of the Civil Rights Act of 1964 which prohibits discrimination in workplaces on the basis of race, sex, religion, and national origin. Two years after its passage the U. S. Supreme Court ruled that Title VII of the Act includes sexual harrassment.[9]

More recently the Court outlined a broad definition of sexual harrassment that permit workers to win court suits without having to prove that their being harrassed injured them psychologically and led to their being unable to do their work properly.[10]

The case with the decision containing that definition arose in Nashville, Tennessee, where Teresa Harris, manager of Forklift Systems, Inc., was often insulted and subjected to sexual innuendos. In a unanimous decision in her favor, the Supreme Court ruled that "Title VII of the Civil Rights Act is violated when the workplace is permeated with discriminatory intimidation, ridicule, and insult, sufficiently severe or pervasive to alter the conditions of the victim's employment and create an abusive working environment."

---

9. Monitor Savings Bank v. Vinson, (1986).
10. Harris v. Forklift Systems, Inc., Docket No. 92-1168 (November 9, 1993).

CHAPTER
3

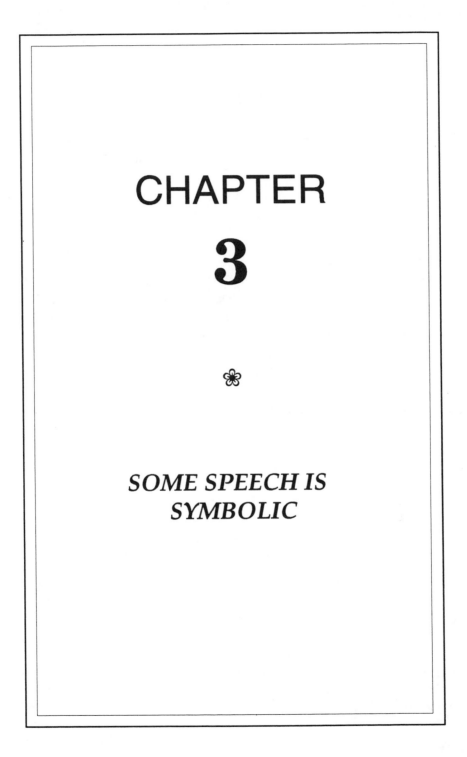

SOME SPEECH IS
SYMBOLIC

SOME SPEECH IS SYMBOLIC

❀

Freedom of speech ends, whether it is spoken, written, or symbolic, when it assaults someone, or is libelous or obscene, when it incites people to violence and disturbs the peace, and when it involves criminal trespass, personal injury, damage to property, conspiracy and other unlawful acts. Although the courts have generally protected the right of free speech, even when the speech is odious, the law does not protect speech that becomes disorderly conduct or vandalism such as painting a swastika on a Jewish synagogue.

Symbolic speech of an extreme nature, however, such as desecration of the American flag, has been upheld by the U.S. Supreme Court. Three convictions for disrespect for the flag occurred during the turbulent times of the late 1960s and early 1970s when the nation was racked by riots and demonstrations in protest to the war in Vietnam; the Court reversed all three convictions.

One of the cases involved the burning of an American flag by Sidney Street in Brooklyn on June 6, 1966, after he heard on the radio that James Meredith had been shot by a sniper in Mississippi. Meredith had enrolled four years earlier as the first black student in the University of Mississippi. When he heard the news about Meredith, Street took his American flag to a nearby street corner and set it afire. When a group gathered to watch Street announced, "Yes, that is my flag; I burned it. If they let that happen to Meredith, we don't need no damn flag."

Street was arrested by a policeman who had observed the incident and charged him with malicious mischief under a law that made it illegal to mutilate the flag or to cast contempt upon it by words or conduct. He was subsequently convicted and given a suspended sentence. The case was then appealed, finally reaching the U.S. Supreme Court in 1969 when in a 5-to-4 decision overturned the conviction on the grounds that the New York law was too broad in that it permitted punishment for speech that was protected under the First and Fourteenth Amendments.[1]

The next year a man named Valarie Goguen was arrested in Massachusetts for appearing in public with a small American flag sewn to the seat of his pants. He was found guilty, but the U.S. Supreme Court reversed the conviction on the grounds that the Massachusetts law making contemptuous treatment of the flag a crime was not constitutional since it did not draw reasonably clear lines between the kinds of nonceremonial treatment of the flag that are criminal and those that are not.[2]

Another case arose when a man named Harold Spence was arrested in Seattle for violating a Washington statute that prohibited defacement of the flag. Spence had affixed a large peace symbol to the flag and then hung the flag upside down outside his window as a protest against the U.S. invasion of Cambodia and the killing of four students at Kent State University in 1970. He, too, was convicted; but the conviction was overturned by the U.S. Supreme Court in 1974 on the basis that his conduct was a form of symbolic speech protected by the First Amendment.[3]

The actions of the accused persons in those three cases were in one sense political statements; that is, they were

---

1. Street v. New York, 394 U.S. 576 (1969).
2. Smith v. Goguen, 415 U.S. 566 (1974).
3. Spence v. Washington, 418 U.S. 405 (1974).

symbolic objections to government policies and events that arose as a result of those policies. A decision in this area of "speech" that attracted nationwide attention was the case of *Texas v. Johnson*. It began while the Republican National Convention was in session in 1984 in Dallas, Texas, when a man named Gregory Lee Johnson poured kerosene on an American flag and set it afire in front of the Dallas City Hall. While it was burning he and about a hundred of his followers chanted, "America, red, white, and blue, we spit on you."

Johnson was arrested for violating a Texas law prohibiting "desecration of a venerated object," tried, found guilty, and sentenced to a year in prison. Upon appeal the Texas Court of Criminal Appeals reversed the decision. The case was then appealed to the U.S. Supreme Court which in a 5-to-4 decision ruled that "no law could prohibit political protesters from burning an American flag."

In dissent, one justice stated that "no other American symbol has been as universally honored as the flag; its value as a symbol cannot be measured," implying that desecrating that symbol should be a violation of law. That is apparently the feeling of most legislators since the federal government and all but two states have laws prohibiting desecration of the flag. This Supreme Court decision has in effect made those laws unconstitutional.

Burning or otherwise desecrating "Old Glory," the revered symbol of our country, is highly offensive to great numbers of Americans — so offensive that the decision in the *Texas v. Johnson* case was immediately followed by a groundswell of demands for a constitutional amendment to protect the flag, with President Bush joining in the demand.

The majority of the Court, however, saw protection of the First Amendment guarantee of free speech as paramount to the indignation resulting from disrespect for the flag. Justice Brennan, in the majority opinion, stated:

"We do not consecrate the flag by punishing its desecration, for in doing so we dilute the freedom that this cherished emblem represents. . ."

"If there is a bedrock principle underlying the First Amendment, it is that the Government may not prohibit the expression of an idea simply because society finds the idea itself offensive or disagreeable . . ."

After the Supreme Court decision in 1989, Congress promptly passed the Flag Protection Act which states, "Whoever knowingly mutilates, defaces, physically defiles, burns, maintains on the floor or ground, or tramples upon any flag of the United States shall be fined . . . or imprisoned for not more than one year, or both." President George Bush refused to sign the bill on the ground that it was probably unconstitutional, and it became law without the president's signature.

It wasn't long before the law was tested in Seattle and in Washington, D.C., and in both cases convictions were reversed by Federal District Courts. The U.S. Supreme Court heard both cases together, and on June 11, 1990, handed down a decision supporting the rulings of both district courts and declaring that the new federal law making it a crime to burn or deface the American flag violates the First Amendment guarantee of freedom of speech.[4] The decision was by a vote of 5-to-4, the same as that in the decision on June 21, 1989. The Court held, in a brief majority opinion by Justice Brennan, that the government cannot prohibit the burning of the flag "simply because society finds the idea itself offensive or disagreeable."

The Court is convinced, he said, that burning the flag to make a political statement "will not endanger the special role played by our flag or the feelings it inspires."

The dividing line between what is legally permissible and what is not is sometimes tenuous. An example is erotic nude dancing in barrooms and night clubs. A case arose in Indiana which has a law that prohibits dancing that displays male or female genitals, buttocks, and female nipples. When JR's Kitty

---

4. U.S. v. Eichman and U.S. v. Haggerty, 110 L. Ed. 2d 287 (June 11, 1990).

Kat Club in South Bend was charged with violating that law, the Club, several dancers, and an adult bookstore argued that the law was in violation of their constitutional right of free speech. An appeals court agreed, stating that nude dancing is "inherently expressive," conveying an emotional message of eroticism and sensuality and thus protected by the First Amendment.

The case was then appealed to the U.S. Supreme Court which in a 5-to-4 decision handed down on June 21, 1991, upheld the Indiana law, holding that such dancing is "within the outer perimeters of the First Amendment" but "only marginally so," and is overridden by public indecency statutes "designed to protect morals and public order." [5]

In the majority opinion written by Chief Justice William H. Rehnquist, the Court stated that "public nudity is an evil that the State seeks to prevent, whether or not it is combined with expressive activity." Requiring a dancer to wear pasties and a G-string, he said, does not deprive the dance of whatever erotic message it conveys; it simply makes the message less graphic.

Symbolic speech is expressed through action rather than by the spoken word. Whether the First Amendment guarantees freedom for such action has been questioned notably by Hugo L. Black, associate justice of the U.S. Supreme Court for 34 years from 1937 to 1971. In the Carpentier Lectures he presented in the spring of 1968, he said, "It is time enough for government to step in to regulate people when they *do* something, not when they *say* something. Marching back and forth, though utilized to communicate ideas, is not speech and therefore is not protected by the First Amendment." [6]

Spreading a bag of horse manure over the carpeted lobby of the town hall doesn't qualify as symbolic free speech, Judge Herman Harding, justice of the town Salina, New York, ruled in July 1977. Henry Kindt had expressed himself in that

---

5. Barnes v. Glen Theatre, Inc., 115 L. Ed 2d 504 (June 21, 1991).
6. *Time*, April 5, 1968, page 81.

manner to protest action by the city officials of Onondaga, New York, in permitting construction of a riding stable next to his home. The judge sentenced Kindt to a year's probation for that act, stating, "Symbolic speech is not protected when it involves tangible property and threatens public health, safety, and welfare." A state law in Georgia makes it a misdemeanor for Ku Klux Klan members to wear masks in public, a law designed to prevent violence and intimidation. The Georgia Supreme Court ruled on December 5, 1990, that the law is constitutional, that it does not violate the right of free speech.

What constitutes free speech is sometimes debatable. For example, does freedom of speech include begging for money? The courts have generally upheld the right to solicit contribuions for charitable purposes, but beggars can be an annoyance thereby infringing on another person's right to privacy.

Although there has long been an ordinance against begging on subway cars in New York City, apparently little effort was made to enforce it until the Metropolitan Transportation Authority attempted in the fall of 1989 to ban all begging anywhere within the subway system, a move designed to attract more riders. In the following January, Judge Leonard Sand of the Federal District Court in Manhattan overturned the ordinance by ruling that begging is speech protected by the U.S. Constitution. The case then went to the Second Circuit Court which reversed that decision by holding that begging is personal conduct, not speech, and thus can be legally prohibited. The U.S. Supreme court refused to accept an appeal, thus letting that decision stand.

In quite different reasoning, the U.S. Supreme Court two years later upheld the right of the Port Authority of New York and New Jersey to prohibit begging in the three New York-area airports which it operates.[7] At the same time however,

---

7. International Society for Krishna Consciousness v. Lee, Docket No. 91-155, June 26, 1992.

the court ruled that handing out literature at the airports is permissible.[8]

Both decisions resulted from a suit filed 17 years earlier by members of Hare Krishna against the Port Authority after the Authority attempted to stop all solicitation in the airports. The action was taken because the Port Authority believed that such activities cause delays in passenger movement, increase congestion, facilitate fraud, and invade privacy. The Hare Krishna members objected to the Port Authority action because they are required as part of their religious duties to solicit contributions and to hand out literature regarding their beliefs.

In deciding the case, the Court was divided in regard to speech on property that may be used as "public forums." Such places include public parks and streets that traditionally have been open to unrestricted speech; but the Court ruled 6 to 3 that the airports are not public forums. In the majority opinion, Chief Justice William H. Rehnquist stated that "the tradition of airport activity does not demonstrate that they have historically been made available for speech activities."

The Court divided 5 to 4 in ruling that handing out literature at the airports is permissible. In dissent Chief Justice Rehnquist said it is just as reasonable to ban the distribution of literature as to ban begging. "The weary, harried or hurried traveler may have no less desire and need to avoid the delays generated by having literature foisted upon him than he does to avoid delays from a financial solicitation," he said.

Justice Sandra Day O'Connor, however, contended that pamphleteering is compatible with the multipurpose environment of airports, noting that the JFK airport even has two

---

8. Lee v. International Society of Krishna Consciousness, Docket No. 91-339, June 26, 1992.

branches of Bloomingdale's. "The Port Authority is operating a shopping mall as well as an airport," she stated.

As indicated earlier, freedom of speech does not allow the use of insults, profanity, threatening gestures, or "fighting words," whether face to face, by letter, or by other such means that provoke others to violence. A person can be sent to jail for assaulting another, or for using words that cause a breach of the peace.[9]

An example is a case that occured in Rochester, New Hampshire, when a Jehovah's Witness named Walter Chaplinsky provoked a public disturbance while handing out religious tracts and saying that another religion besides his own was "a racket." A traffic officer decided to take Chaplinsky to the police station for his safety, and the city marshal joined in. Chaplinsky called the marshal " a God damned racketeer" and "a damned Fascist" among other things. For those violent words which he admitted he spoke, (although he denied using the word "God"), Chaplinsky was found guilty of violating a city ordinance which read:

> ■ No person shall address any offensive, derisive or annoying word to any other person who is lawfully in any street or other public place, nor call him by any offensive or derisive name . . . with intent to deride, offend or annoy him, or to prevent him from pursuing his lawful business or occupation.

The U.S. Supreme Court unanimously upheld the conviction. In the majority opinion by Justice Frank Murphy, the Court stated:[10]

---

9. In law, *assault* means threatening to do bodily harm; *battery* means doing bodily harm. The word *assault* in that context is a noun. As a verb, *assault* means to attack.
10. Walter Chaplinsky v. State of New Hampshire, 315 U.S. 568 (March 9, 1942).

■ There are certain well-defined and narrowly limited classes of speech, the prevention and punishment of which has never been thought to raise any Constitutional problem. These include the lewd and obscene, the profane, the libelous, and the insulting or "fighting" words — those which by their very utterance inflict injury or tend to incite an immediate breach of the peace. It has been well observed that such utterances are no essential part of any exposition of ideas, and are of such slight social value as a step to truth that any benefit that may be derived from them is clearly outweighed by the social interest in order and morality.

Hate-speech, as it is sometimes called, is widely condemned. Many cities and most states — all but Alaska, Nebraska, Utah, and Wyoming — have enacted ordinances and laws against it. Further, more than a dozen states have laws that permit courts to impose longer jail sentences for crimes motivated by prejudices and hatred based on religion, ethnicity, gender and sexual orientation.

Such laws are constitutional, the U.S. Supreme Court agreed unanimously in a decision handed down on June 11, 1993[11]. Chief Justice William H. Rehnquist stated in the Court opinion, "The question presented in this case is whether this penalty enhancement is prohibited by the First and the Fourteenth Amendment. We hold that it is not."

The case with that decision began with an ugly crime described in *The New Yorker* as follows:[12]

■ On October 7, 1989, a group of black men and boys had gathered outside an apartment complex. Todd Mitchell, then aged 19, was discussing a scene from the movie, "Mississippi Burning," in which a white man beat

---

11. Wisconsin v. Mitchell (June 11, 1993), The United States Law Week - Supreme Court, Vol. 61, No. 46.
12. The New Yorker, June 21, 1993, pages 4, 6.

a black boy who was praying. Mitchell asked the others, "Do you feel hyped up to move on some white people?"

A short time later Gregory Riddick, a 14 year old white youth, happened by. Seeing him, Mitchell said, "There goes a white boy. Go get him." He then counted to three, and the group set upon the white boy and beat him until he was unconscious.

Mitchell was later arrested on a charge of aggravated battery, tried and convicted, and sentenced to two years in prison. The sentence was then increased to four years under a provision of a Wisconsin hate-crime law that permits sentence enhancement for crimes when the victim is chosen on the basis of race, religion, color, disability, national origin or ancestry, or sexual orientation.

In commenting on this case, *The New Yorker* pointed to possible results of hate-crime status that provide for sentence enhancement: "It is not hard to imagine a hate-crime investigation in which a prosecutor might quite reasonably think himself obliged to look at a defendant's political beliefs or even the books he reads ... The prospect of such inquiries by the police is one that civil libertarians correctly call chilling...it is always a little alarming when what people think, as distinct from what they do, becomes an object of the attention of policemen and prosecutors."

In its decision, the Court stated, "While a sentencing judge may not take into consideration a defendant's abstract belief, however obnoxious to most people, the Constitution does not erect a per se barrier to the admission at sentencing of evidence concerning one's beliefs and associations simply because they are protected by the First Amendment."

Yet wording a prohibition that distinguishes between proscribed and protected speech is delicate, with the courts at times failing to delineate clear distinctions.

Litigation involving an ordinance in St. Paul, Minnesota, provides an example. Titled "Bias-Motivated Crime Ordinance," it read:

31

■   Whoever places on public or private property a symbol, object, appellation, characterization or graffiti, including, but not limited to, a burning cross or Nazi swastika, which one knows or has reasonable grounds to know arouses anger, alarm or resentment in others on the basis of race, color, creed, religion or gender commits disorderly conduct and shall be guilty of a misdemeanor.

The case originated when several white youths burned a crude cross about 2 o'clock in the morning of June 21, 1990, on the front lawn of the home of Russ and Laura Jones and their five children, the only black family in that neighborhood in St. Paul. The youths were soon arrested and charged with violating the hate-crime ordinance. One of them, Robert A. Viktora, moved that the case be dismissed because the ordinance was so "substantially overbroad and impermissibly content based," it was unconstitutional.

The trial court granted the motion, but the Minnesota Supreme Court reversed that decision in 1991. It held that the modifying phrase, "arouses anger, alarm or resentment in others" limited the reach of the ordinance to conduct that amounts to "fighting words," that is, "conduct that itself inflicts injury and tends to incite immediate violence," citing the ruling in *Chaplinsky v. New Hampshire* in 1942.

The next year the U.S. Supreme Court overturned that decision, ruling unanimously that the St. Paul ordinance was unconstitutional.[13] The justices were divided, however, on why it was unconstitutional, with four disagreeing with the reasoning of the Court opinion. The result tended to confuse rather than to clarify the manner in which laws and ordinances can be formulated without infringing on the First Amendment guarantee of freedom of speech.

Justice Antonin Scalia, who delivered the opinion of the Court, found the ordinance to be unconstitutional because of

---

13. R.A.V. v. St. Paul, Docket No. 907675, June 22, 1992.

its content-based discrimination. "We conclude that the ordinance is facially unconstitutional in that it prohibits otherwise permitted speech solely on the basis of the subjects the speech addresses," he wrote. He stated further:

■ The FirstAmendmentgenerally prevents government from proscribing speech, or even expressive conduct, because of disapproval of the ideas expressed. Content-based regulations are presumptively invalid . . .

The First Amendment does not permit St. Paul to impose special prohibitions on those speakers who express views on disfavored subjects . . .

St. Paul has not singled out an especially offensive mode of expression. It has not, for example, selected for prohibition only those fighting words that communicate ideas in a threatening (as opposed to a merely obnoxious) manner. Rather, it has proscribed fighting words of whatever manner that communicate messages of racial, gender, or religious intolerance. Selectivity of this sort creates the possibility that the city is seeking to handicap the expression of particular ideas.

The four justices who disagreed with that reasoning held that the St. Paul ordinance was unconstitutional because it was so broad that it might prohibit speech that deserved constitutional protection. They differed with Justice Scalia who contended that while "fighting words," defamation, and obscenity can be banned, the government does not have the right to make distinctions within the categories on the basis of "hostility, or favoritism, toward the underlying message expressed." Justice Byron R. White asserted that the government should indeed be free to make such distinctions in categories that do not deserve constitutional protection.

Justice Harry A. Blackmun said, "I see no First Amendment values that are compromised by a law that prohibits hoodlums from driving minorities out of their homes by burning crosses on their lawns, but I see great harm in preventing the people of St. Paul from specifically punishing

33

the race-based 'fighting-words' that so prejudice their community."

Four years later on June 15, 1995, the Florida Supreme Court agreed in general with Justice Blackmun by upholding the constitutionality of a Florida state law that banned the burning of a cross without permission of the property owner. In the decision the Court said, "The threat of violence shines so clearly from a burning cross that the terrifying symbol can be outlawed without violating free speech . . . Few things can chill free expression and association to the bone like night-riders outside the door and a fiery cross in the yard."

Arriving at a decision regarding the St. Paul ordinance was not the first time the Court had debated the matter of "hate speech" in relation to the First Amendment. In *Chaplinsky* (1942) the majority agreed, "All ideas having even the slightest redeeming social importance...even ideas hateful to the prevailing climate of opinion — have the full protection of the guarantee of free speech and the press."

In *Garrison v. Louisiana* (1964), the Court agreed, "Debate on public issues will not be uninhibited if the speaker must run the risk that it will be proved in court that he spoke out of hatred, even if he did speak out of hatred, utterances honestly believed contribute to the free exchange of ideas and the ascertainment of truth."[14]

---

14. Garrison v. Louisiana, 370 U.S. 64 (1964).

CHAPTER
4

CONGRESS SHALL MAKE
NO LAW . . .

CONGRESS SHALL MAKE
NO LAW . . .

❀

When you read this portion of the First Amendment to the U.S. Constitution, emphasize the first word, on this manner:

■ *Congress* shall make no law . . . abridging the freedom of speech or of the press . . .

Read that way, the sentence implies that Congress is prohibited from abridging freedom of speech and of the press, but that other law-making bodies such as state legislatures and city councils are not prohibited from doing so. Curiously, that is what it does mean. The First Amendment, in fact, the first ten amendments, apply to the federal government, not to the states.

That curiosity, if that is what it is, resulted from the fact that citizens of this country, unlike citizens of other countries, live under two sovereign governments, one federal and one state. Each has its own sphere of authority, although those spheres overlap in a number of respects and states are limited in their sovereignty by being subordinate to the federal government in a number of respects. Their sovereignty is provided in the Tenth Amendment to the Constitution, which reads:

■ The powers not delegated to the United States by the Constitution, nor prohibited by it to the States, are reserved to the States respectively, or to the people.

The federal government has power over such national and international matters as war, treaties, immigration, interstate commerce, postal service, and coinage of money while states and their subdivisions have authority over such local matters as public education, police and fire protection, marriages, divorces, property records, and licensing of businesses and professional practitioners.

The origin of that division of power dates back more than 200 years to the struggle of the thirteen states, after declaring independence from England, to become united as one nation. While they realized the importance of being united as one country, they were largely unwilling to give up their autonomy. Much of that unwillingness resulted from the fear that a strong central government could become tyrannical, and they had had enough tyranny under English kings.

A tentative step toward union came with the meeting of the First Continental Congress on September 5, 1774, called as the result of discontent with British rule. That was only a beginning, as fifteen painful years would pass before the United States of America became a functioning reality with the first Congress meeting on April 4, 1789, followed by the inauguration of George Washington on April 30 as the first president. Here is the chronology:

■ May 10, 1775 — The Second Continental Congress met.

■ July 4, 1776 — The Colonies declared independence from England.

■ July 12, 1776 — The Continental Congress appointed a committee to develop a plan for the union of the States. (After they had declared independence, they considered themselves States, not Colonies.)

■ March 1, 1781 — The Continental Congress became a constitutional body with the adoption of the Articles of Confederation.

37

■ October 17, 1781 — The surrender of Lord Cornwallis effectively ended the Revolutionary War, although a peace treaty was not signed until September 3, 1783.

The Continental Congress struggled for seven years under the Articles of Confederation, which it came to realize were unbalanced by giving too much power to the states and too little to the national government. Article II was clear on that point, stating that "each state retains its sovereignty, freedom and independence." The Congress was therefore powerless to raise money, control foreign and interstate commerce, and enforce its laws — in short, unable to operate effectively as the government of a unified nation.

The Congress finally resolved on February 21, 1787, that a convention should meet in May of that year in Philadelphia to revise the Articles of Confederation. The delegates convened on May 25 and during the long hot summer behind closed doors drafted what became the Constitution of the United States of America. The completed document contained several compromises, mostly regarding the rights of states, large and small, and was finally approved by the delegates as "the supreme law of the land" (Article VI). It was sent to the states on September 28 for their approval and became effective on June 21, 1788, with ratification by New Hampshire, the ninth state to do so. The last ratification was two years later on May 29, 1790, by Rhode Island.

Those dates, however, give no inkling of the intense debate that raged throughout the land over ratification of the proposed constitution. The people were divided, with the Federalists favoring a strong central government and the Anti-Federalists arguing that a concentration of power in a national government would endanger the liberties of the people and deny rights that properly belonged to state and local governments.

They realized that with the adoption of the Constitution the people would be living under two constitutions and two governments, one state and one federal. They felt that the rights of citizens would be protected by the constitutions of the states, but how would such rights be protected against possible tyranny of the federal government? To assure such protection, the states recommended that the Constitution be amended to guarantee certain "unalienable rights."[1]

Congress adopted the recommendation, and on September 25, 1789, it passed the ten Amendments that comprise the Bill of Rights and sent them to the states for ratification. Approval by eleven states was necessary for adoption; and on December 15, 1791, Virginia became the eleventh state to give its approval.[2] The Bill of Rights became a part of the Constitution at that time — but applicable only to the federal government.

That was affirmed in a U.S. Supreme Court decision in 1833 in the case of *Barron v. Baltimore*.[3] Chief Justice John Marshall, who served on the court for 34 years from 1801 to 1835, made it fairly clear in the majority opinion he wrote in this case that the Bill of Rights applied only to the federal government. That opinion has never been totally reversed by the Supreme Court.

The difference over states' rights vs. a strong national government, which led to the adoption of the Bill of Rights, continues in one form or another to this day. It led to the secession of 11 states from the Union in 1861 and consequently to the Civil War in 1861-1865 with the question of

---

1. An inalienable right is one so essential to human welfare that it cannot be given up or taken away, not even for the benefit of society at large. The Declaration of Independence speaks of *unalienable* rights, but the meaning is the same as inalienable.
2. Vermont was admitted as a State on March 4 1791, making a total of fourteen States in the United States of America at that time. Three of them — Georgia, Connecticut, and Massachusetts — did not ratify the Bill of Rights until 1939.
3. Barron v. Baltimore, 7 Pet. 243 (1833).

slavery as a major point of contention. The Thirteenth Amendment to the U.S. Constitution abolishing slavery became effective on December 18, 1865; and the Fourteenth Amendment, ratified on July 9, 1868, gave citizenship to all persons born or naturalized in the United States, which included all former slaves. In fact, a major purpose of the Amendment was to guarantee equal protection of the laws for newly freed slaves. Section 1 of the Fourteenth Amendment also states:

■ No State shall make or enforce any law which shall abridge the privileges or immunities of citizens of the United States; nor shall any State deprive any person of life, liberty, or property, without due process of law; nor deny to any person within its jurisdiction the equal protection of the law.

This amendment, and especially the "due process" and "equal protection of the law" clauses, added a significant new dimension to the guarantees of fundamental human rights in the United States, including the right of free speech and of the press. The U.S. Supreme Court has cited it numerous times in upholding the rights of citizens; and in 1925 in the case of *Gitlow v. New York*, the Court implied that freedom of speech is protected by the Fourteenth Amendment from unwarranted action by the states.[4]

In the majority opinion Justice Edward T. Sanford stated:

■ For present purposes we may and do assume that freedom of speech and of the press — which are protected by the First Amendment from abridgment by Congress — are among the fundamental personal rights and "liberties" protected by the due process clause of the Fourteenth Amendment from impairment by the States.

---

4. Gitlow v. New York, 268 U.S. 495 (1925).

That extension of the First Amendment guarantee of freedom of speech and press to include state and local governments has prevailed ever since. In the U.S. Supreme Court decision in the case of *Near v. Minnesota* in 1931, discussed in Chapter 7, Chief Justice Charles Evans Hughes said, "It is no longer open to doubt that the liberty of the press and of speech is within the liberty safeguarded by the due process clause of the Fourteenth Amendment from invasion by State action."

In the majority opinion of the Court in the case of *Joseph Burstyn, Inc. v. Wilson* in 1952, Justice Tom C. Clark stated:[5]

■ In a series of decisions beginning with *Gitlow v. New York*, this Court held that the liberty of speech and of the press which the First Amendment guarantees against abridgment by the federal government is within the liberty safeguarded by the Due Process Clause of the Fourteenth Amendment from invasion by state action. That principle has been followed and affirmed to the present day . . .

In 1975 Justice Harry A. Blackmun stated flatly in the majority opinion in the case of *Bigelow v. Virginia*, "The First Amendment . . . is applicable to the states through the Fourteenth Amendment."[6]

In a number of cases some U.S. Supreme Court justices have contended that the Fourteenth Amendment covers all the first eight constitutional amendments guaranteeing certain human rights. In the case of *Adamson v. California* decided in 1947, for example, four of the justices urged extending the coverage of the Bill of Rights en bloc to the states, but they failed to convince the other five; and so far a majority of the justices have not agreed to that.

---

5. Joseph Burstyn, Inc. v. Wilson, 343 U.S. 495 (1952).
6. Bigelow v. Virginia, 421 U.S. 809 (1975). Discussed further in Chapter 26.

The case concerned a man convicted of murder in the first degree, with the conviction affirmed by the Supreme Court of California. In his appeal he contended that he should be protected from state action by the Fifth Amendment to the Constitution, but the Court held that the amendments in the Bill of Rights applied only to the federal government, not to the states. In the majority opinion, Justice Stanley F. Reed stated:[7]

■ It is settled law that the clause of the Fifth Amendment protecting a person against being compelled to be a witness against himself is not made effective by the Fourteenth Amendment as a protection against state action on the ground that freedom from testimonial compulsion is a right of national citizenship or because it is a personal privilege or immunity secured by the Federal Constitution as one of the rights of man that are listed in the Bill of Rights.

Whether the Bill of Rights, especially the First Amendment, applies only to the federal government and not to the states usually has little practical significance, however, because the constitutions of all the states contain those safeguards. Although not worded precisely alike, all are similar. Here are examples regarding freedom of speech:

■ Indiana: No law shall be passed, restraining the free interchange of thought and opinion, or restricting the right to speak, write, or print, freely, on any subject whatever; but for the abuse of that right, every person shall be responsible.

■ Montana: No law shall be passed impairing the freedom of speech; every person shall be free to speak, write, or publish whatever he will on any subject, being responsible for all abuse of that liberty.

---

7. Admiral Dewey Adamson v. People of the State of California, 332 U.S. 46 (June 23, 1947).

CHAPTER
5

❁

BUT IT HAS DONE SO

BUT IT HAS DONE SO

❄

Government has the right and the duty to protect itself against its enemies, both foreign and domestic; but attempts at such protection can result in infringement on the right of free speech and have done so in the United States despite the constitutional guarantee that "Congress shall make no law . . ."

The Alien and Sedition Acts of 1798, enacted less than a decade after the adoption of the Bill of Rights, were the first passed by Congress that inhibited freedom of speech and of the press and trampled on civil rights.

One of the two Alien Acts, applying only in peace time and effective for two years, empowered the President "to order all such aliens as he shall judge dangerous to the peace and safety of the United States to depart." If anyone refused to leave the country, the President could order that person to be imprisoned for three years; and if such person should return after sent away, the President could determine what punishment should be meted out.

The other Alien Act applied only when war was declared or invasion threatened and was in effect for the duration of war. It stated that "all natives, citizens, denizens, or subjects of the hostile nation or government, being males of the age of 14 years and upwards, who shall be within the United States, and not actually naturalized shall be liable to be apprehended, restrained, secured, and removed, as enemy aliens."

The Sedition Act made it illegal to impede any officer in the execution of his duty, or to attempt to form any conspiracy, insurrection, or unlawful assembly against the government. It also made it illegal to print, publish, or quote any false, scandalous, or scurrilous writings against the U.S. government, the President, or either house of Congress in order to stir up hatred against them.

Repressive laws such as the Alien and Sedition Acts are most likely to be enacted in times of stress, in times of emergency, and on occasions of mass hysteria and mob rule. It is then that liberty is in greatest jeopardy, and the climate was right for such laws at the end of the 18th century with the country in turmoil.

It was a time of bitter dissension between the Federalists, who favored a strong central government, and the Republicans, who favored local control. The Federalists were in office, with John Adams as president; and the Alien Act was aimed at foreign-born Irish and English residents editing anti-Federalist newspapers. The Sedition Act was aimed at native-born Americans attacking the administration through their newspapers.

The condition in this country at the time was exacerbated by the war between England and France, which began in 1793 and continued intermittently until after the defeat of Napoleon at Waterloo on June 18, 1815. Both countries were seizing American ships and confiscating their cargo, and the British were impressing American sailors into their naval service. The United States, in existence only ten years under its new constitution, did not yet have a navy strong enough to maintain its neutrality. The United States and France were on the verge of war; and although it was never declared, the two countries fought several small naval battles. The conflict with England finally culminated in the War of 1812, which officially ended with the signing of a peace treaty on December 24, 1814.

President Adams never invoked the Alien Acts or deported anyone, but about 25 persons were indicted for violating the Sedition Act and ten of them were tried and convicted. Seven of the ten were newspaper editors. Among them was Dr. Thomas Cooper, an editor who wrote that President Adams was incompetent and as president had tried to influence the course of justice. That does not sound very dangerous; but Dr. Cooper was found guilty of criminal libel, fined $400 and sentenced to six months in jail. Another indicted and tried was James Callender, accused of bringing President Adams into disrepute by calling him a monarchist and a toady to British interests in a pamphlet titled *The Prospect Before Us*.

The Alien and Sedition Acts were widely recognized as bad legislation and were allowed to expire in 1801, and they were an important factor in the Federalists' losing to the Republicans in the presidential election of 1800. The laws, however, did contain two provisions on points of law argued in the Peter Zenger case more than sixty years earlier and are today accepted principles in libel cases. One is that truth is a defense; the other is that the jury determines both the law and the fact, under direction of the court.

More than a hundred years would pass before more laws restricting speech and the press were enacted, although those years of the 19th century brought more troubled times, including a bloody Civil War in 1861-65.[1] There was, as could be expected, press censorship in the time of war; but such censorship in the United States was conducted primarily by military authorities and voluntarily by journalists themselves, without legal restraint.

As early as 1815, after the Battle of New Orleans, General Andrew Jackson had the editor of the *Louisiana Gazette*

---

1. At the outbreak of the Civil War, Congress enacted a law making conspiracy or use of force to overthrow the government or to prevent the execution of any law a crime, but it did not contain provisions restricting speech.

46

imprisoned for publishing an article on the peace treaty between the United States and England at the close of the War of 1812.

Northern generals suppressed several newspapers in Southern states during the Civil War on the grounds of treason after the cities in which the papers were being published had been taken over by the Union Army. A few Northern newspapers were also suppressed by the military. One was the *Philadelphia Evening Journal,* with the editor, Albert D. Boileau, arrested on January 27, 1863, for criticizing President Lincoln. Although Boileau had been critical of the Lincoln administration, early in January he published an editorial which described the war as having entered a phase with "no other purpose than revenge, and thirst for blood and plunder of private property." General Robert Schenck, commander of the Middle Department of the Army, then ordered his arrest. Boileau was taken to Ft. McHenry where he recanted and promised that no editorials of that kind would appear in the future. He was released and the paper soon resumed publication.

Another was the *Chicago Times*, which was suppressed on June 1, 1863, for criticizing the government. In New York the offices of the *Journal of Commerce* and of the *World* were cordoned off by guards on May 18, 1864, with publication stopped for several days and the editors placed in jail because they had published a false presidential proclamation regarding the draft.

Although the word "treason" was used in closing some Southern newspapers, the word has a limited application in the United States to limit free speech. As defined by the U.S. Constitution, treason "shall consist only in levying War against them, or in adhering to their Enemies, giving them Aid and Comfort." Congress thus cannot pass any law that makes any act treasonable except as stated in the Constitution, so few if any publications can be censored on that account.

There were no guidelines on censorship for military officers to follow in shutting down newspapers and punishing editors; each officer decided for himself whether a reporter or an editor was guilty of hindering the war effort. The procedure became more formalized in the early part of the 20th century. After the U.S. Navy blockaded Mexico in 1913 in support of revolutionaries there and occupied the city of Vera Cruz the next year, the War Department began exercising censorship over military information regarding U.S. relations with Mexico.

In 1917, with America's entry into World War I in Europe, a censorship board was established to control information related to the war effort; and an Office of Censorship was created after the United States entered World War II in 1941. The press cooperated in both wars, but journalists often felt that censorship was too strict and that on occasion information was censored to cover up mistakes by government agencies and officials rather than to keep it from the enemy.

Since a law creating government censorship would be in conflict with the First Amendment, censorship offices during the two world wars were established by presidential executive orders, with authority to do so implied in such Congressional legislation as the Espionage Act of 1917, Trading with the Enemies Act, Alien Registration Act of 1940, and the War Powers Act of 1941.

A number of repressive provisions were contained in laws enacted in the first half of the 20th century prohibiting the overthrow of the government by force and violence. The laws were in response to the effects of a social ferment that began in Europe in the latter half of the 19th century and gradually spread to the United States. The ferment gave rise to such social reform movements as syndicalism, anarchy, socialism, and communism, all of which posed a threat to the American government and way of life.

Syndicalism is an economic theory in which workers own and manage the industries in which they work, with strikes, terrorism, and sabotage advocated as a way to achieve the system. That movement was accompanied by the theory of anarchy, which holds that coercive government as it exists should be destroyed and replaced by the cooperative and voluntary association of individuals and groups as the chief mode of society. Socialism and communism are similar in that they call for establishing a society in which there is no private property, with the means of production owned and controlled by the state and all goods owned in common and available to all as needed.

Those movements were marked by the publication of *Das Kapital* by Karl Marx in Germany in 1867, a book on which 20th Century Communism was based, and by the establishment of the Fabian Society in England in 1884 devoted to the spread of socialism by peaceful means. In the United States the movements were connected primarily with labor organizations. The Knights of Labor, a secret society, was formed in 1869, the Federation of Trades and Labor Unions in 1881, the Social Democratic Workingmen's Party about 1897, and the Independent Workers of the World (I.W.W.) in Chicago in June 1905, as organized labor struggled to find a place in American society.

The frightening aspect of those social reform movements was the violence that accompanied their efforts, including notably the bloody Haymarket Square riot in Chicago in 1886. The movements arose, no doubt, in protest to the harsh working conditions created by the Industrial Revolution which began about 1760 in England and later in other countries, and also to the widespread poverty among workers in contrast to the few immensely wealthy industrialists and "robber barons."

It is not surprising that government viewed those radical movements with alarm as they were frequently accompanied by violence. The assassination of President McKinley by an anarchist named Leon Czolgosz spurred legislators into action. The President was shot on September 6, 1901, and died eight days later. By the next year the New York State Legislature had passed a criminal anarchy act, and soon several other states enacted similar laws. The New York law defined criminal anarchy as "the doctrine that organized government should be overthrown by force or violence, or by assassination of the executive head or any of the executive officials of government, or by any unlawful means." The law made it a felony to advocate criminal anarchy by speech or by printing and distributing any material advocating or teaching it.

There is a difference between advocating change in government and in using force to effect a change. In advocating change, a person is exercising his right of free speech; but he does not have that freedom when his advocacy is accompanied by violence or when it incites or is intended to incite others to violence. As each case is different, the trial courts must decide who is guilty of violating advocacy laws, and the appeals courts must rule on the application and the constitutionality of the laws.

The U.S. Supreme Court, however, did not have occasion to rule on a case involving advocacy of the overthrow of the government by force before it was confronted by another kind of case regarding freedom of speech. That kind centered on protests to America's participation in World War I.

A real emergency arose when the United States entered the war in April 1917. A joint resolution declaring war on Germany was adopted by the Senate on April 4 that year and by the House of Representatives on April 6. Congress passed a law on May 18 instituting the draft; and on June 14 it enacted the National Defense Law, which is generally known as the Espionage Act of 1917. The Act was designed not only to prevent spying by and for the enemy but also to curb any dissent that might weaken the war effort. The Act reads in part:

■ Whoever, when the United States is at war, shall willfully make or convey false reports or false statements with the intent to interfere with the operation or success of the military or naval forces of the United States or to promote the success of its enemies;

And whoever, when the United States is at war, shall willfully cause or attempt to cause insubordination, disloyalty, mutiny, or refusal of duty in the military or naval forces of the United States;

Or shall willfully obstruct the recruiting or enlistment service of the United States, shall be punished by a fine of not more than $10,000 or imprisonment for not more than twenty years, or both.

On May 16, 1918, the Espionage Act was amended to broaden prohibition of dissent. The law then stated in part:

■ Whoever shall say or do anything except by way of bona fide and not disloyal advice, to obstruct the sale of bonds or other securities of the United States; or

Shall willfully utter, print, write, or publish any disloyal, profane, scurrilous, or abusive language about the form of government of the United States, the military or naval forces of the United States, the flag of the United States, the uniform of the army or navy of the United States, or any language intended to bring the foregoing into contempt, scorn, contumely, or disrepute;

Or shall willfully utter, print, write or publish any language intended to incite, provoke, or encourage resistance to the United States, or to promote the cause of its enemies; or advocate any curtailment of production essential to the prosecution of the war; or shall teach, advocate, or defend any of these acts;

Or whoever shall by word or act support or favor the cause of any country with which the United States is at war, shall be punished by a fine of not more than $10,000 or imprisonment for not more than twenty years, or both.

In other words, anyone who voiced any complaint about the war or the government did so at his own peril. Some, however, felt so strongly about compulsory drafting of men

51

into military service and about other aspects of the war that they refused to remain silent. As a result, there were numerous arrests and court trials. Seven of those cases reached the U.S. Supreme Court on appeal, with decisions handed down in 1919 and 1920 and with the convictions upheld in all but one.

Two of the cases, *Charles T. Schenck v. United States*[2] and *Elizabeth Baer v. United States*,[3] were heard together as both defendants had been convicted of the same violations of law. Those cases arose when the Executive Committee of the Socialist Party in the United States authorized the publication of 15,000 copies of a leaflet to be sent to men who had been accepted for military service by draft boards.

The leaflet, protesting conscription for military service, stated that "a conscript is a little better than a convict." In impassioned language it said that drafting men into the army and navy was "despotism in its worst form and a monstrous wrong against humanity, in the interest of Wall Street's chosen few." It warned, "If you do not assert and support your rights, you are helping to deny or disparage rights which it is the solemn duty of all citizens and residents of the United States to retain."

Schenck, who was general secretary of the Socialist Party, and Baer, the secretary who took notes of the meeting of the Executive Committee, and several others were arrested and tried for violating the Espionage Act of 1917. They were charged with conspiracy to attempt to cause insubordination in the military and naval forces and to obstruct recruiting and enlistment and of using the mails to send matter declared to be non-mailable.

---

2. Charles T. Schenck v. United States of America, 249 U.S. 47 (March 3, 1919).
3. Elizabeth Baer v. United States of America, 249 U.S. 47 (March 3, 1919).

In the unanimous decision upholding the convictions, Justice Oliver Wendell Holmes introduced the "clear and present danger" test for statements held dangerous to the government and the public welfare. The opinion reads in part:

■ We admit that in many places and in ordinary times the defendants, in saying all that was said in the circular, would have been within their constitutional rights. But the character of every act depends upon the circumstances in which it is done. The most stringent protection of free speech would not protect a man in falsely shouting fire in a theater, and causing a panic. It does not even protect a man from an injunction against uttering words that may have all the effects of force.

The question in every case is whether the words used are used in such circumstances and are of such a nature as to create a clear and present danger that they will bring about the substantive evils that Congress has a right to prevent. It is a question of proximity and degree. When a nation is at war many things that might be said in time of peace are such a hindrance to its effort that their utterances will not be endured so long as men fight, and that no court could regard them as protected by constitutional right.

Another arrested and jailed for speaking too freely in those troubled times was Eugene Victor Debs, leader of the Socialist Party USA during the first two decades of the 20th century. In a speech in Canton, Ohio, in 1917 he criticized war in general and World War I then in progress in particular, urging "Workers of the world to unite" and to "refuse to kill your comrades in other lands!" He said, "The masters have always declared the war, they have always sent the workers to fight for them. We object to murdering the citizens of other countries; they are our brothers."

Debs was not talking to soldiers and he did not urge listeners to resist the draft. Still, for that anti-war speech he was arrested, tried, convicted, and sentenced to ten years in prison for "attempting to incite insubordination, disloyalty, mutiny, and refusal of duty in the armed forces and for attempting to obstruct the recruiting and enlistment service of the United States in violation of the Espionage Act of 1917." In his trial Debs told the jury that he had been accused of opposing the war, and he said, "I admit it. Gentlemen, I abhor war. I would oppose war if I stood alone."

The U.S. Supreme Court upheld the conviction by a unanimous vote, even though the facts did not indicate a "clear and present danger."[4] The decision was handed down on March 10, 1919, just a week after the Court had upheld the conviction of Charles T. Schenck and Elizabeth Baer for violating the Espionage Act in a decision in which Justice Holmes had enunciated the "clear and present danger" doctrine.

Unlike some of the "radicals" caught in Espionage Act net, Debs was no unknown person. At the turn of the century his Social Democratic Party and the Socialist Labor Party had merged to form the Socialist Party USA; and as a result of his leadership, he had become a national political figure. As such, he was the Socialist Party's candidate for the office of President of the United States in the elections from 1900 to 1920, and in 1920 while he was still in prison he received more than 900,000 votes.

Still another case also decided by the U.S. Supreme Court in 1919 had its origin in a protest to President Wilson's sending troops to Vladivostok and Murmansk in the summer of 1918 to help the Russians put down the Bolshevik Revolution. The protesters were Jacob Abrams, Hyman Lachowsky, Samuel Lipman, and Mollie Steimer, all immigrants from Czarist Russia. They believed the revolution would bring freedom to Russia, so they considered America's intervention to be wrong. They also objected to the manufacture of

---

4. Debs v. United States, 249 U.S. 211 (1919).

munitions in this country, although the United States at the time was fighting in World War I, and they called for a general strike.

As a means of protesting, they had several thousand leaflets printed, in English and in Yiddish, and on the evening of August 22, 1918, they threw a large number of them from the roof of a building on the Lower East Side of New York.

In reference to the U.S. intervention in Russia, one leaflet said: "Awake! Awake, you workers of the world. Revolutionists. There is only one enemy of the workers of the world and that is capitalism. It is a crime for workers in America to fight the workers' republic in Russia."

The other leaflet was headed, "Workers — Wake Up!" and it stated in part: "Workers in the ammunition factories, you are producing bullets, bayonets, cannon to murder not only Germans, but also your dearest, best, who are in Russia fighting for freedom." It ended with a call for a general strike.

The four were arrested, tried, and convicted on four counts of conspiracy — conspiracy to publish abusive language about the form of government of the United States, to publish language intended to bring the form of government into contempt, to encourage resistance to the United States, and to incite curtailment of production of ordnance and ammunition necessary for prosecution of the war. The men were sentenced to 20 years in prison and the woman to 15 years. In 1921, however, the four were released on condition that they return to the Soviet Union.

Although the U.S. Supreme Court had been unanimous in upholding the convictions in the Schenck and Debs cases, only seven justices voted to uphold the convictions of those four "conspirators." In the majority opinion Justice John H. Clarke held that the printing and distribution of the leaflets were not protected within the meaning of the First Amendment.

The dissent by Justice Holmes, joined by Justice Louis D. Brandeis, was more significant in regard to freedom of expression than was the majority opinion. He wrote in part:[5]

■ It is only the present danger of immediate evil or an intent to bring it about that warrants Congress in setting a limit to the expression of opinion where private rights are not concerned. Congress certainly cannot forbid all effort to change the mind of the country. Now nobody can suppose that the surreptitious publishing of a silly leaflet by an unknown man, without more, would present any immediate danger that its opinions would hinder the success of the government arms or have any appreciable tendency to do so . . .

I think we should be eternally vigilant against attempts to check the expression of opinions that we loathe and believe to be fraught with death, unless they so imminently threaten immediate interference with the lawful and pressing purposes of the law that an immediate check is required to save the country.

Besides the three cases discussed here, and not including cases in which the Post Office Department had denied mailing privileges to publications opposing the war, the Supreme Court upheld convictions for violations of the Espionage Act of 1917 in two other cases. They were *Frohwerk v. United States*, 1919,[6] for publication of twelve newspaper articles opposing the war, and *Pierce v. United States*, 1920,[7] for circulation of copies of a four-page pamphlet attacking the purposes of the war and the United States' participation in it.

In still another case, *Schaefer v. United States*, 1920,[8] for publication of a German-language newspaper with allegedly

---

5. Jacob Abrams v. United States, 250 U.S. 616 (November 10, 1919).
6. Frohwerk v. United States, 249 U.S. 204 at 208-209 (1919).
7. Pierce v. United States, 252 U.S. 239 (1920).
8. Schaefer v. United States, 251 U.S. 466 (1920).

false articles critical of capitalism and the war, five persons were tried as one. The Supreme Court upheld the convictions of three of them and reversed the convictions of two.

The 1918 amendment to the Espionage Act of 1917 that contained the restrictions on speech and the press under which those seven cases were tried was repealed in 1921. That brought to an end prosecutions for sedition under those provisions of the law. The repeal did not end cases involving freedom of speech, however. There still remained state laws prohibiting advocacy of the overthrow of the government by force.

That kind of advocacy, often accompanied by violence, came from socialist, syndicalist, and anarchist organizations, with their activities in the early part of the century portrayed by newspaper cartoons depicting bearded "Bolsheviks" carrying smoking bombs and in articles about the radical Independent Workers of the World (I.W.W.).

Add to that the effects of the Russian Revolution in 1917, which deposed the Tzar and established a system of communism with the avowed intention of conquering the world. That alone resulted in a paranoia in this country that persisted for most of the 20th century, leading to such excesses as the "Red Scare" in 1919-1920 and the televised McCarthy hearings in 1954 into alleged Communist influence in the Army. Both destroyed reputations of innocent persons and wantonly violated individuals' constitutional rights.

The Soviet Third International organized in the spring of 1919, set world revolution as its goal, an action followed by the organization of two communist parties in the United States, the Communist Party and the Communist Labor Party. Those events, plus labor unrest accompanied by violence, more than two dozen bombings aimed at high government officials, and race riots in Cleveland and Washington, D.C. combined to create a climate of near hysteria throughout the country. Reacting to what many perceived as "a Red conspiracy to destroy the American way of life," steps were taken in the name of national security that severely infringed on American freedoms.

Thirty-two states enacted "red flag" laws in 1920 and another state in 1921, making it illegal to carry a red flag in a parade or to display a banner or emblem of an organization distinctive of bolshevism, anarchism, or radical socialism. About 70 sedition bills carrying varying degrees of severity were introduced in Congress in the winter of 1919-1920, although none were enacted.

Acting under provisions of the Alien Registration Act of 1918, Attorney General A. Mitchell Palmer authorized a series of raids by federal officers in November 1919 that resulted in the arrest of hundreds of aliens and suspected "Reds," 249 of whom were deported within a month. Then on the night of January 2, 1920, federal officers carried out raids in 33 cities in 23 states, making wholesale arrests of more than 4,000 aliens and others suspected of being aliens, many of whom were harshly treated in the process. Hundreds of warrants had been run off on mimeograph machines in preparation for the raids, and frequently names were filled in after arrests were made. Large numbers of others were held for a time without being charged.

Attorney General Palmer had been able to persuade the Department of Labor to change Rule 22 regarding immigration, so that arresting officers no longer needed to inform aliens of either their right to counsel or the charge against them. In all, 556 aliens were deported as a result of the arrests, with the others being released.[9]

In commenting years later on this event, *The New York Times* stated in an editorial, "Attorney General A. Mitchell Palmer in 1920 swept aside all constitutional restraints and

---

9. For a detailed account, read "The Great Red Scare" by Allan L. Damon, *American Heritage*, Vol. xix, February 1968.

momentarily took the United States to the brink of totalitarianism."[10]

A total of nine cases involving criminal syndicalism and anarchy reached the U.S. Supreme Court during that period of national paranoia. The Court upheld convictions in five of the cases but ruled that the state statutes under which prosecution had been made in four cases were unconstitutional or had been unconstitutionally applied.

Among those indicated and tried were Benjamin Gitlow and three other members of the Socialist Party who had published a 34-page pamphlet titled "*The Revolutionary Age*" that contained a manifesto, which is a public declaration of intentions. The pamphlet predicted that "the mass struggle of the proletariat was coming into being" and it urged mass strikes and action by the proletariat. The men had 16,000 copies printed, and they mailed some and sold others.

The four men were charged with violating the New York Criminal Anarchy Act that forbade the publication or distribution of material that advocates, advises, or teaches the duty, necessity or propriety of overthrowing organized government by force. The men were found guilty and sentenced to serve from five to ten years at hard labor.

The case, *Gitlow v. New York*,[10] mentioned in the previous chapter, eventually reached the U.S. Supreme Court on appeal, where in 1925 the Court upheld the convictions by a vote of 7-to-2. In the majority opinion, Justice Edward T. Sanford stated in part:

■ By enacting the present statute the State has determined, through its legislative body, that utterances advocating the overthrow of organized government by force, violence and unlawful means, are so inimical to the

---

10. June 3, 1971, page 16E.
11. Benjamin Gitlow v. People of the State of New York, 268 U.S. 652 (June 8, 1925).

general welfare and involve such danger of substantive evil that they may be penalized in the exercise of its police power . . .

That utterances inciting the overthrow of organized government by unlawful means, present sufficient danger of substantive evil to bring their punishment within the range of legislative discretion, is clear. Such utterances, by their very nature, involve danger to the public peace and ultimate revolution. And the immediate danger is none the less real and substantial, because the effect of a given utterance cannot be accurately foreseen . . .

We cannot hold that the present statute is an arbitrary or unreasonable exercise of the police power of the State unwarrantably infringing the freedom of speech or press; and we must and do sustain its constitutionality.

The State Legislature of California passed a Criminal Syndicalism Act in 1919 which defined criminal syndicalism as "any doctrine or precept advocating, teaching or aiding and abetting the commission of crime, sabotage . . . , or unlawful methods of terrorism as a means of accomplishing a change in industrial ownership or control, or affecting any political change." The law also made it a crime for anyone who taught or advocated criminal syndicalism or who disseminated written material advocating it, or any person who associated with persons who proposed to advocate criminal syndicalism.

In the next five years 504 persons were arrested for violating that sweeping law and 204 of them were tried in court. Among them was Anita Whitney who had participated in a convention that organized the Communist Labor Party of California. She was tried and convicted on the ground that the Communist Party was formed to teach criminal syndicalism, and as a member she participated in the crime.

The case was appealed to the U.S. Supreme Court which in 1927 upheld the conviction on the ground that concerted action by an organization or a large group poses a greater threat to public order than statements by individuals.[12]

Miss Whitney, in her defense, claimed that although she had attended the convention and had in fact been named an alternate member of the executive committee, she did not agree with the majority who favored the use of violence and that her presence at the convention should not be considered a crime.

This was another of a number of cases in which the Court was confronted by the question of freedom of speech vs. the right of government to protect itself. Justice Brandeis concurred with the majority decision in this case, but he wrote a separate opinion in which he commented further on the "clear and present danger" test which he had first stated in the Schenck case in 1919. Because of its significance, somewhat extended excerpts are quoted here:

■ The statute (under which Miss Whitney was convicted) restricted the right of free speech and of assembly . . .

. . . the statute aims, not at the practice of criminal syndicalism, nor even directly at the preaching of it, but at association with those who propose to preach it . . .

. . . although the rights of free speech and assembly are fundamental, they are not in their nature absolute. Their exercise is subject to restriction, if the particular restriction proposed is required in order to protect the state from destruction or from serious injury, political, economic, or moral.

. . . This court has not yet fixed the standard by which to determine when a danger shall be deemed clear; how remote the danger may be and yet be deemed present; and what degree of evil shall be deemed sufficiently substantial to justify resort to abridgment of free speech and assembly as the means of protection.

---

12. Charlotte Anita Whitney v. People of the State of California, 274 U.S. 357 (May 16, 1927).

To reach sound conclusions on these matters, we must bear in mind why a state is, ordinarily, denied the power to prohibit dissemination of social, economic and political doctrines which a vast majority of its citizens believes to be false and fraught with evil consequences.

To justify suppression of free speech there must be reasonable ground to fear that serious evil will result if free speech is practiced. There must be reasonable ground to believe that the danger apprehended is imminent. There must be reasonable ground to believe that the evil to be prevented is a serious one.

In order to support a finding of clear and present danger it must be shown either that immediate serious violence was to be expected or was advocated, or that the past conduct furnished reason to believe that such advocacy was then contemplated.

Only an emergency can justify repression.

Although Miss Whitney was found guilty and her conviction upheld by the U.S. Supreme Court, she was pardoned a few months later by the Governor of California.

On the same day on which the Supreme Court handed down the decision in the Whitney case, it ruled for the first time that a state criminal syndicalism law was unconstitutional. In that case it reversed the conviction of Harold B. Fiske, an organizer for the International Workers of the World (I.W.W.), who had been found guilty of violating the Kansas Criminal Syndicalism Act.[12]

Section 3 of the Kansas statute read, "Any person who, by word of mouth, or writing, advocates, affirmatively suggests or teaches the duty, necessity, propriety or expediency of criminal syndicalism, or sabotage . . . is guilty of a felony . . ."

In delivering the opinion of the Court, Justice Sanford stated, "As applied the Act is an arbitrary and unreasonable

---

12. Fiske v. Kansas, 274 U.S. 380 (May 16, 1927).

exercise of the police powers of the State, unwarrantably infringing the liberty of the defendant in violation of the due process clause of the Fourteenth Amendment."

The decision marked a turning point, as the Supreme Court subsequently reversed three more convictions in cases testing the constitutionality of state criminal syndicalism laws, and criminal syndicalism quietly faded away — to be replaced by other perceived threats.

CHAPTER

6

IN THE NAME OF NATIONAL SECURITY

IN THE NAME OF
NATIONAL SECURITY

❀

World War II began in September 1939 with Germany's invasion of Poland and soon engulfed most of Europe. Although the United States declared its neutrality, there was a real probability of its eventual entry in the war. Among those who opposed aid to England and war on Germany was a man named Elmer Hartzel who wrote several short articles of protest some time before the United States declared war on Japan on December 8 and on Germany and Italy on December 11, 1941.

In the articles, which he mimeographed and mailed to several hundred well-known persons and organizations, he made scurrilous and vitriolic attacks on the English, on the Jews, and on the President of the United States, urging Americans not to ally themselves with the English. Only a German victory, he wrote, would bring "increased stability and safety to the West."

In 1942, after America's entry into the war, Hartzel wrote more articles filled with calumny and invective. They depicted the war as a gross betrayal of America, they denounced the English allies and the Jews, and they assailed in reckless terms the integrity and patriotism of the President of the United States. Hartzel and two colleagues mimeographed the articles and mailed them to about 600 addresses.

When authorities discovered the articles, they reached back 25 years to the Espionage Act of 1917 as amended and indicted Hartzel and his colleagues on seven counts of violating the Act. The dissent (sedition) part of the Espionage Act as amended in 1918 had been repealed in 1921, and many of those convicted for violating it, including Eugene V. Debs, were given pardons or reduced sentences. That portion of the Espionage Act that made illegal any attempt to incite insubordination in the armed forces, however, remained in effect and was used in this case.

Shortly after being taken into custody, Hartzel signed a statement in which he claimed that "the prime motive which impelled me in writing and distributing the articles was the hope that they might tend to create sentiment against war amongst the white races and in diverting the war from them, to unite the white races against what I consider to be the more dangerous enemies, the yellow races."

Hartzel and his colleagues were found guilty and sentenced to five years in prison. The convictions were upheld on appeal, and the case eventually reached the U.S. Supreme Court which reversed the convictions.[1]

In a 5-to-4 decision handed down in June 1944, the Court stated that there was nothing in the pamphlets to indicate that the defendants intended specifically to cause insubordination, disloyalty, mutiny, or refusal of duty in the military forces, or to obstruct the recruiting and enlistment services. "They contain, instead, vicious and unreasoning attacks on one of our military allies, flagrant appeals to false and sinister racial theories and gross libel of the President," the Court stated.

It ruled in the majority opinion that "such ideas enunciated by a citizen are not enough to warrant a finding of criminal intent... An American citizen has the right to discuss these matters either by temperate reasoning or by immoderate and vicious invective without running afoul of the Espionage Act of 1917."

---

1. Elmer Hartzel v. United States, 322 U.S 680 (June 12, 1944).

On June 28, 1940, with the United States on the brink of entering World War II and the fear of communism unabated, Congress enacted even more stringent restrictions on speech and the press by passing a revision of the Espionage Act of 1917. The law bears the innocent-sounding title, Alien Registration Act; but Title I, called the Smith Act, contains restrictions similar to the 1918 amendment to the Espionage Act of 1917. The Smith Act states, in part, that it is unlawful:

■ To interfere or impair the loyalty, morale, or discipline of the naval or military forces of the United States,

■ To advise, counsel, urge or cause insubordination, disloyalty, or refusal of duty by any member of the naval or military forces of the United States,

■ To distribute any written or printed matter which advises, counsels, or urges insubordination, disloyalty, mutiny, or refusal of duty of any member of the naval or military forces of the United States,

■ To knowingly or willfully advocate, abet, advise, or teach the duty, necessity, desirability, or propriety of overthrowing or destroying any government in the United States by force or violence, or by the assassination of any officer of any such government,

■ With the intent to cause the overthrow or destruction of any government in the United States, to print, publish, edit, issue, circulate, sell, distribute, or publicly display any written or printed matter, advocating, advising, or teaching the duty, necessity, desirability or propriety of overthrowing or destroying any government in the United States by force or violence,

■ To organize or help to organize any society, group, or assembly of persons who teach, advocate, or encourage the overthrow or destruction of any government in the United States by force or violence , or to be or become a member of, or affiliated with, any such society, group, or assembly of persons, knowing the purpose thereof.

A considerable number of persons have been prosecuted under the Smith Act, including 29 for conspiracy and several others for being members of the Communist Party. As the law has never been repealed, there could be more in the future.

Among the cases that reached the U.S. Supreme Court on appeal was one in which Eugene Dennis, Secretary of the Communist Party, and ten fellow Communists had been tried and convicted for conspiracy.[2] They had been charged with "willfully and knowingly conspiring (1) to organize the Communist Party of the USA as a society, group, and assembly of persons who teach and advocate the overthrow and destruction of the Government of the United States by force and violence, and (2) to advocate and teach the necessity of overthrowing the Government by force and violence" during the period of April 1945 to July 1948 in violation of the Smith Act. They were indicted on the latter date.

This was a landmark case in which the Supreme Court continued to grapple with the conflict between freedom of speech and the right of government to protect itself from harm or destruction and to prevent violence. Because of the wording of the law, virtually all the cases arising under the Smith Act involved the question of freedom of speech and the press and the right peaceably to assemble, as guaranteed in the Bill of Rights.

It was not until the passage of the Espionage Act of 1917, however, that the Supreme Court was seriously confronted with cases involving freedom of speech. Chief Justice Fred Vinson, in the majority opinion in *Dennis v. United States*, wrote: "No important case involving free speech was decided by the U.S. Supreme Court prior to *Schenck v. United States*

---

2. Eugene Dennis, John B. Williamson, Jacob A. Satchel, Robert G. Thompson, Benjamin J. Davis, Jr., Henry Winston, John Gates, Irving Potash, Gilbert Green, Carl Winter, and Gus Hall v. United States, 341 U.S. 494 (June 4, 1951).

in 1919 . . . It was not until the classic dictum of Justice Holmes in the Schenck case that speech per se received that emphasis in a majority opinion . . ."

In the *Dennis v. United States* case, he held that "the Smith Act does not inherently . . . violate the First Amendment," and he justified that opinion as follows:

■ That it is within the power of the Congress to protect the Government of the United States from armed rebellion is a proposition which requires little discussion . . .

The question with which we are concerned here is not whether Congress has such *power*, but whether the *means* which it employed conflict with the First and Fifth Amendments to the Constitution.

The very language of the Smith Act . . . is directed at advocacy, not discussion . . . the trial judge properly charged the jury (in this case) that they could not convict if they found the petitioners did "no more than pursue peaceful studies and discussion or teaching and advocacy in the realm of ideas.". . . Congress did not intend to eradicate the free discussion of political theories, to destroy the traditional rights of Americans to discuss and evaluate ideas without fear of government sanction. Rather Congress was concerned with the very kind of activity in which the evidence showed these petitioners engaged.

The mere fact that from the period 1945 to 1948 petitioners' activities did not result in an attempt to overthrow the Government by force and violence is of course no answer to the fact that there was a group that was ready to make the attempt.

Petitioners intended to overthrow the Government of the United States as speedily as the circumstances would permit. Their conspiracy to organize the Communist Party and to teach and advocate the overthrow of the Government of the United States by force and violence created a "clear and present danger" of an attempt to overthrow the Government by force and violence. They were properly and constitutionally convicted for violation of the Smith Act. The judgments of conviction are affirmed.

In concurring with the majority opinion, Justice Felix Frankfurter wrote in part:

■ Few questions of comparable import have come before this Court in recent years. The appellants maintain that they have a right to advocate political theory, so long, at least, as their advocacy does not create an immediate danger of obvious magnitude to the very existence of our present scheme of society. On the other hand, the Government asserts the right to safeguard the security of the Nation by such measures as the Smith Act. Our judgment is thus solicited on a conflict of interests of the utmost concern to the well-being of the country.

The Court voted 7-to-2 to uphold the convictions, with Justices William O. Douglas and Hugo L. Black dissenting. In his dissent, Justice Black said in part:

■ The indictment is that they conspired to organize the Communist Party and to use speech or newspapers or other publications in the future to teach and advocate the forcible overthrow of the Government. No matter how it is worded, this is a virulent form of prior censorship of speech and press, which I believe the First Amendment forbids . . .

Justice Douglas in his dissent, said:

■ Petitioners were charged not with a "conspiracy to overthrow" the Government. They were charged with a conspiracy to form a party and groups and assemblies of people who teach and advocate the overthrow of our Government by force or violence and with a conspiracy to advocate and teach its overthrow by force and violence. . .
    The Act, as construed, requires the element of intent — that those who teach the creed believe in it. The crime then depends not on what is taught but on who the teacher

is. That is to make freedom of speech turn not on *what is said*, but on the *intent* with which it is said. Once we start down that road we enter territory dangerous to the liberties of every citizen.

Less than a year later the Supreme Court reinforced the Dennis decision by ruling in another case that "the Alien Registration Act of 1940 did not deprive aliens of due process of law . . . and did not abridge freedoms of speech and assembly in contravention of the First Amendment."[3]

In the five years following the Dennis decision, 16 minor Communist officials were prosecuted, but the Supreme Court heard no more cases involving convictions under the Smith Act for the next four years. In 1955 it agreed to accept the case of *Yates v. United States* in which 14 Communist Party leaders including Oleta Yates had been convicted for conspiring to advocate the overthrow of the government and for conspiring to organize the Communist Party as a society with the intent of overthrowing the government by force and violence as soon as conditions would make that possible.[4]

In its decision, handed down in 1957, the Court by a vote of 5-to-2 reversed convictions of five and ordered new trials for the rest of them, an order that often results in dismissal of the charges. The majority decision was contrary to that in the Dennis case in which the Court upheld the convictions. The difference, as indicated in the majority opinion by Justice John M. Harlan, lay in the trial court's interpretation of advocacy. He stated, in part:

---

3. Harisiades v. Shaughnessy, Mascitti v. McGrath; and Coleman v. McGrath, 342 U.S. 580 (March 10, 1952).
4. Oleta O'Connor Yates, Henry Steinberg, Loretta Starvus Stack v. United States of America; William Schneiderman v. United States of America; Al Richmond and Philip Marshall Connelly v. United States of America, 354 U.S. 298 (June 17, 1957).

■ We are thus faced with the question whether the Smith Act prohibits advocacy and teaching of forcible over-throw as an abstract principle, divorced from any effort to instigate action that leads to that end, so long as such advocacy or teaching is engaged in with evil intent. We hold that it does not.

The distinction between advocacy of abstract doc-trine and advocacy directed at promoting unlawful action is one that has been consistently recognized in the opin-ions of this Court . . . the District Court appears to have been led astray by the holding in Dennis that advocacy of violent action to be taken at some future time was enough . . . In other words, the District Court apparently thought that Dennis obliterated the traditional dividing line be-tween advocacy of abstract doctrine and advocacy of action. This misconceives the situation confronting the Court in Dennis and what was held there.

The decision in the Yates case weakened if it did not completely reverse the Dennis case. In Dennis, conviction was based on the belief that the accused were "a group ready to make the attempt" to overthrow the government. In Yates the Court held that the Smith Act forbade only "the sort of advocacy which incites to action." The difference is signifi-cant, and the prosecutions under the Smith Act diminished in number after the Yates decision; but the Act, never declared unconstitutional, remains in force.

In the next year after the Yates case, the Supreme Court handed down another decision involving freedom of speech, although this case centered on the right to remain silent. In the 1950s when the Un-American Activities Committee of the House of Representatives was holding hearings on Commu-nist infiltration into education, one of the witnesses was Lloyd Barenblatt, who had been a graduate student at the University of Michigan. When he was asked whether he was or ever had been a member of the Communist Party, he refused to answer on the grounds that the First Amendment protected his right to silence. For doing so, he was convicted for violation of a federal statute that makes it a misdemeanor for a witness before a Congressional committee to refuse to answer questions that pertain to the subject being investigated.

The U.S. Supreme Court upheld the conviction in a 5-to-4 decision handed down in 1959.[5] In the majority opinion Justice John Marshall Harlan balanced one right against another, stating that "where First Amendment rights are asserted, the issue always involves a balancing by the courts of the competing private and public interests at stake." In this case, he concluded, "the balance must be struck in favor of the government."

In a dissenting opinion, Justice Hugo Black objected to the principle of balancing one interest or right against another. He said, in part:

■ At most it balances the right of the government to preserve itself, against Barenblatt's right to refrain from revealing Communist affiliations. Such a balance, however, mistakes the factors to be weighed. In the first place, it completely leaves out the real interest in Barenblatt's silence, the interest of the people as a whole in being able to join organizations, advocate causes and make political "mistakes" without later being subjected to government penalties for having dared to think for themselves . . .

It is these interests of society, rather than Barenblatt's own right to silence, which I think the Court should put on balance against the demands of the government, if any balancing process is to be tolerated.

A case involving the membership clause of the Smith Act came before the U.S. Supreme Court three years later in 1961, in which a man named Junius Irving Scales had been convicted for being a member of the Communist Party in violation of the Smith Act.[6] Scales was chairman of the North and

5. Lloyd Barenblatt v. United States, 360 U.S. 109 (June 8, 1959).
6. Junius Irving Scales v. United States, 366 U.S. 978 (June 8, 1961).

South Carolina Districts of the Party, had recruited members, and had taught violence in a secret school. The Court upheld the conviction, also by a vote of 5-to-4.

Eight years later in 1969 the Court was back to the question of advocacy in the case of *Brandenburg v. Ohio*, ruling here as it did in *Yates* that the State may not prohibit advocacy of the use of force or violation of law unless such advocacy "is directed to inciting or producing imminent lawless action."[7]

That was in contrast to the Gitlow decision 44 years earlier in 1925. In that case, the Court held that words may be punishable because of their undesirable nature regardless of whether they are intended to incite immediate violence, which is the opposite of the "clear and present danger" test. It thus appears that over the years the Court gradually reached the position that advocacy at some future time is legal but advocacy of immediate lawless action is not permissible.

The cases cited in this chapter illustrate how the highest court in the land tried to reach decisions that allow government to protect itself from danger and destruction without infringing on the right of free speech and assembly. It may be noted, however, how few decisions were unanimous, as viewpoints and interpretations of law varied among the justices.

Repressive laws enacted in times of high emotion and the use of unwise or unrestrained police power tend to destroy the very freedoms they are intended to protect. In such cases, as Pogo once wisely observed, "The enemy is us." It is especially in such instances that the highest court in the land serves as protector of justice and defender of human rights.

Laws to protect government from criticism and invective always pose a threat to freedom of speech because of the

---

7. Clarence Brandenburg v. State of Ohio, 395 U.S. 444 (June 9, 1969).

manner in which they can be interpreted. The fact was aptly stated by Zechariah Chafee Jr. some years ago in these words:[8]

■ The truth is that the precise language of a sedition law is like the inscription on a sword. What matters is the existence of the weapon. Once the sword is placed in the hands of the people in power, then, whatever it says, they will be able to reach and slash at almost any unpopular person who is speaking or writing anything that they consider objectionable criticism of their policies.

8. Zechariah Chafee Jr., *Free Speech in the United States*, Harvard University Press, 1967, p. 467.

CHAPTER

7

YOU CAN'T PRINT THAT!

YOU CAN'T PRINT THAT !

❀

The basic right of the press guaranteed in the First Amendment is freedom from government censorship. In other words, no level of government is permitted to say in advance what may be published and what may not be published. Censorship is a form of *prior restraint.*

It has long been recognized, perhaps ever since printing first began, that censorship or prior restraint is inimical to freedom of the press. More than two hundred years ago Sir William Blackstone, noted English jurist, wrote:

> ■ The liberty of the press is indeed essential to the nature of a free state; but this consists in laying no previous restraints upon publications . . . Every free man has an undoubted right to lay what sentiments he pleases before the public; to forbid this is to destroy the freedom of the press; but if he publicizes what is improper, mischievous or illegal, he must take the consequences.

Still it was almost 150 years after the adoption of the U.S. Constitution in 1788 before the U.S. Supreme Court extended the prohibition against prior restraint to include state and local governments. That came in the landmark case of *Near v. Minnesota* in 1931.

The Minnesota State Legislature passed a law in 1925 which stated in part that "any person who . . . shall be engaged in . . . publishing, selling, or giving away an obscene, lewd or lascivious newspaper, magazine, or other periodical, or a malicious, scandalous and defamatory newspaper, magazine, or other periodical is guilty of a nuisance and . . . may be enjoined . . ."

Jay M. Near and Howard A. Guilford began publishing a weekly newspaper, the *Saturday Press*, in Minneapolis on September 24, 1927, a paper "to expose graft, corruption, and all other forms of wrongdoing in local government." It was severe and unrelenting in attacks on officials including the mayor, the chief of police, the county attorney, and the grand jury, and even the Jewish people.

Floyd B. Olson, prosecuting attorney for Hennepin County, Minnesota, in which Minneapolis is located, brought suit against the paper; and the district court adjudged the paper to be a public nuisance and enjoined the defendants "from producing, editing, publishing and circulating any publication whatsoever which is a malicious, scandalous, or defamatory newspaper as defined by law."

The Minnesota Supreme Court upheld the decision; and the case was then appealed to the U.S. Supreme Court which by a 5-to-4 vote reversed the lower court decision.[1] By doing so, the Supreme Court in effect declared the Minnesota law unconstitutional and by extension any law that imposes prior restraint is unconstitutional. Chief Justice Charles E. Hughes wrote in the majority opinion that "the object of the (Minnesota) statute is not punishment in the ordinary sense but suppression of the offending newspaper or periodical." The opinion continues in part:

■ The statute not only operates to suppress the offending newspaper or periodical but to put the publisher under an effective censorship.

. . . the operation and effect of the statute in substance is that public authorities may bring the owner or publisher

---

1. J.M. Near v. State of Minnesota Ex Rel. Floyd B. Olson, 283 U.S. 697 (June 1, 1931).

of a newspaper or periodical before a judge upon a charge of conducting a business of publishing scandalous and defamatory matter . . . and unless the owner or publisher is able and disposed to bring competent evidence to satisfy the judge that the charges are true and are published with good motives and for justifiable ends, his newspaper or periodical is suppressed and further publication is made punishable as a contempt. This is of the essence of censorship . . .

Charges of reprehensible conduct, and in particular of official malfeasance, unquestionably create a public scandal, but the theory of the constitutional guarantee is that even a more serious evil would be caused by authority to prevent publication . . .

For these reasons we hold the statute . . . to be an infringement of the liberty of the press guaranteed by the Fourteenth Amendment.

Although the decision in *Near v. Minnesota* appears to make all prior restraint by government on the press unconstitutional, that is not quite true. In the Court opinion in that case, Chief Justice Charles Evans Hughes said:

■ Liberty of speech and of the press is not an absolute right . . . the protection even as to previous restraint is not absolutely unlimited. But the limitation has been recognized only in exceptional cases . . . No one would question but that a government might prevent actual obstruction to its recruiting service or the publication of sailing dates of transports or the number and location of troops.

On similar grounds, the primary requirements of decency may be enforced against obscene publications. The security of the community life may be protected against incitements to acts of violence and the overthrow by force of orderly government . . .

Another case involving prior restraint centered on a law in Alabama that prohibited newspapers from publishing election editorials on election day.[2] James E. Mills, editor of the *Post-Herald* in Birmingham, was found guilty of publishing an editorial on election day in 1962, urging voters to vote in favor of a mayor-council plan of city government rather than a commissioner plan. Justice Hugo L. Black stated in the majority opinion of the U.S. Supreme Court in this case:

■ The Constitution specifically selected the press, which includes not only newspapers, books, and magazines, but also humble leaflets and circulars, to play an important role in the discussion of public affairs. Thus the press serves and was designed to serve as a powerful antidote to any abuses of power by governmental officials and as a constitutionally chosen means for keeping officials elected by the people responsible to all the people whom they were selected to serve . . .

We hold that no test of reasonableness can save a state law from invalidation as a violation of the First Amendment when the law makes it a crime for a newspaper editor to do no more than urge people to vote one way or another in a publicly held election . . .

Those two cases, in Minnesota and in Alabama, involved attempts by state governments to exercise prior restraint on publications. An attempt by the federal government was made in 1971 to prevent publication of what were widely known as "The Pentagon Papers."

The case occurred during a time when the nation was experiencing bitter dissension over America's fighting a war in Vietnam. Opposition began to rise in the early 1960s and grew in intensity as greater numbers of troops were sent there and casualties increased without any sign of victory. The protests became acrimonious; violent demonstrations and

---

2. Mills v. Alabama, 384 U.S. 214 (1966).

riots, many on college campuses, became commonplace; numerous young men eligible for the draft burned their draft cards in public defiance; and hundreds fled to Canada to escape military service.

By 1967 doubts about the wisdom of engaging in a war in Vietnam had reached the point where Robert McNamara, then Secretary of Defense, ordered a thorough study of the policies and actions that had led to the war. A group of researchers including civilians, Pentagon personnel, and Rand Corporation experts spent more than a year on the project.

When the study was completed in the middle of 1968, it consisted of 7,000 pages bound in 47 volumes. Titled *History of U.S. Decision Making Process on Vietnam Policy*, the study was essentially a long narrative of American involvement in Southeast Asia dating back more than 30 years, with an appendix that contained a large number of secret documents. The entire study was then classified "Top Secret — Sensitive," which means that unauthorized possession would be a violation of the Espionage Act and thus a criminal offense.

Fifteen copies were made and apparently lay unread and undisturbed for more than two years before the study became the subject of litigation involving prior restraint when some of the documents and summaries and extracts were published by *The New York Times* and the *Washington Post*. Publication began after a man named Daniel Ellsberg, an employee of the Rand Corporation, gave a copy to *The New York Times*.

Dr. Ellsberg (Ph.D., Harvard) had formerly been an analyst in the Department of Defense, and as one of the Rand Corporation experts he had been for a while a member of the group that made the historical study which came to be called "The Pentagon Papers." Originally strongly in favor of American military intervention in Southeast Asia, he gradually became disillusioned with the war, to the extent of becoming a highly vocal opponent going about the country giving speeches and taking part in demonstrations against the war.

Dr. Ellsberg apparently believed that the government had not told and was not telling the American people the truth, or at least not the whole truth, about the war. To help inform the people and indirectly to hasten disengagement in Vietnam, he removed a set of the Pentagon Papers from the Rand Corporation offices and took the set to a small advertising agency in Los Angeles where he made a copy. He was assisted in the work by a man named Anthony J. Russo, Jr. After returning the original set to the Rand Corporation offices, he offered the copied set to *The New York Times* in April 1971.

Immediately a small group of writers was assigned by *The Times* to work secretly on the study. The result was five long articles which included verbatim copies of a number of secret documents. The first of the articles was published about three months later on Sunday, June 13, 1971. The second was published on Monday and the third on Tuesday — and then publication was stopped by a court order issued at the request of the federal government.

After the second article appeared, U.S. Attorney General John Mitchell, in a telegram to *The New York Times*, asked that publication of the articles be stopped for national security reasons and that the classified papers be returned, citing a provision of the Espionage Act regarding disclosure of classified information. *The New York Times* refused to comply with the request.

Assistant Attorney General Robert Mardian then petitioned the U.S. District Court for the Southern District of New York to issue a temporary restraining order to stop publication. Judge Murray I. Gurfein agreed to do so and issued the order about 5:30 p.m. Tuesday, which was after the third article had been published; and he set Friday as the date for a hearing to consider issuance of a permanent injunction.[3] It

---

3. An injunction is a court order requiring someone to do or to refrain from taking a particular action.

was the first time in the 182 years of the United States history that a federal judge had exercised prior restraint to prevent publication of all or part of a newspaper and the first time that a president of the United States had asked the courts through the Department of Justice to stop a publication.

The New York Times, commenting on the order in an editorial on Wednesday, June 16, called the action "an unprecedented example of censorship." The editorial contended that "the documents in question belong to history" and stated, "We believe that it is in the interest of the people of this country to be informed."

After the matter had been finally decided by the Supreme Court, *The New York Times* defended its publishing the Pentagon Papers in an editorial on July 4 which read in part:

■ The Times felt that the documents, all dating from 1968 or earlier, belonged to the American people, were now a part of history, could in no sense damage current military operations or threaten a single life, and formed an essential element in the understanding by the American people of the event that has affected them more deeply than any other in this generation, the Vietnam war.

In the hearing in the District Court on Friday, the Government argued that publication of the Pentagon Papers should be stopped permanently because their publication (a) was a violation of espionage laws, (b) would pose a grave and irrevocable threat to the national security, and (c) would hinder future diplomatic negotiations because officials of foreign countries would be afraid to speak confidentially to American officials.

Judge Gurfein was not convinced by those arguments and ruled in favor of *The New York Times.* Refusing to grant a permanent injunction, he stated that "no cogent reasons were advanced as to why publication of these documents . . . would vitally affect the security of the nation." *The Times* was not able to continue publication of the Pentagon Papers, however, because Judge Irving M. Kaufman of the U.S. Court of Appeals for the Second Circuit issued a temporary restraining order the same day. The order was effective until noon Monday to give the Justice Department time to appeal Judge Gurfein's decision. In issuing the order, Judge Kaufman said that "the ultimate disposition of this case must be made by a panel of at least three judges."

In the meantime, the matter was becoming more complicated by the fact that the *Washington Post* had been able to obtain a large portion of the Pentagon Papers and began publishing articles based on them. The first of the articles appeared Friday morning, June 18, the day Judge Gurfein had set for hearings in *The New York Times* case in New York. In addition, the article in the *Post* went to 365 newspapers across the country that were subscribers to the Los Angeles-Washington Post News Service; and both the Associated Press and the United Press International news services picked up the story and sent it to their client newspapers, which numbered in the hundreds. Among large newspapers that began publishing articles based on the Pentagon Papers were the *Boston Globe,* the *Los Angeles Times*, and Knight Newspapers in Miami, Philadelphia, and Detroit.

The same day the first article appeared in the *Washington Post,* the government petitioned Judge Gerhard Gesell of the District Court for the District of Columbia Circuit in Washington to issue a restraining order to stop further publication of the Pentagon Papers by the *Post.* The Judge refused to do so, ruling that "the government had no right to impose prior restraint on publication of essentially historical data."

Even with this ruling, the *Post* was unable to continue publishing the articles because the government immediately took the case to the appeals court which ruled that same day by a vote of 2-to-1 that publication could not be resumed until the matter was decided after a full hearing.

Litigation over the publication of the Pentagon Papers then went into the second week and resulted in two appeals courts making opposite decisions. The nine-member Court of Appeals for the District of Columbia decided in favor of the *Washington Post*; but the eight-member Court of Appeals for the Second Circuit in New York voted 5-to-3 to send the case back to Judge Gurfein for him to decide which parts of the Pentagon Papers were all right to publish and which should be prohibited from publication. It gave the judge until July 3 to examine the documents and make the decision.

That wasn't at all satisfactory to *The New York Times*, so its attorneys asked John M. Harlan, a justice of the U.S. Supreme Court, to vacate the order of the Court of Appeals in New York and to request an immediate hearing by the Supreme Court with all nine justices present and participating. Justice Harlan agreed to do so, and the Supreme Court met in an extraordinary session on Saturday of that week, June 26, to hear arguments. One of the justices, William O. Douglas, who was on the Pacific Coast at the time, flew back to Washington so the full court would be present. Two cases were argued that day. One was *New York Times v. United States*; the other, *United States v. Washington Post*.[4]

Four days later at 2:30 p.m., Wednesday, June 30, Chief Justice Warren E. Burger announced the decision of the Supreme Court, which consisted of a 6-to-3 vote in favor of the newspapers. In the majority decision, the Court stated that "the Government had failed to carry its heavy burden of proof necessary for imposing prior restraint." With that decision, newspapers were then free to continue publishing the Pentagon Papers.

The case attracted nationwide attention during those three weeks in June 1971, not only because it centered on a vital aspect of freedom of the press but also because it came at a time when feeling was running high concerning the war in

---

4. New York Times v. United States and United States v. Washington Post 403 U.S. 713 (1971).

Vietnam. It appeared that there was widespread belief that the government was more concerned about being embarrassed by publication of the Pentagon Papers than it was about the effects publication would have on national security. On June 20, *The New York Times* stated, "There can be no doubt that the publication . . . will temporarily embarrass the United States Government in the eyes of the world and its own citizens . . ."

Justice Douglas, in his opinion, said in part:

■ The dominant purpose of the First Amendment was to prohibit the widespread practice of governmental suppression of embarrassing information. It is common knowledge that the First Amendment was adopted against the widespread use of the common law seditious libel to punish the dissemination of material that is embarrassing to the powers-that-be . . .

The present case will, I think, go down in history as the most dramatic illustration of that principle. A debate of large proportions goes on in the nation over our posture in Vietnam. The debate antedated the disclosure of the contents of the present documents. The latter are highly relevant to the debate in progress.

Secrecy in government is fundamentally anti-democratic, perpetuating bureaucratic errors. Open debate and discussion of public issues are vital to our national health.

The three justices who dissented from the majority did so not so much on the question of prior restraint as on the speed with which the case was being decided. They felt that the Court should have been allowed more time to consider a case as important and complex as this one. The Chief Justice himself wrote in his opinion:

■ A great issue of this kind should be tried in a judicial atmosphere conducive to thoughtful, reflective deliberation, especially when haste, in terms of hours, is unwarranted in the light of the long period The New York Times . . . deferred publication.

Justice John Marshall Harlan agreed, stating in his opinion:

■ These are difficult questions of fact, of law, and of judgment; the potential consequences of erroneous decisions are enormous. The time which has been available to us, to the lower courts, and to the parties has been wholly inadequate for giving these cases the kind of consideration they deserve . . .

In one sense, the case illustrates that one freedom or right may conflict with another freedom or right. In this case, freedom of the press was in conflict with what the government claimed was its right and duty to protect the country from its enemies. The U.S. Constitution grants a number of freedoms and rights, but it does not list any one as being superior to another. That was stated by Justice Harry A. Blackmun in his dissenting opinion in these words:

■ Each provision of the Constitution is important, and I cannot subscribe to a doctrine of unlimited absolutism for the First Amendment at the cost of downgrading other provisions (of the Constitution).

The case did not set a precedent that would apply to future cases of the same nature. In this case the Court issued a brief unsigned judgment and each of the nine justices wrote his own opinion, which had never occurred before. As no one of those opinions received the support of a majority of the justices, no one of the opinions set a precedent for the future. Although this case centered on the question of prior restraint, the Supreme Court in prohibiting it this time made it fairly clear that there may be times when the imposition of prior restraint might be imposed legally.

Eight years later in 1979 the federal government did attempt to exercise prior restraint based on law, in contrast to the attempt to suppress publication of the Pentagon Papers on the grounds of "national security." This time the action was based on a provision of the Atomic Energy Act of 1954 which authorizes the Attorney General to obtain a court injunction to prevent the publication of anything that he believes will violate the Atomic Energy Act "to the endangerment of national security."

At the request of the U.S. Attorney General, Judge Robert Warren of the Federal District Court in Wisconsin issued a temporary restraining order to stop the publication of an article titled "The H-Bomb Secret: How We Got It, Why We Are Telling It" by *The Progressive*, a monthly magazine published in that state. The government claimed that the technical information in the article on how the hydrogen bomb is designed and operates would aid other countries to make such bombs more quickly and thus "modern civilization would be one step closer to its potential destruction in a nuclear holocaust."

Seventeen days later on March 26, the judge changed the ruling into a preliminary injunction, the first ever issued against the press in the United States. The order against *The New York Times* in the Pentagon Papers case in 1971 was a temporary restraining order. In issuing the injunction, Judge Warren said, "What is involved here is information dealing with the most destructive weapon in the history of mankind, information of sufficient destructive potential to nullify the right of free speech and to endanger the right to life itself."

The editor, Erwin Knoll, insisted that the article contained no classified, secret information since the author, Howard Morland, had obtained the information for it by reading literature available to the public, by interviewing scientists, and by taking part in government-conducted tours of nuclear plants.

The purpose of the article, the editor said, was "to show how much unnecessary secrecy is being maintained in the name of national security." He said that the secrecy deprives the public of information they need regarding the environmental hazards of nuclear materials and the health and safety risks they pose. Some scientists agreed that the article contained no information that was not already widely known; others disagreed and recommended censorship of the article.

The American Civil Liberties Union, in defense of *The Progressive*, argued that the law invoked by Judge Warren is unconstitutional because it is so vague that no one can know precisely what is prohibited. The section of the law under which the government moved against *The Progressive* states that all information, even if lawfully obtained, is restricted when it comes into being and may not be made public until it is declassified. As the government is not required to give notice of declassification, and procedures for declassification themselves are secret, it is difficult if not impossible to know what is illegal to publish.

The constitutionality of the law was never tested in court, however, as the case never came to trial. The case dragged on for more than six months, in contrast to the Pentagon Papers case which was resolved in 15 days. In the meantime some newspapers had published material on atomic energy that duplicated much of the information in the article in question. Then on September 16 the *Press Connection* in Madison published a letter by an independent nuclear weapons researcher that repeated much of what was contained in the article in *The Progressive*. After those publications, the information was no longer "secret," so the Justice Department moved on September 17 to drop the injunction. In so doing, however, a spokesman for the Department said, "In this particular effort we have been thwarted, but we intend to keep on trying to stop the spread of such information."

A second instance of prior restraint of that kind by a federal judge[5] arose in November 1990 in connection with the

---

5. Judge Warren in *The Progressive* case was the first. Gurfein in the Pentagon Papers case was a State judge.

impending trial of General Manuel Antonio Noriega, former Panamanian leader who at that time was in prison in Miami, Florida. Two years earlier on February 4, 1988, he had been indicted on drug charges by federal grand juries in Miami and Tampa. That was after the invasion of Panama by U.S. military forces on December 4, 1989, and the capture of Noriega two weeks later on January 3, 1990.

In November 1990, Cable News Network (CNN) obtained seven tape recordings of telephone conversations between Noriega and his defense lawyers and on November 8 broadcast a segment of them. Noriega's lawyers immediately petitioned Federal District Judge William A. Hoeveler in Miami to issue a restraining order to prevent further use of the tapes, contending that their being broadcast would impair a fair trial for their client. The judge complied, issuing the order on the same day the first tapes were broadcast.

CNN then appealed to the U.S. Supreme Court to have the order vacated, but ten days later on November 18 the Court upheld the restraining order in a 7-to-2 decision issued without a formal opinion.[6] The decision was in contrast to the decision in the Pentagon Papers case in 1971 and was unprecedented in American history.

This particular case was complicated by the fact that revealing privileged conversations between attorney and defendant or client is illegal. CNN had not recorded the conversations, however. Apparently they had been tape-recorded by prison officials, as tape-recording of telephone calls by prisoners is standard procedure by the U.S. Bureau of Prisons, even though in this case the conversations were supposed to be private. Apparently copies of the tapes were sent to an official in Panama who then made them available to CNN.

---

6. Cable News Network, Inc. et al v. Manuel Antonio Noriega and the United States 111 S. Ct. 451, 112 L. Ed. 2d 432 (November 18, 1990).

The flap ended three weeks later on November 28 when Judge Hoeveler lifted the restraining order, giving CNN the right to make its own decision on broadcasting them. In so doing, the judge said he had decided, after reading a transcript of the tapes, that there was no need to keep them off the air any longer.

"Gag orders" are occasionally issued by state judges in criminal cases to insure that trials are unprejudiced by publicity, with contempt powers available to enforce those restraints.[7] In such instances, judges order prosecuting and defense attorneys, criminal justice officials, and court staff members not to talk for publication on any aspects of a particular case. Forbidding the publication of specific information, however, is a different matter as it involves prior restraint which has traditionally been considered unconstitutional.

Occasionally some judge will issue an order that nothing is to be published about a particular case, although such order is unconstitutional. Even so, it can effectively restrict publication of news. If the news media disobey the order and publish some information about the case, they can be cited for contempt. If they file suit to have the order rescinded, the litigation could take days, even months or years — so much time that the information is not longer news.

As an example, a case of that kind occurred in Louisiana in 1971. Two reporters from Baton Rouge, Larry Dickinson of the *Sun Times*, and Gibb Adams of the *Morning Advocate,* were assigned to report on a case in the U.S. District Court in New Orleans in which a man accused of murder insisted that the state was prosecuting him, not with the expectation of finding him guilty but rather for the purpose of harassing him.

The judge, E. Gordon West, ruled that "no report of the

---

7. Prejudicial publicity is discussed further in Chapter 13.

testimony in this case shall be published in any newspaper or by radio or television or by any other media."

The testimony was given on November 1, 1971. The two reporters considered the order unconstitutional, so they wrote stories which were published in their papers the next day. Then in the next week, they were convicted of criminal contempt and fined $300 each. The U.S. Court of Appeals for the Fifth Circuit ruled that Judge West's order was unconstitutional as a violation of the First Amendment, but that the reporters were still liable for the punishment for contempt.

The case then went back to Judge West who again convicted the reporters and upheld the fines. In an appeal this time, the Court of Appeals ruled that the order had been unconstitutional but it let the fines stand. The case then went to the U.S. Supreme Court which on October 23, 1973, voted not to hear the case, an action that let the decision of the Appeals Court stand.

That was almost three years after the case started; and by that time it was no longer news but had become history. The initial court order and contempt citation had been effective as "prior restraint."

A significant case of a judge's attempt at suppression of information arose in Nebraska several years ago, not regarding national security but rather to insure a fair trial. There, after witnesses had testified in a preliminary hearing that Erwin Charles Simants had confessed to having murdered six members of a farm family, the trial judge ordered that that information not be published because he believed its publication would jeopardize a fair trial for Simants. His order was upheld upon appeal, but the U.S. Supreme Court overturned the order in a unanimous decision handed down on June 30, 1976.[8] In the opinion in that case written by Chief Justice Warren Burger, the Court stated that "past cases demonstrate

8. Nebraska Press Association v. Stuart, 427 U.S. 539 (June 30, 1976).

that pretrial publicity — even pervasive, adverse publicity — does not inevitably lead to an unfair trial . . . . It is clear that the barriers to prior restraint remain high unless we are to abandon what the Court has said for nearly a quarter of our national existence and implied throughout all of it."

The Chief Justice pointed out, however, that the freedom the press enjoys has an accompanying responsibility. He said, "The extraordinary protections afforded by the First Amendment carry with them something in the nature of a fiduciary duty to exercise the protected right responsibly . . . It is not asking too much to suggest that those who exercise First Amendment rights in newspapers or broadcasting enterprises direct some effort to protect the rights of an accused to a fair trial by unbiased jurors."

He also reminded readers of the decision that the guarantee of free speech and free press by the First Amendment is not necessarily unlimited. "This Court," he wrote, "has frequently denied that First Amendment rights are absolute and has consistently rejected the proposition that a prior restraint can never be employed."

CHAPTER

8

YOU HAVE A RIGHT TO KNOW

YOU HAVE A RIGHT
TO KNOW

❊

The First Amendment guarantee of a free press is not granted as a favor to printers and publishers but rather as a benefit to the people, as essential to their role as citizens in a democracy. The word *democracy* is from two Greek words, *demos* which means people and *kratein* which means to rule. Democracy is thus rule by the people; and to rule wisely they must be informed on what their government is doing in order to make intelligent decisions and to cooperate in governing.

The fact that the press is given no special privileges means that everyone has the same freedom to gather information and to publish it as he wishes without first getting permission from a government office. If publishers were given special privilege, then anyone who wanted to publish a newspaper or bulletin of any kind would have to apply at a government office for that privilege and applications could be denied for a variety of reasons government officials believe appropriate.

No special privileges means that a reporter or an editor has no more legal right to information than any other citizen. The right to know is not written in the Constitution. The U.S. Supreme Court stated in 1972, "It has generally been held that the First Amendment does not guarantee the press a constitutional right of special access to information not available to the public generally."[1]

---

1. United States v. Caldwell, 408 U.S. 665 (1972).

Anyone who wishes to attend a public meeting being conducted by a unit of government has only to walk in and take a seat. In some instances a pass may be required such as for visitors' galleries in Congress. The passes are for crowd control, not to keep out the public.

Although meetings are open, news reporters are often given privileges not accorded to the general public. In fact, some states have provided journalists with some limited statutory privileges, but most have not done so. Reporters do, however, customarily have the use of press boxes in football stadiums and basketball courts, press galleries in state legislatures and Congress, special tables reserved for their use in city council chambers, and in many ways are given access to information and aid in their work.

Police departments routinely issue press passes to reporters which permit them to cross fire lines, barricades that cordon off accidents and disasters, and to attend certain kinds of restricted events. Authority to issue the passes carries with it control over which reporters and news organizations are allowed immediate access to breaking news. That authority is apparently legal, even to the extent of denying passes to some, as the U.S. Supreme Court in 1971 let stand a California ruling that no constitutional rights had been violated when the Los Angeles police department refused to issue press cards to reporters of an underground newspaper operating there at the time.

The reason for passes and other forms of deference accorded the press results from the unique position it occupies in society in its influence and the service it performs in facilitating the exchange of ideas and in informing the public of all sorts of events including actions and policies of government. Its function in reporting on government was described a number of years ago in a speech by William F. Thomas, then editor of the *Los Angeles Times*, as follows:[2]

---

2. Quoted from *Editor & Publisher*, January 13, 1973.

■ We, the press, are your only avenue of information (about your government) for all practical purposes.

■ If you want to know what the government did today — without the press you will have to listen to the governor himself and his friends and opponents.

■ Without the press, if you want to know what happened in city council, you will need press releases from the parties involved.

■ If you want to know what happened in the courtroom — without the press, you must rely on the judge to explain and evaluate his own actions, and each attorney to do the same — provided the judge will permit you to hear anything at all.

The press today includes radio and television as well as newspapers and magazines. The unique place of the press in society gave rise long ago to the term, "The Fourth Estate." It came into being in the 18th century when Sir Edmund Burke, in a speech in the British Parliament, said: "There are three estates in Parliament, but in the Reporters' Gallery yonder there sits a Fourth Estate more important far than they all. It is not a figure of speech or witty saying; it is a literal fact, very momentous to us all in these times."[3]

To fulfill its function in a democracy, the press must have access to information about government at all levels. The

3. Sir Edmund Burke, Irish statesman, orator, and writer, lived from 1729 to 1797. The word *estate* as he used it means a class of people vested with political power. The expression Fourth Estate, was also later attributed to Thomas Babington Macaulay, English historian, author, and statesman, who lived from 1800 to 1859. He is quoted as saying, "The Fourth Estate ranks in importance equally with the three estates of the realm, the Lords Spiritual, the Lords Temporal, and the Lords Common."

guarantee of freedom of the press is meaningless without the means of exercising that freedom. The right to know is as important as is the right to publish.

Although the U.S. Constitution does not provide for the right to know, legislative and judicial proceedings ranging from meetings of the city council to Congress and from traffic court to the U.S. Supreme Court are open to the public and so also are records of those proceedings. The principle is mandated in a number of states by Open Meetings and Sunshine laws that prohibit executive sessions and secret meetings of boards, councils, committees, and other such government bodies. Congress passed a Sunshine Act in 1976 requiring federal government meetings to be open to the public.

Some records kept by government employees and officials are not strictly *public* records. For example, the California Supreme Court ruled in July 1991 that the appointments calendar of the governor in that state is not a public record. The police blotter, which is log of daily transactions and occurrences, is public record in some states; but not in others. In most states, such matters as internal memorandums, correspondence, and resumes of job applicants are not classed as public records.

Secrecy is incompatible with democracy, and it can be used to cover up ineptitude and corruption in government. In recognition of the need of the people to know, the vast majority of both government meetings and government records are open and available to the public, with openness generally required by state law and city ordinances. Court trials, both civil and criminal, with minor exceptions, are open as are sessions of Congress and state legislatures and meetings of legislative committees, city councils, county commissioners, and board of directors of public schools, parks, and libraries.

Even so, the necessity for some secrecy has been written into law and upheld by the courts. Laws establishing the

Central Intelligence Agency and the Atomic Energy Agency contain provisions for secrecy. Business and industry have the legal right to protect trade secrets and manufacturing processes. By law, federal income tax returns may not be disclosed unless so directed by the President. Other government areas that include some degree of secrecy are these:

■ Diplomatic negotiations with foreign governments (but not secrecy of treaties, agreements, and covenants after they have been completed).

■ Intelligence operations, including information that could compromise foreign governments or American friends and agents in foreign lands.

■ Development of new weaponry, and in time of war, military plans and troop movements.

■ Undercover investigations of criminal activities and grand jury deliberations.

■ Official plans and decisions which if disclosed prematurely would lead to land and property speculation, private gains, and higher cost to government.

■ Personnel records, confidential doctor-patient data, and other personal information the disclosure of which would constitute an invasion of privacy.

Those are generally accepted as legitimate subjects for confidentiality, although every one has been misused to cover up poor judgment, mismanagement, and dishonesty on the part of government offices and officials. Also some, perhaps many, government officials regard government business as their own business, so they are inclined to release only such information as they think the public should have and to withhold information that is "not to the public benefit."

All jury deliberations are secret. Grand jury proceedings are secret to encourage both witnesses and jurors to speak freely without fear that what they may say will be made public or that they may later be sued for slander. Secrecy also protects the privacy of persons who are discussed in the hearings but are not indicted. Another reason for secrecy is to prevent the escape of accused persons. If the hearings were open to the public, a criminal could learn that he was being indicted and flee from arrest. Usually indictments are not announced until after the arrests have been made.

A bill in indictment, also known as a *true bill*, is an accusation endorsed by a grand jury which considers the evidence sufficient to justify a hearing. An indictment initiates a criminal case and is usually required for a serious offense. Its purpose is to inform the accused person of the charge against him so he can prepare his defense.

Grand jury secrecy, although necessary under present procedures, tends to give prosecutors control of the proceedings, allowing them to present such evidence as they wish and to avoid prosecuting cases they do not want to prosecute.

Laws in at least 16 states prohibit witnesses from ever revealing their testimony in grand jury hearings which makes it possible for unscrupulous prosecutors in those states to "gag" news reporters and investigators in the process of uncovering corruption and malfeasance. All the prosecutor has to do is to call them before a grand jury as witnesses, which would subject them to a lifetime ban on discussing what they know about a particular wrongdoing.

Laws forbidding grand jurors and witnesses from ever discussing testimony were limited somewhat by the U.S. Supreme Court in its decision in the case of *Butterfield v. Smith* in 1990. In that case Robert A. Butterfield, a newspaper reporter, was a witness in a grand jury hearing, and afterwards petitioned for the right to use his testimony in a feature story he planned to write.[4]

---

4. Robert A. Butterfield, Jr. vs Michael Smith, 108 L. 2d Ed. 2d 572 (March 21, 1990).

The U.S. Court of Appeals for the Eleventh Circuit held "the statute prohibiting a witness from ever revealing his testimony in a grand jury hearing to be unconstitutional to the extent that it applied to witnesses who speak about their testimony after the grand jury investigation is completed."

On certiorari[5], the U.S. Supreme Court unanimously affirmed that decision. In its opinion, Chief Justice William H. Rehnquist said that "the law violated the First Amendment insofar as it prohibited grand jury witnesses from disclosing their own testimony after the term of the grand jury had ended — at least in situations other than those in which the investigation continues with another grand jury."

The grand jury, which may range from 12 to 33 persons, depending upon the court, has a venerable history and an important function in the American criminal justice system. Its purpose is to make impartial inquiries into alleged violations of law and to decide whether there is sufficient evidence in each case to warrant a trial by a petit (petty) jury. It has authority to issue subpoenas and to cite disobedient witnesses for contempt.

All federal indictments for serious offenses must be made by a grand jury to comply with the Fifth Amendment which states, "No person shall be held to answer for a capital,[6] or

---

5. A writ of certiorari (pronounced sur-shee-a-rair-ee) is a legal document requesting the records of a case in a lower court so the case may be reviewed. To obtain a review of a case by the Supreme Court that is not eligible for automatic appeal, a person must petition for a writ of certiorari. If it is granted, the Court reviews the case. If it is denied, the decision of the lower court stands.

6. A capital crime is one for which the death penalty may be imposed. The words *felony, crime,* and *misdemeanor* are general terms with no precise definitions. A felony is a serious offense punishable by death or imprisonment for more than a year. A misdemeanor is a less serious offense than a felony. Murder, arson, rape, and armed robbery are examples of felonies; exceeding the speed limit and

otherwise infamous crime, unless on a presentment or indictment of a Grand Jury..." The same principle applies to the
states.

Despite laws requiring government meetings to be open
and records available to the public and to news reporters,
accessibility is not perfect. At times and in some places, short
notices or no notice of meetings are published; high fees are
charges for copying records, and restrictions make copying
difficult; also some meetings are closed to the public and to
press representatives.

In a recent study the Reporters Committee for Freedom of
the Press found more than a hundred instances between
March 1991 and March 1992 in which federal government
offices and agencies attempted to limit or conceal information. In commenting on those findings, *Editor & Publisher*
stated, "Secrecy in our government is an insidious and permanent feature. In spite of all the Sunshine and Freedom of
Information Acts, government officials have the compulsion
to cover their actions with secrecy; and the higher the official,
the worse the offense."[7]

Typical, perhaps, of the attitude of many, maybe most,
government officials is a comment made by Philip Young,
chairman of the U.S. Civil Service Commission, in hearings
held by the U.S. House of Representatives Subcommittee on
Government Information in 1955-56. He said, "I believe that
dirty linen should be washed within your own office and your
own family and not in public."[8]

Among methods used to maintain secrecy in government
besides out-and-out refusal to answer questions are claims of

---

disturbing the peace are examples of misdemeanors. Criminal laws
usually state whether a violation is a felony or a misdemeanor.

7. *Editor & Publisher*, April 11, 1992.
8. Virgin Miller Newton, Jr., "Executive Privilege Still Info Problem,"
   Editor & Publisher, November 19, 1966, page 42.

executive privilege or endangering national security or invasion of privacy. One method is lying, which is unwise because the truth will eventually be revealed, resulting in embarrassment or dismissal of the official who told the untruth. It has been tried many times at all levels of government, often with disastrous results. The CIA on occasion has been especially guilty of passing false information, and telling outright lies to the press to prevent the truth from being known, or to influence public opinion, or "to mislead the enemy." If government does lie occasionally, how are the people and the press to know when it is telling the truth? Lying destroys credibility.

A relatively recent example of secrecy in federal government was presented in a report of an extensive investigation of the Iran-Contra affair. The report, released on January 18, 1994, by Lawrence E. Walsh, special prosecutor, accuses a number of government officials, including two presidents, of dissembling, evading questions, and failing to be truthful in regard to sales of weapons to Iran in 1985 and subsequent diversion of funds from the sales to rebels, known as "contras," who were fighting the leftist government in Nicaragua.

Another method of maintaining secrecy is "misplacing" documents or shredding them. Still another is issuing order prohibiting the publication of specific information, which constitutes prior censorship and is unconstitutional in the United States. Even so, it has been attempted through court orders a number of times, mostly by trial judges, but seldom successfully. The most publicized case was that of The Pentagon Papers in 1971, discussed in Chapter 7.

Still another method of maintaining secrecy in the federal government is requiring employees and contractors to sign lifetime agreements to submit for prior approval before publication any books, articles, or speeches they write or give that pertain to their work in government service. Failure to do so gives the government the right to sue in court. More than 50 agencies require that restriction on employees' freedom of speech, and more than 4 million people in government and in companies with federal government contracts have signed such agreements. A recent survey by the General Accounting Office found that the number is increasing. The 48 agencies in the survey reported that during the six-month period from October 1, 1989, to March 31, 1990, a total of 143,531 federal employees had signed the secrecy oath. The GAO also reported that 1,455,430 workers in companies with government contracts signed the secrecy oath during 1988 and 1989.[9]

Use of the oath is not new, but it gained momentum in 1972 when the government was successful in obtaining a court order prohibiting the publication of a book about the CIA. The case involved Victor L. Marchetti who resigned from the CIA after 14 years of service and in collaboration with John Marks wrote an exposé of the agency for publication by Alfred A. Knopf, Inc. He had signed a secrecy oath, so agents of the CIA seized the manuscript from Knopf and deleted about a fifth of the material in it.

Eight years later in 1980 the use of the secrecy oath was reinforced by the decision in the case of Frank W. Snepp III, a former CIA agent who, as a condition of employment in 1968, had signed an agreement not to publish any information or material relating to the agency during or after the term of his employment without specific prior approval by the agency. After leaving the agency, Mr. Snepp disregarded the agreement by writing and publishing a book about CIA activities in South Vietnam without submitting it for review in advance.

The CIA brought suit to obtain an injunction on all his future writings and asking that all profits from anything he published in violation of his agreement to go to the agency.

---

9. Angus Mackenzie, "The Secrecy Obsession," *Columbia Journalism Review*, November-December 1991.

Mr. Snepp argued that his agreement with the agency was unenforceable because it represented prior restraint on freedom of speech; but both the U.S. District Court for the Eastern District of Virginia and the U.S. Court of Appeals for the Fourth District ruled that he had breached his position of trust and they enjoined future breaches. The U.S. Supreme Court in a 6-to-3 decision agreed, holding that "the agent having entered a trust relationship had breached his fiduciary obligation" and that "his violation of trust did not depend on whether the book actually contained classified information."[10]

The most common and most misused method of maintaining secrecy by the federal government is the classification of records and documents as Restricted, Confidential, Secret, and Top Secret, with "classified" meaning "held for reasons of national security." Under the guise of "national security," millions of government documents dating back for years are still classified and thus unavailable to writers and reporters, historians, consumer groups, and other interested persons.

Classification of government documents can be traced as far back as the War of 1812. At first, authority for classification was based on general orders of the War and Navy Departments. In 1940, President Roosevelt issued an executive order authorizing the classification of papers relating to military intelligence; and the National Security Act of 1947 gave statutory authority for classification. In 1951 President Truman signed an executive order that extended classification beyond the military, authorizing any executive department or agency to withhold information considered "necessary in the interest of national security."

---

10. Frank W. Snepp III v. United States, 444 U.S. 507 (February 19, 1980). An excellent discussion by Taylor Branch, Washington editor of *Harper's* magazine, of the background and implications of this case and the book appears in the January 1974 issue of *Harper's*.

The floodgates opened wider two years later in 1953 when President Eisenhower signed Executive Order 10501 which, while withdrawing authority to classify documents from 29 agencies and limiting the authority to classify documents to the heads of 16 other agencies, provided no effective control over classification and no procedures for declassification.

Classification grew exponentially so that by 1962, almost 20 years after Eisenhower's order, more than a million federal employees had authority to stamp permanent security designations on all kinds of documents. The kinds of documents that require classification and the designation of who is authorized to classify or declassify material are not specified by law; rather they are spelled out only by Executive Order, so the process became freewheeling, varying from agency to agency.

In the summer of 1971 a retired Pentagon official said in testimony before the Foreign Operations and Government Information Subcommittee of Congress that he estimated that the Pentagon files alone contained about 20 million classified documents. He added that he believed that less than five per cent of them contained information the release of which would be "prejudicial to the defense interests of the United States."

In an article in *The Wall Street Journal* on June 25, 1971, Richard J. Levine wrote, "Today, some 26 years after the end of World War II, U.S. archives still hold some 100 million pages of classified war records that remain beyond the public's reach." The National Archives is the chief depository for historical records and contains secret documents dating back to 1913. Also there are regional Archives; and the Federal Records Center in Suitland, Maryland, is a depository for spillover from various agencies.

Concern over the rapid drift toward secrecy in government grew because logically there just could not be so many secrets necessary to national security. Not only was so much secrecy unnecessary, it was a denial of the right of access to information by the public and by a free press. In a panel discussion at a meeting of the American Society of Newspaper Editors in April 1972, Jack Anderson, investigative reporter and columnist, said he had been told by numerous government sources that 95 to 98 percent of material that is classified should not be. "This is not national security," he said. "This is political security."

Earlier, Lester Markel, Sunday editor of *The New York Times*, in commenting on the need for access to information by the press, wrote:[11]

■ In a democracy the press is vital as a watchman of the government, to make certain that any deceptions or chicaneries or corruptions are disclosed, so that correction can be achieved. The press cannot do this job of surveillance unless it has free access to the news, clear channels of investigation and verification; in sum, there must be complete freedom of the press in normal times.

Congress has long recognized that need, and as far back as 1946 it enacted a federal public information law as Section 1002 of the Administrative Procedures Act. However, the law contained three exemptions that were so vaguely stated that federal agencies and offices had no difficulty withholding any information they chose to keep secret. The exemptions read: (1) Any function of the United States requiring secrecy in the public interest; (2) Any matter relating solely to the internal management of the agency; and (3) Information held confidential for good cause.

Twenty years later, disturbed by the enormous increase in classified documents, Congress passed the Freedom of Information Act in 1966 to allow legal access by the public to records of federal agencies.[12] President Lyndon B. Johnson

---

11. *Saturday Review*, February 9, 1963, page 50.
12. A copy of the Freedom of Information Act may be obtained by sending a request to Freedom of Information Clearinghouse, P.O. Box 19367, Washington, D. C.

signed the bill into law on July 4, 1966, to become effective on that date a year later. The Act was strengthened by amendments eight years later, with the amendments to become effective on February 19, 1975. Another amendment in October 1986 made particular kinds of organized-crime files unavailable to the public.

The law gives any persons the right to request and receive any document file, or other record in the possession of any agency of the federal government, subject to nine specific exemptions. The exemptions are national security; internal agency memorandums, personal privacy; investigatory records; any two special-interest exemptions relating to banking and oil well information.

The FOI Act applies to any federal agency but not to Congress or to the federal courts or to any executive office that advises or assists the President. It exempts investigatory files, records regarding national defense and foreign policy, and those that contain private personal information, trade secrets, and financial data obtained in confidence.

Requests for information must be made by certified letter addressed to the FOI officer of the agency from which the information is desired and must describe in some detail the kinds of records requested. A request will be acknowledged within ten days, but record searches may take weeks. Agencies are permitted to charge for making searches and copying material.

The law allows wide diversity of policy from agency to agency regarding the release of information, and it limits access to records to "persons properly and directly concerned," which permits agencies to decide who may have access to records. It is possible to seek a court order requiring the release of specific records, but that takes time and is successful only if the court is willing to issue the order.

In several respects the law has not been entirely effective in facilitating the release of government records. Requests may be refused on the grounds that they fall within one or more of the nine categories of information exempted by the law. Delays have run up to a year or more, and requests for information have been denied because they are not specific enough or because they infringe on matters considered confidential or classified. Also, the Freedom of Information Act does not mention computer data, and an enormous amount of information has been stored in computers since the FOI Act became law.

Six years after the passage of the FOI Act, President Nixon in 1972 signed an executive order effective June 1, 1972, that reduced from 38 to 12 the number of agencies outside the White House that can use the Top Secret designation and limited to 12 others use of the Secret stamp. It also reduced from 5,100 to 1,860 the number of officials authorized to classify documents. The order tightened rules for classifying documents, made the process of declassifying documents faster, and provided that Top Secret papers could be made public within ten years after their classification, Secret papers within eight years, and Confidential papers within six years. The ten-year limit, however, on opening Top Secret papers means that it will be at least two years after any president has left office before the public can know the contents of such documents so classified during his administration.

Despite that order, classification has continued virtually unabated. In 1989, for example, 6,796,501 government documents were classified, according to the U.S. Information Security Oversight Office, with only three percent marked with a declassification date.[13] While classified documents pile up, declassification is also going on, but at a slow pace. Not only is it a tedious process, but is all the slower by a lack of urgency and a lack of funds to employ sufficient staff. As a result, an enormous backlog exists.

---

13. Morton H. Halperin and Jeanne M. Woods, "Ending the Cold War at Home," *Foreign Policy,* Winter 1990-91.

Critics have pointed out that in no statute or executive order is there a definition of "national security" so that the term can be and has been interpreted so broadly as to extend far beyond the protection of documents which, if revealed, would pose actual danger to the nation. National security has been used as a pretext for tapping telephones, opening mail, deceiving Congress, and putting thousands of American citizens under surveillance besides classifying millions of government documents.

The classification system has been used to protect government officials from embarrassment and ineptitude, and it has been misused by documents being "leaked" or revealed to the press when an official believes that public disclosure would be advantageous in some manner.

Government's managing the news through withholding some and revealing other information, either openly or through "leaks," has broader implications than merely denying the right of the press to know. It indicates a distrust of the people and an attitude that "we know best what to do."

Arthur Sylvester, Assistant Secretary of Defense for Public Affairs, has been quoted as saying on October 30, 1962, "News generated by actions of the government as to content and timing are part of the arsenal of weapons that the President has in the application of military sources and related forces to the solution of political problems or to the application of international political pressure."[14]

An example of government deceptive action was a report of a test of an ICBM in June 1984, in which a rocket was launched at Vandenberg Air Force Base in California in a test to destroy a rocket launched in Kwajalein Island thousands of miles away in the Pacific Ocean. This was part of the Strategic Defense Initiative, called Star Wars, to place a defense curtain against

---

14. Lester Markel, "The Management of News," *Saturday Review,* Ferruary 9, 1963, page 50.

nuclear ballistic missiles. The test was reported perfect, with the equivalent of a bullet hitting a bullet at the great distance; but on August 30, 1993, *The New York Times* reported that results has been rigged and the results were a fraud.

Another example: Hazel O'Leary, Secretary of the Department of Energy, revealed in December 1993, that secret nuclear tests over the past 45 years had exposed thousands of persons to dangerous radiation levels. Also, the DOE and the Army admitted that during the 1940s and 1950s the government had lied about radiation fallout from 12 atomic bombs detonated in the atmosphere over Utah to test radiation warfare against enemy troops.

In commenting on the effects of news management, Senator William J. Fulbright said in 1971, "Secrecy and subterfuge are themselves more dangerous to a democracy than the practices they conceal." He added, "When a government refuses to put its trust in the people, the people will in turn withdraw their trust from that government."

CHAPTER

9

SOME COMMUNICATION IS PRIVILEGED

SOME COMMUNICATION
IS PRIVILEGED

❀

A privilege is both a right and an immunity. As an example, members of Congress have the right to say whatever they wish in either House and have immunity from being sued for libel for doing so.[1] That privilege is granted in Article I of the U.S. Constitution, which reads in part:

■ The Senators and Representatives shall ... in all cases, except treason, felony, and breach of the peace, be privileged from arrest ... and for any speech or debate in either House, they shall not be questioned in any other place.

Statements by the President of the United States or the governor of a state in executive proceedings or functions, even if false and defamatory, are ordinarily privileged. Such immunity extends to members of state and local legislative bodies and to judges, attorneys, and witnesses in court trials, provided what they say is related to the case being tried. A prosecuting attorney, for example, may call an accused person on trial a murderer, or a liar, or a thief, and not be held accountable, even though the jury later finds that person not guilty.

---

1. U.S. Representatives and Senators may be sued for libel for actions or statements made outside official sessions, whether the actions or statements are connected with their duties or not.

Confidentiality of communication between the President of the United States and his aides is known as *executive privilege*. That means that oral discussions and written communications between the president and his staff are privileged and may not be revealed without his approval.

Virtually every president has claimed executive privilege as inherent in his position, beginning with George Washington who refused to release to Congress papers relating to the controversial Jay Treaty with England in 1795. This privilege was invoked by President Eisenhower in 1954 when he directed the Secretary of Defense to order his subordinates not to testify regarding certain matters brought up in the highly publicized Army-McCarthy hearings; and by President Kennedy who refused a request by a special Senate subcommittee for the names of persons assigned to edit speeches of military leaders.

On the other hand, Presidents Washington, Lincoln, and Wilson all agreed to appear before Senate groups to answer questions. Chief Justice John Marshall once ruled that "in proper circumstances a subpoena could be issued to a President," but that was not a firm ruling. When he subpoenaed President Thomas Jefferson to produce a letter he had received for use by Aaron Burr in his treason trial, Jefferson provided an edited version but with a statement that the Court had no authority to compel him to do so.

Executive privilege is not mentioned in the U.S. Constitution; and, although practiced by presidents, the term did not enter into the language until 1958 when it was first used in a U.S. Supreme Court decision. It was obliquely recognized by the U.S. Supreme Court on July 24, 1974, when the Court ruled 8-to-0 that President Richard M. Nixon must turn over 64 tape recordings of White House conversations requested by Watergate Special Prosecutor Leon Jaworski. While tacitly agreeing that executive privilege exists, the Court held that information absolutely essential to an authorized proceeding takes precedence over executive privilege.

Richard M. Nixon was the only president to have claims of executive privilege rejected by the Supreme Court. The case arose when Nixon filed suit, after he had left the office of president, to challenge the constitutionality of the Presidential Recordings and Materials Preservation Act. The Court ruled in the majority opinion by Justice Brennan that (1) the Act did not violate the principle of separation of powers, (2) did not work impermissible intrusion on the doctrine of presidential privilege, (3) did not impermissibly infringe on the former president's privacy interest, (4) did not infringe on the former president's First Amendment right of association, and (5) did not constitute a bill of attainder.[2]

The exercise of executive privilege has, at times, created conflict between the President and the Congress. Congress has investigative and subpoena[3] powers similar to those of a grand jury, not to indict but to hold hearings, with authority to summon witnesses and to cite for contempt[4] those who refuse to attend or to answer questions or to submit documents and evidence as directed.

Everyone except the President of the United States must appear when issued a subpoena by a judge, a legislative

---

2. Richard M. Nixon v. Administrator of General Services, 433 U.S. 425 (June 28, 1977).
3. A *subpoena* is a writ commanding the person named in it to appear in a legal proceeding. The word comes from the Latin sub poena, which means *under penalty* and now means that the person named will be punished if he does not obey. A *subpoena duces tecum* is a writ commanding a person to bring to a legal proceeding such as a court trial certain kinds of documents and evidence. The words *duces tecum* may be translated as "thou shalt bring with thee."
4. *Contempt,* which is willful disobedience to or open disrespect for the rules or orders of a court, a judge, or a legislative body, is the only offense for which a person may be jailed without a trial—except in cases where a guilty plea is entered.

committee, or by a grand jury. Failure to do so makes a person subject to contempt. It is generally accepted that the President is not required to obey such summons under the separation of powers.

The President can also refuse to permit members of his staff to testify and can refuse to make subpoenaed materials available to a Congressional committee on the basis of executive privilege or separation of powers or national security. One instance of such refusal arose in the Congressional investigation of the Watergate scandal during the Nixon administration. Another was in a similar investigation of the sale of arms to Iran and the diversion of funds to Nicaraguan Contras during the Reagan administration.

Just as most government meetings are open to the public, so also are the records of meetings and actions of the government at all levels open to the public. Among public records which anyone may see and copy are those of court proceedings, tax collections, government expenditures, property deeds, mortgages, transfers of real estate, wills filed for probate, marriage licenses, divorce petitions, election results, and many others.

The right to see government records is limited in several ways. One is in regard to access because the work of an office could be disrupted by large numbers of people asking to see records out of idle curiosity. Records are almost always available, however, to anyone who has a good reason for wanting to see them. The other limitation is that some records are confidential and thus not open to the public at all. Examples are reports of police investigations, adoptions of children, individual income tax returns, and records protected by privacy laws.

Governmental proceedings and records are *privileged*, the meaning of which in this context is the opposite of *privileged communication*, which is secret and confidential. That is to say, the word *privilege* has opposite meanings. In one context, it means confidential; in the other, it means non-

117

confidential, with the right to reveal or publish.

Communication between doctor and patient, lawyer and client, and pastor and communicant is privileged. Privileged communication in that sense means that no judge in a courtroom or any other government officials may require such communication to be revealed. There are some exceptions, and the laws vary from state to state; but in general, privileged communication is that which cannot legally be disclosed.

Technically, in the opposite meaning privilege is not so much the right to publish as it is the right to be free from legal liability for libel. In other words, privilege is a defense against a charge of libel. Here again, laws vary, but that is the general rule. There are basically two defenses against a charge of libel. One is truth, discussed in Chapter 16. The other is privilege.

If, for example, someone brings suit for defamation based on publication of an article the contents of which came from public records, the reporter, the editor, and the publisher can defend themselves legally by showing that the information came from public records, from records that are open for anyone to see. There are some exceptions, however, as privilege may be qualified or conditional rather than absolute.

Suppose, for example, a man files suit for a divorce charging his wife with adultery, and the newspaper publishes that information, which is public record but has only qualified privilege. It is qualified because the man could withdraw the suit before it goes to trial. If he did so, it would be safe to publish the fact that he sued for divorce, but not that his wife was accused of adultery. That would not become privileged information until after it was sworn testimony in court.

CHAPTER
10

YOU HAVE A RIGHT NOT TO SPEAK

YOU HAVE A RIGHT
NOT TO SPEAK

❀

Freedom of speech includes freedom not to speak. Legally you don't have to answer questions asked you by a news reporter or by anyone else. That applies to everyone, from an ordinary citizen to the President of the United States. You don't have to tell your name, where you are going or what you are thinking, not even to a policeman. You don't have to pledge allegiance to the flag or join in singing the National Anthem or in public prayer. Silence may not be the best for you, and it may make people angry at you; but you don't break the law by keeping quiet.

A person arrested for a misdemeanor or a felony or for any other reason doesn't have to say even one word if he chooses not to. That right is a part of the Fifth Amendment to the U.S. Constitution which reads:

■ No person . . . shall be compelled in any criminal case
to be a witness against himself.

"Taking the Fifth" became part of the American language as the result of witnesses in televised hearings refusing to answer questions "on the grounds that they may tend to incriminate me."

In a preliminary hearing, an accused person asked whether he pleads guilty or not guilty doesn't have to speak. If he remains silent, a plea of not guilty is entered in the record.

To encourage witnesses or accused persons to speak, courts and legislative committees occasionally offer grants of immunity, provided the information needed is important and there apparently is no other way of obtaining it. Immunity means that the person will not be held liable for the misdeeds he confesses he committed in connection with the case in question. Immunity may be total or limited; and it may be refused by witnesses or accused persons for fear of reprisal if they talk, or of losing friends and reputation, or of jeopardizing their position at work.

The United States has had a federal immunity law since 1857. As amended by the Immunity Act of 1954, it enables the Senate and the House of Representatives by majority vote or a Congressional committee by two-thirds vote to grant immunity to witnesses in investigations concerning national security provided the Attorney General is notified in advance and given an opportunity to object and an order is first obtained from a U.S. district court judge. Immunity was granted, for example, to Lt. Col. Oliver North and others in the Congressional hearings in the Iran-Contra Affair in the summer of 1987, hearings that received widespread publicity.

The reach of the Fifth Amendment right to remain silent, combined with the Sixth Amendment guarantee of a fair trial, is broad, and has been at the heart of numerous appeals including a landmark decision by the U.S. Supreme Court in 1966. That case involved a 25-year-old man named Ernesto A. Miranda who had been convicted in Arizona of kidnapping and raping an 18-year-old girl and given a jail sentence of 20 to 30 years. There was little doubt of his guilt. He was arrested at his home on March 13, 1963, by Phoenix police and taken to the station house where he was identified in a lineup. He was then taken to an interrogation room and questioned by two police officers.

After two hours the officers had a signed confession and with it a typed paragraph stating that "the confession was made voluntarily with full knowledge of his legal rights and with the understanding that anything he said might be used against him." In the trial the confession was admitted as evidence, over objection by Miranda's attorney; but the officers who had questioned Miranda admitted that he had not been advised that he had a right to have an attorney present.

Although the Arizona Supreme Court upheld the conviction, the U.S. Supreme Court reversed the conviction by a 5-to-4 vote and ordered another trial for Miranda..[1] In the majority opinion handed down on June 13, 1966, the Court held that Miranda's confession to the police was inadmissible as evidence in his trial because "he was not in any way apprised of his right to counsel nor was his privilege against self-incrimination effectively protected in any other manner."

Procedures that should be used in questioning accused persons were stated by Chief Justice Earl Warren in the majority opinion:

■ Prior to any questioning, the person must be warned that he has a right to remain silent, that any statement he does make may be used as evidence against him, and that he has a right to the presence of an attorney, either retained or appointed.

The defendant may waive effectuation of these rights, provided the waiver is made voluntarily, knowingly and intelligently. If, however, he indicates in any manner and at any stage of the process that he wishes to consult with an attorney before speaking, there can be no questioning. Likewise, if the individual is alone and indicates in any manner that he does not wish to be interrogated, the police may not question him. The mere fact that he may have answered some questions or volunteered some statements

---

1. Here the Court grouped four cases together, all similar in that the persons convicted had confessed without being fully advised of their constitutional rights. The decision is commonly known by the first name on the list: Miranda v. State of Arizona, Vignera v. State of New York, Westover v. United States, and State of California v. Stewart, 384 U.S. 436 (1966). Miranda was retried, as the Court ordered, and reconvicted.

on his own does not deprive him of the right to refrain from answering any further inquiries until he has consulted with an attorney and thereafter consents to be questioned.

Four of the justices expressed strong dissent to the majority opinion; and there was an immediate outcry by law enforcement agencies that the court decision would tie the hands of police and make obtaining confessions very difficult if not impossible. Many persons accused the Warren Court of coddling criminals and failing to give the public adequate protection. It was, *The New York Times* said, "the most heatedly debated and widely publicized issue to divide judges, lawyers, and scholars of criminal law in decades."[2]

Regardless of protests, the decision stood and, galling as it appeared to police departments, they had no choice but to follow the guidelines laid down by the Supreme Court. So they began issuing billfold-size cards to their officers as a guide in the interrogation of suspects. One side of a typical card would read:

MIRANDA WARNING

1. You have the right to remain silent.
2. Anything you say can and will be used against you in a court of law.
3. You have the right to advice of a lawyer before being questioned and the presence of a lawyer here with you during questioning.
4. If you cannot afford to hire a lawyer, one will be appointed to represent you before any questioning if you desire one.

(This warning is mandatory, to be given to all persons you interview before questioning.)

---

2. *The New York Times*, October 2, 1966.

The other side of the card would read:

WAIVER OF CONSTITUTIONAL RIGHTS

The burden is upon the officer to show that the waiver is made voluntarily, knowingly, and intelligently.

Therefore ask (after warning and before questioning):

1. Do you understand each of these rights I have explained to you?
2. Having these rights in mind, do you wish to talk to us now without a lawyer?

(If the suspect indicates in any manner, prior to or during questioning that he wishes to remain silent, or that he wishes an attorney, the interrogation must cease, unless permission is given by his attorney.)

Despite later modifications of the decision in the Miranda case, the Miranda Warning remains today a part of police procedure throughout the United States. While it is not necessary or generally used at the time of arrest, the Warning is mandatory before questioning begins.

The Miranda decision, and those in other self-incrimination cases, have centered on the word "compelled" in the Fifth Amendment. The purpose of that part of the Amendment is to prevent the use of coercion to obtain confessions. Coerce, which means "to bring about by force or threats," can take many forms, ranging from torture, hypnosis, and mind-altering drugs to persistent questioning, cajoling, and promises of leniency. The use of coercion is an ugly thread running throughout history. Fiendishly cruel instruments of torture can be seen in museums in Europe; and the term "rubber hose" came from the use of "physical persuasion" by overly zealous police in this country. In the Miranda decision, the Court made clear that a confession must be entirely voluntary to be used as evidence in a trial, and that a confession is invalid and not admissible as evidence if it has been obtained by the use of flattery, deception, psychological pressure, or physical abuse.

The matter of involuntary or "compelled" confessions, however is so complex that few decisions by the U.S. Supreme Court in such cases have been unanimous. The Miranda decision itself was approved by a majority of only one. Since no two cases are alike, it is often debatable in any particular instance whether coercion was used, and if so, how and to what extent and under what conditions. While accused persons and criminals have rights that must be respected, those rights need to be balanced against the rights of society and of victims of crime.

For more than a hundred years after the adoption of the Fifth Amendment, the U.S. Supreme Court was not faced with self-incriminating cases, but in this century it has been confronted by a number of them, deciding for the defendant in some cases and for the prosecution in others.

In 1934, the Court handed down a unanimous decision in which it reversed the conviction of Ed Brown, a 17-year-old black youth, for murder in Mississippi. He had been seized by a lynch mob that threatened his life by hanging, actually suspending him twice with a rope and then whipping him until he admitted to being guilty.[3] There was no question but what his confession had been "compelled."

In the summer of 1944, the Court ruled in favor of the prosecution in two self-incriminating cases and for the plaintiff in one. In May of that year it ruled, again unanimously, that a confession by E. E. Ashcraft, accused of murder in Tennessee, had been coerced and therefore his confession was not admissible as evidence in this trial.[4] There police had turned a searchlight on Ashcraft and questioned him in relays for 36 hours before he confessed.

---

3. Brown v. Mississippi, 297 U.S. 278 (1934).
4. Ashcraft v. State of Tennessee, 320 U.S. 728 (1944).

In June of 1944 the Court upheld the conviction of W.D. Lyons for multiple murders in Oklahoma.[5] Lyons had confessed twice, with the second confession coming 12 hours after the first; and it was on the basis of the second confession that he was found guilty. Justice Frank Murphy, in a strong dissent to the majority decision upholding the conviction, described the kind of pressure the police had placed on Lyons. His dissent reads in part:

> ■ . . . even assuming that there was no violence surrounding the second confession, it was inconceivable under these circumstances that the second confession was free from the coercive atmosphere that admittedly impregnated the first one . . . To conclude that the brutality inflicted at the time of the first confession suddenly lost all of its effect in the short space of twelve hours is to close one's eyes to the realities of human nature.
>
> An individual does not that easily forget the type of torture that accompanied petitioner's previous refusal to confess, nor does a person . . . so quickly recover from the gruesome effects of having a pan of human bones placed on his knees in order to force incriminating evidence from him.

In another decision in the same month, the Court held that the Fifth Amendment did not apply to an organization such as a labor union in the same way as it does to an individual.[6] In that case, the District Court for the United States for the Middle District of Pennsylvania issued a subpoena directing Local No. 542, International Union of Operating Engineers, to produce to the grand jury on January 11, 1943, copies of its constitution, bylaws, and certain financial records. The subpoena was served on the president of the union, who refused to produce the records as "they might tend to incrimi-

---

5. Lyons v. Oklahoma, 322 U.S. 596 (June 1944).
6. United States v. White, 322 U.S. 694 (June 1944).

nate him." He argued that the order constituted "unreasonable search and seizure," and that he could not legally be compelled in any criminal case to be a witness against himself.

The District Court found him guilty of contempt and sentenced him to 30 days in prison. Upon appeal, the U.S. Supreme Court upheld the conviction, ruling that "the constitutional privilege against self-incrimination is essentially a personal one, applying only to natural individuals, and cannot be utilized by or on behalf of any organization, such as a corporation."

A case reviewed by the U.S. Supreme Court in 1945 illustrates extreme coercion.[7] Morris Malinski, arrested for the murder of a New York police officer, was taken to a Brooklyn hotel, stripped naked, threatened, questioned throughout the day, and was not permitted to see an attorney or relatives or friends. Police boasted that Malinski "was not hard to break," and they succeeded in getting an oral confession from him. But that was not enough; wanting a written confession, they continued to badger him from the time of his arrest Friday evening until 2 o'clock the next Tuesday morning. The only concession they made was to permit him to wear his clothes. They got a written confession, but the conviction obtained by the confession was reversed by the U.S. Supreme Court.

In stating the position of the Supreme Court in regard to coerced confessions, Justice Frank Murphy said in dissent in the case of Taylor v. Alabama in June 1948:[8]

■ Wherever a confession is shown to be the product of mental or physical coercion rather than reasoned and voluntary choice, the conviction is void. And it is void even though the confession is in fact true and even though

---

7. Malinski v. New York, 324 U.S. 401 (March 1945).
8. Taylor v. Alabama, 335 U.S. 253 (June 1948).

there is adequate evidence otherwise to sustain the conviction.

This principle reflects the common abhorrence of compelling any man, innocent or guilty, to give testimony against himself in a criminal proceeding. It is a principle which was written into the Constitution because of the belief that to torture and coerce an individual into confessing a crime, even though that individual be guilty, is to endanger the rights and liberties of all persons accused of crime.

History has shown that once tyrannical methods of law enforcement are permitted as to one man such methods are invariably used as to others. Brutality knows no distinction between the innocent and the guilty. And those who suffer most from these inquisitorial processes are the friendless, the ignorant, the poor and the despised.

Other cases followed, but none have been so definitive and so far-reaching in effect as the Miranda decision in 1966. That decision, however, has been modified by legislation and later court decisions. The Omnibus Crime Control and Safe Streets Act passed by Congress in 1968, for example, states that confessions in particular kinds of cases are admissible as evidence whether the Miranda Warning was given or not.

The California Supreme Court ruled in June 1972 that police must stop questioning a minor who asks to talk with his parents. The U.S. Supreme Court held in the case of *Oregon v. Hass* in 1975 that the Miranda Warning is not required by the U.S. Constitution but is a necessary procedural device.[9] A year later in the case of *United States v. Mandujano*, the Court ruled that the Warning and legal counsel are not necessary in connection with the subpoena of a suspect before a grand jury.[10]

---

9. Oregon v. Haas, 420 U.S. 714 (1975).
10. United States v. Mandujano, 425 U.S. 564 (1976).

In decisions before and after the Miranda case, the U.S. Supreme Court generally but not invariably upheld the right of accused persons not to talk, not to incriminate themselves. In so doing, it established the principle that a coerced confession used as evidence in a criminal trial automatically invalidated a conviction. Then on March 26, 1991, in the case of *Arizona v. Fulminante* it ruled that that was not necessarily so.[11]

The case began when Oreste C. Fulminante reported to the police in Mesa, Arizona, that his 11-year-old stepdaughter, Jeaneane Michell Hunt, was missing. Two days later her body was found in the desert east of the city. She had been shot twice in the head.

The police suspected Fulminante but were unable to find sufficient evidence to arrest him. Fulminante soon moved to New Jersey, where he was later arrested and found guilty of a firearms violation and was sent to a federal prison in New York.

While in that prison the rumor spread that he was a child killer, and by one account he was roughed up by some inmates because of that reputation. Fulminante was then befriended by Anthony Sarivola, another "inmate" who was reputed to have Mafia connections, but unknown to Fulminante, was in fact a former policeman and now an informer for the FBI.

Sarivola told Fulminante that he could protect him, but he could do so only if Fulminante told him truthfully what had happened in Arizona. Frightened, Fulminante told how he had taken the girl out into the desert, sexually assaulted her, and then shot her to death. Later he repeated the story to Sarivola's fiancé.

With that evidence available, authorities returned Fulminante to Arizona where he was tried, found guilty of

---

11. Arizona v. Fulminante, 111 S. Ct. 1246, 113 L Ed. 2d 302 (March 26, 1991).

murder, and sentenced to die. Upon appeal, the Arizona Supreme Court reversed the decision and ordered a new trial on the grounds that the confession had been coerced by "a credible threat of physical violence." The case then went to the U.S. Supreme Court, which in a 5-to-4 decision upheld the Arizona Supreme Court ruling.

In another aspect of the ruling, however, the Court held by a majority of 5 to 4 with a somewhat different alignment of justices that a coerced or involuntary confession can be excused as "a harmless error" if it can be shown that other evidence, obtained independently of the confession, was also introduced at the trial and was sufficient to sustain a verdict of guilty.

Four of the justices strongly dissented with that opinion. Justice Byron R. White took the unusual step of reading his dissent from the bench, stating that the majority had overruled "a vast body of precedent" and in so doing had dislodged "one of the fundamental tenets of our criminal justice system." He cited 14 Supreme Court decisions that supported his dissent, including *Chapman v. California* in 1967.

In that case Ruth Elizabeth Chapman and Thomas LeRoy Teale were accused of robbery, kidnapping, and murder, but refused to testify in their trial. The California State Constitution provides that "failure of an accused person to explain or to deny any evidence or facts in the case against him may be commented on by the court or counsel, and may be considered by the court or the jury."

In their trial the prosecuting attorney accordingly made extensive adverse comments on their refusal to testify and the judge suggested certain inferences that could be drawn from their silence. The jury found the two guilty, with the woman sentenced to life imprisonment and the man to death. The U.S. Supreme Court reversed the verdicts and remanded the case for retrial, stating in the majority opinion that "the right of defendants not to be punished for exercising their Fifth and Fourteenth Amendment rights to be silent is a federal right which, in the absence of appropriate congressional action, is the responsibility of the Supreme Court to protect by fashioning the necessary rule."[12]

Cases involving confessions, whether coerced or alleged to be involuntary, point up the conflict that often exists between the right of accused persons to remain silent and the responsibility of the criminal justice system to enforce the law. Although police at times feel hindered by the Miranda decision, it is generally agreed that the Miranda Warning has resulted in more professional action by police with less dependence on coercion and more effort at obtaining independent evidence.

Although the Fifth Amendment prohibition against compelling anyone to be witness against himself has been variously interpreted, the fact remains that everyone has the right not to speak, the right to remain silent when questioned by police or on any other occasion. One important exception is that a witness in a court trial or a legislative inquiry is required to answer the questions asked and to give testimony as directed.

Refusing to do so makes a person liable to being cited for contempt, which is punishable by a fine or jail or both. A legal way to avoid answering questions under oath is to "take the Fifth."

As a witness a person swears or affirms "to tell the truth, the whole truth and nothing but the truth, so help me God." Holding up one's hand and swearing to tell the truth is taking an oath. A person also takes an oath by signing a document such as a deposition or an affidavit attested to by a notary public. Not telling the truth under oath is perjury, which is a criminal offense.

---

12. Ruth Elizabeth Chapman and Thomas LeRoy Teale v. State of California, 368 U.S. 18 (February 20, 1967).

CHAPTER

11

❀

YOU HAVE A RIGHT FOR AN ATTORNEY TO SPEAK FOR YOU

YOU HAVE A RIGHT FOR
AN ATTORNEY TO
SPEAK FOR YOU

❀

Anyone arrested for a misdemeanor or a felony in this country has the right to be represented by an attorney. The Sixth Amendment to the U.S. Constitution states in part:

■ In all criminal prosecutions, the accused shall have the right . . . to have Assistance of Counsel for his defense.

If one does not have the money to hire a lawyer, the Court will provide one and pay the cost. In almost every city or county there is a Public Defender's office staffed by one or more attorneys to act as counsel for indigent persons accused of breaking the law.

It has not always been that way, and the right to counsel is not always that simple. In Colonial days the people were governed by English common law, which did not allow a person accused of a felony to be represented by counsel. The men who drew up the Bill of Rights believed that to be unjust, and they made sure that would not be the practice under the newly adopted Constitution of the United States.

They did so for good reasons. One is that the criminal justice system in this country is adversarial, with the prosecution and the defense taking opposite sides. Anyone who does not know what his rights are and is uninformed in regard to court procedures and legal technicalities is at a disadvantage — and that includes most people.

Frank Murphy, as a justice of the U.S. Supreme Court, stated the need in this fashion:[1]

■ The ordinary person accused of crime has little if any knowledge of law or experience in its application. He is ill prepared to combat the arsenal of statutes, decisions, rules of procedure, technicalities of pleading and other legal weapons at the ready disposal of the prosecutor. Without counsel, many of his elementary procedural and substantive rights may be lost irretrievably in the intricate maze of a criminal proceeding. Especially is this true of the ignorant, the indigent, the illiterate and the immature defendant.

Equal protection under the law is for everyone. It applies to both children and adults, to the weak and the strong, the mentally handicapped, the sick and the crippled, the poor and discouraged, to the drunkard and the drug addict as well as to the mentally alert, the physically able, and the affluent. It applies to the alien in this country as well as to the citizen.

The person who has committed a heinous crime and is clearly guilty has as much right to equal protection under the law as does the law-abiding citizen, although such protection might seem to conflict with the rights of the public. To deny a despised person his or her rights is to deny the rule of law, even though there may be widespread indignation and a feeling that that criminal should be hanged on the nearest tree limb.

If a defense attorney knows that his client is guilty, he is not at liberty to reveal that fact. His responsibility is to see that his client receives a fair trial; and if his client is found guilty, to see that the state proves the guilt beyond doubt.

Protection as guaranteed by the U.S. Constitution is important at the time of arrest and questioning by police as well

---

1. Canizio v. New York, 327 U.S. 82 (February 1946).

as in court. Being arrested and questioned generally places a person under such psychological stress that clear thinking and considered judgment are difficult if not impossible. That is especially true of anyone who is sick or injured, is under the influence of alcohol or drugs, or is mentally handicapped.

If justice is to be served, such protection is necessary because no lone individual, no group of persons, not even the governor of a State can resist the awesome power of government. At its command are thousands of police officers and sheriffs' deputies, State Police, the National Guard, the Secret Service, the FBI, and in extreme cases, the U.S. Army to enforce laws and to compel compliance with court orders.

Although mandated by the U.S. Constitution, assistance of legal counsel came slowly for the poor, for accused persons unable to hire an attorney to defend them — and even for some who were financially able. A major reason was the widelyheld interpretation that the Bill of Rights applied only to the federal government; and since most litigation did, and still does, take place in state and local courts, the Sixth Amendment under that interpretation protected relatively few defendants.

In extending "assistance of counsel" to virtually everyone accused of a crime, the U.S. Supreme Court in its decisions relied on the "due process" clause of the Fourteenth Amendment, Section 1, which is stated in Chapter 4 and repeated in part here:

■ . . . nor shall any State deprive any person of life, liberty, or property, without due process of law; nor deny any person within its jurisdiction the equal protection of the law.

Consideration by the U.S. Supreme Court of the "due process" clause of the Fourteenth Amendment, but not necessarily of the Sixth Amendment, was significant in its decision in the highly publicized "Scottsboro Case"[2] in 1931-1932. In that case the Court ruled that counsel must be provided in any case involving a capital crime in which the defendant is ignorant, illiterate, and unable to hire an attorney.

The case originated when a group of black youths and a group of white youths got into a fight while riding a freight train in Alabama. All the white youths except one were thrown off the train, and two white girls who were aboard were then allegedly raped by the black youths.

The incident became known immediately and caused great excitement locally. A message was sent ahead, and the train was met by a sheriff's posse before it reached Scottsboro. The black youths were tried without delay and sentenced to death. In the trial each of the two girls testified that she had been assaulted by six different Negroes in turn, and the girls identified seven of the defendants as being among that number.

The convictions were reversed by the U.S. Supreme Court. In the opinion written by Justice George Sutherland, the black youths had been denied due process and equal protection of the law by "being denied the right to counsel; by not being given a fair, impartial and deliberate trial; and by being tried before juries from which qualified members of their own race were systematically excluded."

In the opinion, he also stated, "The United States by statute and every state in the union by express provision of law, or by determination of its courts, make it the duty of the trial judge, where the accused is unable to employ counsel to appoint counsel for him."

The interpretation that the Sixth Amendment applied only to the federal government was affirmed by the U.S.

---

2. Powell v. Alabama, Patterson v. Same, and Weems v. Same, 287 U.S. 45 (November 7, 1932).

Supreme Court in 1942 in the case of *Betts v. Brady*.[3] In that decision the Court held that counsel for a defendant is not a constitutional right but rather policy supported by law. Thus, it ruled, a state is not required by the Sixth Amendment to provide counsel for an indigent in a criminal case.

The case arose when Smith Brady, a farm worker in Maryland, was arrested for robbery. Having no money to hire a lawyer, he asked the court to appoint one. The judge refused, stating that he was permitted to appoint a defense attorney only in cases of murder or rape. Brady was found guilty and sentenced to eight years in jail. On June 1, 1942, the U.S. Supreme Court upheld his conviction by a majority of 6-to-3, contending that the Sixth Amendment was applicable only in federal courts, not in state courts.

That decision was in turn reversed, however, twenty-one years later in the landmark case of *Gideon v. Wainwright* when the U.S. Supreme Court ruled on March 18, 1963, that every poor person charged with a serious crime in this country must be provided a lawyer for his defense.[4] In the majority opinion, Justice Hugo L. Black stated:

■ In our adversary system of justice, any person hauled into court who is too poor to hire a lawyer cannot be assured a fair trial unless counsel is provided for him . . . That government hires lawyers to prosecute and defendants who have the money hire lawyers to defend are the strongest indications of the widespread belief that lawyers in criminal courts are necessities, not luxuries . . . The right of one charged with crime to counsel may not be deemed fundamental in some countries, but it is in ours.

The case arose when Clarence Earl Gideon was arrested in 1961 and charged with breaking into the Bay Harbor Poolhall

---

3. Betts v. Brady, 316 U.S. 455 (1942).
4. Gideon v. Wainwright, 372 U.S. 335 (March 1, 1963).

in Panama City, Florida, and taking about $65 in coins from a vending machine and a juke box, a couple of six packs of beer, a dozen bottles of Coca-Cola, and four-fifths of wine. At his trial, Gideon insisted that he was entitled to an attorney to defend him. The judge, Robert L. McCrary Jr., replied:

■ Mr. Gideon, I am sorry but I cannot appoint counsel to represent you in this case. Under the laws of the State of Florida, the only time the court can appoint counsel to represent a defendant is when that person is charged with a capital offense.

Gideon made an opening statement, cross-examined the State's witnesses, declined to testify himself, and made a short argument "emphasizing his innocence to the charge contained in the information filed in the case." The jury found him guilty, and the judge sentenced him to five years in jail.

Described as a friendly, talkative white man with a frail body and white hair who had been in and out of jail much of his life, Gideon eked out a living by gambling and occasional thefts. In this case he believed he was being denied his constitutional right to defense counsel, and that rankled; so about a year and a half after being imprisoned in the Union Correctional Institution in Raiford, Florida, he took action. With a pencil he hand-lettered a petition on ruled prison paper, asking the U.S. Supreme Court to review his trial. He was helped with some of the wording of the petition by a fellow inmate, Joe Peel, a former lawyer who had been a city judge in West Palm Beach, Florida, and had been convicted of murder.

Although the Supreme Court declines to review scores of appeals it receives each year, it accepted Gideon's unimpressive petition; and it appointed Abe Fortas, who himself was later appointed a justice of the Supreme Court, to represent Gideon. In its decision, the Court ordered a new trial for

Gideon; and in that trial, he was acquitted.[5]

The *Gideon v. Wainwright* decision requiring state and local courts to appoint attorneys to defend indigent persons accused of serious crimes was far-reaching, affecting all criminal justice systems in the country. It brought a flood of petitions to state courts from prisoners who had been convicted without benefit of counsel, asking that their cases be reviewed. Florida quickly passed a public-defender law, and several other states that did not require counsel for indigent defendants in felony cases passed similar laws.

The case embodied elements of drama, with the highest court in the land willing to hear the plea of one of the country's humblest citizens. It resulted in a book titled *Gideon's Trumpet* by the Pulitzer-prize winning journalist Anthony Lewis and a movie of the same title starring Henry Fonda as Gideon.

The Sixth and the Fourteenth Amendments took on new meaning with the decision of the Supreme Court in the Gideon case. The original purpose of the Sixth Amendment, as stated previously, was to prevent the adoption by the new U.S. government of the English system of barring defense lawyers in criminal cases. Now, under this decision attorneys for the defense are not only permitted to participate, they are required whenever defendants want them.

The ruling in this case was presaged the year before by a decision of the U.S. Supreme Court in the case of *Chewning v. Cunningham* overturning a conviction obtained in a trial without counsel for the defense.[6] The right to legal counsel was extended and clarified in later decisions of the U.S. Supreme Court.

---

5. Gideon died nine years later on January 18, 1972, in a Ft. Lauderdale (Florida) hospital.
6. Morgan C. Chewning v. W.K. Cunningham, Jr., Supt. of the Virginia State Penitentiary, 368 U.S. 443 (February 19, 1962).

Among them was the decision in the case of *Escobedo v. Illinois* which came in the next year after the Gideon decision and attracted national attention.[7] In that case Danny Escobedo, a 22-year-old man of Mexican extraction, had been convicted in the Criminal Court of Cook County, Illinois, of murdering his brother-in-law, Manuel Valtierra, on January 19, 1960, and sentenced to 20 years in the penitentiary.

In being questioned after his arrest, Escobedo had not been advised of his right to remain silent, had been denied several requests to see his attorney, and after persistent questioning by the police, had made incriminating statements that were used in testimony against him in the trial. Upon appeal, the Supreme Court of Illinois upheld the conviction; but on June 23, 1964, the U.S. Supreme Court by a majority of 5-to-4 reversed the conviction and remanded the case to the lower court for retrial. The majority opinion of the Court written by Justice Arthur J. Goldberg stated that Escobedo had been denied his rights under the Sixth and Fourteenth Amendments. The Court held not only that the confession must be voided but also that every arrested person has the right to consult an attorney as soon as police investigation makes him or her a prime suspect.

The next year the Supreme Court ruled in *Pointer v. Texas* that defendants in criminal cases have the right not only to legal counsel but also to cross-examine witnesses against them.[8] The Miranda decision in 1966, discussed in the previous chapter, held that a suspect must be informed of his rights before being questioned by the police and has the right to legal counsel during questioning.

In 1970 in *Coleman v. Alabama* the Court extended a suspect's rights by ruling that a suspect has a right to legal

---

7. Escobedo v. Illinois, 378 U.S. 478 (1964).
8. Pointer v. State of Texas, 380 U.S. 400 (April 5, 1965).

counsel in a preliminary hearing held to determine whether there is probable cause to believe that the suspect has committed a crime.[9]

Further extension came on June 12, 1972, when the U. S. Supreme Court ruled in the case of *Argersinger v. Hamlin* that "no person may be imprisoned for any offense unless he was represented by counsel at his trial, or had waived the right to an attorney."[10]

That Court decision reversed the conviction of Jon Richard Argersinger, who had been found guilty of carrying a concealed weapon and sentenced to pay a fine of $500 or serve three months in the Leon County jail in Florida but had not been asked if he wished legal counsel to defend him. The sentence was upheld by the Florida Supreme Court, stating that a court-appointed defense attorney was not required in cases carrying prison sentences of less than six months.

In this opinion, the Court ruled that while judges could impose fines, they could not impose a jail sentence of any length on an indigent defendant unless the defendant had been provided a defense attorney or had waived his right to one. A year earlier the Court ruled that no one could be sent to jail for inability to pay a fine.

The next year in *Gagnon v. Scarpelli* the Court held that a prisoner has the right to legal counsel in some kinds of parole and probation revocation proceedings.[11]

In 1981, the Court ruled that once an accused person requests legal counsel, officials may not start questioning again "until counsel has been made available." In that case, Robert Edwards had been convicted of robbery, burglary, and first-degree murder. He had confessed, but before his trial he had moved to suppress his confession on the ground that his

---

9. Coleman v. Alabama, 399 U.S. 1 (June 22, 1970).
10. Jon Argersinger v. Raymond Hamlin, Sheriff of Leon County, Florida, 407 U.S. 25 (1972).
11. Gagnon v. Scarpelli, 411 U.S. 778 (1973).

rights had been violated in regard to his right to counsel. The U.S. Supreme Court agreed, stating in its decision that "it is inconsistent with Miranda for authorities to reinterrogate an accused in custody if he has clearly asserted his right to counsel."[12]

In a somewhat similar case, the Court ruled on December 3, 1990, by a 6-to-2 majority that a suspect in custody who asks for an attorney when police officers try to question him may not be questioned later when the attorney is no longer present, even if the suspect does not ask for his attorney to be present at the later questioning.[13]

In that case, Robert Minnick and another prisoner had escaped from a Mississippi jail in 1976, broke into a mobile home looking for guns, and killed the owner and another person. Minnick was arrested and questioned with his attorney present, but later he was questioned without his attorney being present and at that time he confessed to his part in the killings. With that evidence he was convicted and sentenced to death. Upon appeal, the U.S. Supreme Court reversed the conviction because Minnick's attorney was not present at the later questioning; and it remanded the case to the lower court for retrial but without Minnick's confession available for evidence.

In its opinion, the Court stated, "When counsel is requested, interrogation must cease, and officials may not reinstate interrogation without counsel present, whether or not the accused has consulted with his attorney."

In other cases the Supreme Court has held that prisoners cannot be prevented from obtaining legal aid from fellow prisoners who have some knowledge of law, and it ruled that a state cannot keep law students and legal assistants from

---

12. Edwards v. Arizona, 451 U.S. 477 (1981).
13. Minnick v. Mississippi, 111 S. Ct. 486 (December 3, 1990).

entering a prison to aid inmates.

Appeals are a part of the criminal justice system, and in 1963, the Supreme Court ruled that legal assistance must be provided in the first appeal of a conviction.[14]

Appeals are submitted as habeas corpus petitions that challenge the constitutionality of convictions and prison sentences. They are the only means by which federal courts are permitted to review convictions by state courts.

There has been no limit to the number of appeals a prisoner may make; and it is estimated that about 40 percent of all death sentences are overturned by federal judges who find constitutional "errors" in sentences and convictions. As a result of the appeals process on the average eight years go by from the time a prisoner is sentenced to death until he is executed.

Apparently moving toward eliminating or decreasing the number of habeas corpus petitions submitted to federal courts, the Supreme Court ruled in 1976 that federal courts may not accept petitions from prisoners who argue that they were convicted on the basis of evidence that had been illegally seized and should not have been presented at their trials. Such ruling would hold, however, only if the prisoners had had "a full and fair" chance to make the argument in state appeal courts.[15]

In a decision handed down April 16, 1991, the U.S. Supreme Court further curtailed the flow of appeals by limiting death row inmates to one round of federal court review after state court appeals had been exhausted.[16] It ruled that further appeals must be dismissed unless the petitioner can show cause for not presenting the matter earlier and that he has suffered "actual prejudice" from the constitutional error he is trying to prove.

Specifically, the Court ruled that a Federal district court

14. Douglas v. People of the State of California, 372 U.S. 353 (1963).
15. Stone v. Powell, 96 S Ct/ 3037 (1976).
16. McCleskey v. Zant, 111 S. Ct. 1464 (April 16, 1991).

judge in Georgia should have dismissed the second habeas corpus petition filed in 1987 by Warren McCleskey who had been found guilty of armed robbery and murder in 1978. In dissent, Justice Thurgood Marshall, joined by Justices Harry A. Blackmun and John Paul Stevens, argued that limitation of appeals to Federal courts should be imposed by Congressional legislation rather than by ruling of the Supreme Court.

Against that background, a decision handed down on April 21, 1993, came as somewhat of a surprise.[17] Rather than limiting appeals, the Court in a 5-to-4 decision written by Justice David H. Souter, ruled that federal courts could accept habeas corpus petitions from state prisoners who claim that they had not been told of their right to remain silent as required in the Miranda decision.

Establishing the right of "asssistance of counsel" for everyone covered many years, and so did the development of public-defender systems accompanying that right. By 1913 public-defender systems were functioning in a few jurisdictions, but they were rare. Some jurisdictions appointed legal counsel for indigent persons accused of serious crimes, but generally the courts depended upon attorneys' volunteering their services in such cases. Today virtually everyone held for questioning or tried for a crime is assured legal counsel if he or she wishes it. In recognition of the need of some defendants for financial assistance, Congress provided for modest compensation for counsel in criminal cases in federal courts through the Criminal Justice Act of 1964.

The fair trial concept extends beyond the criminal to include civil cases such as tenant versus landlord. In civil litigation a poor person who is unable to hire a lawyer is at considerable disadvantage when pitted against a wealthy person or a corporation. Recognition of that kind of inequity led to the formation of legal aid societies that function today

---

17. Withrow v. Williams, Docket No. 91-1030 (April 21, 1993).

in most communities throughout the country.

Although injustice can occur in civil cases, courts are not required by statute or by judicial precedent to provide attorneys for indigent litigants in civil cases. That was tested in 1967, when the U.S. Supreme Court denied certiorari in the case of *Williams v. Shaffer,* which involved eviction proceedings against a poor tenant.[18] In dissent to that action by the Court, Justice William O. Douglas said:

■ ... the promise of equal justice for all should be an empty phrase for the poor, if the ability to obtain judicial relief were made to turn on the length of a person's purse. ... The Equal Protection Clause of the Fourteenth Amendment is not limited to criminal prosecutions. Its protection extends as well to civil matters.

Seven years later in 1974 Congress created the Legal Services Corporation to provide legal assistance in non-criminal proceedings to persons financially unable to afford an attorney. The corporation gives financial assistance to more than 300 legal-aid providers at the local level. Additional funds are available through other federal agencies as well as from state and local governments. Even so, recent studies have shown that only about 20 percent of the non-criminal legal needs of poor people are being met.

Following a surge of death sentences and a lack of funds, a shortage of legal counsel to assist indigent condemned inmates in making final appeals has developed, according to a report in *The New York Times.*[19] There were 2,729 prisoners on death row in this country in the spring of 1993, many without legal representation, the article stated.

---

18. Williams v. Shaffer, 385 U.S. 1037 (1967).
19. June 4, 1993, page B 11

CHAPTER
12

❀

SOME SPEECH IS CONFIDENTIAL

SOME SPEECH IS CONFIDENTIAL

❧

The right to remain silent is not absolute because participants in some kinds of legal proceedings are required to speak, to give testimony, to answer questions. Such proceedings include court trials, grand jury hearings, coroners' inquests, and legislative inquiries. A person who refuses to speak when directed to do so on such occasions can be cited for contempt and fined and/or jailed.

When a person does speak in a legal proceeding, he must be honest because he has sworn "to tell the truth, the whole truth, and nothing but the truth." Telling a falsehood under oath is known as perjury, which is a criminal offense.

The authority of a presiding judge, a committee chairman, or a jury foreman to require responses has some limits. Communication between doctor and patient, lawyer and client, pastor and communicant, and husband and wife is "privileged" as a matter of common law as well as by statute in more than two thirds of the states.[1] That means that such communication is confidential and restricted, so that no government officer or agency has the authority to force anyone to reveal what has been said in those circumstances.

---

1. Husband and wife may not be compelled to testify to confidential communication with one another made during the course of their marriage, but they can be required to testify regarding observed acts of each other.

Confidentiality in law, medicine, the church, and the home have long been established precepts because the benefits to society are considered greater than those that would result from public revelation of such communication. It was a tradition in Roman law, for example, that a lawyer could not be a witness against his client; and the attorney-client privilege dates back to English common law in the 17th century. The principle of confidentiality, however, is not absolute. A conversation in which a client seeks advice from his lawyer regarding a criminal or fraudulent activity, for example, would not be privileged. As another example, the U.S. Supreme Court ruled in a case in 1986 that the Sixth Amendment right to legal counsel was not violated by an attorney's refusal to cooperate with an accused person in presenting perjured testimony at his trial.[2]

A related area struggling with limited success for juristic recognition lies in journalism, involving the right of reporters not to be required to reveal confidential sources of news. Journalists often find it advantageous and at times necessary to promise people who provide them with sensitive information that they will not divulge their sources — a necessary practice because otherwise they could not get the information. That kind of confidentiality is a basic tool of journalism, without which some essential sources of news might not be forthcoming.

Professional journalists pride themselves on their reputation for not violating such confidences. In 123 years between 1848 and 1971 judicial records show only four instances in which newsmen threatened with jail for remaining silent revealed their confidential sources of news.[3] One arose in the

---

2. Crispus Nix v. Emanual Charles Whitehead, 475 U.S. 157 (February 26, 1986). It would also obviously be wrong for an attorney to misrepresent facts, make false statements, and further fraud for a client.
3. David Gordon, "The Confidences Newsmen Must Keep," *Columbia Journalism Review*, November/December 1971.

investigation of a grand jury leak in Hawaii in 1914, another during a murder trial in Pennsylvania in 1930, a third in 1931 in connection with an investigation in Texas of the alleged beating and kidnapping of two Communist organizers, and the fourth during a labor dispute in 1961 in Minnesota.

Promises of confidentiality by reporters may and sometimes do lead to a conflict between the right of the press, on the one hand, to gather and publish news and the authority of courts and legislative bodies, on the other hand, to compel witnesses to reveal the sources of their information. One of the earliest instances of such conflict was in 1848 when a Washington correspondent was sent to jail for refusing to tell the Senate where he obtained information regarding a proposed treaty between the United States and Mexico.[4] That action, however, was based chiefly on whether the Senate could legally punish anyone for contempt rather than being based on the question of protecting the confidentiality of sources of news.

In 1894 two reporters were cited for contempt when they refused to tell a U.S. Senate committee where they had obtained information for articles published in the *Philadelphia Press* and the *New York Mail* that indicated that bribery had been used in an attempt to influence votes on a tariff bill. A few other cases occurred during the 1800s, but confidentiality for news reporters, or reporters' privilege as it is usually called, did not become a subject of considerable debate until the latter part of this century.

A widely discussed case arose over a column titled, *TV-Radio Today* by Marie Torre, published on January 10, 1957, in the *New York Herald Tribune*. The column contained statements about actress Judy Garland which Miss Torre

---

4. The Treaty of Guadeloupe Hidalgo ending the war with Mexico was signed February 2, 1848, and approved by the U.S. Senate on March 10 that year.

attributed to an executive of the Columbia Broadcasting System, but she did not name the executive. Because of some of the statements, Miss Garland filed a $10 million libel suit against CBS, alleging that the statements in the column were 'false, defamatory, and highly damaging to her reputation."

CBS filed an answer and a counterclaim, denying among other things that it had made the alleged statements or caused them to be published. In a deposition in pretrial discovery proceedings, Miss Torre testified that the statements about Miss Garland in her column were "exact words" made to her over the telephone by a CBS informant, but under repeated questioning she refused to give the name of the "network executive," asserting that to do so would violate a confidence.

In the proceedings in the district court, Miss Torre was ordered to state the name of her informant; and when she refused to do so, she was cited for criminal contempt. In her defense she contended that the act of compelling newspaper reporters to disclose confidential sources of information would encroach upon the freedom of the press as guaranteed by the First Amendment because "it would impose an important practical restraint on the flow of news to the media and thus diminish the flow of news to the public." [5]

Upon appeal, the U.S. Court of Appeals upheld the contempt citation, stating, "We hold that the Constitution conferred no right to refuse an answer." As a result, Miss Torre spent ten days in jail.

That was the first case in which the First Amendment was used in defense of news reporter privilege, although it has been used numerous times since. In ruling in that case on that aspect of defense, the Appeals Court stated:

■ ... at the foundation of the Republic the obligation of a witness to testify and the correlative right of a litigant to

---

5. Garland v. Torre, 259 F. 2d 545 (2nd Cir. 1958).

enlist judicial compulsion to testimony were recognized as incident to the judicial power of the United States . . . Whether or not the freedom to invoke this judicial power be considered an element of Fifth Amendment due process, its essentiality to the fabric of our society is beyond controversy . . . Without question, the exaction of this duty impinges sometimes, if not always, upon the First Amendment freedom of the witness. Material sacrifice and the invasion of personal privacy are implicit in its performance. The freedom to choose whether to speak or to be silent disappears. But the personal sacrifice involved is a part of the necessary contribution of the individual to the welfare of the public. . .

If an additional First Amendment liberty — the freedom of the press — is here involved, we do not hesitate to conclude that it too must give place under the Constitution to a paramount public interest in the fair administration of justice.

Fourteen years after the Torre case the U.S. Supreme Court accepted the task of deciding the limits of news reporters' privilege in three cases considered together.[6]

In one case Paul M. Branzburg, a reporter for the *Courier-Journal,* Louisville, Kentucky, was issued subpoenas by two separate grand juries to testify regarding alleged drug violations he had told about in stories he had written for the newspaper.

The first subpoena followed publication of a story under his byline in the *Courier-Journal* on November 15, 1969, that described in detail his observations of two young residents of Jefferson County synthesizing hashish from marijuana, an activity which they said brought them about $5,000 in three

----

6. Paul M. Branzburg v. John P. Hayes, Judge et al; In the Matter of Paul Pappas; and United States v. Earl Caldwell, 408 U.S. 665 (June 29, 1972).

weeks. The article stated that the reporter had promised not to reveal the identity of the two hashish makers. When Branzburg appeared before the Jefferson County grand jury, he refused to identify them on the grounds that he was protected from doing so by the Kentucky reporters' privilege law. An order by the trial court judge that he answer the questions asked by the grand jury was upheld by the Kentucky Court of Appeals.

The second subpoena followed publication of a story on January 10, 1971, in which Branzburg described in detail the use of drugs in Frankfort, Kentucky. The article stated that he had "spent two weeks interviewing several dozen drug users in the capital city" and had seen some of them smoking marijuana. When the Franklin County grand jury subpoenaed him to testify "in the matter of violation of statutes concerning the use and sale of drugs," he moved that the summons be quashed, arguing that if he were forced to appear before the grand jury or to answer questions regarding the identity of informants or disclose information given to him in confidence, his effectiveness as a reporter would be greatly damaged. The motion to quash was denied by the Court of Appeals.

In another case Paul Pappas, a television reporter-photographer working out of the Providence, Rhode Island, office of a New Bedford, Massachusetts, television station, was called to New Bedford on July 30, 1970, to report on civil disorders there which involved fires and other turmoil. He intended to cover a Black Panther news conference at the group's headquarters in a boarded-up store, where after some difficulty in gaining entrance he recorded and photographed a prepared statement read by one of the Black Panther leaders about 3 p.m. About 9 p.m. he was allowed to return and remain inside; but as a condition, he agreed not to disclose anything he saw or heard inside except for an anticipated police raid. There was no raid, and Pappas did not write a story or reveal to anyone what had occurred in the store while he was there.

Two months later he was summoned before the Bristol

County Grand Jury where he answered questions about what he had seen and heard outside the Black Panther headquarters, but he refused to answer any questions about what had taken place inside, claiming that the First Amendment afforded him a privilege to protect confidential informants and their information. His motion to quash on First Amendment and other grounds was denied by the trial judge, a denial affirmed by the Supreme Judicial Court of Massachusetts.

Still another case arose from a subpoena issued to Earl Caldwell, a reporter for *The New York Times*, on February 2, 1970, by a federal grand jury in the Northern District of California. Caldwell had been assigned to cover the Black Panther Party and other black militant groups in the San Francisco area. The summons ordered him to appear before a grand jury to testify and to bring with him his notes and tape recordings of interviews of officers and spokesmen of the Black Panther Party concerning the aims, purposes and activities of the organization.

A continuance was granted regarding the first subpoena, but a second subpoena was issued on March 16, ordering him to appear and testify, but it omitted the requirement that he bring notes and tape recordings. Caldwell and *The New York Times* moved to quash, contending that appearing in secret before the grand jury would destroy his working relationship with the Black Panther Party and "suppress vital First Amendment freedoms by driving a wedge of distrust and silence between the news media and the militants."

On April 6, the District Court denied the motion to quash; but the term of the grand jury soon expired and the new grand jury issued a new subpoena on May 22. A motion to quash this subpoena was denied, and the court issued an order to show cause why Caldwell should not be held in contempt.

The Court of Appeals reversed that order. Viewing the issue as whether Caldwell was required to appear before the grand jury at all, rather than the scope of permissible interrogation, the Court of Appeals determined that the First

Amendment provided a qualified testimonial privilege to journalists. In its view, requiring a reporter like Caldwell to testify would deter his informants from communicating with him in the future and would cause him to censor his writings in an effort to avoid being subpoenaed.

The Court also held, for First Amendment reasons, that, absent some special showing of necessity by the Government, attendance by Caldwell at a secret meeting of the grand jury was something he was privileged to refuse because of the potential impact of such an appearance on the flow of news to the public.

The litigation in those three cases illustrates the legal complexity involved in reporters' confidentiality with their news sources, with two appeals courts deciding that journalists must obey subpoenas and testify before grand juries and another deciding otherwise. The U.S. Supreme Court in considering these three cases together split 5-to-4 with the majority deciding against the reporters' privilege.

In the majority opinion on those three cases, Justice Byron R. White stated: "The issue in these cases is whether requiring newsmen to appear and testify before a state or federal grand jury abridges the freedom of speech and press guaranteed by the First Amendment. We hold that it does not . . . We are asked . . . to grant newsmen a testimonial privilege that other citizens do not enjoy. This we decline to do . . ."

The majority opinion reads in part:

■ The sole issue before us is the obligation of reporters to respond to grand jury subpoenas as other citizens do and to answer questions relevant to an investigation into the commission of crime . . . Neither the First Amendment nor any other constitutional provision protects the average citizen from disclosing to a grand jury information that he has received in confidence.

Requiring newsmen to appear and testify before state and federal grand juries does not abridge the freedom of speech and press guaranteed by the First Amendment; and a newsman's agreement to conceal criminal conduct of his news sources, or evidence thereof, does not give rise to any constitutional testimonial privilege with respect thereto.

We do not question the significance of free speech, press, or assembly to the country's welfare. Nor is it suggested that news gathering does not qualify for First Amendment protection; without some protection for seeking out the news, freedom of the press could be eviscerated. But these cases involve no intrusions upon speech or assembly, no prior restraint or restriction on what the press may publish, and no express or implied command that the press publish what it prefers to withhold. . .

While Justice White presented cogent reasoning in the majority opinion for denying journalists the automatic right to refuse to testify before grand juries and in court, Justice Potter Stewart in dissent presented a three-way test for determining whether a journalist's refusal should be accepted or denied, a test that has been adopted in a number of jurisdictions. He said:

■ . . . when a reporter is asked to appear before a grand jury and reveal confidences, I would hold that the government must —

1. show that there is probable cause to believe that the newsman has information that is clearly relevant to a specific probable violation of law;

2. demonstrate that the information sought cannot be obtained by alternate means less destructive of First Amendment rights; and

3. demonstrate a compelling and overriding interest in the information.

Justice Stewart stated further:

■ . . . when government officials possess an unchecked power to compel newsmen to disclose information received in confidence, sources will clearly be deterred from giving information, and reporters will clearly be deterred from publishing it, because uncertainty about the exercise of the power will lead to "self-censorship." The uncertainty arises, of course, because the judiciary has traditionally imposed virtually no limitations on the grand jury's broad investigatory powers.

After today's decision, the potential informant can never be sure that his identity or off-the-record communications will not subsequently be revealed through the compelled testimony of a newsman. The public spirited person inside government, who is not implicated in any crime, will now be fearful of revealing corruption or other governmental wrongdoing, because he will now know he can subsequently be identified by use of compulsory process. The potential source must, therefore, choose between risking exposure by giving information or avoiding the risk by remaining silent.

Following that decision, a number of bills were introduced in Congress to protect reporters from having to reveal confidential sources of information, but none have been enacted so far. Twenty-eight states, however, do have shield laws, as they are called, with the first such law passed in Maryland in 1896. Also, court rulings based on the First Amendment give some protection to journalists in all U.S. states and territories.

State shield laws were approved by the U.S. Supreme Court in 1972 in the majority opinion in the three cases just cited, in which it stated:

■ There is merit in leaving state legislatures free, within First Amendment limits, to fashion their own standards ... with respect to the relations between law enforcement officials and the press in their own areas.

Provisions of shield laws vary somewhat from state to state, with some protecting both print and broadcast reporters and some including a prohibition against the subpoena of unpublished information such as notes, files, photographs, and outtakes of television tape and motion picture film.

As an example, one section of the Ohio Revised Code reads:

■ No person engaged in the work of, or connected with, or employed by any newspaper or any press association for the purpose of gathering, procuring, compiling, editing, disseminating, or publishing news shall be required to disclose the source of any information procured or obtained by such person in the course of his employment, in any legal proceeding, trial, or investigation before any court, grand jury, petit jury, or any officer thereof, before the presiding officer of any tribunal, or his agent, or before any commission, department, division, or bureau of this state, or before any county or municipal body, officer or committee thereof.

Another section of the Ohio Code gives the same protection to broadcasters.

Many but not all members of the press favor statutory protection. Those that do maintain that being required to reveal confidential sources of information in court trials and grand jury hearings hinders their ability to obtain news because the threat of subpoena power tends to intimidate. It tends to cause them to refrain from reporting on such sensitive matters as waste and dishonesty in government, and it limits their independence. Such governmental control and interference, they insist, has the effect of abridging the constitutional guarantee of freedom of the press.

Confidentiality involves a conflict between society's need for an independent, informative press on the one hand and a fair, effective judicial system on the other. Shield laws cannot resolve the conflict totally and satisfactorily, a major reason being in deciding who should have such statutory protection. Lawyers and doctors are licensed by the states, ministers are ordained, and even husbands and wives must obtain licenses to be married; but reporters have no such distinction. Licensing them would be unconstitutional. Anyone has a right to report as he or she wishes without government sanction or approval. Legally, a person who writes a report of a meeting of the ladies' aid society for the church bulletin is as much a reporter as is a correspondent for a large daily newspaper.

As illustrated in the Ohio law, shield laws proposed or enacted so far generally apply to persons employed "as a reporter, editor, commentator, journalist, writer, correspondent, announcer, or other person directly engaged in the gathering or presentation of news for any newspaper, periodical, press association, newspaper syndicate, wire service, or radio or television station."

That kind of definition extends the privilege of confidentiality to only one class of writers. If a law were to provide protection to all who write, or may write, or are free to write without government approval, it would have to include potentially everyone. An absolute statute, as Clark Mollenhoff, former writer for the *Des Moines Register*, said several years ago, "would have to include every person who had written a book, an article, a pamphlet, or anyone who could claim he was gathering information for a book, an article, or a pamphlet."[7] In other words, anyone in the world could claim to be a writer and thus entitled to confidentiality, which would make the law meaningless.

The difficulty in providing absolute protection to reporters was pointed out in a decision of the Supreme Court of Oregon in the case of *State v. Buchanan* in 1968.[8] Two years earlier Annette Buchanan, as managing editor of the *Daily Emerald*, The University of Oregon student newspaper, had written an article in which she quoted seven unnamed mari-

---

7. Quoted in *Time*, March 19, 1973.
8. State v. Buchanan, 250 Oregon 244, 436 P 2d 729 (1968).

juana users, one of whom said that hundreds of students smoked marijuana on the campus.

When Miss Buchanan refused to reveal the names of those seven students when she was questioned by a grand jury, she was cited for contempt and fined $300. On appeal, the Oregon Supreme Court upheld the conviction. In its decision, the Court explained the difficulty of enacting and enforcing a law that gives protection to one class of journalists and not to another. The decision reads in part:

■ . . . it would be dangerous business for courts . . . to extend to an employee of a "respectable" newspaper a privilege which would be denied to an employee of a disreputable newspaper; or to an episodic pamphleteer; or to a free-lance writer seeking to sell a story on the open market; or, indeed, to a shaggy nonconformist who wishes only to write out his message and nail it to a tree.

The same difficulty in determining who should be protected by a confidentiality or privilege law was echoed by the U.S. Supreme Court in the Branzburg case in 1972. The majority opinion reads in part:

■ Sooner or later it would be necessary to define those categories of newsmen who qualified for the privilege, a questionable procedure in the light of the traditional doctrine that liberty of the press is the right of the lonely pamphleteer who uses carbon paper or a mimeograph just as much as of the large metropolitan publisher who utilizes the latest photo composition methods . . . The press in its historic connotation comprehends every sort of publication which affords a vehicle of information and opinion.

Subpoenas served on communication companies, editors, and reporters have become increasingly common. A survey by the Reporters Committee for Freedom of the Press shows that in 1989 alone, 4,408 subpoenas were served on 703 newspapers and 339 television stations, with about half of them in states that have shield laws.[9]

A major reason for the large number of subpoenas is that prosecutors and defense attorneys, upon reading news stories or hearing broadcasts about cases they are involved in, are tempted to use the subpoena power to see if they can obtain information from the mass media that will help them win their cases. One newspaper is quoted in the Reporters Committee survey report as saying that "subpoenas are often simply a means that lawyers use to get newspapers to do their legwork for them." Grand juries also often look upon reporters as sources of additional information regarding cases they are investigating. Journalists are also on occasion subpoenaed because as trained observers and skilled reporters they are excellent witnesses.

Authority to issue subpoenas is not limited to the judicial and legislative branches of government. Forty-seven federal agencies have subpoena power, which they can use legitimately or as a means of intimidation. Those agencies can issue an official request for secrecy along with subpoenaing information from banks, telephone companies or other sources of information, with the secrecy effective for 90 days and renewable for 90-day periods. They are not required to inform journalists or any other citizens that the subpoenas have been issued.

Journalists dislike receiving subpoenas and are sometimes resentful because responding takes time and is expensive especially in attorney fees when the subpoenas are challenged. That is not to say, however, that journalists do not cooperate with attorneys and grand juries; they often do. They do so as their civic duty, and they do so because attorneys and law enforcement officials are important news sources themselves with whom they want to maintain a working relationship. In its survey, the Reporters Committee

---

9. *Editor & Publisher*, February 9, 1991, and February 20, 1993.

found that the media had complied with more than half, almost 2,500, of the 4,408 subpoenas they received in 1989.

Also, courts often decide in favor of journalists. Judges do not invariably send reporters to jail for refusing to reveal confidential news sources, and they do not enforce every subpoena. That is shown in the Reporters Committee survey of 1989 which found that judges quashed three-fourths of the 348 subpoenas challenged by the news media, and trial and appellate courts blocked one-fourth of those not quashed.

Legal action against the media served with subpoenas is relatively rare with only six cases reported in the 1991 survey. Three were against newspapers including one in Arizona and two others, one in California and another in Arizona, the two being ordered to pay fines for each day they failed to comply, plus three newspaper reporters in South Carolina jailed for refusing to respond to subpoenas.

Journalists know that there are limits to confidentiality. They know they have an obligation as citizens to serve justice. They know they have no right to reveal information that is secret by law or pertains to espionage or to national security. Also they know that they, as well as non-journalists, have no right legally and morally to shield criminals and criminal activities, or to keep secret any information that if revealed would endanger human life or property.

In obtaining news, journalists need be careful to avoid being involved in any way in criminal conspiracy, which is the planning by two or more persons to commit a crime. Conspiracy is in itself a crime; and just being present in the room while the planning is taking place, without taking part, is a criminal act.

Justice White alluded to the legal limitations and civic responsibilities of journalists in the majority opinion in the Branzburg case in 1972 by stating:

■ It would be frivolous to assert . . . that the First Amendment, in the interest of securing news or other-

wise, confers a license on either the reporter or his news
sources to violate valid criminal laws. Although stealing
documents or private wiretapping could provide newsworthy information, neither reporter nor source is immune from conviction for such conduct, whatever the
impact on the flow of news. Neither is immune, on First
Amendment grounds, from testifying against the other,
before the grand jury or at a criminal trial.

Keeping sources of information confidential in libel cases
poses a dilemma for reporters, especially if the defense is
based on the source. If a newspaper is sued for libel as the
result of an article it has published and the reporter refuses to
divulge the source of his information, the jury may conclude
that there was no source, that the reporter fabricated what he
wrote, and thus find for the defendant.

Libel differs from contempt in that libel involves civil
action, which carries damages, while contempt is a criminal
act for which a person can be sent to jail. The reporter who
refuses to name the source of his information in a libel suit
runs the risk of being found guilty, with the result that he and
his newspaper will have to pay a large amount in damages.

Journalists know that the terms of confidentiality may be
misunderstood or misinterpreted, that an informant may claim
that a reporter has broken his promise, not by revealing the
name but by details in the story he writes that make clear who
the informant is, or that he or she was not sufficiently
camouflaged on television to conceal the identity.

There is the chance, remote but possible, that the editor
may decide to print an informant's name even though the
reporter has promised confidentiality. An instance occurred
in Minnesota in 1982 involving Dan Cohen, a public relations
executive in Minneapolis and adviser to Wheeler Whitney,
Republican candidate for governor. Four days before the
election Cohen offered reporters copies of some documents
that reflected negatively on Marlene Johnson, a candidate for
lieutenant-governor on the Democratic Farm-Labor Party

ticket, provided they would not use his name in the stories they wrote or broadcast. The documents he offered consisted of court records showing that Ms. Johnson had been arrested in 1969 for unlawful assembly and convicted for petty theft in 1970.

Although Lori Sturdivant of the *Minneapolis Star & Tribune* and Bill Salisbury of the *St. Paul Pioneer Press* agreed to keep Cohen's identity secret, their editors independently of each other decided that the source of the information about Ms. Johnson was as important as the information itself, and each paper printed Cohen's name with the story. The Associated Press used the story without identifying Cohen, and a local television station did not use the information at all.

After the stories were published with his name, Cohen brought suit against Cowles Media Company, publisher of the *Star & Tribune*, and Knight-Ridder Company, publisher of the *Pioneer Press*, claiming that the reporters' promise of confidentiality was legally binding as a "contract." At the trial the jury agreed, and it awarded him $200,000 in compensatory damages and $500,000 in punitive damages for breach of contract. The State Appeals court upheld the verdict but threw out the award for punitive damages. Then the Minnesota Supreme Court in July 1990 overturned the verdict on the basis that it violated the First Amendment guarantee of freedom of speech, thus finding for the newspapers and wiping out the award for damages. One of the justices, however, pointed out in dissent that the press usually asks for protection in order to keep names of news sources confidential but this time was asking for protection for just the opposite.

Cohen then appealed to the U.S. Supreme Court to decide whether a promise of news source confidentiality is legally enforceable as a contract. The Supreme Court ruled that it is. In a 5-to-4 decision handed down on June 24, 1991, the Court reversed the decision of the Minnesota Supreme Court by holding that the First Amendment guarantee of a free press "does not confer on the press a constitutional right to disregard promises that would otherwise be enforced under state law as contracts."[10]

In the majority opinion written by Justice Byron R. White, the Court stated that "generally applicable laws do not offend the First Amendment simply because their enforcement against the press has incidental effects on its ability to gather and report news . . . The publisher of a newspaper has no special privilege to invade the rights and liberties of others . . .

"There can be no doubt that the Minnesota doctrine of promissory estoppel is a law of general applicability. It does not target or single out the press."

The U.S. Supreme Court remanded the case to the Minnesota Supreme Court for further proceedings, and in 1992 that Court reinstated the $200,000 in damages under a common law doctrine which holds that some promises are legally binding.

Three instances, all in 1972, illustrate the collision that occasionally occurs between the mass media and the judicial system. One involved Peter J. Bridge, a reporter for the *Evening News*, Newark, New Jersey, who spent 22 days in jail in October that year for refusing to answer questions in a grand jury hearing that went beyond the stories he had written about corruption in the Newark Housing Authority. He answered more than 50 questions but balked when questioning went beyond what had been published, because, by doing so, he would betray the confidentiality of his news sources and because he felt that the grand jury was on "a fishing expedition" to which he did not want to be a party.

John Lawrence, Washington bureau chief for *The Los Angeles Times,* was ordered jailed for refusing to hand over tapes of interviews with the chief prosecution witness in the

10. Dan Cohen v. Cowles Media Co., 115 L Ed. 2d 586, 111 S. Ct. 2513 (June 24, 1991).

Watergate bugging case. The witness was FBI agent Alfred Baldwin III, and Baldwin was named in the story, but the defense attorney wanted the tapes on the chance that some unused portions might help discredit the FBI agent as a witness.

Edwin Goodman, manager of Radio Station WBAI in New York City, became the first broadcaster ever jailed for refusing to release tape recordings of news programming after being issued a subpoena by the district attorney on January 25, 1972, ordering him to do so. The recordings were made during riots in October 1970 in the Manhattan House of Detention in New York, commonly known as the Tombs. Station WBAI in reporting the event called the prison office which the prisoners had taken over and broadcast telephone talks with the prisoners round the clock for about 30 hours, preempting regular programming.

The district attorney's office believed that the tape recordings would be of help in prosecuting the rioters, some of whom had threatened to kill hostages. Goodman, grandson of a founder of the fashionable Bergdorf Goodman store in New York who had gone into broadcasting, refused to sell the tapes, so the district attorney's office obtained a subpoena ordering him to surrender them. When he refused to do so on March 3, he was sentenced to 30 days in jail and the station was fined $250. Goodman was released, however, after two days in jail on a writ of habeas corpus pending appeal of the case.

In refusing to release the tapes, the radio station contended that the subpoena "seeks information in violation of the First, Fourth, and Fourteenth amendments that guarantee freedom of the press and prohibit unreasonable search and seizure." It also argued that the material was privileged under the New York Civil Rights law as amended in 1970, which protects a newsman who refuses to disclose "news or the source of any news coming into his possession in the course of gathering or obtaining news."

The district attorney's office in rebuttal pointed out that the material had already been broadcast to the public, so there was nothing confidential about it. In response, Goodman said, "I think if you had to say before every phone call you receive, 'we'd like to warn you that anything you say on this call will be broadcast and may be held against you in a court of law months or even two years from now,' the quality of public discussion on the air would diminish radically."

CHAPTER
13

✽

RIGHTS CAN CONFLICT IN FREE PRESS / FAIR TRIAL

RIGHTS CAN CONFLICT IN
FREE PRESS / FAIR TRIAL

❀

A crime story in the newspaper does not give all the facts for the simple reason that the police do not tell all they know. Before an arrest, they withhold information that might hinder the investigation and the apprehension of a criminal or criminals; and after the arrest, they withhold information that might cause an unfair trial.

Although it does not use those words, the U.S. Constitution guarantees a fair trial for everyone accused of a crime. It does that in the Sixth Amendment, which reads in part:

■ In all criminal proceedings, the accused shall enjoy the right to a speedy and public trial by an impartial jury . . .

That right was gained over centuries of struggle and is still denied millions of peoples in many other countries. In the U.S. it is a simple statement; yet it has two aspects that have caused considerable debate. The two are *public trial* and *impartial jury.*

Public means that trials may not be secret, that persons besides officials may attend, and that newspapers and broadcast stations are free to publish court proceedings. *Impartial* means that the members of the jury selected to decide the case are not prejudiced for or against the defendant, and that the jurors have not decided before they hear the case whether the accused is innocent or guilty. A jury is expected to base its verdict on the evidence presented during the trial, not on statements or rumors heard or read outside the courtroom.

Press freedom makes it possible for newspapers, radio, and television to publish lurid details of a crime, which may inflame the public against the person accused of the crime. In such a climate of opinion, it may be difficult, if not impossible, for the accused to have a fair trial. That would be especially true if the persons selected for the jury have been influenced by what they read in newspapers or hear on radio and television.

To illustrate: A prominent woman is stabbed to death in her apartment. She is well known to great numbers of residents in the community through her social life and civic activities and as moderator of a popular television talk show.

After two days a 24-year-old assistant electrician at a local factory is arrested for the murder. He is shown on television and in the newspaper while being arrested. He refuses to make any statement, but the prosecuting attorney tells reporters, "We've got our man." Later he fails a polygraph test, which is taken as further proof of his guilt.

As days go by, pictures of the scene of the crime and the life history of the murdered woman are published, and employers and relatives are interviewed on television and their comments are published in the newspapers. The story is kept alive as prospective witnesses are quoted while preparations are being made for the trial.

Publicity is so widespread and continuous, all pointing to the man's guilt, that the entire community assumes there is no doubt he is the murderer. In view of that condition, will it be possible to empanel a jury of unbiased and impartial citizens? Can a sufficient number of residents be found for the jury who have not already made up their minds about the case? In other words, can the accused man receive a fair trial in that community where a barrage of publicity has pointed to his guilt?

A situation of that kind does not occur very often. Most criminal cases, perhaps 90 to 95 percent, never go to trial because defendants plead guilty, some as the result of plea bargaining in which the accused person agrees to plead guilty in exchange for a lesser charge or lighter sentence or both. When a person pleads guilty, there is no need for a trial.

Also, comparatively few criminal cases are reported by newspapers and broadcast stations for two reasons. One is that newspapers do not have enough space and broadcast stations enough time to report all or even a large percentage of such cases, which number into the thousands annually. The other reason is that few criminal cases are of sufficient public interest to be published.

Occasionally, however, one comes along that attracts widespread attention. An example was the trial of Bruno Hauptmann for the kidnapping-murder of the infant son of Charles A. Lindbergh. As Lindbergh had become a national hero for flying the Atlantic Ocean solo in 1927, the entire country followed that case with keen interest all the way to the conviction and execution of Hauptmann.

Among other cases that got nationwide publicity were the trial of Lizzie Bordon for the ax slaying of her father and her stepmother in Fall River, Massachusetts, on August 4, 1892: and of Alger Hiss for espionage and perjury in 1948-50.

In some of the cases that developed into circuses of media publicity and avid public interest, convictions have been appealed on the basis that extensive pretrial publicity influenced the outcome. One such highly publicized case, ultimately appealed all the way to the U.S. Supreme Court on that basis, was that of Dr. Samuel H. Sheppard in Cleveland, Ohio.

On July 4, 1954, Sheppard's wife Marilyn, young, pretty, and pregnant, was found bludgeoned to death in their lakeside home in Bay Village, a fashionable suburb of Cleveland. Dr. Sheppard, an osteopath, claimed that he had been knocked unconscious by a bushy-haired intruder who had slain his wife.

The police in Bay Village, an independent municipality, accepted his account of the crime, but a number of persons were skeptical. Among them was Louis B. Seltzer, editor of *The Cleveland Press*, who was quoted as saying that "a conspiracy existed to defeat the ends of justice." Some days after the murder *The Press* carried a banner headline which read, "Why Isn't Sam Sheppard in Jail?" with a long article stating reasons for believing that the police should take action against him.

That was followed by more front-page stories, including an editorial which read in part, "Now proved to be a liar, still free to go about his business, shielded by his family, protected by a smart lawyer who had made monkeys out of the police and authorities, carrying a gun part of the time, left free to do whatever he pleases . . ." The case continued to build as other newspapers and radio and television stations joined in, so after a time the Bay Village police turned the case over to the Cleveland police, who promptly arrested Dr. Sheppard.

The case became a sensation as new developments were revealed and public interest grew. One revelation was that Dr. Sheppard had been having an illicit love affair with another woman in the weeks before his wife's murder. Publicity increased in intensity in the months before the trial started, and the trial itself was characterized by a frenzy of reporters and photographers attempting to outdo one another in covering the event. The trial took nine weeks and ended with the jury finding Dr. Sheppard guilty of second-degree murder and recommending a life sentence.

The verdict was then appealed on the basis that the press coverage was so prejudicial that the trial was unfair and the conviction void. The conviction was upheld by both the Ohio Supreme Court and the U.S. Court of Appeals for the Sixth District, with both courts pointing out that there was no proof that the jury had been influenced by the publicity.

The case then went to the U.S. Supreme Court where the justices were confronted for the first time to decide whether press coverage can be so prejudicial as to void a conviction. The Supreme Court ruled 8 to 1 that Dr. Sheppard should have a new trial within a reasonable time or the case should be dismissed. (When a new trial was held, the jury found Dr. Sheppard not guilty.)

173

The majority opinion of the Supreme Court, handed down on June 6, 1966, was written by Justice Tom C. Clark. The decision he wrote contains a description of some of the conditions that prevailed at the Sheppard trial, excerpts of which read:[1]

■   A long temporary table was set up inside the bar, in back of the single counsel table. It ran the width of the courtroom, parallel to the bar railing, with one end less than three feet from the jury box.

Approximately 20 representatives of newspapers and wire services were assigned seats at this table by the court. Behind the bar railing there were four rows of benches. These seats were likewise assigned by the court for the entire trial. The first row was occupied by representatives of television and radio stations, and the second and third rows by reporters of out-of-town newspapers and magazines.

One side of the last row, which accommodated 14 people, was assigned to Sheppard's family and the other to Marilyn's. The public was permitted to fill vacancies in this row on special passes only.

Representatives of the news media also used all the rooms on the courthouse floor, including the room where cases were ordinarily called and assigned for trial. Private telephone lines and telegraphic equipment were installed in these rooms so that reports from the trial could be speeded to the papers.

Station WSRS was permitted to set up broadcasting facilities on the third floor of the courthouse next to the jury room, where the jury rested during recesses in the trial and deliberated. Newscasts were made from this room throughout the trial, and while the jury reached its verdict.

On the sidewalks and steps in front of the courthouse, television and newsreel cameras were occasionally used

1. Sheppard v. Maxwell, 384 U.S. 333 (1966).

to take motion pictures of the participants in the trial, including the jury and the judge . . .

The jurors themselves were constantly exposed to the news media. Every juror, except one, testified . . . to reading about the case in the Cleveland papers or having heard broadcasts about it.

The fact is that bedlam reigned at the courthouse during the trial, and newsmen took over practically the entire courtroom, hounding most of the participants in the trial, especially Sheppard.

For months the virulent publicity about Sheppard and the murder made the case notorious.

Another case in which an appeal was based on a claim of prejudicial pretrial publicity was that of Leslie Irvin, who was arrested in 1955 on a charge of murder committed on December 23, 1954, in Vanderburgh County, Indiana.[2] After the police chief in Evansville announced that Irvin had confessed not only to the murder but also to five others, the media had a field day for six months before the trial began. The case was kept alive by articles, pictures, and cartoons in the newspapers and by broadcasts on radio and television. One radio station went so far as to ask listeners to say whether they thought Irvin was guilty and to say what punishment he should receive. Irvin was found guilty, the case was appealed and in 1961 the U.S. Supreme Court reversed the verdict.

In this and other cases where the U.S. Supreme Court has reversed convictions in appeals based on the claim of an unfair trial because of prejudicial pretrial publicity, the Court has not laid primary responsibility at the doorstep of newspapers, radio, and television. Rather, the Court in effect placed the blame on the criminal justice system for assisting in the publicity and in failing to conduct trials with decorum.

Rather than denigrating the role of the press in criminal

---

2. Leslie Irvin v. A.F. Dowd 366 U.S. 717 (June 5, 1961).

justice, Justice Clark in the majority opinion in the Sheppard case said:

■ The principle that justice cannot survive behind walls of silence has long been reflected in the "Anglo-American distrust for secret trials." A responsible press has always been regarded as the handmaiden of effective judicial administration, especially in the criminal field...

The press does not simply publish information about trials but guards against the miscarriage of justice by subjecting the police, prosecutors, and judicial process to extensive public scrutiny and criticism. The Court has, therefore, been unwilling to place any direct limitations on the freedom traditionally exercised by the news media, for "what transpires in the court room is public property."

In the Sheppard case, the Supreme Court did not remand on the basis of prejudicial publicity but rather on the manner in which the trial was conducted. In his opinion on that case, Justice Clark wrote, "The carnival atmosphere of the trial could easily have been avoided since the courtroom and the courthouse premises are subject to control by the court."

His statement points up the fact that in the American legal system the judge (sometimes called "the court") has absolute control over the courtroom during a trial and during a recess of a trial. He may cite anyone for contempt who refuses to obey an order he gives; and contempt is the one offense for which a person may be sent to jail on the order of a judge — without a trial.

Contempt, which is disobedience or disrespect for the judge, the court, or a legislative body, is classified as civil or criminal. Civil contempt is failure to obey an order of the judge or refusal to carry out the terms of a court decision or to obey the verdict in a civil suit.

Criminal contempt is an act that interferes with the orderly process of the court. The act may be misbehavior in court during a trial or during the recess of a trial, or it may be an act or acts outside the courtroom that interfere with, delay, or obstruct justice. A newspaper or broadcast station can be in contempt of court before a case comes to trial, during the trial, after the verdict or decision has been reached, and while a motion for a new trial or an appeal is pending.[3]

In most states there is no limit on the amount of time a person can spend in jail for civil contempt, but the U.S. Supreme Court ruled in 1971 that a person may not be kept in prison for more than six months for criminal contempt without a jury trial.

Quelling disturbances and keeping order in the courtroom is in some respects much simpler than attempting to control news and comment before and during a trial because attempts of that kind can conflict with the First Amendment guarantee of freedom of speech and the press. A judge cannot, for example, safely cite a newspaper or even an individual for criticizing the conduct of a trial because such criticism falls under the rubric of fair comment. Yet the judge has the authority to cite as contemptuous any publication, true or false, that has a tendency to interfere with the orderly process of the court, that contains grossly inaccurate reports of court proceedings, or that scandalizes the judge and participants in the trial. Always, however, there is the question of whether the publication is fair comment or contemptuous.

The same freedom of expression allowed the press also extends to police officials and attorneys, but that freedom is accompanied by the responsibility of not jeopardizing fairness for persons accused of crimes. It is expected that police and prosecutors try to make themselves appear competent by announcing arrests, giving interviews, holding press conference, and releasing information regarding crimes. Most pretrial publicity comes from criminal justice officials; some, but to a lesser degree, reaches the press through investigation

---

3. Adapted from William R. Arthur and Ralph L. Crosman, *The Law of Newspapers*, McGraw-Hill Book Co., 1940, pp. 357-380.

by news reporters. Most states have established rules on what attorneys may say about pending cases in which they are involved but there is little uniformity in those rules across the country.

The conflict between the bar and the press is exacerbated by the adversarial nature of the American judicial system, with the prosecuting attorney trying to prove the defendant guilty and the accused person defending his innocence; with one side trying to prove that the charges are true while the opposing side tries to prove them false.

The free press / fair trial conflict was of sufficient concern to the American Bar Association in 1964, which was two years before the Supreme Court decision in the Sheppard case, that it appointed an Advisory Committee on Fair Trial and Free Press to develop standards that would strengthen the right to a fair trial without abridging freedom of speech and the press. Paul C. Reardon, then Associate Justice of the Supreme Judicial Court of Massachusetts, was named chairman of the Committee.

The Committee report, known as *The Reardon Report*, was adopted by the House of Delegates of the American Bar Association at the midyear meeting in Chicago in February 1968 and by the Judicial Conference of the United States later that year.

In summary, the standards recommended in *The Reardon Report* state that police and lawyers for the defense and the prosecution should not release information concerning the prior criminal record, if any, of a person accused of a crime; his character or reputation; the contents of a confession or that he has confessed or may possibly plead guilty; the result of a polygraph test or any other examination; the identity or testimony of prospective witnesses; and any opinion regarding the accused person's guilt or innocence.

The Report recommended that "law enforcement agencies in each jurisdiction adopt internal regulations imposing similar restrictions on the personnel; and where they fail to do so, such regulations should be made effective by rule of court or legislative bodies."

The kinds of information that may be released, the Report stated, are facts and circumstances of the arrest, including time and place, resistance, and use of weapons; identity of the investigating officer or agency; any physical evidence seized; a brief description of the offense charged; public records of the court case, to be quoted without comment; scheduling of hearings and trial; and requests for assistance in obtaining evidence.

The Report further recommended that contempt power be used, with considerable caution, "against a person who publishes anything beyond the public record of the court that is willfully designed to affect or seriously threatens to affect the outcome of the trial," and "against any person who knowingly violates a valid judicial order not to disseminate specific information referred to in certain sections of this report until after completion of the trial."

The adoption of *The Reardon Report* by the American Bar Association was immediately protested by representatives of the press as being too restrictive. Press freedom, they pointed out, rather than being an obstruction to a fair trial is actually a means of guaranteeing justice. The press was granted the freedom it has in order to act as a watchdog or a check on government, including the criminal justice system as a branch of government.

If the press were restricted to reporting only what occurs in the courtroom and what appears in public records, they contended, many facts about a case might never become known. Records can easily and conveniently be lost or misplaced; and the adoption of rules such as those in *The Reardon Report* could become a means of secrecy behind which an accused person could be railroaded or released through political or powerful influence.

Among comments by journalists when the proposed report was released more than a year earlier, George Beebe,

Managing Editor of the *Miami Herald*, said, "The cure suggested by the American Bar Association to assure fair trial is far more dangerous than the suspected ailment." Arville Schaleben, Associate Editor of the *Milwaukee Journal*, wrote, "The ABA committee report is seemingly judicious but it would be more damaging than helpful." Editors in general described the proposals as a definite infringement of press freedom and the public's right to know.[4]

Even in cases where the police are not involved in a cover-up, where the criminal justice process is carried out honestly, rules restricting the release of legitimate information to protect an accused person can have the opposite effect. An example of an actual case was that of Larry E. Bunten, chief petty officer, USN, who was arrested in New Mexico in 1967 for a double murder and held in prison for 18 days because of misidentification.[5]

Bunten was on leave and visiting relatives of his wife on the Acoma Indian Reservation when a robbery attempt at the Budville Trading Post, 60 miles from Albuquerque, ended in the killing of two persons in the store. By coincidence, because Bunten and the murderer not only looked alike but were wearing similar clothes, two witnesses who had survived the shooting identified Bunten as the killer.

He was able to prove his innocence, but not before spending more than two weeks behind bars. The police, after his arrest, operated under the kind of rules recommended by *The Reardon Report* and thus released the name and age of the person arrested, the fact that he was unarmed and offered no resistance, and the reason for the arrest, but nothing more.

The fact that Bunten had offered an alibi was not revealed, so the newspapers could not check on that. No information that might have raised doubts and led to further investigation

---

4. *The New York Times*, October 9, 1966, page 89.
5. Tony Hillerman, "The Budville Murders: Reardon Rules in Action," *The Quill*, October 1968, pages 12-15.

by reporters was available. Police were sure they had the murderer in custody, and the press had so little information that there was no reason to question whether the police were right.

In this case the police were not trying to cover up any facts, but the secrecy they maintained, designed to protect the accused person, caused an innocent person much anguish and inconvenience.

The press-bar conflict over pretrial publicity has diminished in recent years. The American Bar Association amended its *Standards Relating to Fair Trial and Free Press* in 1978 and further modified its standards pertaining to pretrial publicity in its *Model Rules of Professional Conduct* adopted on August 2, 1983. The ABA Rules have been adopted in whole or in part in more than half the states. Those rules admit that "no body of rules can simultaneously satisfy all interests of fair trial and all those of free expression."

In the comments, the *Model Rules* state: "Preserving the right to a fair trial necessarily entails some curtailment of the information that may be disseminated about a party prior to trial... On the other hand, there are vital social interests served by the free dissemination of information about events having legal consequences and about legal proceedings themselves."

Responsible editors and publishers recognize that the publication of some kinds of information can be prejudicial, so in some communities representatives of the news media and the legal profession have cooperatively developed voluntary guidelines for reporting criminal law proceedings. In fact, within four years after the Bar Association's adoption of *The Reardon Report*, voluntary fair trial-free press guidelines had been agreed upon between state bar associations and news media organizations in 23 states. Together, the press and the bar, including representative judges, attorneys, and police, have agreed upon the kinds of information that should be published or broadcast for the benefit of the public and what should be withheld so as not to jeopardize the rights of accused persons or to protect innocent persons and their right to privacy.

What is published in newspapers and on broadcasts is controlled primarily by editors who decide what to publish or broadcast and by law enforcement officers who decide what information to release and what to withhold.

At all times, however, they must operate within laws that require or prohibit the release of certain kinds of information. All state, county, and municipal records, except for some listed as confidential, are open to the public. On the other hand, privacy laws prohibit the release of some kinds of information, and some states have laws that restrict the release of some kinds of information about children. Juvenile court hearings are frequently private, but not secret. In most states the names of juveniles taken into custody are not made public, and some states have laws that prohibit publication of their names.[6]

In general, here are what a police-related story in a newspaper or on a radio or television station reports and does not report:

■ The kind or nature of such events as a fire, accident, homicide, suicide, shooting, robbery, theft, assault, rape, hostage taking, explosion, flood, strike, and riot, including time and place.

---

6. Laws that impose prior restraint are often difficult to enforce. For example, West Virginia had a law that made it a crime to publish the names of juvenile offenders without written approval of the juvenile court. When two newspapers in Charleston published the name of a 14-year-old boy arrested for the murder of another boy, they were indicted and found guilty. The U.S. Supreme Court affirmed the decision of the West Virginia Supreme Court of Appeals that the state statute operated as a prior restraint on speech, and the state's interest in protecting the identity of juvenile offenders did not overcome the constitutionality of such prior restraint. Robert K. Smith et al v. Daily Mail Publishing Co., 443 U.S. 97, (June 26, 1979).

- The number of persons killed or injured, but not their names until after the next of kin have been notified.

- The amount of money and property lost, damaged, and destroyed and their value, but usually nothing about the personal wealth of those who suffered the loss.

- Facts about a sex crime, an abduction, or a case of spouse or child abuse, but not the name of the victim or any kind of information that could lead to the victim's identity.

- Who, when, and where regarding a suicide, but not why; and if there is a suicide note, not its contents.

- The adoption of an abandoned baby, but not the names or address of the couple who adopted the baby.

- The name, age, residence, employment, marital status, and similar personal information about an adult who has been arrested and charged with a crime; but not the name and address of a juvenile, unless he or she is charged with a felony or has a record of habitual lawbreaking.

- The nature of the charge against the person arrested, such as would be contained in a complaint or an indictment, and the name of the complainant, if there is one.

- Circumstances of an arrest, including time and place, method of apprehension, resistance and any resulting injuries, possession and use of weapons, and description of items or contraband seized.

- Names of officers who made the investigation and arrest, but not their home addresses or telephone numbers, and not photographs or places of employment of their wives or husbands, and not the names and location of the schools their children attend.

- Names of one or more prospective witnesses who will testify regarding the crime, but no statements by the police regarding the character or reputation of the person arrested.

- Amount of bail, scheduled court dates, and place of detention of the accused person.

- A photograph of a person who has been arrested, but not one in which he has been deliberately posed with police officers.

- Indictments returned by a grand jury, naming persons indicted and the charges against them; but nothing about the grand jury hearings, which are always conducted in secret.

- That a jury has been selected, but not the names of the jury members.

- An interview in the newspapers or on radio or television of someone arrested and held in prison, but only with that person's permission.

Because of the likelihood of prejudicing or influencing a trial, it is usually inappropriate for a news story about someone arrested for a crime to report that the accused person is expected to plead guilty, or has confessed, or to publish the contents of a confession, or the results of a polygraph test or other examination, or refusal to take such test. Also, such news stories rarely contain comments by police or attorneys regarding the guilt or innocence of the accused person, or the names of jurors selected for the trial, or the identity of witnesses; and, during the trial, arguments made in the absence of the jury and any evidence ruled inadmissible by the judge.

CHAPTER
14

❀

CAMERAS MAY BE
PROHIBITED IN THE
COURTROOM

CAMERAS MAY BE PROHIBITED
IN THE COURTROOM

❧

With few exceptions, trials are open to the public. If the courtroom is not overcrowded, all a person needs do to attend is to walk in and take a seat. He may sit and listen, and he may take notes; but it would not be wise to have a camera of any kind with him because the question of whether photography is permitted in the courtroom is still not fully answered after more than half a century of debate. Also, tape recording by observers may be forbidden.

The question of photography stems from the conflict between the right of the press to report the news and the right of an accused person to a fair trial. The photojournalism aspect of the conflict heated up in 1937 when the American Bar Association adopted a rule prohibiting photography in the courtroom. The action was taken after the trial of Bruno Hauptmann in 1935, mentioned in the previous chapter, for the kidnapping and murder of the infant son of Mr. and Mrs. Charles A. Lindbergh. As the Lindberghs were a famous and popular couple, the trial became one of the most highly publicized ever. Described as a "media circus," the trial was conducted in an atmosphere of sensationalism, with the sheriff permitted to sell seats to the public and women bringing lunches so they would not need to leave at noon recesses. The lack of decorum at the trial has been cited as a major reason for the American Bar Association's subsequent adoption of *Judicial Canon 35,* which ruled against photography in courtrooms, although press photographers were not permitted to take pictures in the courtroom during the Hauptmann trial. The Canon read:

■ Proceedings in the court should be conducted with fitting dignity and decorum. The taking of photographs in the courtroom during sessions of the court or recesses between sessions, and the broadcasting of court proceedings are calculated to detract from the essential dignity of the proceedings, degrade the court and create misconceptions with respect thereto in the mind of the public and should not be permitted.

The Canon was updated in 1963 to include television.

All but three states adopted the Canon, either by law or by their supreme courts as court rules. Rule 53 of the *Federal Rules of Criminal Procedure* prevented photography in federal courts; and cameras in the U.S. Supreme Court was, and remains, an absolute no-no. However, copies of tape-recordings of arguments made before the Court are available to the public.

Television as a new medium was regarded as entertainment as were motion pictures in their infancy, and not as an important medium of communication. Publishers and editors argued for the right of press photography to replace artists with sketch pads, and television broadcasters asked why public court proceedings should be limited to relatively small court and hearing rooms when they could be seen by thousands by means of television.

The bulkiness of the equipment and the bright lights necessary in the early days of television and the flash lighting necessary in still photography could be disturbing elements; but as television and photography equipment became less intrusive through technical developments and as television became a more familiar medium, rules against photography in the courtroom began to relax, slowly and haltingly.

By 1992 cameras and recorders were being permitted to some extent in courtrooms in 46 states, but forbidden totally in Indiana, Mississippi, South Dakota, and the District of

Columbia. A two-year experiment in the use of cameras in selected trial courts in Missouri began on January 1, 1994. Trial courts have proved to be the most sensitive areas in regard to photography with more than a dozen states forbidding the use of cameras in their trial courts. In Illinois, for example, photography is permitted in the state Supreme Court and in appellate courts, but not in trial courts.

A three-year experiment began July 1, 1991, in the use of television cameras in half dozen federal district courts and in a couple of federal appeal courts. Virtually all state legislatures permit televising of their floor activities. Both the U.S. House of Representatives and the Senate now make television recordings of selected proceedings, with some sessions and committee hearings broadcast on C-SPAN (Cable-Satellite Public Affairs Network). Virtually all state legislatures permit televising of their floor activities.

Examples of "first steps" include approval in 1956 by the Colorado Supreme Court of a recommendation that trial judges in that state be allowed to decide for themselves whether to permit trials in their courts to be televised or broadcast by radio. In Mason, Michigan, a three-month experiment was conducted in 1971 in televising courtroom proceedings "to provide true-to-life instant replay of key testimony," thus drastically reducing delay over the time it would take to prepare typewritten transcripts.

In 1972 a probate court judge in Portage County, Ohio, began videotaping hearings to save a court reporter from having to sit throughout the proceedings and enabling the judge to replay any part of the hearings on a television set. In 1973 a Common Pleas Court judge in Sandusky, Ohio, had all testimony in 14 civil cases taken by video tape to show to jurors when they were empaneled. The jurors watched the tapes and rendered verdicts without ever having seen any of the witnesses in person.

Police in Lake Charles, Louisiana, were too clever, the U.S. Supreme Court decided, when they made a motion picture of an "interview" with a bank robber in 1961. The Supreme Court decision in that case, and in another two years later, contain reasons for the reluctance of the justices to allow cameras in the courtroom. The case began in the evening of February 16, 1961, when Wilbert Rideau robbed a bank in Lake Charles, kidnapped three of the bank employees, and killed one of them. Later that day the filmed "interview" was broadcast over a television station in Lake Charles, with an estimated 24,000 people in the community seeing and hearing the broadcast. The film was shown again on television the next day to an estimated audience of 53,000. The following day the film was broadcast again.

Rideau was later convicted by the Calcasieu Parish trial court and sentenced to death on a murder charge. The conviction was affirmed by the Supreme Court of Louisiana, but it was reversed by the U.S. Supreme Court in 1963.[1] In the majority opinion, Justice Potter Stewart said:

■ For anyone who has ever watched television the conclusion cannot be avoided that this spectacle, to the tens of thousands of people who saw and heard it, in a very real sense was Rideau's trial—at which he pleaded guilty to murder. Any subsequent court proceedings in a community so pervasively exposed to such a spectacle could be but a hollow formality.

The most highly publicized trial involving television was the Billie Sol Estes case in Tyler, Texas, in October 1962. Estes, a nationally known Texas financier, was tried and convicted for theft, swindling, and embezzlement involving the federal government. The pretrial publicity was so massive that 11 volumes of press clippings were on file with the Clerk of Courts.

---

1. Rideau v. Louisiana, 373 U.S. 723 (1963). He was later retried and again found guilty.

Texas was a state that had not adopted Canon 35 of the American Bar Association but operated under Canon 28 of the Integrated State Bar of Texas, which left telecasting and photographing of court proceedings to the discretion of the trial judge. In this case Judge Otis T. Dunagan allowed Station KLTV in Tyler, Texas, to televise the proceedings, over the objection of attorneys for Estes.

A hearing on a pretrial motion in September was carried live by both radio and television and news photography was permitted throughout. At least 12 cameramen were engaged in the courtroom throughout the hearing, taking motion and still pictures and televising the proceedings. Cables and wire were snaked across the courtroom floor, three microphones were on the judge's bench, and others were beamed at the jury box and the counsel table. The activities of the television crews and news photographers led to considerable disruption of the hearings.

The proceedings of the first day were televised live and repeated on tape later that evening in lieu of the usual late-night movie, reaching an estimated 100,000 local viewers, as well as a potential network audience in the millions. There were 15 sponsors for the local program.

Estes objected to the televising and broadcasting of the proceedings; and because of his continued objections, live telecasting was prohibited during a great portion of the actual trial. Only the opening and closing arguments by the state, the return of the jury's verdict, and its receipt by the trial judge were carried live with sound. Although videotaping of the entire proceedings was allowed without sound, the cameras operated only intermittently, recording various portions of the trial for broadcast on regularly scheduled newscasts later in the day and evening. Because of varying restrictions, telecasts of the trial were confined largely to film clips shown on the station's regularly scheduled news programs.

Estes appealed his conviction to the Texas Court of Criminal Appeals, contending that he had been deprived of his right under the Fourteenth Amendment to due process of law by the televising and broadcasting of his trial. The Appeals Court upheld the conviction, so he appealed to the U.S. Supreme Court, which on June 7, 1965, reversed the conviction with a majority agreeing that the televising and broadcasting portions of his trial had indeed deprived him of "due process of law."[2] It was a bare majority, however, with only five of the nine justices agreeing to reverse the conviction for that reason.

In the majority opinion, Justice Tom C. Clark said in part:

■ The chief function of our judicial machinery is to ascertain the truth. The use of television, however, cannot be said to contribute materially to this objective. Rather its use amounts to the injection of an irrelevant factor into court proceedings.

He listed four situations in which television in the courtroom might cause actual unfairness to accused persons. In brief, he said:

1. The potential impact of television on the jurors is perhaps of the greatest significance . . . From the moment the trial judge announces that a case will be televised, it becomes a cause celebre . . .while it is practically impossible to assess the effect of television on jury attentiveness, those of us who know juries realize the problem of jury "distraction."

2. The impact upon a witness with the knowledge that he is being viewed by a vast audience is simply incalculable. Some may be demoralized and frightened, some cocky and given to overstatement may be severely undermined.

3. A major aspect of the problem is the additional responsibilities the presence of television places on the

_____

2. Estes v. Texas, 381 U.S. 532 (1965).

trial judge . . .

4. We cannot ignore the impact of courtroom television on the defendant . . . A defendant on trial for a specific crime is entitled to his day in court, not in a stadium, or a city or nationwide arena.

Chief Justice Earl Warren, in concurring, said in part:

■ I believe that it violates the Sixth Amendment for Federal courts and the Fourteenth Amendment for State courts to allow criminal trials to be televised to the public at large . . . The televising of trials would cause the public to equate the trial process with the forms of entertainment regularly seen on television and with the commercial objectives of the television industry.

Justice Potter Stewart, in dissenting from the majority opinion, said, "I cannot now hold that the Constitution absolutely bars television cameras from every criminal courtroom"; and Justice William J. Brennan Jr., in dissent, said, ". . . today's decision is *not* a blanket constitutional prohibition against the televising of state criminal trials."

A significant decision by the U.S. Supreme Court in 1981 gave impetus to television in the courtroom by removing the constitutional barrier the Court had established ten years earlier.[3] The case involved the conviction of Noel Chandler and Robert Granger, former Miami Beach policemen, of conspiracy to commit burglary, grand larceny, and possession of burglary tools. Over their objection, part of the trial was televised.

Canon 35 of the American Bar Association prohibiting photography in the courtroom had been embodied in Canon 3A (7) of the *Florida Code of Judicial Conduct*, but in January 1975 Post-Newsweek Florida, Inc., had petitioned the Su-

---

3. Chandler v. Florida, 449 U.S. 560 (January 26, 1981).

preme Court of Florida for a change in that rule. The Court acceded to the extent of permitting experimental televising of trials, which began in 1977.

The next year the Committee on Fair Trial-Free Press of the American Bar Association proposed a revision in Canon 35 to permit coverage of trials by electronic media under control of the judge "but only if such coverage was carried out unobtrusively and without affecting the conduct of the trial." That proposal was approved by the ABA House of Delegates in February 1978.

The Florida District Court of Appeals found no evidence that the presence of a television camera in the courtroom had hampered Chandler and Granger in presenting their case, deprived them of an impartial jury, or impaired the fairness of the trial. The Florida Supreme Court denied review. The case then went to the U.S. Supreme Court, which in January 26, 1981, upheld the conviction unanimously. In the opinion of the Court, Chief Justice Warren Burger stated: "We hold that the Constitution does not prohibit a state from experimenting with the program authorized by Florida Canon 3A (7), which permits television in the courtroom.

CHAPTER
15

LYING ABOUT SOMEONE IS MALICIOUS

LYING ABOUT SOMEONE
IS MALICIOUS

❀

The belief that it is wrong to say something that injures another person dates back for centuries. One of the Ten Commandments reads:

- Thou shalt not bear false witness against thy neighbor.[1]

Shakespeare wrote in the play *Othello:*

Who steals my purse steals trash; 'tis something, nothing;
'Twas mine, 'tis his, and has been slave to thousands;
But he that filches from me my good name
Robs me of that which not enriches him,
And makes me poor indeed.

Speaking, writing, or printing statements that damage or destroy someone's reputation is called *defamation.* When it is written or printed, defamation is called *libel.*[2] When it is spoken, it is called *slander.*

---

1. Deuteronomy Chapter 5.
2. *Libel* is from the Latin *libellus*, a diminutive of *liber* meaning *book.* When a Roman wanted to defame someone, he issued a little book, poster, or broadside, stating the alleged misdeeds of that person. In Middle English libel meant a handbill, especially one that attacked or defamed someone. Today the word means defamation in writing or printing, although it doesn't have to be in words. It can be representational, as in a cartoon, effigy, etc.

Defamation is not protected by the First Amendment to the U.S. Constitution. A person guilty of defaming another person cannot claim that his right of free speech is guaranteed by the Constitution.

Each state has its own laws regarding libel and slander, but those laws do not necessarily define defamation with precisely the same words from state to state. All agree, however, that to defame is to harm the reputation of someone by libel or slander; and doing so is a civil offense.

The law in California, for example, defines libel as "false and unprivileged publication . . . which exposes any person to hatred, contempt, ridicule, or obloquy, or which causes him to be shunned or avoided, or which has a tendency to injure him in his occupation."

Libel is defined in one court decision in these words:[3]

■ A publication, if false, which is calculated to deprive a person of public confidence . . . to degrade and disgrace him, and to injure his rights of friendly and business intercourse with others is libelous.

Another court spoke as follows:[4]

■ A person injured by the publication of a libelous article, or the speaking of false and slanderous words, is entitled to compensation for the injury sustained, whether the person speaking the words or publishing the article did so maliciously or not.

Note the word *false* in those statements. Freedom of speech does not include *freedom* to tell lies, especially lies that defame another person or persons. Even if a person believes what he is saying or writing is true but is actually

---

3. Patchell v. Jaqua, 6 Ind. App. 70 33 NE 132.
4. Wabash Printing and Publishing Co. v. Crumrine, 123 Ind. 89 21 NE 904.

false, he can be in trouble. Believing it to be true is no excuse; it must be true, and it must be said or published without malice.

To be slanderous or libelous, a statement must be heard or read by more than one person besides the speaker or writer or publisher. Publication involves two or more persons. When only two persons are involved, it is one person's word against the other; and in that case it is not possible to prove what was said or published.

To publish is to place before the public, and legally more than one person constitutes the public. A letter, for example, sent to someone does not constitute publication. In such case, the letter becomes the property of the receiver, but the right of publication remains with the writer-sender.

Note that the definition of libel contains the word *publication*, and publication means being available to more than one person. Publication has been defined in this manner:[5]

■ Exhibiting a libelous letter and proclaiming its contents, or giving it to others to read, constitute publication.

Repeating a slanderous or libelous statement is as bad as stating it in the first place. A person can say that he is only repeating what someone else told him, but that is no defense. The person who is slandered can bring suit against anyone and everyone who repeats a statement that defames him. That has been upheld by the courts numerous times. Here are two examples:

■ Every person who repeats a slander, unless upon a justifiable occasion, is liable therefor; and no one can exempt himself from damages by proving that when he repeated the slander he gave the name of the author.[6]

---

5. McCallester v. Mount, 73 Ind. 559.
6. Gates v. Kellogg, 9 Ind. 506.

■ A person who copies primary libelous matter and publishes or otherwise distributes copies thereof is guilty of publishing a new libel for the consequences of which he is responsible to the exclusion of the makers of the primary publication.[7]

Also anyone who aids in disseminating a libel is legally liable. If a defamatory statement is published in a newspaper, for example, everyone connected with the publication could be sued by the offended person. Everyone could include the company that owns the newspaper, the publisher, the editor, the reporter, the workers who operated the press, and even the carrier who delivered the paper. In actual practice, that does not happen; generally only the company or the person who owns the newspaper is sued.

Libel does not have to be intentional. The lines under two pictures in a newspaper, for example, might accidentally be switched so that an innocent person is labeled as a criminal, and a criminal as an innocent person. The innocent person could bring suit for damages, and the claim that the error was accidental and unintentional would be a weak defense.

One example of mistaken identity, among many, that led to a libel suit occurred years ago and involved Annie Oakley, who had acheived fame as an expert rifle shot, charming and amazing thousands by her performances in Buffalo Bill's Wild West Show in the latter part of the past century. The case had its origin on August 8, 1903, when a man named Charles Curtis filed a complaint in the Harrison Street Police Court in Chicago, stating that a toothless hag named Lillie Cody had stolen his pants to get money to buy cocaine.

Lillie was arrested on a charge of breach of the peace, and in jail in answer to questions she admitted to the matron that she was in fact the Annie Oakley who had been a crack shot

---

7. Sourbier v. Brown, 188 Ind. 554-123 NE 802.

and had toured with the William F. Cody Wild West Show. At her arraignment, the arresting officer told the judge that the woman was Annie Oakley and should be locked up to prevent her from spreading a disease; and the judge agreed.

Here was an irresistible newspaper story! A police reporter for the *Chicago American*, who had once seen Annie Oakley perform, interviewed the woman in jail and, embellishing the facts, told how this once nationally acclaimed woman had fallen so low as to steal the pants of a "Negro" to satisfy her drug habit. Other newspapers in Chicago picked up the story, which was also sent by wire to papers all over the country.

In the meantime, the real Annie Oakley, having retired from show business several years earlier and in poor health, was living in Nutley, New Jersey. When she read the story about herself in her newspaper, she sued not only the *Chicago American* for libel but also 45 others, taking advantage of the principle that repeating a libel is as actionable as stating it the first time. She won all but one of the suits and received thousands of dollars in damages.

There are two kinds of libel. One is *civil*, which involves a person or persons, or in some cases may involve a group, a company, or an organization. The other kind of libel is *criminal*, which involves society in general and the government.

Criminal libel originated centuries ago in English common law and pertained to the prohibition of speaking or writing critical statements about the King or the Church and publishing without a license. Such acts were known as seditious libel. The laws governing criminal libel in the United States vary from state to state, but in general they pertain to speech or publication that causes a breach of the peace, offends public morals, reviles the Deity, or urges the overthrow of the government by force.

In criminal libel, the person brought to trial is accused of a crime for what he or she said or published. In such cases, the state is the plaintiff, and the public prosecutor is the attorney for the state. The accused person, the defendant, must provide his own attorney for the defense, if he is financially able to do so. If he is not, the state will provide a public defender as his attorney.

Civil libel is a *tort,* which in law is a wrongful act that causes injury to someone's person, property, or reputation for which the injured person is entitled to compensation or damages. Thus, a dead person cannot be libeled. Torts include all such injuries except those caused by breach of contract and trust.

In a civil libel suit, a person or even a group of persons files a complaint maintaining that he or they have been defamed and asks that the guilty party be required to pay damages. In such cases, both the plaintiff and the defendant have their own attorneys.

Libel may be classified as libel *per se* or libel *per quod.* The Latin *per se* means "by or in itself," so published words and statements that are clearly defamatory are libelous *per se.* Calling a person a murderer, a thief, or a liar would be libelous *per se*, unless that person had been convicted in court as a murderer, a thief, or a liar. A person who is libeled *per se* does not have to prove in court that he or she has been defamed; the defaming word or words are sufficient. If, on the other hand, a person believes that he has been defamed by a particular printed article which does not contain defaming words, he must prove that he has been libeled and thus entitled to special damages. This is known as libel *per quod.*

Libel *per quod* is so seldom used today that it is virtually an anachronism, but its equivalent in suits claiming defamation by false impression has not disappeared. Such cases arise when a person or a company believes that, although every statement in an article is true, the statements and perhaps photographs are presented in a manner that intentionally and deliberately creates a false and defamatory impression.

Accusing a person of a crime, of violating the law, is libelous *per se*, unless it can be proven as true. For example, a newspaper story stated that Virginia Gentry filed suit asking for damage on the pretense of a back injury. The court held that that was libelous per se, stating "To our way of thinking that statement in the story exposed her to "public hatred, contempt, or obloquy and tended to deprive her of public confidence and is therefore libelous in itself."[8]

Some words may be libelous at one time and in one place but not in another. There was a time in the early 1950s during the McCarthy Era when calling a person a Communist if he was not one, or calling him a Communist sympathizer, was libelous per se. Among words that have been judged libelous *per se* are "drunkard", "liar", "horsethief", "mean coward."[9]

In 1966 a white merchant in a black neighborhood in Washington D.C., sued for damages when he was called a "bigot" in a local newspaper. The jury decided that the word as used was libelous, and he was awarded $500 in damages.

The law allows for three kinds of damages in libel. *Special* damages cover financial loss caused by publication of the libel. *Compensatory*, or *general*, damages compensate for injured feelings, mental anguish, and public humiliation caused by the libel. *Punitive*, or *exemplary*, damages are awarded if malice or gross carelessness is proven, and it is here that catastrophic verdicts occur.

Legal cases involving criminal libel are relatively rare, but civil cases are common, comprising by far the most litigation in this country in regard to freedom of speech. Comparatively few suits for libel against newspapers, magazines, and broad-

---

8. 315 Pac. 2d 715 718 (1960). The name is changed here.
9. Once libel "per se" has been established, the defendant has no defense as to stated facts unless he can persuade the jury that they were true in all their particulars. — Justice William J. Brennan Jr., in the decision in New York Times v. Sullivan, 376 U.S. 254 (1964).

cast companies succeed; but those that do can result in enormous judgments by juries, running into millions of dollars, some sufficiently large to bankrupt smaller companies.

Among relatively recent huge awards was a $58 million judgment by a jury in State District Court in Waco, Texas, on April 20, 1991, the largest ever made in this country, at least up to that time. The award was to Vic Feazel, former District Attorney of Lennan County, Texas, who the jury found had been recklessly defamed by WFAA-TV in 1985 by an 11-part news series that accused him of taking bribes for dropping charges of drunken driving.

The previous high award for libel damages was a $34 million judgment assessed in 1990 against *The Philadelphia Inquirer* by a jury that found the newspaper guilty of defaming Richard A Sprague, a former first assistant district attorney in Philadelphia.

A judgment of $40.2 million was made in 1981 by a jury that found *Hustler* magazine guilty of defaming Robert Guccione, publisher of *Penthouse* magazine. The trial judge, however, reduced the award to $2.8 million, and on appeal the verdict was reversed so that *Hustler* magazine had no damages to pay.

There is virtually no limit to the amount of damages an aggrieved person may ask for in a libel suit. In 1987, for example, the nationally known evangelist Marvin Gorman sued another nationally known evangelist, Jimmy Swaggart, for $90 million for falsely accusing him of numerous adulterous affairs.[10] Even that amount is small compared with the $4 billion asked by Arthur Jones, inventor of the Nautilus exercise machines, in a libel suit filed the same year against the American Broadcasting Company. His complaint was in

---

10. On September 12, 1991, a jury in New Orleans found Swaggart *et al* guilty of defamation and awarded Gorman $10 million in damages.

reference to a "20/20" television program that told of the fate of 63 baby elephants which Jones had airlifted from Zimbabwe to his estate in Ocala, Florida, in the summer of 1984.

Jury awards running into the millions of dollars have been relatively rare, and most such verdicts have been reduced or overturned upon appeal. Before 1980 there were only two known libel awards of $1 million or more, according to a survey by the Libel Defense Resource Center in New York.[11] The survey indicates that this may be changing, however, as the average libel award increased from $432,000 in 1987-1988 to $4.5 million in 1989-1990. The trend continued in 1990-1991 with more than one in four jury awards exceeding $10 million compared with only 2 percent reaching that figure in the 1980s.

"Despite their growing size," the survey stated, "libel judgments against the media rarely survive the appeals process intact. In the decade through 1990, only 28.7 per cent of the libel awards were upheld on appeal, and they were reduced to an average of $359,419 on appeal, from original verdicts averaging $2 million." The hazard of libel lies not so much in enormous damage judgments as it does in the high cost of litigation; that is, in defending against libel suits. Cases that run on for months or years can be extremely expensive in court costs and attorney fees; and all suits must be defended to avoid losing them by default.

---

11. *Editor & Publisher*, October 12, 1991, September 5, 1992.

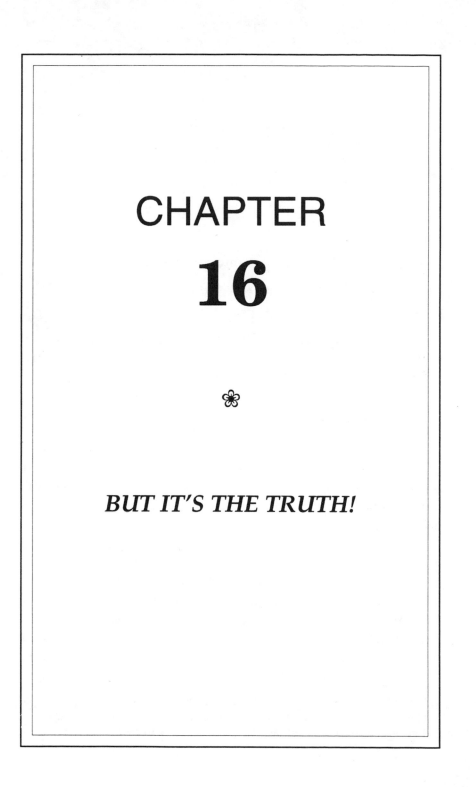

CHAPTER
16

❀

BUT IT'S THE TRUTH!

BUT IT'S THE TRUTH !

❀

LOUISE: Our butcher is selling tainted meat.

MOTHER: You shouldn't say things like that.

LOUISE: But, Mother, it's true!

If it's true, you can say it; but if it's false, don't. In other words, you can defend yourself, as Louise did, if what you say is true; but you can get into trouble if it isn't true.

Truth, however, has not always been a defense in libel and slander, especially if what was said or published was derogatory to government or church officials. In such cases, whether it was true or not made no difference. Rulers have always been sensitive to criticism, have demanded respect and obedience, and have seldom hesitated to inflict such punishment as they could on their critics — a condition that continues to the present time.

On the other hand, people have traditionally believed that persons in high places should be treated with respect and deference. As stated in Acts of the Apostles 23:5, "For it is written, Thou shalt not speak evil of the ruler of thy people."

To assure respect and obedience, the notorious Star Chamber was established in England in 1487, primarily to punish people accused or guilty of sedition[1] and seditious statements.

---

1. Sedition is an act or statement that causes or tends to cause people to refuse to obey lawful authority or rebel against the government.
   Under English common law criticism of the King was seditious.

It operated under the principle that "truth is immaterial" and "the greater the truth the greater the libel." Although the Star Chamber was abolished as a court in 1641, English common law on libel retained that principle for another 150 years.

The kind of thinking which permitted a person to be punished for telling the truth was never accepted in the American colonies and in the new country they formed. The first significant court case pointing to freedom of speech and the press in what is now the United States, including truth as a defense in libel, took place in New York while New York was still one of the British colonies and thus governed under English common law. The case included the trial in 1735 of John Peter Zenger, who was accused of publishing criminally libelous statements about William Cosby, the British-appointed Governor of New York.[2]

Governor Cosby, intensely disliked by many in New York, was arbitrary in making decisions and in some instances unethical if not downright dishonest. One of his acts, for example, was claiming back salary immediately upon his arrival from England that some felt was not rightfully his. His predecessor, Governor Montgomerie, died in office on July 1, 1731, and the position was filled temporarily by a man named Rip Van Dam, a merchant of Dutch descent and a member of the Executive Council.

Van Dam's appointment as acting governor was logical as the Dutch had originally claimed Manhattan and established a settlement there in 1623 and named it New Amsterdam. The British took the island by threat of force 41 years later in 1664,

---

2. The next year, in 1736, Zenger published an account of the trial in his newspaper under the title "A Brief Narrative of the Case and Trial of John Peter Zenger." Among books on the trial are *A Brief Narrative of the Case and Trial of John Peter Zenger,* by James A. Alexander, 1969; *John Peter Zenger: His Press, His Trial; A Bibliography,* by Livingston Rutherfurd, 1970; and *The Trial of John Peter Zenger,* by Vincent Buranelli, 1976.

renamed it New York, and governed it until the American colonies became an independent country.

Van Dam served as acting governor until Cosby arrived in May 1732. Shortly afterward, Cosby claimed that half of the salary and fees accumulated during those months belonged to him, not to Van Dam. That was only one of a number of decisions and actions he took that inflamed the public against him, to the extent that some community leaders decided to start a newspaper that would present facts about Cosby and oppose *The Gazette*, which supported the Governor or at least played it safe by not criticizing him.

The opposition newspaper they started publishing in 1733 was named the *New-York Weekly Journal*, and John Peter Zenger, a printer and German immigrant, was employed as its printer and publisher. The paper was indeed harsh in its criticism of the administration of Governor Cosby. In one issue, for example, one article read in part:

■ We see men's deeds destroyed, judges arbitrarily displaced, new courts erected without the consent of the legislature, by which it seems to me, trials by juries are taken away when a governor pleases; men of known estates denied their votes . . . Who is there in the province that can call anything his own, or enjoy any liberty longer than those in the administration will condescend to let him do it.

The *Journal* published articles in this vein on freedom of the press, trial by jury, and other rights of the people, most if not all of which Governor Cosby considered seditious. He tried to get a grand jury to indict Zenger, which it wouldn't do; he had the sheriff seize a number of copies of the *Journal* and burn them, but he couldn't get officials to attend the burning; and finally on November 17, 1734, he issued a warrant for the arrest of Zenger for "printing and publishing several seditious libels." Bail was set at 600 pounds, which was more than Zenger could post, so he remained in jail until his trial and release eight months later on August 5, 1735.

His arrest did not stop publication of the *Journal*, however. It missed one issue, and then Zenger's wife and some supporters continued publication weekly until the trial ended and Zenger could take over again.

In the trial, held in Federal Hall at Wall and Nassau streets in New York City, the Attorney General who prosecuted the case argued that Zenger should not be permitted to continue attacking His Excellency the Governor, who was the King's immediate representative and the supreme magistrate of the Province, and that Zenger should desist from disturbing the peace with criminal libels.

Andrew Hamilton, an experienced and highly respected attorney in Philadelphia, represented Zenger in the trial. He admitted that the articles alleged to be libelous had indeed been published by Zenger, although the Attorney General had said that the truth could make the libel greater.

Under English common law Zenger was clearly guilty, and Hamilton knew it. Zenger had published articles disrespectful of the Governor, who was a representative of the Crown. That is all it took to be guilty. Whether the articles were true or false made no difference.

So Attorney Hamilton, instead of pleading the case to the judge, spoke to the jury, arguing that people have a right to know what their government is doing and to complain when they believe that government officials are guilty of misconduct. He said, in part:

■ It is natural, it is a privilege . . . it is a right which all free men claim, that they are entitled to complain when they are hurt, they have a right publicly to demonstrate against the abuses of power in the strongest terms.

He was eloquent in his argument that truth should be a defense and in his appeal to the jury to decide the law itself:

■ Gentlemen of the jury, it is to you we must now

appeal for witnesses to the truth of the facts we have offered, and are denied the liberty to prove . . . The law supposes you are to be summoned out of the neighborhood where the fact is alleged to be committed . . . because you are supposed to have the best knowledge of the fact that is to be tried; and were you to find a verdict against my client, you must take upon you to say that the papers referred to in the information, and which we acknowledge we printed and published, are false, scandalous and seditious; but of this I have no apprehension . . . the facts which we offer to prove were not committed in a corner. They are notoriously known to be true; and, therefore, in your justice lies our safety . . .

Hamilton was persuasive in his presentation. The judge could have stopped him, even cited him for contempt for taking that line of reasoning, which was contrary to existing law, but he did not do so. As a result, the jury ignored instructions from the judge and returned a verdict of "Not guilty."

Zenger was set free, and the verdict encouraged writers and editors in the American colonies to be bolder, less fearful, in writing about government and government officials. Although the case received widespread attention and pointed the direction that press freedom would take later in the United States, the trial did not change English common law — not in the colonies and not in England. It would be 57 years later in 1792 that the Parliament would pass the Fox Act assuring greater freedom of the press by leaving it to the jury to decide what constitutes seditious libel.[3]

It would be 67 years after the Zenger trial that a court case in 1803 in the United States led to the enactment of laws

---

3. It was not until 1843 that the Parliament passed the Lord Campbell's Act which allowed truth to be a defense in criminal libel, provided the publication was for "a public benefit."

governing libel in this country, including the principle that truth is a defense. The case, tried in Columbia County, New York, was the *People v. Croswell*.[4]

The trial resulted from dissension between two political parties in the early days of the nation. A major difficulty in the framing and the adoption of the U.S. Constitution in 1787 and 1788, which would determine what kind of government the new country would have, lay in the difference of opinion regarding what has been called states' rights vs. a strong federal government. As a consequence of that difference, two political parties came into being. (mentioned briefly in Chapter 4.) One party was the Federalists, created by Alexander Hamilton; the other was the Democratic-Republicans, led by Thomas Jefferson. The Federalists favored a strong central government; the Democratic-Republicans favored protecting the rights of states against a centralized government.

Both George Washington, who served as the first president from 1789 to 1797, and John Adams, the next president who served from 1797 to 1801, were Federalists. Then Thomas Jefferson, a Democratic-Republican who was inaugurated president in 1801 and served until 1809, wanted to unite the states in opposing a national concentration of power.

Following the election at the turn of the century, contention between the two parties reached what historians have called a fever pitch, with virtually unrestrained acrimony. Accusations were much more vituperative than anything that appears in the press today.

James T. Callendar, a Democratic-Republican, published a pamphlet titled "The Prospect Before Us" that mercilessly slandered both Washington and Adams, and he wrote in the

---

4. A complete account of the Croswell trial appears in *American Heritage*, Vol. XIX, December 1967, under the title, "A Scandalous, Malicious and Seditious Libel."

Richmond Examiner that "Mr. Washington has twice been a traitor." Alexander Hamilton and a group of Federalists, in order to publicize their beliefs and denounce their opponents, started the *Evening Post* in New York.

Among Federalists at the time was a young man 22 years of age named Harry Croswell, who was editor of *Balance*, a newspaper in Hudson, New York. In addition to editing the *Balance*, he started a small newspaper he called *The Wasp*, presumably to "sting" the opposition; and he published articles in it under the penname of Robert Rusticoat. Among the articles that appeared in *The Wasp* was one from the *New York Evening Post*, which read in part:

■ Jefferson paid Callendar for calling Washington a traitor, a robber, a perjurer; for calling Adams a hoary-headed incendiary and for grossly slandering the private characters of men he knew well were virtuous.

That was too much; and Croswell was indicted on two counts of libel, with the indictment stating in part, " . . . the said Harry Croswell on September 9, 1802, did wickedly, maliciously, and seditiously print and publish . . . certain scandalous malicious, and seditious libel, in a certain paper or publication entitled 'The Wasp.' "

The trial was held in the summer and lasted several weeks, with Chief Justice Morgan Lewis as the presiding Judge. He ruled that the truth of the statements published by Croswell "could not be given in evidence as justification" for publication. Croswell's attorneys objected to the ruling, arguing that this was a case of public libel in which the truth was a vital consideration. The judge's ruling held, and the jury was instructed to decide only one thing: Did Harry Croswell publish the statements in *The Wasp*, or didn't he? He did, of course; so the jury had no choice but to find him guilty.

On appeal the case went to the New York Supreme Court which, after a hearing, would decide whether to let the guilty verdict stand or order a new trial for Croswell. For the defense the Federalists were able to get Alexander Hamilton to serve as an attorney. Hamilton, not related to Andrew Hamilton who defended Zenger, was one of the most brilliant men of his time and had been Secretary of the Treasury under George Washington.

The Supreme Court convened on February 13, 1804, and there again the chief point of disagreement was whether truth could be used as a defense against a charge of seditious libel. What Croswell had published was classed as seditious rather than civil because the statements were about Thomas Jefferson, who was then president of the United States.

Hamilton was eloquent in his argument that anyone has the right to publish the truth, provided it is done with good motives, as a check on government and government officials. He also contended that a country has freedom only when the people have representation in government and trial by jury. He spent most of the day presenting all aspects of the case, holding the audience spellbound with his dazzling oratory.

Decisions by a supreme court are made by the justices, not by a jury as they are in a trial court; and the New York Supreme Court at the time had five justices. For this case, however, there were only four justices on the bench because one had abstained from serving. He was Ambrose Spencer who, only ten days before this hearing began, had been nominated a justice of the Supreme Court. As he had been the attorney general in the trial of Croswell, he quite properly did not take part in this hearing.

When it came to a vote the court was divided, with two justices in favor of a new trial for Croswell and two opposed. Thus the conviction of Croswell by the trial court stood. The next year the Court granted Croswell a new trial, but it was never held and he was not fined or sent to jail. The matter was simply dropped.

The case, however, marked a significant milestone in the history of freedom of the press. The entire case, and especially Hamilton's highly persuasive presentation, had a powerful effect on public opinion and so influenced the members of the state legislature that the legislature began work immediately on legislation that would provide for truth as a defense in libel. That became law in New York in 1805 and before long other states passed similar laws.

Two important legal principles, in effect today, were highlighted by the Zenger and the Croswell trials. One is that truth is a defense in libel. The other is that a jury, not a judge, decides whether the accused is guilty or innocent. This was significant because the colonists had seen too much injustice when court verdicts were made by a magistrate appointed by or representing the King. Decisions by a jury of ordinary citizens would be much fairer, they believed, and would act as a curb on the powers of government.

Today all states have laws governing libel and slander, although they do vary in wording from state to state. In general, truth is a defense everywhere, provided publication is made "with good motives" or "justifiable ends" and not for spite, revenge, or maliciousness. The Florida State Constitution, for example, states:

> ■ In all criminal prosecutions and civil actions for libel, the truth may be given in evidence to the jury, and if it shall appear that the matter charged as libelous is true, and was published for good motives, the party shall be acquitted or exonerated.

Truth is one of two kinds of defense against a charge of libel. The other is privilege, which is discussed in Chapter 9.

Truth is not necessarily a defense against a charge of criminal libel. Statements may be true, but if they cause a disturbance of the peace or otherwise violate law, the speaker or the publisher could be found guilty. Also, truth is not an absolute defense in civil cases, as it is possible to write an article in which all the statements are true but are worded in such manner as to create a false impression.

CHAPTER
17

❀

FAIR COMMENT ISN'T
NECESSARILY FAIR

FAIR COMMENT ISN'T
NECESSARILY FAIR

❀

"Good show!"

"Excellent meal!"

"The speech was so boring I fell asleep."

"Sammy played with the skill of a professional."

It is human nature to evaluate almost everything we come in contact with, whether it is a book we are reading, the food served us in a restaurant, the attitude of a store clerk, the performance of an actor, or the quality of the tires on a car.

Freedom of speech means that everyone has a right to say what he or she thinks about all sorts of things — a play, a concert, a work of art, a book, a speech, a television or radio program, government officials and governmental bodies such as legislatures and city councils, the ability or personality of a teacher, lawyer, doctor, or nurse, and so on and on.

Criticism, whether favorable or unfavorable, is legally called *fair comment*, although what we say or write may not be considered fair by others; and courts have held that such expressions of opinion and judgment are protected by the First Amendment to the U.S. Constitution. In other words, everyone has a legal, constitutional right to be critical.

One of the first court cases to establish the principle of fair comment took place in Des Moines, Iowa, in 1901 as the result of a critical review of a vaudeville act by the Cherry

Sisters published in *The Leader,* a weekly newspaper.[1] Here is a paragraph from that review that so offended the sisters that they sued *The Leader* for libel:

> ■ Effie is an old jade of 50 summers, Jessie a frisky filly of 40, and Addie, the flower of the family, a capering monstrosity of 35. Their long skinny arms, equipped with talons at the extremities, swung mechanically, and anon waved frantically at the suffering audience. The mouths of their rancid features opened like caverns, and sounds like the wailings of damned souls issued therefrom. They pranced around the stage with a motion that suggested a cross between the *danse du ventre* and fox trot — strange creatures with painted faces and hideous mien. Effie is spavined, Addie is string halt, and Jessie, the only one who showed her stockings, has legs with calves as classic in their outlines as the curves of a broom handle.

The Court ruled in favor of the newspaper, maintaining that the published review of the performance was "fair comment," although the Cherry Sisters no doubt felt that the article was not at all fair. The Court stated, "One who goes upon the stage to exhibit himself to the public, or who gives any kind of performance to which the public is invited, may be freely criticized."

It should be noted that the review did not defame the character of the performers. Although the criticism of the sisters and their performance was harsh, it did not say that they were immoral or dishonest, which would be defamatory and therefore libelous. Also the review did not comment on the private lives of the sisters; it expressed opinion only about them as performers. To be ruled as fair comment, a statement or a written comment must be about a subject that has some public interest, although the public may vary from a few persons to many thousands.

---

1. Cherry v. Des Moines Leader, 114 Iowa 298, 86 N. W. 323 (1901).

Fair comment must be based on something factual or real, not on an imaginary event. It must center on the performance and not wander off into some other subject. Fair comment must be free of malice. In other words, it is not fair comment if it is spoken or published to spite or to harm someone or some group. It is not fair comment if it attacks the character of the individual or group being criticized.

Here are two highly critical reviews of television performances by Elvis Presley published in *Time* magazine several years ago.[2] Note that they pertain only to the show and do not defame the character of Elvis or any other performer.

TELEVISION

One of the Worst

Two years in the Army did more for Elvis Presley than relieve him of his 25-lb. sideburns. His name mellowed with absence, and some people cast a friendlier eye on the new image: a clean-cut kid in khaki, his pelvis at parade rest. Last week ABC's *Frank Sinatra Timex Show* spent more than a quarter of a million dollars to welcome Elvis home and performed a highly useful service: it reminded the forgetful just how dreadful Elvis really is.

First briefly introduced in full-dress uniform under waving flags, amid the sound of military trumpets and carefully cued hoyden screams, he had to wait for his big moment until later in the

GI Blues (Paramount), the first movie made by Elvis Presley since his release from the U.S. Army (TIME, March 14) might be expected to answer one of the less pressing questions confronting the U.S. public: Did the Army make a man of him? Maybe so, but it sure didn't make him an actor.

The addition of two years and the subtraction of ten pounds (Uncle Sam shaved off his sideburns) seem to have effected precious little difference in the Tennessee tomcat. At 25 he still looks 17, still holds his li'l ole "gweetar" at crotch level and lets the spasms run through his legs while his eyes glaze and unintelligible phrases spurt from his doll-baby mouth. Between ballads he still looks like the hero of a girl's school *Hamlet*.

---

2. Copyright 1960 by Time, Inc. Reprinted by permission.

show, just after John Cameron Swayze had pulled a heartily ticking Timex watch out of the mouth of a Miami Beach porpoise. Wilder and greasier than the porpoise, Presley came abumping on-screen, wearing boots and a tuxedo, his double-folded forelock bobbing above his head like a Vaseline halo. As he sang *Fame and Fortune* and *Stuck on You*, his feet tapped, his hands clapped, and his hips wrestled with each other. The voice was ordinary whine, on the point of becoming vinegar.

The rest of the show was gaudy, pretentious and dull — one of the worst TV hours in memory. Considering that it was taped almost two months ago in Miami, someone missed a major chance. As it sat on the shelf for seven weeks, some network employee — with guts and a Zippo lighter — could have sacrificed his job for the sake of the industry.

(TIME, May 23, 1960)

Even Elvis deserves a better script than he gets in this sniggery little dogface farce. The G.I. hero (Presley) is stationed, as Elvis was, in Germany; and he has, as Elvis had, more "frowlines" than he can find time for. Then of course he meets the girl he can't have, a hoofer (Juliet Prowse) in a Frankfurt *Kabarett*, and makes a bet he can "get his foot in the door" before the week is out. He wins the bet, loses the girl, wins her back at the fade. Time and again the scriptwriters run out of ideas, and whenever that happens Elvis just hauls off and belts a ballad. There are ten of them, and every last one is goshawful. The dialogue is not much better. She: "How can I ever repay you?" He: "Oh, I'll think of something."

Actress Prowse, a sort of Leslie Caron with vitamins, is absolutely out of place in this picture. She looks human.

(TIME, December 5, 1960)

Fair comment is criticism of someone's performance; libel is impugning someone's character. Fair comment is protected by the First Amendment; libel is not. A newspaper story stating that "a suit was filed by Louise Acton on the pretense of a back injury" was ruled libelous *per se* because it says in effect that she was trying to obtain damages under false pretenses.[3] Ruled as fair comment or non-defamatory

---

3. 315 Pac 2d. 715, 718 (1960).

criticism was an article that characterized a congressman as "hardly dry behind the ears" and that asked whether he was a representative of a district or "merely of a small minority of weak-kneed, jelly-backed, slab-sided parasitical mugwumps."

"It by no means follows that a publication which is unfavorable is also libelous," the Supreme Court of South Carolina stated in absolving the *Columbia State and Record* of a charge of libel in 1968.[4] The action had been brought against the newspaper by a former instructor at the University of South Carolina on the basis of a report, obtained from the police, stating that his wife had shot him in an argument.

The dividing line between fair comment and libel is at times tenuous. Fair comment is primarily a matter of opinion, and the courts have generally held that opinion is not libelous. That principle was supported in a decision by the U.S. Supreme Court in the case of *Gertz v. Robert Welch Inc.*, in 1974 in which the Court stated that "under the First Amendment there is no such thing as a false idea."[5] Just calling an article "opinion" or "editorial" does not mean that it cannot be libelous, however. An example is the case of *Milkovich v. Lorain Journal Company* in which the U.S. Supreme Court ruled on June 21, 1990, that "opinion" is not necessarily protected by the First Amendment guarantee of free speech.[6]

The case had its origin in a fight that broke out after a wrestling match between Maple Heights and Mentor high schools in northeastern Ohio on February 8, 1974, a case that continued over a period of 17 years, reached the U.S. Supreme Court, and finally ended in April 1991 with a cash settlement of more than $100,000 paid by the Lorain Journal Company to Coach Michael Milkovich, Sr., the plaintiff.

Both wrestling teams and the crowd became involved in the melee that followed a controversial call at the meet, and

---

4. *Editor & Publisher*, April 6, 1968.
5. Discussed in Chapter 19.
6. Milkovich v. Lorain Journal Co., 111 L. Ed 2d 1 (June 21, 1990).

several persons were injured. A public hearing was held later, and Maple Heights School was placed on probation by the Ohio High School Athletic Association and Coach Milkovich was censured — penalties that were lifted by a judge the next year. J. Theodore Diadiun, sports writer for *The Lake County News-Herald*, wrote several columns about the hearing, in one of which he stated in part:

> ■ A lesson was learned (or relearned) yesterday by the student body of Maple Heights High School, and by anyone who attended the Maple Heights-Mentor wrestling match.
>
> A lesson which, sadly, in view of the events of the past year, is well they learned early.
>
> It is simply this: "If you get in a jam, lie your way out. If you're successful enough and powerful enough, and can sound sincere enough, you stand an excellent chance of making the lie stand up, regardless of what really happened."
>
> The teachers responsible were mainly Maple wrestling coach, Mike Milkovich, and former superintendent of schools, H. Donald Scott.
>
> Anyone who attended their meet, whether he be from Maple Heights, Mentor or an impartial observer, knows in his heart that Milkovich and Scott lied at the hearing after each having given his solemn oath to tell the truth. But they got away with it.

Coach Milkovich sued the Lorain Journal Company, owner of the *News-Herald*, for libel. The Lorain Journal Company, in defense, argued that what Diadiun had written was not libelous in that it was opinion and thus protected by the First Amendment. It appeared in a format that included a photo of Diadiun and a logo that read, "T. D. Says." The columnist, it was contended, was sending a message to students, "If you get in a jam, lie your way out."

The Ohio Supreme Court agreed, ruling in favor of the Lorain Journal Company and stating in part in its decision,

"Sharp criticism of a governmental official produces a far greater good in a democracy than does artificial respect fostered by suppression of such opinion."

On the third appeal to the U.S. Supreme Court, litigation ended with the Court deciding in favor of Milkovich by a majority of 7-to-2, holding that newspaper columns and other forms of opinion may be libelous if they contain statements that can be interpreted as actionable, regardless of the way they are labeled.

In the majority opinion, Chief Justice William H. Rehnquist discussed the origin of fair comment, stating:

■ Since the latter half of the 16th century, the common law has afforded a cause of action for damage to a person's reputation by the publication of false and defamatory statements . . .

The common law generally did not place any additional restrictions on the type of statement that could be actionable. Indeed, defamatory communications were deemed actionable regardless of whether they were deemed to be statements of fact or opinion . . .

However, due to concerns that unduly burdensome defamation laws could stifle valuable public debate, the privilege of "fair comment" was incorporated into the common law as an affirmative defense to an action for defamation . . .

The Court was unwilling to rule, however, that the claim of fair comment or opinion protects against libelous statements. The Chief Justice quoted this sentence from the Gertz decision of 1974: "However pernicious an opinion may seem, we depend for its correction not on the conscience of judges and juries but on the competition of other ideas." He then said, "We do not think this passage was intended to create a wholesale exemption for anything that might be labeled 'opinion'."

The Chief Justice also referred to the decision in *New York Times v. Sullivan* case, discussed in Chapter 18, which contains the statement, "The privilege of 'fair comment' for expression of opinion depends on the truth of the facts upon which the comment is based." He then said, "Even if the speaker states the facts upon which he bases his opinion, if those facts are either incorrect or incomplete, or if his assessment of them is erroneous, the statement may still imply a false assertion of fact. Simply couching such statements in terms of opinion does not dispel these implications; and the statement, 'In my opinion Jones is a liar', can cause as much damage to reputation as the statement, 'Jones is a liar'."

Deciding whether a statement or a publication is fair comment or libel is sometimes difficult since criticism can be coarse and vitriolic, even vulgar, yet not libelous. An example is a raunchy "parody" of an advertisement for Campari Liqueur published in the inside front cover of the December 1983 issue of *Hustler*, a sex-oriented magazine published by Larry C. Flynt. The parody was modeled after actual Campari ads that include interviews with various celebrities about their "first times." Although it is apparent by the end of each interview that this meant the first time they sampled Campari, the ads clearly played on the sexual entendre of "first times."

Copying the form and layout of the Campari ads, the editors chose the Rev. Jerry Falwell, nationally known Baptist television evangelist and founder of *The Moral Majority*, as the featured celebrity. In the "alleged" interview with him, he states that his "first time" was during a drunken incestuous rendezvous with his mother in an outhouse, and says, "I always get sloshed before I go out to the pulpit." The advertisement bears his name and picture and portrays Falwell and his mother as drunk and immoral, suggesting that he is a hypocrite who preached only when he is drunk. At the bottom of the advertisement in small type is this notice: "Ad parody — not to be taken seriously"; and the table of contents lists the advertisement as "Fiction: Ad and Personality Parody."

Criticism and comment can hardly be more vicious than that, but the U. S. Supreme Court ruled unanimously in 1988 that Falwell, as a public figure, could not recover damages for distress that results from "speech that is patently offensive and is intended to inflict emotional injury."[7]

After publication of the advertisement, Falwell brought suit in the U.S. District Court for the Western District of Virginia against *Hustler Magazine, Inc.*, Larry C. Flynt and Flynt Distributing Company, asking for damages on three counts: libel, invasion of privacy, and intentional infliction of emotional distress. The Court granted a directed verdict in favor of Flynt in regard to invasion of privacy. The jury turned down the libel claim, but it did rule for the claim of intentional distress, stating that Falwell should be awarded $100,000 in compensatory damages and $50,000 each in punitive damages, for a total of $200,000. That judgment was upheld by the U. S. Court of Appeals for the Fourth Circuit in Richmond on the basis that, although the parody was not libelous because it was not presented as factual and would not be understood by readers as factual, it was "sufficiently outrageous" to justify a damage award for "intentional infliction of emotional distress."

In its decision reversing the judgment of the Court of Appeals and ruling in favor of Flynt, the Supreme Court stated in part in the opinion written by Chief Justice William H. Rehnquist:

■ This case presents us (the U.S. Supreme Court) with a novel question involving First Amendment limitations upon a state's authority to protect its citizens from the intentional infliction of emotional distress. We must decide whether a public figure may recover damages for emotional harm caused by the publication of an ad parody offensive to him, and doubtless gross and repugnant in the eyes of most . . .

---

7. Hustler Magazine and Larry C. Flynt v. Jerry Falwell, 485 U. S. 46 (February 24, 1988).

Justice Felix Frankfurter put it succinctly in (the Court's majority opinion in the case of *Baumgartner v. United States* in 1944) when he said, "One of the prerogatives of American citizenship is the right to criticize public men and measures." Such criticism inevitably will not always be reasoned or moderate; public figures as well as public officials will be subject to "vehement, caustic and sometimes unpleasantly sharp attacks."

The Rev. Mr. Falwell argued that a standard different from the one that applies to public figures should apply in this case because here the plaintiff was seeking redress for severe emotional distress suffered as a victim of an offensive publication, not the ordinary tort of defamation. Also, he contended, the caricature in question was so "outrageous" as to distinguish it from more traditional political cartoons.

The Court, in the words of Chief Justice Rehnquist, admitted that not all "speech" is protected by the First Amendment, by stating:

■ We (the Court) recognized in our decision in *FCC v. Pacifica Foundation* in 1978 that speech that is "vulgar," "offensive," and "shocking" is not entitled to absolute constitutional protection under all circumstances . . .

Yet in deciding this case, he stated:

■ We conclude that public figures and public officials may not recover for the tort of intentional infliction of emotional distress by reason of publications such as the one here at issue without showing in addition that the publication contains a false statement of fact which was made with "actual malice" . . . it reflects our considered judgment that such a standard is necessary to give adequate "breathing space" to the freedoms protected by the First Amendment.

Key words in the decision are "a false statement of fact." As the parody in *Hustler* was opinion, not a statement of fact, it could not be false because "there is no such thing as a false opinion or idea."

CHAPTER
18

❁

YOU HAVE A RIGHT TO CRITICIZE OFFICIALS

YOU HAVE A RIGHT TO CRITICIZE OFFICIALS

❀

For almost a hundred years after the adoption of the Thirteenth and Fourteenth Amendments to the Constitution abolishing slavery and guaranteeing all citizens due process and equal protection of the law, racial segregation was still common in Southern states. Blacks were not permitted to eat in the same restaurants, attend the same schools, or use the same parks, public restrooms, and railway and bus waiting rooms as white persons.

In protest of that condition, a wave of sit-ins began on February 1, 1960, when four black students were refused service at a Woolworth store lunch counter in Greensboro, North Carolina. Inspired by the leadership of the Rev. Dr. Martin Luther King, Jr., more than 70,000 blacks and whites had participated in sit-ins and freedom marches throughout the South by September that year.

They were met by violent opposition; and newspapers and television carried news and pictures of helmeted police on horseback and on foot with billy clubs, attack dogs, and fire hoses harassing marchers. It was a gripping time, marking the beginning of significant social changes.

To raise funds and solicit participation in this movement for civil rights for blacks, a group titled "Committee to Defend Martin Luther King and the Struggle for Freedom in the South" purchased space for a full-page advertisement in *The New York Times*, which was published on March 29, 1960.

The advertisement carried the names of the officers of the committee, the names of 64 public figures as signers, plus 16 others, all but two of whom were identified as clergymen in various Southern cities. The advertisement read in part:

■ As the whole world knows by now, thousands of Southern Negro students are engaged in wide-spread non-violent demonstrations in positive affirmation of the right to live in human dignity as guaranteed by the U. S. Constitution and the Bill of Rights. . .

In Montgomery, Alabama, after students sang "My Country 'Tis of Thee" on the State Capitol steps, their leaders were expelled from school, and truckloads of police armed with shotguns and tear-gas ringed the Alabama State College Campus. When the entire student body protested to state authorities by refusing to re-register, their dining hall was padlocked in an attempt to starve them into submission . . .

Again and again the Southern violators have answered Dr. King's peaceful protests with intimidation and violence. They have bombed his home almost killing his wife and child. They have assaulted his person. They have arrested him seven times — for "speeding," "loitering," and similar "offenses." And now they have charged him with "perjury" — a felony under which they could imprison him for ten years . . .

The advertisement did not name any individual as being responsible for the "unprecedented wave of terror" and other actions opposing those who were demonstrating for integration and civil rights. Rather, it used such designations as "truckloads of police," "Southern violators," "state apparatus," and the pronouns "they" and "their."

Even so, L. B. Sullivan, one of the three elected Commissioners of the city of Montgomery, Alabama, felt that the advertisement libeled him because one of his responsibilities as Commissioner was supervision of the Montgomery Police Department. He therefore filed suit against *The New York*

Times, and four of the clergymen named in the advertisement, and asked that he be awarded $500,000 in damages for libel.

The trial was held in the Circuit Court of Montgomery County where the jury found the defendants guilty and awarded Mr. Sullivan the half-million dollars he had sought. The Alabama State Supreme Court upheld the decision of the Circuit Court; and *The Times* then appealed to the Supreme Court of the United States.

All that litigation took time, so it was four years later in March 1964 when the U.S. Supreme Court handed down its decision — a decision that reversed the findings of the lower courts and was a landmark in defense against charges of libel brought by public officials.[1] A landmark is an event or development that marks a turning point, and this decision was indeed that. The key point in the Supreme Court decision was that a public official could not recover damages unless he proves "actual malice," often a difficult thing to do.

Justice William J. Brennan, Jr., in the majority opinion of the Court, wrote, "The Constitutional guarantees require, we think, a federal rule that prohibits a public official from recovering damages unless he proves that the statement was made with 'actual malice' — that is, with knowledge that it was false or with reckless disregard of whether it was false or not . . ."

That did indeed mark a turning point. Previously, the matter of libel had been left to the states. Now, Justice Brennan stated in the first paragraph of the opinion, "We (the U. S. Supreme Court) are required in this case to determine for the first time the extent to which the constitutional protections for speech and press limit a state's power to award damages in a libel action brought by a public official against criticism of his official conduct."

---

1. New York Times Co. v. L. B. Sullivan and Ralph D. Abernathy v. L. B. Sullivan, 376 U. S. 254 (March 9, 1964).

The extent to which one has the right to criticize government and its officials, as stated in this decision, is broad:

■ The general proposition that freedom of expression upon public questions is secured by the First Amendment has long been settled by our decisions ... we consider this case against the background of a profound national commitment to the principle that debate on public issues should be uninhibited, robust, and wide open, and that it may well include vehement, caustic, and sometimes unpleasantly sharp attacks on government and public officials.

Reversal of the state-court decision against *The New York Times* meant that *The Times* did not have to pay the half-million dollars in damages awarded by the trial court. In that connection, Justice Brennan stated: "We hold today that the Constitution delimits (places a limit on) a State's power to award damages for libel in actions brought by public officials against their critics of their official conduct."

Justice Hugo Black, joined by Justice William O. Douglas in concurring with the majority opinion, stated, "I doubt that a country can live in freedom where its people can be made to suffer physically or financially for criticizing their government, its actions, or its officials."

Mr. Sullivan argued that the statements published in *The New York Times* were not protected by the First Amendment guarantee of free speech and press because they appeared in a paid advertisement. The Court rejected that argument by holding that the publication was not a commercial advertisement because it "communicated information, expressed opinion, recited grievances, protested claimed abuses, and sought financial support on behalf of a movement whose existence and objectives are matters of the highest public interest and concern."

It stated further: "That *The Times* was paid for publishing the advertisement is as immaterial in this connection as is the fact that newspapers and books are sold. Any other conclusion would discourage newspapers from carrying 'editorial advertisements' of this type, and so might shut off an important outlet for the promulgation of information and ideas by persons who do not themselves have access to publishing facilities — who wish to exercise their freedom of speech even though they are not members of the press."

Mr. Sullivan also argued that as truth is a defense against libel, the defendants were guilty because the advertisement contained statements that were not true. As examples, the students on the State Capitol steps sang the National Anthem, not "My County 'Tis of Thee"; nine students were expelled by the State Board of Education for demanding service at a lunch counter in the Montgomery County Court House, not for leading a demonstration at the Capitol; the campus dining hall was not padlocked at any time; Martin Luther King had been arrested only four times, not seven as stated in the advertisement; and although police were stationed near the campus on three occasions, they did not "ring the campus."

The Supreme Court admitted that the advertisement contained factual errors, but it still ruled against Mr. Sullivan. "A rule compelling the critics of official conduct to guarantee the truth of all their factual assertions — and to do so on pain of libel judgment virtually unlimited in amounts — leads to a comparable 'self-censorship'," the Court ruled. "Would-be critics of official conduct may be deterred from voicing their criticism, even though it is believed to be true and even though it is in fact true, because of doubt whether it can be proved in court or fear of the expense of having to do so."[2]

The decision was significant in making publishing less precarious, less liable to be sued for libel, and thus not

---

2. A complete account of this landmark case is presented in *Make No Law: The Sullivan Case and the First Amendment*, by Anthony Lewis, Random House, 354 pages, 1991.

incurring the expense of defending against such suits. Previously the spectre of disastrous libel suits brought by public officials could result in caution that tended to inhibit the "robust, wide open sharp attacks on government and government officials" which the Court implied are not only permitted but actually encouraged by the First Amendment.

Freedom is restricted when it is accompanied by the possibility, or the probability, of severe punishment for unintentional or accidental mistakes. Even if a newspaper or a broadcast station wins a libel suit, attorney fees and other defense costs can be high — so high that they can bankrupt a small newspaper or broadcast station.

An example of cost of defense is a case in 1917 when Henry Ford, noted automobile manufacturer, sued the *Chicago Tribune* for calling him an "anarchist." The trial jury found the *Tribune* guilty but awarded Mr. Ford only six cents in damages. Still, the *Tribune* spent more than a half-million dollars in defending the suit.

If the U. S. Supreme Court had not decided in favor of *The New York Times* in the Sullivan case, it would have cost *The Times* the half-million dollars in damages awarded by the trial jury plus the costs of defense. That would have been only the beginning, because four other suits were brought against *The New York Times* on the basis of the same advertisement. Shortly after Mr. Sullivan filed his libel suit, the two other Commissioners, the Mayor of the City of Montgomery, and the Governor of the State of Alabama each brought suit for libel. The Governor asked for a million dollars in damages. Clearly, the cost to *The New York Times* would have been extremely high had the Supreme Court not reversed the verdict of the Circuit Court.

Justice Brennan addressed that directly in the majority opinion:

■ The judgment awarded in this case — without the need for any proof of actual pecuniary loss — was one

233

thousand times greater than the maximum fine provided by the Alabama criminal statute, and one hundred times greater than that provided by the Sedition Act. And since there is no double jeopardy limitation applicable to civil lawsuits, this is not the only judgment that may be awarded against petitioners for the same publication.

Whether or not a newspaper can survive a succession of such judgments, the pall of fear and timidity imposed upon those who would give voice to public criticism is an atmosphere in which the First Amendment freedoms cannot survive.

Prior to this decision, it had generally been assumed that elected and appointed government officials were in the same class as other persons in regard to libel and slander. Now they were set apart, making possible more severe criticism of officials than of private citizens. As *Time* magazine stated it, "The decision granted the U.S. citizen dramatic new immunity in the exercise of his classic right to sound off against his chosen leaders." [3]

Although that is true, that immunity, that freedom to criticize and to comment unfavorably, is not unlimited. Justice Abe Fortas emphasized that fact in dissent to a decision in 1968 when he said, "The First Amendment should not be a shelter for character assassination." [4] His dissent was in a case that hinged on "reckless disregard to the truth." In the majority opinion in that case the Court held that if a person sued for libel had good reason to believe that the damaging statements were true, mere failure to investigate their veracity thoroughly did not of itself constitute reckless disregard.

A comment similar to that by Justice Fortas was made years later in a decision in which the Supreme Court upheld

---

3. March 20, 1964.
4. Phil A. St. Amant v. Herman A. Thompson, 390 U. S. 727 (April 29, 1968).

a $200,000 judgment against the *Journal News* in Hamilton, Ohio.[5] There the Court agreed unanimously with the trial court jury that charges appearing in the newspaper during a political campaign were defamatory and false and published with actual malice. In the opinion of the Court, Justice John Paul Stevens said, "We have not gone so far as to accord the press absolute immunity in the coverage of public figures or elections. If a false or defamatory statement is published with knowledge of falsity or a reckless disregard to the truth, the public figure may prevail."

5. Harte-Hanks Communications, Inc. v. Daniel Connaughton, 491 U.S. 657 (June 22, 1989).

CHAPTER
19

*BUT NOT WITH ACTUAL
MALICE*

BUT NOT WITH ACTUAL MALICE

❀

A drastic change in the defense of libel suits brought by public officials was mandated by the U. S. Supreme Court decision in *The New York Times v. Sullivan* case in 1964. As stated in the previous chapter, the Court ruled that a public official cannot recover damages for a defamatory falsehood relating to his official conduct unless he proves that "the statement was made with actual malice — that is, with knowledge that it was false or with reckless disregard of whether it was false or not."

Before this decision, a person who sued for libel had only to read the publication in court, and the publisher had to prove that the statement or statements were true. Now the person bringing the suit has to prove that the statement or statements are not only false and defamatory, but also that they were written with malice, as defined above.

It is important to note the phrase, "relating to his official conduct," in the Supreme Court decision as that seems to rule out anything pertaining to an official's private life. The dividing line between official conduct and private life, how-ever, is often difficult to discern; and frequently actions in private life can and do affect official conduct.

The decision in that *New York Times* case had the effect of abolishing seditious libel in the country. It became legally safe to criticize government and government officials. But which officials? Almost any, the Court held a couple of years later.[1] In the opinion delivered by Justice Brennan, the Court stated:

■ We remarked in *New York Times* that we had no occasion, "to determine how far down into the lower ranks of government employees the 'public official' designation would extend for purposes of this rule, or otherwise to specify categories of persons who would or would not be included." No precise lines need be drawn for the purpose of this case . .

Criticism of government is at the very center of the constitutionally protected area of free discussion. Criticism of those responsible for government operations must be free, lest criticism of government itself be penalized.

It is, therefore, that the "public official" designation applies at the very least to those among the hierarchy of government who have, or appear to the public to have, substantial responsibility of or control over the conduct of governmental affairs.

Both the "public official" rule and the "malice" aspect have been debated in a number of cases since the *New York Times* decision in 1964. The word "malice" has traditionally meant ill will or intent to do harm. In journalism, publishing a defamation with the intention of harming someone is "malice in fact"; and publishing anything that is libelous per se, intentionally or unintentionally, presumes malice and is known as "malice in law." The *New York Times* decision, however, gave the word a different meaning, to wit, "with the knowledge that it was false or with reckless disregard of whether it was false or not."

The term "public official" has been puzzling, too. In concurring with the majority opinion in the Rosenblatt case,

---

1. Alfred D. Rosenblatt v. Frank P. Baer, 383 U. S. 75 (1966).

Justice William O. Douglas expressed his difficulty in determining who is and who is not a public official, saying, "I see no way to draw lines that exclude the night watchman, the file clerk, the typist, or, for that matter, anyone on the public payroll."

Among cases in which those terms were considered were two, both highly publicized, that were decided together by the U.S. Supreme Court in 1967.[2] One case arose out of an Associated Press dispatch giving an eyewitness account of events on the campus of the University of Mississippi on the night of September 30, 1962, when a massive riot erupted because of federal efforts to enforce a court decree ordering the enrollment of James Meredith, a black man, as a student in the university. The incident attracted national attention when three thousand troops were sent in to quell the rioting.

The Associated Press stated in its report that General Edwin Walker (U. S. Army, Ret.) had taken command of the violent crowd, had encouraged rioters to use violence, had provided rioters with technical advice on combating the effects of tear gas, and had personally led an assault on the federal marshals.

Charging libel, General Walker sued the Associated Press for $2 million and other newspapers and broadcast stations that carried the AP news reports for a total of $33 million in damages. A jury in a trial court in Texas awarded him $500,000 in general damages and $300,000 in exemplary or punitive damages. The judge, seeing no malice in the news reports, dismissed the punitive damage award, leaving the verdict at half a million dollars. That was affirmed by the Texas Court of Civil Appeals; but as the Texas Supreme Court denied certiorari, the case was appealed to the U.S. Supreme Court.

---

2. Curtis Publishing Company v. Wallace Butts and Associated Press v. Edwin A. Walker, 388 U. S. 130 (1967).

The other case had its origin in what was claimed to be a telephone conversation between Wallace ("Wally") Butts, athletic director of the University of Georgia, and Paul ("Bear") Bryant, head football coach of the University of Alabama. An insurance salesman named George Burnett said he had overheard the conversation due to an electronic quirk when he picked up the receiver in a pay telephone station and heard the two men conspiring to "fix" a football game between the teams of the two universities.

The Saturday Evening Post obtained the information from Burnett, and in the March 23, 1963, issue published an article titled "The Story of a College Football Fix." The article was prefaced with a comment by the editors stating: "Not since the Chicago Black Sox threw the 1919 World Series has there been a sports story as shocking as this one . . . Before the University of Georgia played the University of Alabama . . . Wally Butts . . . gave (to its coach) . . . Georgia's plays, defensive patterns, all the significant secrets Georgia's football team possessed."

The article stated that Burnett had accidentally overheard, because of an electronic error, a telephone conversation between Butts and Bryant, that took place about a week prior to the game.

Burnett said he listened while Butts outlined Georgia's offensive plays, told how Georgia planned to defend, and mentioned both players and plays by name. The article went on to describe the game and the players' reaction to the game, concluding that "the Georgia players, their moves analyzed, and forecast like those of rats in a maze, took a frightful physical beating."

The article said that the players, and other sideline observers, were aware that Alabama was privy to Georgia's secrets. It told of Butts' resignation from the university's athletic affairs, for health and business reasons; and concluded with the statement, "The chances are that Wally Butts will never help any football team again . . . The investigation is continuing; where it will end no one so far can say. But careers will be ruined, that is sure."

Butts sued the Curtis Publishing Company, publishers of *The Saturday Evening Post*, in the federal courts in Georgia for libel, asking for $5 million in compensatory damages and an equal amount in punitive damages, for a total of $10 million. The jury found the Curtis Publishing Co. guilty and returned a verdict of $60,000 in general damages and $3 million in punitive damages.

Soon after the trial, the U.S. Supreme Court handed down its decision in the *New York Times v. Sullivan* case; and the Curtis Publishing Co. moved for a new trial, contending that Butts was a public official. The trial judge rejected the motion, as he did not consider Butts to be a public official. The Curtis Publishing Co. then appealed to the U.S. Supreme Court.

The Supreme Court handed down decisions on those two cases on June 12, 1967, ruling unanimously in favor of the Associated Press, thus denying General Walker any damages; and deciding against *The Saturday Evening Post* by a 5-to-4 vote, thus in effect clearing Wally Butts' name.

In these cases, the Court was primarily concerned with two aspects of the *New York Times v. Sullivan* decision. One was the "public official" aspect; the other was "malice," which translates essentially to "reckless disregard for the truth." In the majority opinion written by Justice John M. Harlan, the Court stated, "We brought these two cases here to consider the impact of that decision on libel actions instituted by persons who are not public officials, but who are 'public figures' and involved in issues in which the public has a justified and important interest." That was indeed relevant, as both men were prominent figures. As the Court stated, "Both, in our opinion, would have been labeled 'public figures' under ordinary tort rules."

As athletic director of the University of Georgia at the time the article was published, Butts had overall responsibility for the administration of the athletic program. Georgia is a state university; but Butts was employed by the Georgia Athletic Association, a private corporation, rather than by the state itself. He had previously served as head football coach of the university and was a well-known and respected figure in coaching ranks. He had maintained an interest in coaching and was negotiating for a position with a professional team at the time of publication.

General Walker was a private citizen at the time of the riot. He had pursued a long and honorable career in the U.S. Army before resigning to engage in political activity and had, in fact, been in command of federal troops during the school segregation confrontation in Little Rock, Arkansas, in 1957. He had his own following, the "Friends of Walker," and could fairly be deemed a man of some political importance.

In its decision, the Court, in effect, created a "public figure" category similar to the "public official" category. Chief Justice Earl Warren, in concurring with the majority opinion, stated, "To me, differentiation between 'public figures' and 'public officials' and adoption of separate standards of proof for each has no basis in law, logic, or First Amendment policy."

The matter of "reckless disregard for the truth" was of significance in the decision in favor of the Associated Press and against *The Saturday Evening Post*. In delivering the opinion, Justice Harlan commented as follows on such "disregard" by *The Post:*

■ Elementary precautions were ignored. The Saturday Evening Post knew that Burnett (who provided the information for the article) had been placed on probation in connection with bad check charges, but proceeded to publish the story without substantial independent support. Burnett's notes were not even viewed by any of the magazine's personnel prior to publication.

■ No attempt was made to screen the films of the game to see if Burnett's information was accurate, and no

243

attempt was made to find out whether Alabama had adjusted its plans after the alleged divulgence of information.

■   The Post writer assigned to the story was not a football expert and no attempt was made to check the story with someone knowledgeable in the sport . . .

■   *The Saturday Evening Post* was anxious to change its image by instituting a policy of "sophisticated muckraking," and the pressure to produce a successful expose might have induced a stretching of standards. In short, the evidence is ample to support a finding of highly unreasonable conduct constituting an extreme departure from the standards of investigation and reporting ordinarily adhered to by responsible publishers.

The reporting that General Walker objected to was different. The Associated Press reporter, Van Savell, was competent and experienced. He was present during the rioting, able to see firsthand what was happening, and he sent in his report immediately. The Supreme Court said in part:

■   In the case of Walker, the trial court found evidence insufficient to support more than a finding of even ordinary negligence . . . The Associated Press received the information from a correspondent who was present at the scene of the events and gave every indication of being trustworthy and competent. His dispatches, with one minor exception, were consistent . . . We therefore conclude that General Walker should not be entitled to damages from the Associated Press.

CHAPTER
20

❁

LIBEL SUITS MAY BE CIVIL OR CRIMINAL

LIBEL SUITS MAY BE
CIVIL OR CRIMINAL

❀

Both the Butts and the Associated Press cases were civil libel suits. How the decision in the *New York Times v. Sullivan* case applied in a criminal libel suit was considered by the U.S. Supreme Court a few months after handing down the decision in the Butts and Associated Press cases.

The case involved Jim Garrison, district attorney of Orleans Parish, Louisiana.[1] During a dispute with eight judges of the Criminal District Court of the parish, Garrison held a press conference in which he attributed the large backlog of pending criminal cases to inefficiency, laziness, and excessive vacations of the judges; and he said that by their refusing to authorize disbursements to cover the expenses of undercover investigations of vice in New Orleans, the judges had hampered his efforts to enforce the vice laws.

"The judges have now made it eloquently clear where their sympathies lie by refusing to authorize the use of the DA's funds to pay for the costs of closing down the Canal Street clip joints," he said. "This raises interesting questions about the racketeer influences on our eight vacation-minded judges."[2]

For those statements Garrison was convicted of criminal

---

1. Jim Garrison v. State of Louisiana, 379 U.S. 61 (Nov. 23, 1964).
2. Quoted from *Seminar*, A quarterly Review for newspapermen by Copley Newspapers, March 1970, page 6.

libel, and the Supreme Court of Louisiana upheld the conviction. The U.S. Supreme Court, however, reversed the conviction without dissent. Justice William J. Brennan Jr., who wrote the opinion, said in part:

■ At the outset, we must decide whether . . . *The New York Times* rule also limits state power to impose criminal sanctions for criticism of the official conduct of public officials. We hold that it does.

Where criticism of public officials is concerned, we see no merit in the argument that criminal libel statutes serve interests distinct from those secured by civil libel laws, and therefore should not be subject to the same limitations.

In succeeding years, the U.S. Supreme Court considered how the decision in *The New York Times v. Sullivan* case applied in a variety of civil libel suits brought by public officials. Among them was a case that arose on June 27, 1962, when a man named Phil A. St. Amant, in a televised speech in Baton Rouge, Louisiana, read answers to some questions he had asked J. D. Albin, a member of a Teamsters Union local.[3] Part of Albin's answers accused Herman A. Thompson, a deputy sheriff, of criminal conduct and called him an "ex-convict" and a "labor Chieftain" who had misused and stolen union funds and had been involved in a hit-and-run accident with a union car.

Thompson denied those charges and filed a libel suit against St. Amant. He won the case in the trial court; but the U.S. Supreme Court in a decision handed down in 1968, four years after *The New York Times v. Sullivan* case, reversed the judgment, concluding that "nothing referred to by the Louisiana courts indicates an awareness by St. Amant of the prob-

---

3. Phil A. St. Amant v. Herman A. Thompson, 390 U.S. 727 (April 29, 1968).

able falsity of Albin's statement about Thompson."

In the lone dissent to that decision, Justice Abe Fortas said, "The occupation of public office holder does not forfeit one's membership in the human race. The public official should be subject to severe scrutiny and to free and open criticism. But if he is needlessly, heedlessly, falsely accused of crime, he should have a remedy in law."

In four decisions handed down in 1971, seven years after *The New York Times* case, the Supreme Court extended its ruling on libel beyond government officials to include candidates for public office, no matter how minor the office; to prominent persons who are not government officials; and to private individuals who become involved in matters or events of public interest; and in two of the cases it ruled on questions of official conduct versus private life.

One of those cases arose when *The Monitor* in Concord, N. H., published a column by Drew Pearson on September 10, 1960, that characterized Alphonso Roy, a candidate for the U.S. Senate, as "a former small-time bootlegger."[4] Roy bought suit for libel. The jury decided in his favor and granted a judgment of $10,000 against *The Monitor* and the American Newspaper Alliance, which distributed the Pearson column. In reaching the verdict, the jury decided that the reference to bootlegging, an activity dating back to the Prohibition era of the 1920's, pertained to Roy's private life and was not relevant to his candidacy.

The U.S. Supreme Court disagreed, and in a unanimous decision handed down on February 24, 1971, ruled in favor of *The Monitor,* stating that any accusation of criminal conduct concerning an official or a candidate for public office is relevant to his public life and that private activities are often clues to the qualifications of candidates to hold office. The

---

4. Monitor Patriot Co. v. Roselle A. Roy, 401 U.S. 265 (February 24, 1971).

opinion, written by Justice Potter Stewart, reads in part:

■ The principal activity of a candidate in our political system, his "office," so to speak, consists in putting before the voters every conceivable aspect of his public and private life which he thinks may lead the electorate to gain a good impression of him.

A candidate who, for example, seeks to further his cause through the prominent display of his wife and children can hardly argue that his qualities as a husband and father remain of "purely private" concern. And a candidate who vaunts his spotless record and integrity cannot convincingly cry "foul!" when an opponent or an industrious reporter attempts to demonstrate the contrary.

On the same day the Court ruled, again unanimously, on a case in which the *Star-Banner* in Ocala, Florida, had stated that Mayor Leonard Damron of Crystal City, a candidate for county tax assessor, had been charged in a federal court "with perjury in a civil rights case." [5] That was an error; the charge had been made against Damron's brother. The Mayor sued for libel, and the jury awarded him $22,000 in damages on the basis that the charge of perjury did not relate to the Mayor's official conduct.

The U.S. Supreme Court, however, ruled in favor of the newspaper. In the majority opinion, also by Justice Stewart, the Court quoted in part from the *Monitor Patriot v. Roy* decision: "A charge of criminal misconduct against an official or a candidate, no matter how remote in time or place, is always 'relevant to his fitness for office' for purposes of applying *The New York Times* rule of knowing falsehood or reckless disregard of the truth." Leonard Damron, the Court held, was also to be considered a public official "in his status

---

5. Ocala Star Banner Co. v. Leonard Damron, 401 U.S. 295 (February 24, 1971).

as a candidate for the office of county tax assessor."

In a third case decided on the same day, the Court ruled in favor of *Time, Inc.*, which had been sued for libel by Frank Pape, Deputy Chief of Detective, in Chicago.[6] *Time* magazine had published an article summarizing a report by the U.S. Commission on Civil Rights titled *Justice* which stated that Pape had been guilty of brutality after entering a home "ostensibly investigating a murder." The trial court dismissed the case as the article was not clearly false, but the appeals court ruled that failure of *Time* to use the word "alleged" constituted a false report and that a jury should decide whether the article had been published with "actual malice."

In an 8-to-1 decision, the U.S. Supreme Court held that "making a rational, if inexact, interpretation of an ambiguous document does not constitute falsity . . . *Time's* conduct reflected at most an error of judgment."

Then on June 7 of that year the Supreme Court in a 5-to-3 decision broadened the constitutional protection of the press against libel in a case in which an individual's privacy was claimed.[7] In so doing, the Court strictly limited the right of private individuals to collect damages for libelous news accounts about them if they were involved in matters of public interest.

The case arose from a series of news broadcasts by radio station WIP in Philadelphia in 1963 regarding a crackdown by the Special Investigation Squad of the Philadelphia Police Department on persons believed to be violating the city's obscenity laws. George A. Rosenbloom was among several newsstand operators arrested on October 1, and he was arrested again on October 4 when the police seized "nudist magazines" from a barn he had rented to use as a warehouse.

---

6. Time, Inc. v. Frank Pape, 401 U.S. 1015 (February 24, 1971).
7. George A. Rosenbloom v. Metromedia, Inc. 403 U.S. 29 (June 7, 1971).

After the second arrest, Police Captain Clarence Ferguson, who was in charge of the raid, called station WIP and described the raid and arrests.

In reporting the story, the radio station said, "Captain Ferguson says he believes they have hit the supply of the main distributor of obscene material in Philadelphia." Rosenbloom felt that that was libelous. He also objected to the statement, "The girlie-book peddlers say the police crackdown and continued reference to their borderline literature as smut or filth is hurting their business." Rosenbloom sued Metromedia, Inc., owner of station WIP, claiming that he had been defamed by such statements.

The jury decided that he had indeed been libeled, and it awarded him $25,000 in general damages and $725,000 in punitive damages; but the trial judge reduced the latter figure to $250,000.

A case with a judgment of that amount would certainly be appealed, and it was, with the key question being whether the standard set in *The New York Times v. Sullivan* decision applied in this case. The Federal District Court ruled that it did; the Court of Appeals ruled that it did not. The case then went to the U.S. Supreme Court, which ruled in favor of Metromedia, stating that radio station WIP had the right to report and comment on such official actions as arrests, even though an individual's privacy was concerned.

Rosenbloom had argued that as a private individual he enjoyed more protection of his reputation than does a public figure. That argument was rejected by the Court, which stated in the majority opinion written by Justice William J. Brennan Jr.:

■ We honor the commitment to robust debate on public issues, which is embodied in the First Amendment, by extending constitutional protection to all discussion and communication involving matters of public or general concern, without regard to whether the persons involved are famous or anonymous . . .

Drawing a distinction between "public" and "private" figures makes no sense in terms of the First Amendment guarantees.

In that decision the Supreme court extended the freedom of news media to comment on individuals involved in matters of public interest even though those individuals are not public figures. It also imposed limits on judgments for damages, stating:

■ In libel cases we view an erroneous verdict for the plaintiff as most serious. Not only does it mulct the defendant for an innocent misstatement — the three-quarter-million-dollar jury verdict in this case could rest on such an error — but the possibility of such error, even beyond the vagueness of the negligence standard itself, would create a strong impetus towards self-censorship which the First Amendment cannot tolerate.

After the three Supreme Court decisions on libel were announced on February 24, 1971, the *Saturday Review* observed, "Libel suits are no longer as successful as they once were, thanks in large measure to recent decisions by the Supreme Court of the United States."[8] After the Rosenbloom decision on June 7 that year, *The New York Times* said, "The Court has extended its free-press doctrine to news about private individuals — the millions of anonymous 'little men' who make up the vast majority of the population."[9] Regarding that decision, *Editor & Publisher* went so far as to say, "The United States Supreme Court this week came close to making state libel laws extinct."[10]

That was, of course, an overstatement as libel suits are not extinct and continue to be filed in courts across the land, but

8. April 10, 1971.
9. June 13, 1971.
10. June 12, 1971.

with stricter limits on the hazards faced by broadcast and print media. In its decision in the Rosenbloom case, the Court acknowledged that it "was aware that the press has, on occasions, grossly abused the freedom it is given by the Constitution, and all must deplore such excesses." However, it continued, "to insure the ascertainment and publication of the truth about public affairs, it is essential that the First Amendment protect some erroneous publications as well as true ones."

Three years later, in 1974, the Supreme Court made more changes in the rules regarding liability by enlarging protection of private persons against defamation. These came in a decision on a case that had its genesis in 1968 in the shooting and killing of a youth named Nelson by Richard Nuccio, a Chicago policeman.[11] For that act Nuccio was prosecuted and convicted of murder in the second degree. The Nelson family filed a civil suit against Nuccio, retaining Elmer Gertz., a reputable attorney, to represent them.

In the meantime, *American Opinion*, published monthly by Robert Welch, Inc., as an outlet for the views of the John Birch Society, started a series of articles to warn about what it regarded as a nationwide conspiracy to discredit local law enforcement agencies and to create in their stead a national police force capable of supporting a communist dictatorship. As part of the continuing effort to alert the public to this perceived danger, the managing editor of *American Opinion* commissioned an article on the murder trial of Officer Nuccio.

That article, published in *American Opinion*, stated that Elmer Gertz had been an official of the "Marxist League for Industrial Democracy, originally known as the Intercollegiate Socialist Society, which has advocated the violent seizure of our government." It also stated that Gertz had been an officer of the National Lawyers Guild, described as a

---

11. Elmer Gertz v. Robert Welch, Inc., 418 U.S. 323 (1974).

communist organization that "probably did more than any other outfit to plan the Communist attack on the Chicago police during the 1968 Democratic convention."

Those statements contained serious inaccuracies, and the implication that Mr. Gertz had a criminal record was false. He had been a member and officer of the National Lawyers Guild 15 years earlier, but there was no evidence that he or that organization had taken any part in planning the 1968 demonstrations in Chicago. There was also no basis for the charge that he was a "Leninist" or a "Communist-fronter." Also, he had never been a member of the "Marxist League for Industrial Democracy" or the "Intercollegiate Socialist Society." The managing editor had made no effort to verify or substantiate the charges against Gertz.

In a 5-to-4 ruling in favor of Attorney Gertz and against the *American Opinion* magazine, the U.S. Supreme Court gave greater protection to private individuals against libel, as contrasted to the public official and the public figure, by refusing to apply the principle it had stated in the *New York Times* case. In the majority opinion, Justice Lewis F. Powell Jr. stated:

■ The principal issue in this case is whether a newspaper or broadcaster that publishes defamatory falsehoods about an individual who is neither a public official nor a public figure may claim a constitutional privilege against liability for the injury inflicted by those statements . . .

In support of the ruling that private individuals should have greater protection against libel than do public officials and public figures, the Court made these points:

■ Public officials and public figures usually enjoy significantly greater access to the channels of effective communication and hence have a more realistic opportunity to counteract false statements then private individuals normally enjoy. Private individuals are therefore more vulnerable to injury, and the state interest in protecting them is correspondingly greater.

■   An individual who decides to seek government office must accept certain necessary consequences of that involvement in public affairs. He runs the risk of closer public scrutiny than might otherwise be the case.

■   Those classed as public figures stand in a similar position . . . Some occupy positions of such persuasive power and influence that they are deemed public figures for all purposes. More commonly, those classed as public figures have thrust themselves to the forefront of particular public controversies in order to influence the resolution of issues involved. In either event, they invite attention and comment.

■   No such assumption is justified with respect to a private individual . . . He has relinquished no part of his interest in the protection of his own good name, and consequently he has a more compelling call on the courts for redress of injury inflicted by defamatory falsehood. Thus, private individuals are not only more vulnerable to injury than public officials and public figures; they are also more deserving of recovery . . .

In commenting on injury by defamation, the Court stated:

■   The common law of defamation is an oddity of tort law, for it allows recovery for purportedly compensatory damages without evidence of actual loss . . . Indeed, the more customary types of actual harm inflicted by defamatory falsehood include impairment of reputation and standing in the community, personal humiliation, and mental anguish and suffering. . .

Regarding punitive damages, the Court said:

■   We also find no justification for allowing awards of punitive damages against publishers and broadcasters held liable under state-defined standards of liability for defamation. In most jurisdictions jury discretion over the amounts awarded is limited only by the gentle rule that they not be excessive. Consequently, juries assess punitive damages in wholly unpredictable amounts bearing no necessary relation to the actual harm cause. And they remain free to use their discretion selectively to punish expressions of unpopular views... They are not compensation for injury. Instead, they are private fines levied by civil juries to punish reprehensible conduct and to deter its future occurrence.

A libel suit can arise over misquoting someone, especially if the quotations are defamatory or the person quoted considers them defamatory. Accusations of "I was misquoted" are fairly common, giving rise to the question of how precise a writer must be in quoting someone he or she has interviewed or heard speak. Journalists customarily "clean up" quotations by correcting grammar and omitting what could be considered vulgar or libelous, but in doing so they are careful not to change the meaning.

Among court cases involving accuracy in quotations was one that arose after a two-part article by Janet Malcolm was published in *The New Yorker* in December 1983 and later expanded and published in 1984 by Alfred A. Knopf, Inc., as a book titled *In The Freud Archives*. The subject of the article and the book was Jeffrey M. Masson, a psychiatrist, and his relationship with the Sigmund Freud Archives in Maresfield Garden outside of London. Dr. Masson was hired as projects director of the Archives in 1980, but was dismissed by the Board of Directors the next year.

In obtaining information for the article and the book, Malcolm tape recorded a number of interviews in 1982 with Masson and others who had been associated with him, with some interviews in person and others by telephone. The result was a work that portrayed Masson in a most unflattering light; and Masson accused the author of deliberately misquoting him. One of the narrative devices she used consisted of enclosing lengthy passages attributed to Masson in quotation marks.

Masson, a resident of Berkeley, California, brought suit for libel under California law in the U.S. District Court for the Northern District of California, claiming that various passages in the published works were false and defamatory. In the trial no identical statements of the disputed passages appeared in the 40 hours of tape-recorded interviews, but Malcolm, in defense, claimed to have taken notes in unrecorded interview sessions.

The District Court held that the alleged inaccuracies did not raise a jury question, or were "one of a number of possible rational interpretations of a conversation or event that bristled with ambiguities," and thus were entitled to constitutional protection. The Court therefore issued a summary judgment in favor of the author and the publishers.

The Court of Appeals for the Ninth Circuit affirmed the decision, with one of the three judges dissenting. He argued that any intentional or reckless alteration would prove actual malice, so long as a passage within quotation marks purports to be a verbatim rendition of what was said, contains inaccuracies, and is defamatory.

"To invoke the right to deliberately distort what someone else has said is to assert the right to lie in print," the judge said.

The U.S. Supreme Court granted certiorari, and on June 20, 1991, it decided in favor of Masson, thus reversing the decisions of the lower courts.[12] The Court held that fabricated quotations may injure reputation by attributing untrue factual assertion to the speaker, or by the manner of expression or even the fact that the statement could indicate a negative personal trait or an attitude the speaker does not hold.

In the opinion delivered by Justice Anthony M. Kennedy, the Court set some standards for evaluating disputed quota-

---

12. Jeffrey M. Masson v. New Yorker Magazine, Inc., Alfred A. Knopf. Inc., and Janet Malcolm, 115 L. Ed 2d 447 (June 20, 1991).

tions, stating in part:

■ We reject the idea that any alteration beyond correction of grammar or syntax by itself proves falsity in the sense relevant in determining actual malice under the First Amendment. An interviewer who writes from notes will attempt a reconstruction of the speaker's statement. The author would, we may assume, act with knowledge that at times she had attributed to her subject words other than those actually used. . .

If an author alters a speaker's words but effects no material change in meaning, including any meaning conveyed by the manner or fact of expression, the speaker suffers no injury to reputation that is compensable as a defamation . . .

We conclude that a deliberate alteration of (spoken) words does not equate with knowledge of falsity . . . unless the alteration results in a material change in the meaning conveyed by the statement.

Deliberate or reckless falsification that comprises actual malice turns upon words and punctuation only because words and punctuation express meaning.

The author's use of quotation marks was apparently pivotal in the Supreme Court decision, with the opinion stating:

■ Where a writer uses a quotation, and where a reasonable reader would conclude that the quotation purports to be a verbatim repetition of a statement by the speaker, the quotation marks indicate that the author is not involved in an interpretation of the speaker's ambiguous statement, but attempting to convey what the speaker said. This orthodox use of a quotation is the quintessential "direct account of events that speak for themselves." More accurately, the quotation allows the subject to speak for himself.

In conclusion the Court said, "we must assume . . . that

Malcolm reported with knowledge or reckless disregard of the difference between what petitioner said and what was quoted... The judgment of the Court of Appeals is reversed, and the case is remanded for further proceedings."

The case was reinstated in April 1992 for trial by jury. The trial opened in a federal court in San Francisco in May 1993, with *Masson v. Malcolm* labeled by *Newsweek* as "the Libel Trial of the Century, as a tale of sex, lies and more than 40 hours of audio tape."[13]

The trial ended June 3, 1993 with the jury finding Janet Malcolm guilty of defaming Jeffery Masson by fabricating five quotations in the article she wrote about him for publication in *The New Yorker*. The jurors agreed that she had acted with "reckless disregard" for the truth, but they did not agree on the amount of damages Masson should receive.

In criminal law, an accused person is presumed to be innocent until proven guilty. In a libel case, the role is reversed. There the publisher of an alleged libel must prove that the person who claims to have been libeled is guilty of the offense stated in the offending publication. That is what the defendant, Janet Malcolm, failed to do in the case discussed above.

As stated in Chapter 16, truth if published for a good purpose is a defense in libel. So the person accused of publishing a libel is presumed guilty until he or she proves that the offending statement or statements are true.

Libel generally involves one person, but it is possible to libel a group. A court suit charging defamation can be filed if the group is small enough to permit identification of individual members. That is necessary so that each member can prove that he or she is a member of the group and can show how the libel applies to him or her. No suit is possible by a group so large that its members are sufficiently anonymous to make personal identification impossible.

---

13. *Newsweek*, May 17, 1993, page 56.

Some states, however, have laws to protect racial, ethnic, religious, and political groups from defamation, laws that call for criminal action.

As stated before, the dead cannot be libeled. It has been stated that "the dead have no rights and can suffer no wrongs."

However, if defamatory statements are made about survivors in publications about the dead, the survivors can sue for damages.

CHAPTER
21

❋

YOU HAVE A RIGHT TO BE LET ALONE

YOU HAVE A RIGHT TO
BE LET ALONE

❀

Assume that while walking along the street you notice someone taking pictures of persons passing by, and you believe that you are among those photographed. You forget the incident until you are surprised a few weeks later to see your picture in the newspaper in an advertisement for clothing.

You could sue the advertiser for invasion of privacy and most likely obtain a court injunction prohibiting further use of your photograph without your permission, and also you could probably collect damages.

Using a person's picture or name without permission in advertising or in an endorsement of a product is a form of invasion of privacy that is unlawful virtually everywhere in the United States, either by common law, statutory law, judicial precedent, or all three. In New York State, for example, the *Civil Rights Law* reads in part:

■ Sec. 50 - Right of Privacy

A person, firm or corporation that uses for advertising purposes, or for the purposes of trade, the name, portrait or picture of any living person without first having obtained the written consent of such person . . . is guilty of a misdemeanor.

■ Sec. 51 - Action for Injunction and for Damages

Any person whose name, portrait or picture is used

within this state for advertising purposes or for the purposes of trade without... written consent... may sue and recover damages ...

Another scenario: While walking along the street you hear a loud crash; you hurry to the corner, where you see that two cars have collided and that one of the passengers has been injured. As you watch, an emergency vehicle arrives, and soon you see a photographer taking pictures of the scene. The next day a photograph of the accident appears in your newspaper, clearly showing you in the background. Again, you did not give permission for your picture to be published, but this time there is no cause for action.

The difference is that this time, although you were only a bystander, you were part of a news event; and there is no law that prohibits the use of photographs associated with news events. You could argue that you were not really a part of the event, but the fact of your being there watching made it so.

Like all principles governing free speech and a free press, rules regarding the use of photographs are complex. The prohibition against the use of photographs, names, and endorsements in advertising is fairly clear; but wide latitude is given for the use of photographs of persons in articles and publications of public interest, even though the photographs may not pertain to recent news events. Simply stated, the distinction lies between an article or publication of general interest and one published for trade purposes or financial gain.

Privacy — the right to be let alone — includes more than the unauthorized use of a person's photograph and name for financial gain, however. It means being secure in one's home, safe from unwarranted prying into one's affairs, and freedom from harassment by government officials. Intrusion upon a person's seclusion or solitude, placing a tap on someone's telephone, using devices for listening to private conversations, gaining access to private records and information, public disclosure of embarrassing incidents and aspects of one's life, and publicity that places a person in a false light are invasions of privacy.

Privacy as a constellation of rights brought together under a single category within the past century has a rather insubstantial legal foundation. At least 30 states, however, have given common law recognition to some aspects of privacy, some have enacted laws; and four — Alaska, California, Florida, and Montana — have adopted amendments to their constitutions to give privacy legal status. The Florida amendment reads:

■ Every natural person has the right to be let alone and free from government intrusion into his private life except as otherwise provided herein. This section shall not be construed to limit the public's right of access to public records and meetings as provided by law.

Legally, privacy is still searching for definitude. Devising and enacting laws to protect the rights of privacy have been halting and difficult, one reason being its relative newness, the other the multiplicity of possible "invasions" to protect against. Another complicating factor lies in determining where the rights of the individual end and the rights of society and the needs of government begin in regard to the various aspects of privacy and public records.

The matter of privacy has been an element in a number of Supreme Court decisions. In one opinion, delivered in 1973 by Chief Justice Warren Burger, the Court stated:[1]

■ Our prior decisions recognizing a right to privacy guaranteed by the Fourteenth Amendment included "only

---

1. Paris Adult Theatre I v. Slaton, 413 U.S. 49 (1973).

those persons' rights that can be deemed 'fundamental' or 'implicit' in the concept of ordered liberty". . . .This privacy right encompasses and protects the personal intimacies of the home, the family, marriage, motherhood, procreation, and child rearing.

Such offenses as murder or bank robbery are usually obvious, but determining whether the publication of certain kinds of information about an individual is invasion of privacy or is legally permissible can be a matter of debate. The difficulty of legislation is reflected in the New York Civil Rights Law, mentioned on page 262. Section 50 is titled "Right of Privacy," but the word "privacy" appears nowhere else in the law.

Although the U.S. Constitution does not mention privacy, the U.S. Supreme Court has recognized it as legal protection that derives from "penumbras" of the Bill of Rights. In a decision in 1965 the Court stated:[2]

■ Various guarantees create zones of privacy. The right of association contained in the penumbra of the First Amendment is one . . . The Third Amendment in its prohibition against the quartering of soldiers "in any house" in time of peace without the consent of the owner is another facet of that privacy.

The Fourth Amendment explicitly affirms the "right of the people to be secure in their persons, houses, papers, and effects, against unreasonable searches and seizures." The Fifth Amendment in its Self-Incrimination Clause enables the citizen to create a zone of privacy which government may not force him to surrender to his detriment.

The Ninth Amendment provides: "The enumeration in the Constitution, of certain rights, shall not be con-

---

2. Griswold v. Connecticut, 381 U.S. 479 (1965).

strued to deny or disparage others retained by the people."

The Fourth Amendment provides protection against intrusion by government agents. A policeman does not have the right to enter a home without express or implied permission, and no one has to answer any questions the policeman may ask. If he forces his way in, he is guilty of criminal trespass unless he has a search warrant and presents it. A search warrant is a court order, so a person can be arrested for resisting or preventing an officer with a warrant from entering and searching.

Unreasonable searches and seizures extend beyond the home, to include one's person, an automobile, and other property, although laws and court decisions regarding such searches vary widely. In general, everyone has the right to be let alone and not searched unless he gives permission or the officer has a search warrant. Also, any evidence such as papers, contraband, illegal drugs, or stolen property cannot be used as evidence in court if obtained by unauthorized search.

In a decision in 1914, the U.S. Supreme Court ruled that evidence obtained in an illegal search could not be used as evidence in a federal criminal court trial.[3] Then, 47 years later in 1961, the Court ruled in the case of *Mapp v. Ohio* that such evidence could not be used in state and local criminal trials, either.[4] Those decisions established what is known as "the exclusionary rule," which is aimed at discouraging illegal searches and seizures and in protecting accused persons against unfairly obtained evidence.

The rule has led to endless protests by law enforcement officials and to a barrage of court rulings in legal methods of obtaining evidence. Even so, it continues as an essential element in criminal trials, with its role reaffirmed by the U.S.

---

3. Weeks v. United States, 232 U.S. 383 (1914).
4. Mapp v. Ohio, 367 U.S. 643 (1961).

Supreme Court in a 5-to-4 decision handed down on January 10, 1990.[5] In the majority opinion in that case, Justice Brennan stated:

> ■ So long as we are committed to protecting the people from the disregard of their constitutional rights during the course of criminal investigations, inadmissibility of illegally obtained evidence must remain the rule, not the exception.

The genesis of privacy as a legal concept is attributed to an article titled "The Right to Privacy," published in the *Harvard Law Review* on December 15, 1890. It was written by Samuel D. Warren and Louis D. Brandeis, law partners and members of prominent families in Boston. Mr. Brandeis later was appointed to the U.S. Supreme Court, where he served with distinction from 1916 to 1939.

Their article was a protest against reports in local newspapers on social events in their homes. Mr. Warren was especially distressed by the detail in which the papers reported on plans and preparations for his daughter's wedding. In the article Mr. Warren and Mr. Brandeis wrote, "The press is overstepping in every direction the bounds of propriety and decency (with) column upon column filled with idle gossip, which can only be procured by invasion upon the domestic circle."

If Mr. Warren were alive today, he would no doubt be dismayed by the great volume of reporting in newspapers and magazines on the private lives of the rich and famous. Personal information has become an important aspect of ncws, with a gossip column a standard feature of many daily newspapers and news magazines. Some publications are devoted entirely to stories and photographs of prominent and extraordinary men and women. Because people have always been interested in kings and their courts, in the affairs and

---

5. Darryl James v. Illinois, 493 U.S. 307 (January 10, 1990).

activities of the ruling class, the wealthy, and the notable, news of such persons is eagerly read by the public.

Some such reporting, however, can cause embarrassment, anguish, and actual harm. Suppose, for example, a man (call him Mr. Smith) has been a successful businessman in a small city for the past 20 years and has an excellent reputation. He becomes a candidate for a seat on the city council; and a reporter discovers that Mr. Smith had served a 30-day jail sentence some 30 years ago, although he has been a model citizen ever since. In writing a story on the political campaign, the reporter includes the fact of the prison term, much to the distress of Mr. Smith. Or, in another scenario, say that Mr. Smith had undergone treatment in a mental hospital in his youth.

Was the reporter unethical in revealing such personal information about Mr. Smith? Did the newspaper invade Mr. Smith's privacy? Mr. Smith could not successfully sue for libel because the published information is true; and he probably could not prove that the story had been published with malicious intent. His only recourse, if he wishes to take action, would be to sue for invasion of privacy. Libel is defamation of character, it is injury to one's reputation. Privacy, on the other hand, is a wrong that results in injury to one's feelings, which is what the newspaper article did. Libel differs from privacy in that libel is false; a statement that invades privacy is true. Truth is a defense in libel; it is not a defense in privacy.

If Mr. Smith were to sue for damages, the newspaper would argue in defense that the people have a right to know about the past life of a candidate for office. The Court would probably agree, based upon the decision in the *Monitor Patriot Co. v. Roy* case in 1971, discussed in Chapter 20, in which the U.S. Supreme Court ruled that such information is relevant and not libelous.[6] Cases of this kind illustrate that the line

---

6. Monitor Patriot Co. v. Roselle A. Roy, 401 U.S. 265 (1971).

between "invasion of privacy" and "the right of the people to know" is at times difficult to determine.

Among the numerous privacy suits that have been filed in courts across the country, one of the most publicized was *Time, Inc. v. Hill*, which had its origin in the escape of three convicts from the Federal penitentiary in Lewisburg, Pennsylvania, on September 9, 1952.[7] Two days later, after stealing an automobile, shotguns and ammunition, and money, they forced their way into the home of James and Elizabeth Hill in the Philadelphia suburb of Whitemarsh. There they held Mr. and Mrs. Hill, their three daughters, aged 11, 15, and 17, and twin sons aged 4, prisoners in their home for 19 hours on September 11 and 12 before leaving. The convicts were soon apprehended in a widely publicized encounter with the police which resulted in killing of two of them in a gun battle and the capture of the third.

In interviews with reporters, the Hills tried to keep publicity at a minimum, stressing that the convicts had treated the family courteously, had not molested them, and had not been violent or abusive. Two months later the Hills moved to Connecticut. They had refused all requests for magazine interviews and offers of payment for stories for publication, so public interest in their ordeal soon faded away.

The next spring saw the publication of a novel titled *The Desperate Hours* by Joseph Hayes which depicted the experiences of a family of four held hostage by three escaped convicts in the family's suburban Indianapolis home. Unlike what had happened to the Hills, the family in the novel suffered violence in a two-day reign of terror at the hands of the convicts, with the father and the son beaten and the daughter subjected to verbal sexual insults.

The book, which enjoyed a huge sale, was then made into a play, also titled *The Desperate Hours*, with a pre-Broadway

---

7. Time, Inc. v. James J. Hill, 385 U.S. 374 (January 9, 1967).

tryout in Philadelphia, not a great distance from the former Hill home.

The claim of invasion of privacy came as a result of a review of the play in *Life* magazine on February 28, 1955, a review that described the play as a "re-enacted" account of the Hill family experience — which it was not. The review was titled "True Crime Inspires Tense Play," with a subtitle, "The ordeal of a family trapped by convicts gives Broadway a new thriller." The review read in part:

■ Three years ago Americans all over the country read about the desperate ordeal of the James Hill family, who were held prisoners in their home outside Philadelphia by three escaped convicts. Later they read about it in Joseph Hayes' novel, *The Desperate Hours*, inspired by the family's experience. Now they can see the story re-enacted in Hayes' Broadway play based on the book, and next year will see it in his movie, which has been filmed but is being held up until the play has a chance to pay off.

To illustrate the review, *Life* published two pages of photographs of some of the actors taken at the home in Whitemarsh where the Hills had been held prisoner. Among the photographs was one showing the son being "roughed up" by a convict; another showing the daughter biting the hand of a convict in an attempt to make him drop a gun, with the photo titled "daring daughter"; and one showing the father throwing his gun through the door after making "a brave try" to save the family. All were posed pictures; and as the Hills were referred to in the review, they again became front-page news

Viewing the review as fabrication rather than as factual news, published for commercial exploitation and disrupting their lives, the Hills sued Time, Inc., publisher of *Life,* for damages, charging invasion of privacy under the New York Civil Rights Law. After a two-week trial in 1962, the jury awarded the Hills $50,000 in compensatory damages and

$25,000 in punitive damages. On appeal, the Appellate Division of the Supreme Court of New York sustained the jury verdict of liability, but it ordered a new trial as to damages. In regard to liability, the Court stated:

■ Although the play was fictionalized, *Life's* article portrayed it as a re-enactment of the Hills' experience. It is an inescapable conclusion that this was done to advertise and attract further attention to the play, and to increase present and future magazine circulation as well. It is evident that the article cannot be characterized as a mere dissemination of news, nor even an effort to supply legitimate newsworthy information in which the public had, or might have, proper interest.

At the trial on damages, the court awarded $30,000 in compensatory damages but no punitive damages. In brief, the Hills' claim was upheld by a 4-to-1 vote in New York Appellate Division and a 5-to-2 vote in the New York State Court of Appeals.

The U.S. Supreme Court granted the application of *Time, Inc.*, for an appeal; and Richard Nixon was selected as the attorney for the Hills. He had served as vice president of the United States during the time Dwight Eisenhower was president from 1953 to 1961; and after being defeated in the race for governor of California in 1962 had joined a law firm in Washington, D.C., in 1963.

The Supreme Court heard arguments on April 27, 1966, and again on October 18 and 19 that year; and it handed down its decision on January 9, 1967, with a majority of 5 to 4 in favor of *Time, Inc.*[8]

In the majority opinion written by Justice Brennan, the Court stated in part:

---

8. Nixon had lost the case, but two years later on January 20 he was inaugurated President of the United States.

■ The guarantees for speech and press are not the preserve of political expression or comment upon public affairs, essential as those are to healthy government. One need only pick up any newspaper or magazine to comprehend the vast range of published matter which exposes persons to public view, both private citizens and public officials. Exposure of the self to others in varying degrees is a concomitant of life in a society which places a primary value on freedom of speech and of the press.

Although that decision set aside the judgment of the Court of Appeals and remanded the case for further proceedings, that was the end of litigation.

Time, Inc. v. Hill raised difficult questions, as evidenced by five of the justices writing separate opinions. Although the case was highly publicized, its adjudication did little to clarify the right of privacy or point the way to its legal protection. Stating that "the First Amendment principles pronounced in the *New York Times* case guide our conclusion," the majority opinion apparently also hinged on the question of whether *Life* had used the Hill family experience "for financial gain" rather than for information of general interest. In this regard, the opinion states, "The requirement that the jury . . . find that the article was published 'for trade purposes,' as defined in the charge, cannot save the charge from constitutional infirmity." (As stated in the Court's opinion in the case of *Joseph Burstyn, Inc., v. Wilson*), "That books, newspapers and magazines are published and sold for profit does not prevent them from being a form of expression safeguarded by the First Amendment."

Justice Abe Fortas, in dissent from the majority opinion, expressed firm belief that freedom of the press is limited. He stated in part:

■ I believe that freedom of the press, of speech, assembly, and religion, and the freedom to petition are of the

essence of our liberty and fundamental to our values . . .
But I do not believe that whatever is in words . . . is beyond
the reach of the law . . .   I do not believe that the First
Amendment precludes effective protection of the right of
privacy—or, for that matter, an effective law of libel . . .

The courts may not and must not permit either public
or private action that censors or inhibits the press. But
part of this responsibility is to preserve values and
procedures which assure the ordinary citizen that the
press is not above the law . . .

CHAPTER

22

❀

PRIVACY IS A LIMITED RIGHT

PRIVACY IS A LIMITED RIGHT

❦

A privacy case based on placing someone in a false light reached the U.S. Supreme Court in 1974, seven years after *Time Inc. v. Hill.*[1] Its origin was in the collapse of the Silver Bridge across the Ohio River at Point Pleasant, West Virginia, in December 1967, killing 44 persons.

Joseph Eszterhas, a reporter, was assigned by *The Plain Dealer*, a daily newspaper published in Cleveland, Ohio, to cover the disaster. He wrote a feature that focused on the funeral of Melvin Cantrell, who had died in the bridge collapse, and on the impact of his death on the Cantrell family, who lived in the Point Pleasant area.

Five months later Eszterhas returned to Point Pleasant with Richard Conway, a photographer, to get pictures and information for a follow-up feature story. The two men went to the Cantrell residence, where Eszterhas talked with the children and Conway took 50 pictures. Mrs. Cantrell was not home at any time during the 60 to 90 minutes that the men were there.

Eszterhas' story appeared as the lead feature in *Sunday Magazine* of *The Plain Dealer* on August 4, 1968. It stressed the family's abject poverty; the children's old, ill-fitting clothes and the deteriorating condition of their home were

---

1. Margaret Mae Cantrell v. Forest City Publishing Co., 419 U.S. 245 (1974).

detailed in both the text and accompanying photographs. As he had done in his original, prize-winning article on the Silver Bridge disaster, in the follow-up story Eszterhas used the Cantrell family to illustrate the impact of the bridge collapse on the lives of the people in the Point Pleasant area.

The story contained a number of inaccuracies and false statements. Most conspicuously, Mrs. Cantrell was not present when Eszterhas and Conway were there, although Eszterhas wrote: "Margaret Cantrell will talk neither about what happened nor about how they are doing. She wears the same mask of non-expression she wore at the funeral. She is a proud woman. She says that after it happened, the people in town offered to help them out with money and they refused to take it." Other significant misrepresentations were contained in the descriptions of the poverty in which the Cantrells were living and the dirty and dilapidated conditions of the Cantrell home.

Mrs. Cantrell filed suit against Eszterhas, Conway, and the Forest City Publishing Co., publishers of *The Plain Dealer*, for damages, contending that the false feature story about her and her family made them objects of pity and ridicule, causing her and her son William to suffer outrage, mental distress, shame and humiliation.

The jury returned a verdict against all three of the respondents based on the "false light" aspect of privacy. In other words, by publishing a false feature story about the Cantrells, the respondents had made them objects of pity and ridicule, causing them to suffer mental distress, shame and humiliation.

The Court of Appeals for the Sixth District reversed that decision, concluding that there was no evidence that the Forest City Publishing Company had knowledge of any of the inaccuracies contained in the Eszterhas' article.

The U. S. Supreme Court, with only one dissenting vote ruled otherwise. It reversed the decision of the Appeals Court, thus affirming the judgment of the District Court in favor of the Cantrells.

In the majority opinion Justice Potter Stewart stated: "In a false-light case, common-law malice – frequently expressed in terms of either ill will toward the plaintiff or reckless and wanton disregard of the plaintiff's rights – would focus on the defendant's attitude toward the plaintiff's privacy, not toward the truth or falsity of the material published," (as distinguished from the definition of actual malice established by the *New York Times Co. v. Sullivan* case which requires that it be published "with the knowledge that a defamatory statement was false or with reckless disregard of whether it was false or not.")

The right of privacy, like all rights, is of course, limited. A person forfeits much of that right by what he or she does in public in almost any capacity, as an author, an actor, a candidate for office, and in unnumbered other ways. As the U.S. Supreme Court said in a decision in 1968, "There are, however, important limitations on the right of privacy. It does not extend to matters of public interest, or to persons properly in the public eye, at least as to matters other than features of their intimate life."[2]

Privacy involves more than the publication of humiliating and embarrassing personal information. Basically it involves the right of individuals to be let alone and to live in privacy, a right that at times conflicts with the rights of others and of society as a whole.

The controversy over abortion rights is an example of such conflict, with much of the nation and even the Courts sharply divided on that issue. In 1965 in the *Griswold v. Connecticut* case referred to in Chapter 21, the Court struck down a Connecticut law that made the use of birth control devices and even giving advice on the use of such devices, illegal.

Eight years later on January 22, 1973, the Court handed down a ruling in the case of *Roe v. Wade* that a woman's right to privacy permits her to decide whether or not she will have

2. Dodd v. Pearson, 279 U.S. 101 (1968).

an abortion.[3] It held that a State may not prevent a woman from having an abortion during the first six months of pregnancy, and that the right to an abortion is not qualified. In that case, Norma McCorvey, using the fictitious name Jane Roe, sued Henry Wade, District Attorney for Dallas County, claiming that the Texas law on abortion intruded upon her privacy by denying the right of a pregnant woman to decide when to terminate her pregnancy.

Later that same year the Supreme Court overturned a Georgia law on abortion, but ruled that a woman did not have an absolute constitutional right to an abortion upon demand.[4]

As controversy over abortion mounted after that decision, the Court wavered; and on June 19, 1989, by a vote of 5-to-4 in the case of *Webster v. Reproductive Health Services,* it upheld a restrictive Missouri law.[5] The decision has the effect of granting more authority to states in regulating abortions.

The trend continued in the decision handed down on May 23, 1991, in the case of *Rust v. Sullivan* in which the Supreme Court ruled as permissible a government regulation forbidding doctors in federally funded family planning clinics from even discussing abortion as an option with their patients.[6] The regulation pertains to Title X of the Public Health Service Act of 1970, which provides funds for family planning clinics. In 1988 the Department of Health and Human Services, which administers the funds, had announced the regulation but had not enforced it pending a decision by the Supreme Court on whether the regulation constitutes an abridgment of freedom of speech. The Court ruled 5-to-4 that it does not.

---

3. Roe v. Wade, 410 U.S. 113 (1973).
4. Doe v. Bolton, 410 U.S. 179 (1973).
5. Webster v. Reproductive Health Services, 492 U.S. 490 (June 19, 1989).
6. Irving Rust et al v. Louis W. Sullivan, Secretary of Health and Human Services, 111 S.Ct. 1759 (May 23, 1991).

In the majority opinion written by Chief Justice William H. Rehnquist, the Court stated in part:

■ Based on the broad directives provided by Congress in Title X in general and Section 1008 in particular, we are unable to say that the Secretary's construction of the prohibition in Section 1008 to require a ban on counseling, referral, and advocacy within the Title X project, is impermissible.

When we find, as we do here, that the legislative history is ambiguous and unenlightening on the matters with respect to which the regulations deal, we customarily defer to the expertise of the agency . . .

Within far greater limits than the petitioners are willing to concede, when the Government appropriates public funds to establish a program it is entitled to define the limits of that program.

In the following November Congress passed a bill to remove the restriction on discussing abortion as an option, but the bill was promptly vetoed by President Bush and Congress was unable to override the veto. The "gag" thus remained on doctors and other personnel in family planning clinics supported partly or totally by federal funds.[7] That meant, in round numbers, that 4,500 clinics serving about 4 million women annually, were prevented from providing any medical information about abortion. It also raised questions:

■ Do doctors incur legal liability when they do not provide complete medical information to their patients?

■ By logical extension of the decision, can any agency, organization, college or university be restricted in what it may publish or say regarding research or other activities supported in part or totally by federal funds?

■ Is a restriction such as the one imposed by administra-

---

7. It was cancelled by President Clinton in 1993.

tive directive on family counseling clinics a form of censorship that violates the right of free speech in this country?

Apparently because of widespread criticism by medical
and abortion-rights organizations, the Health and Human
Services Department on March 30, 1992, modified its regulations to permit doctors but not nurses or counselors to give
limited advice on abortions.

Respect for the privacy of others is deeply ingrained in the
culture of societies everywhere. It is simply taboo to enter
another's home without knocking, to open someone else's
mail, stare into the windows of homes, and join others at a
table in a public place without asking permission to do so.

The mass media also practice restraints. For example,
they generally do not publish or broadcast the names of rape
victims, as a matter of compassion rather than as a matter of
law, although three states — Florida, Georgia, and South
Carolina — have laws that prohibit the publication of those
names. The tradition of protecting rape victims is long-
standing, with the Florida law dating back to 1911.

Whether such law is constitutional, however, is doubtful.
In October 1991 Judge Robert Parker in Palm Beach County,
Florida, ruled that it is not constitutional after *The Globe*, a
supermarket tabloid, had been charged with violating the law
by revealing the name of the woman who had accused
William Kennedy Smith of raping her in March that year in
that county. The decision applied only to Palm Beach County
and was appealed. The decision that the law is unconstitutional
was upheld by the the appeals court in August 1993.

Publishing the name of a rape victim in violation of a law
would be a criminal offense. In contrast are civil laws which
enable individuals and companies to obtain redress or
compensation for wrongs or injury done them by other
individuals or companies. The government does not enter
into civil suits except to provide the courts and the judges.

The case of *Time, Inc. v. Hill* was civil. Mr. Hill did not
accuse Time, Inc. of violating a law but rather of injuring him

and his family by invading their privacy. The suit brought by Mrs. Cantrell was also a civil case. Mr. Hill and Mrs. Cantrell did not accuse anyone or any company of breaking the law; rather, they felt that they had been injured by their privacy having been invaded. There are, however, civil laws that protect privacy. Missouri and Illinois, for example, have enacted civil laws titled "AIDS Confidentiality Act" prohibiting the disclosure of names of people with AIDS that enables those whose names are disclosed to sue the publisher or broadcaster for damages.

A conflict of rights can occur in connection with laws, either civil or criminal, that forbid the publication of names after those names have become public record — and they become so when they are spoken in open court or appear in official court records. The courts have held that once a name becomes public record, it is "privileged information" and may legally be published. That right was upheld in a decision by the U.S. Supreme Court in 1975 in the case of *Cox Broadcasting Corporation v. Cohn.*[8]

The case had its beginning in August 1971 in Georgia when a gang of six youths raped a 17-year-old girl who died as a result of the attack. The youths were indicted for murder and rape; and while there was substantial press coverage of the crime and its subsequent developments, the identity of the victim was not disclosed pending trial. Section 26-9901 of the Georgia Code makes it a misdemeanor to publish or broadcast the name or identity of a rape victim.

In April 1972, eight months after the rape, the six defendants appeared in court where five of them pleaded guilty to rape or attempted rape, the charge of murder having been dropped. The guilty pleas were accepted by the court, and the trial of the defendant pleading not guilty was set for a later date.

---

8. Cox Broadcasting Corporation v. Martin Cohn, 420 U.S. 469 (1975).

By examining the indictments made available for his inspection in the courthouse, a reporter for Station WSB-TV in Atlanta learned the rape victim's name. Later that day he used her name in a news broadcast and again on the next day.

The father of the victim, Martin Cohn, brought suit, claiming that his right of privacy had been invaded by the television broadcast giving the name of his deceased daughter. Cox Broadcasting admitted the broadcasts but claimed that the information was privileged under both state law and the First and Fourteenth Amendments. The trial court, rejecting those constitutional claims and holding that the Georgia statute provided a civil remedy to those injured by its violation, gave a summary judgment to Mr. Cohn as to liability, with determination of damages to await trial by jury.

In an 8-to-1 decision, the U.S. Supreme Court reversed the decision and found in favor of Cox Broadcasting. In the opinion, written by Justice Byron R. White, the Court stated in part:

> ■ The version of the privacy tort now before us — termed in Georgia "the tort of public disclosure" — is that in which the plaintiff claims the right to be free from unwanted publicity about his private affairs, which, although wholly true, would be offensive to a person of ordinary sensibilities.
>
> The question is . . . whether the State may impose sanctions on the accurate publication of the name of a rape victim obtained from public records — more specifically, from judicial records which are maintained in connection with a public prosecution and which themselves are open to public inspection. We are convinced that the State may not do so.

The U.S. Supreme Court upheld that principle in a decision 14 years later in a rape case in Florida.[9] The case

---

9. The Florida Star v. B. J. F., 491 U.S. 524 (June 21, 1989).

originated when a woman identified as B. J. F. by the Court told the Duval County Sheriff's Department on October 20, 1983, that she had been raped. Someone in the Department mistakenly placed the police report of the incident in the press room, where it was copied verbatim by an intern at *The Florida Star*, a weekly newspaper published in Jacksonville that has since ceased publication. *The Florida Star* then published a one-paragraph story which included the full name of the rape victim, which was in violation of the newspaper's rule never to publish the name of a rape victim and the first time it had ever done so. The publication was also in violation of Florida Statute 794.03 which prohibited publishing the names of rape victims.

Almost a year later, on September 26, 1984, B. J. F. sued *The Florida Star*, Sheriff Dale Carson, and the Sheriff's Department for violating the law in the publication of her name and for emotional distress she had suffered as a consequence. The trial judge ruled that the law did not violate the First Amendment because it applied only to a narrow set of criminal offenses, and he granted a motion for a directed verdict because the newspaper had been negligent per se in violating Florida law.

Although B. J. F. had asked for only $18,000 in damages, the jury awarded her $75,000 in compensatory damages and $25,000 in punitive damages. The First District Court of Appeals upheld the awards, but the U.S. Supreme Court ruled in favor of *The Florida Star*. In the majority opinion, Justice Thurgood Marshall held that finding a newspaper "civilly liable for publishing the name of a rape victim which it had obtained from a publicly released police report" violates the First Amendment. He said that the government cannot constitutionally first give the press a rape victim's name and then prosecute a newspaper for publishing that name; but he modified that by stating that "giving newspapers the privilege of reporting all truthful information would be too broad because the Court cannot anticipate what the effects would be in every case."

In dissent, Justice Byron R. White, joined by Chief Justice William H. Rehnquist and Justice Sandra Day O'Connor, said that by holding that only a state interest of the highest order can be used to challenge publication, the Court, in effect, obliterates "one of the most note-worthy legal inventions of the 20th century, the tort of publication of private facts," or, in other words, the right to sue for the invasion of privacy.

Privacy has been defined as an individual's right to control information about himself. Some of that control was lost, or at least jeopardized, with the advent of computers. Personal information becomes a highly useful and marketable commodity when organized and stored in computer data bases available for rapid retrieval.

Information about virtually everything a person does, from buying a car, obtaining the license plate for the car, subscribing for a magazine, making a telephone toll call, borrowing money, being treated in a hospital, and on and on is fed into hundreds of data bases.

Data bases are owned and operated by credit bureaus, banks, insurance companies, and other corporations that make information available to information companies, from whom it can be obtained for a price by anyone on-line.

Also, the federal government accumulates personal information, with 178 of the largest agencies maintaining about 2,000 data banks, each containing millions of entries.

With surprising prescience, Justice Brandeis more than 60 years ago foresaw the use of such machines as computers. In his dissent in the Olmstead case in 1928, he said:

■ In the application of a Constitution, our contemplation cannot be only on what has been but of what may be.

The progress of science in furnishing the government with means of espionage is not likely to stop with wire tapping. Ways may some day be developed by which the government, without removing papers from secret drawers, can reproduce them in court and by which it will be enabled to expose to a jury the most intimate occurrences of the home.

Law prohibits a person from breaking and entering an office and going through the files there, an act that would be illegal trespass and possibly theft; but with a computer, it is possible to search computer files in other offices without physically entering those offices. As Justice Brandeis foresaw, electronic files can be read by someone who never goes near the office in which they are stored. In fact, millions of employees in the United States today are subject to computer-monitoring of their work, and software programs are available to monitor personal computers secretly.

Another technical development that poses a threat to privacy is the telephone device Caller ID, which displays the number of the telephone from which the call is being made, even if the number is unlisted. Caller ID has an enormous advantage over tracing for obscene calls; but it can be a problem for battered women who fear being traced by their abusive husbands and for social workers and other professionals who want to keep their home phone numbers private from clients.

In October, 1986, Congress took note of the technical advances in communication by extending the protection of privacy given conventional telephones to include cellular telephones operating on high frequency radio waves, transmission by private satellite, paging devices, and "electronic mail," which consists of messages transmitted and stored in computers.

Invasion of privacy by telephone is possible through government subpoena of records of telephone calls as well as by tapping the line to listen to conversations.

Federal agencies such as the IRS or FBI that request or subpoena records from a telephone company are not required to notify the person being investigated that the record of the calls he has made is being examined. Also the telephone company is not required to notify a customer that it has released a record of his calls. In fact, the telephone company will not notify the customer that his records have been obtained by a government agency if that agency has requested the company to keep the matter secret, or if the company has received a court order directing that the matter be kept secret.

With such records obtained in secrecy, it is possible to learn who called whom, when, and how. That kind of secrecy, however, may change as Congress has held hearings on legislation to protect the privacy of telephone users.

Most records, both governmental and non-governmental, relate to financial transactions such as buying and selling, making deposits and writing checks, borrowing money, and paying taxes, and to marriage licenses and divorces, court cases, hospital admissions and treatment, school attendance and grades. Many of them are "nobody's business but your own."

To protect confidentiality, each state has its own laws regarding privacy.

Among laws passed by Congress to protect privacy are:

■ Fair Credit Reporting Act of 1970, which states how financial records of individuals may be used, lists the kinds of information that must be made available to the government, and explains how a person can see his own records kept by credit bureaus and correct any errors he finds in them.

■ The Financial Privacy Act of 1978 which protects the privacy of records kept by financial institutions and prevents unjustified investigation of those records by agencies of the federal government without permission or a warrant.

■ The Family Educational and Privacy Act of 1974, mentioned in the preceding chapter, gives parents the right to see records of their children being kept by the schools and requires parents' written permission for the records to be released to other persons. That applies only to elementary and high school. The law states, "whenever a student has attained 18 years of age, or is attending an institution of post secondary education, the permission or consent required of and the rights accorded to the parents of the student shall thereafter only be required of and accorded to the student."

■ The Federal Age Discrimination in Employment Act prohibits employers from asking an applicant's age, except when it constitutes a legitimate qualification for a job.

Laws designed to protect personal privacy can contain hazards to freedom of the press and the public's right to know. An example was provided by a prize-winning series of articles in *The Atlanta Journal and Constitution* in 1989.[10] In that series Jane Hansen showed how Georgia confidentiality laws designed to protect the privacy of children failed to protect many of them from abuse and in some cases death while being cared for by the state welfare system. What the privacy laws did, she wrote, was to protect the bureaucrats in the welfare system by hiding their failures.

The Family Educational and Privacy Act of 1974 prohibits colleges and universities (institutions of postsecondary education) from releasing information from student records

---

10. James E. Kirtley, "The Cloak Of Privacy," *Columbia Journalism Review*, November-December 1991.

maintained by physicians, psychiatrists, and psychologists to parents without permission of students 18 years of age or older. While that protects privacy, it can prevent institutions from enlisting the cooperation of parents in regard to problems their children may be having if and when students refuse to give permission.

The Act, in toto, was designed to protect individuals from invasion of privacy by federal agencies. The law lists procedures by which a person may learn what personal data have been collected about him. It gives everyone the right to see his or her own records and to correct errors. The law does not apply to records maintained by the CIA, law enforcement agencies, the armed forces, foreign police organizations, and not to state and local governments or to private organizations.

CHAPTER
23

*EAVESDROPPING IS AN
INVASION OF PRIVACY*

EAVESDROPPING IS AN
INVASION OF PRIVACY

❧

"Wiretapping and bugging are 'dirty business,' and it is now clear that they do not help to solve or even prevent much crime. They are expensive, time consuming, and gravely threaten a free society."

Those words by Justice Louis D. Brandeis were in dissent to a noted decision in which the U.S. Supreme Court ruled in 1928, with only five justices agreeing, that wiretapping is not a "search within the meaning of the Fourth Amendment and that words cannot be "seized," so wiretapping without a search warrant does not violate the Fourth Amendment of the Constitution.[1]

The Amendment states in part, "The right of the people to be secure in their person, houses, papers, and effects against unreasonable searches and seizures, shall not be violated . . ."

The four justices in dissent to the majority opinion in this case maintained that "whenever a telephone line is tapped, the privacy of the persons at both ends of the line is invaded."

It was the first wiretapping case ever considered by the U.S. Supreme Court; and it arose during the Prohibition Era (1919-1933) when the possession and sale of alcoholic beverages were illegal. In this case the Supreme Court upheld the conviction of Roy Olmstead, who was directing an extensive

---

1. Olmstead v. United States, 277 U.S. 438 (1928).

business in transporting and selling liquor in Seattle, a business so extensive that he and 72 others were indicted for a conspiracy described as being of "amazing magnitude." It was so large that they were using two seagoing vessels to smuggle in liquor from Canada.

To obtain evidence, police placed wiretaps on telephone lines near Olmstead's home and in the basement of an office building without ever trespassing on his property. Surveillance continued over several months. The Supreme Court held in the majority opinion that "the language of the Fourth Amendment cannot be extended to include telephone wires reaching to the whole world from the defendant's home or office." The majority agreed that there had been no trespass and no seizure of person or property as prohibited by the Fourth Amendment. Disagreeing with that kind of thinking, Justice Brandeis said in dissent:

■ The makers of our Constitution . . . conferred, as against the Government, the right to be let alone — the most comprehensive of rights and the right most valued by civilized men. To protect that right, every unjustifiable intrusion by the Government upon the privacy of the individual, whatever the means employed, must be deemed a violation of the Fourth Amendment.

He said further, "We should try to impose some limits on these pernicious practices (of wiretapping) that would at least bring them within hailing distance of the Bill of Rights."

Half a dozen years later in 1934, that advice was heeded when Congress passed the Federal Communication Act making unauthorized wiretapping illegal. Section 605 of the Act states that "no person not being authorized by the sender shall intercept any communication by wire or radio and divulge or publish its existence, contents, substance, purport, effect, or meaning to any person." The law also applies to radio transmission by police and fire departments as well as conversations on business, marine, aviation, amateur, and other bands. Such communication is considered "private," with some exceptions such as radio messages from ships in distress.

Section 605 consists of one sentence comprised of more than 300 words. In brief, it prohibits interception messages being sent by wire or radio and divulging or publishing the contents of intercepted messages; and it forbids any person "having become acquainted with any intercepted information from using that information for his own benefit or for the benefit of another not entitled thereto."

Although the law is stated simply, the U.S. Supreme Court has been confronted in several cases with determining the meaning and application of various words and phrases. To be a violation, the law requires that a message be intercepted, with the interception unauthorized by the sender, and the content must be divulged or published. The most debated question, naturally, is whether information obtained by intercepting calls may be used as evidence in court.

The word "intercepted" and the phrase "authorized by the sender" sound simple, but in some situations they can be complex. As examples, suppose that one of two persons talking to each other has given permission to a third person to listen in on an extension phone; or police arrange for an informer to talk with a suspected person while they listen; or a switchboard operator listens to calls on company telephones by persons believed to be defrauding the company. Whether information obtained in such situations may be presented as evidence in court must be decided by the presiding judge.

In one case[2] in which the judge had to decide, police had answered the telephone while they were on a raid, and without revealing their identities, they carried on a conversation with the caller. The judge permitted the police to testify at the trial regarding what they had learned about the

---

2. Belleci v. United States, 184 F 2d 394 (D.C. Cir. 1950).

intended recipient of the call ruling that in this situation there had been no interception.

In another case, a man named Rathbun was charged with making a threatening statement in an interstate call in an attempt at extortion. The victim had permitted federal agents to listen to the call on an extension telephone. The agents were permitted to testify in court as to the threat. The judge admitted the evidence they gave, and his decision was sustained by both the Court of Appeals and the U.S. Supreme Court.[3]

One of the first cases arising under Section 605 centered on the words "no person" in the law. The government argued that federal agents could intercept calls and testify as to the content of such calls because of sovereign immunity the federal government was not included in the terms of the Act. "Not so," stated the U.S. Supreme Court, ruling that the prohibition against wiretapping applies to federal officers and agents as well as to other persons.[4] In the same year, the Supreme Court ruled that Section 605 applies to intrastate as well as to interstate communication.[5]

Although the Section mentions only communication by wire or radio, electronic surveillance goes beyond tapping telegraph and telephone lines and listening to radio communication. For example, in one case federal agents installed a dictograph on the wall of a suspect's room and were able to hear conversations from outside. The court held that overhearing statements by the suspect during a telephone conversation did not constitute interception. The judge based his ruling on the view that the law was enacted to protect a specific method of communication and the interception must be by that method to be illegal.[6]

---

3. Rathbun v. United States, 355 U.S. 107 (1957).
4. Nardone v. United States, 302 U.S. 379 (1937); Nordone v. United States, 308 U.S. 338 (1939).
5. Weiss v. United States, 308 U.S. 321 (1939).
6. Goldman v. United States, 316 U.S. 129 (1942).

In another case, a police informer wearing a small radio transmitter entered a laundry to talk with a suspect named Lee. The conversation was broadcast to a treasury agent some distance away. The agent was permitted to testify at the trial regarding what he had heard; and that decision was upheld by the U.S. Supreme Court.[7]

The Supreme Court has also been confronted with the question of whether wiretapping and other forms of electronic eavesdropping are constitutional. Among cases it considered was one in 1953 in which it held that although evidence obtained in wiretapping was not admissible in federal courts, it could be used in state courts.[8] Then 15 years later in 1968 it decided that information obtained illegally by wiretapping could not be used in either state or federal court.[9]

In 1967 the Supreme Court, although still divided on the matter, issued two landmark decisions in which it abandoned the view stated in Olmstead that electronic surveillance and wiretapping are not "searches and seizures" within the scope of the Fourth Amendment. Now it held that they definitely are.

In one case it struck down as unconstitutional a New York law that permitted court-ordered eavesdropping, ruling that although the Fourth Amendment does not absolutely prohibit such searches and seizures "it does prescribe a constitutional standard that must be met before official invasion is permissible."[10] Justice Tom C. Clark stated in the majority opinion that "few threats to liberty exist than the one posed by the use of eavesdropping devices."

In the other case, FBI agents had used an electronic device attached to a telephone booth in Los Angeles to listen and record what Charles Katz said when he gave information on

7. Lee v. United States, 343 U.S. 747 (1952).
8. Schwartz v. Texas, 344 U.S. 199 (1953).
9. Lee v. Florida, 392 U.S. 378 (1968).
10. Berger v. New York, 388 U.S. 41 (1967).

bets and wagers to locations in Boston and Miami. Katz was convicted, but the Supreme Court reversed the conviction,[11] ruling that telephone and other private conversations are protected by the Fourth Amendment, and that eavesdropping by government must be authorized by court warrants to be legal. That was a reversal of the ruling almost 40 years earlier in the Olmstead decision. The Court stated that while the agents had acted with restraint in that case, the restraints must be authorized by a judicial official, not by officers doing the surveillance.

That is a significant point in regard to the American system of justice. As a nation of law, actions and decisions of authorities must conform to law, not to the beliefs and desires of persons in power. When police officers, for example, go beyond the law in their zeal to apprehend criminals, they are violating a basic principle of American government.

That was illustrated in 1972 when Attorney General Richard Kleindienst was asked about the federal government's use of wiretapping without prior judicial approval. He was reported to have said, "Our duty is to prosecute persons who commit crimes. We are acting in good faith."

That was the kind of thinking that got Oliver North in difficulty in connection with the Iran-Contra scandal in the 1980s. He, too, acted in what he considered good faith, but illegally. Kleindienst was forced to resign a year later on April 30, 1973 along with other aides to President Nixon amid charges that the White House was obstructing justice in the Watergate scandal. North was convicted in 1989 on three counts of obstructing Congress, destroying documents, and accepting an illegal gratuity. The next year a U. S. District Court judge dismissed the case against him because Congress had granted North limited immunity.

---

11. Katz v. United States, 389 U.S. 347 (1967).

"Eavesdrop" has been part of the English language for almost four centuries. Eavesdropping, illegal in England in the time of Blackstone and disapproved elsewhere, became easier after the development of the telegraph and the invention of the telephone as it was then no longer necessary to stand under the eaves to listen secretly to private conversation inside the house.

Telegraphy dates back to 1844 and the telephone to 1876 when it was exhibited at the Centennial Exposition in Philadelphia. Telephone use developed rapidly, with the first switchboard for commercial use installed two years later in New Haven, Connecticut. In the early days and for years later tapping telegraph and telephone lines was relatively easy with the wires strung on poles outdoors.

The advantage of tapping telegraph and telephone lines to obtain information before the information becomes widely known was soon recognized by unscrupulous bookmakers betting on distant horse races or boxing matches, and by stock brokers, news reporters, and military intelligence officers. It was considered so important militarily that General Jeb Stuart is reported to have had his own personal telegraph wiretapper travel with him in the field in the Civil War.

Wiretapping and bugging have always been highly tempting, virtually irresistible. As early as 1895, New York police were tapping telephone lines.

Illegal for more than 30 years after the Federal Communication Act of 1934 became law, electronic surveillance continued. The attitude of officials regarding its use has been ambivalent, at least at the federal level. Some U. S. attorneys general have opposed wiretapping. In the wake of the Teapot Dome scandal in 1924, Harlan Stone banned all wiretapping, a decision approved by President Herbert Hoover who called the practice "unethical." Ramsey Clark, attorney general in the Kennedy administration, recommended legislation to prohibit virtually all wiretapping and bugging.

At the state level California enacted legislation as early as

1862 prohibiting the interception of telegraph messages. By the turn of the century a number of states still forbade the use of that method of gathering evidence.

The first wiretapping by a federal agency was in 1908 by the newly created Bureau of Investigation, which later became the Federal Bureau of Investigation (the FBI).[12]

Wiretaps were used extensively during the Prohibition Era in attempts to enforce liquor laws and to apprehend violators. Also wire tapping was widely used as a result of the "Red Scare" in the early 1920s. It was at that time that J. Edgar Hoover started a massive card index file on dissenters and dissidents, with the approval of Attorney General A. Mitchell Palmer.

In 1940 President Roosevelt instructed Attorney General Robert Jackson to use wiretapping to discover any espionage plans of the "Nazi Fifth Column" in this country. The action was no doubt illegal, but it was kept secret from the public. Six years later in 1946, Attorney General Tom C. Clark obtained permission from President Truman to let the FBI use wiretaps on suspected subversives and major criminals, an action also kept secret.

Robert F. Kennedy, after becoming attorney general in 1961, became convinced that organized crime was this country's greatest threat; and he urged the use of "technical equipment" in fighting organized crime. As a result, Hoover

---

12. The information here on eavesdropping by federal officials is largely from "Reflections on Six Years of Legitimated Electronic Surveillance," by Herman Schwartz, Professor of Law, State University of New York at Buffalo, published in *Privacy in a Free Society*, Final Report — Annual Chief Justice Earl Warren Conference on Advocacy in the United States, June 7-8, 1974, Sponsored by the Roscoe Pound-American Trial Lawyers Foundation.

   Another reference is *The Eavesdroppers* by Samuel Dash, De Capo Press, 1971. Also, *The Rights of Americans*, Norman Dorsen, Ed., Pantheon Books, 1971.

intensified bugging and tapping. In May of that year, the FBI had 67 bugs and 85 taps in place, according to a reliable report; almost all installed illegally because they involved break-ins.

In the thirty-some years after the Federal Communications Act of 1934 became law, scores of bills to regulate wiretapping were introduced in Congress. Finally one became law. It is the Omnibus Crime Control and Safe Streets Act, which became effective on June 19, 1968. Title III of the Act legalized certain kinds of eavesdropping for the first time in the history of the United States. The atmosphere conducive to the enactment of a law to regulate electronic eavesdropping was created in large measure by "the war on organized crime" led by Attorney General Robert F. Kennedy earlier in that decade.

The preamble of the law promised that electronic surveillance would be used sparingly, but that was not the case. Statistics show, for example, that in the six-year period from passage of the act in 1968 to 1973, a total of 3,490 wire taps were installed by state and federal agencies, with conversations of 2,131,437 persons monitored.

The law veers in two directions by placing limits to protect the rights of citizens, and by giving almost unlimited authority to the government. In general, the law requires officers to go before a judge and obtain court approval to tap a telephone line or to use electronic surveillance on a suspect. Without the judicial order, the surveillance is illegal, with evidence so obtained inadmissible in court. The law allows persons whose telephones are tapped illegally to sue for damages. In fact, anyone who taps a line illegally risks going to jail or paying a fine or both.

Under the law, a court order to wiretap is harder to get than a search warrant. Officers applying for the order must provide detailed justification and already have practically enough evidence to arrest the suspect. No wiretap order may be for longer than 30 days.

All private wiretapping and bugging with radio devices

are prohibited under the Act. The law lists specific classes of communication that may legally be interpreted and a list of crimes for which electronic surveillance may be used in investigation. It grants states the right to enact similar legislation to allow their police to use electronic surveillance.

Tappers are prohibited from listening to conversations unrelated to the crime they are investigating. A suspect must be informed within 90 days after the court order expires that he or she has been tapped; and police doing the tapping may be required to provide the suspect with a full transcript of any evidence they obtained.

The flip side of the protection the law provides for suspected persons is a section that gives broad, almost unlimited, authority to the President of the United States. It reads:

■ Nothing contained in this chapter or in section 605 of the Communications Act of 1934 (48 Stat. 1143; 47 U.S.C. 605) shall limit the consitutional power of the President to take such measures as he deems necessary to protect the Nation against actual or potential attack or other hostile acts of a foreign power, to obtain foreign intelligence information deemed essential to the security of the United States, or to protect national security information against foreign intelligence activites. Nor shall anything contained in this chapter be deemed to limit the consitutional power of the President to take such measures as he deems necessary to protect the United States against the overthrow of the Government by force or other unlawful means, or against any other clear and present danger to the structure or existence of the Government. The contents of any wire or oral communication intercepted by authority of the President in the exercise of the foregoing powers may be received in evidence in any trial hearing, or other proceeding only where such interception was reasonable, and shall not be otherwise used or disclosed except as is necessary to implement that power.

The section can be questioned on two counts. One is

"national security," which can be interpreted so broadly that it can include whatever the President desires. The other, "the power of the President to take such measure as he deems necessary," appears to give the President virtually dictatorial powers.

During the administration of Richard Nixon, which ran from 1969 to 1974, a time marked by widespread protests to the war in Vietnam, large numbers of Americans were subjected to eavesdropping in the name of national security because Nixon and Attorney General John Mitchell considered them dangerous. Under that administration, officials of the Department of Justice claimed an inherent right in the office of the President to eavesdrop on radical groups and suspected dissidents without first obtaining judicial warrants to do so.

Both President Nixon and Attorney General Mitchell have been criticized for such action but this section of the Omnibus Crime Control and Safe Streets Act may appear to have given them authority to eavesdrop without prior court approval.

The Justice Department in the Nixon Administration, with John Mitchell as Attorney General, held that the term "national security" in the Omnibus Crime law applied not just to foreign powers but also to radical domestic protest groups. Consequently, it was not necessary to obtain prior court warrants to eavesdrop on groups of that kind.

Not so, ruled the U.S. Supreme Court in a decision of a case in which three members of the White Panthers were tried for bombing a CIA office in Ann Arbor, Michigan in 1968.[13]

One of the three, Lawrence (Pun) Plamondon, co-founder of the radical White Panthers, learned that his group had been wiretapped; and he demanded to know what they learned from the taps. The government lawyers refused to give him

---

13. United States vs. District Court, Eastern Michigan, 407 U.S. 297 (June 19, 1972).

that information, arguing that even though the taps had been installed without court-ordered warrants, the warrants were not necessary in cases involving a threat to "national security." A judge, Damon J. Keith, of a Federal District Court, ruled that if the government wished to prosecute Plamondon, it would first have to let him know what it had heard by wiretapping, so no illegally obtained evidence would be used against him.[14]

Challenging the government in this case were William Gossett, former president of the American Bar Association, and Abraham Sofaer, associate professor at Columbia School of Law. They argued that all electronic searches without warrants are clearly in violation of the Fourth Amendment.

The case eventually reached the U.S. Supreme Court, where U.S. Solicitor General Erwin Griswold argued that radical protests within the United States are interrelated with security threats from other countries. In using the wiretaps, he said, the government was only gathering intelligence to protect the nation, not just gathering evidence for criminal prosecution.

In a decision handed down June 19, 1972, the Supreme Court by a vote of 6 to 2, ruled against the government. In the majority opinion, written by Justice Lewis F. Powell Jr., the Court rejected the Justice Department's claim that it did not have to get court approval for electronic surveillance of persons or domestic groups suspected to be subverse.

"The price of lawful public dissent must not be a dread of subjection to unchecked surveillance power," the Court stated. "Nor must the fear of unauthorized official eavesdropping deter vigorous citizen dissent and discussion of government action in private conversation . . private dissent, no less than

---

14. *Time*, March 6, 1972, page 56.

open discussion, is essential to our free society."

"We cannot accept the government's argument that internal security matters are too subtle and complex for judicial evaluation," the opinion stated.

In commenting on the decision, a Justice Department spokesman said, "We took the position that you cannot separate foreign from domestic threats, and we still believe that."

CHAPTER

24

❀

YOU DON'T NEED A LICENSE TO SPEAK OR WRITE

YOU DON'T NEED A LICENSE
TO SPEAK OR WRITE

❊

Johannes Gutenberg and his associates could not have predicted the controversy that would arise over freedom vs. control of the press when they perfected the process of printing by movable type back in the middle of the 15th Century in Germany. For many years government and church officials regarded the printing press as an instrument of the devil, not a blessing for mankind, and some of that feeling still lingers more than five centuries later.

One person making disloyal, seditious, and heretical statements could easily be silenced by being thrown in jail, beheaded, or burned at the stake; but the press added a new and alarming dimension to thought dispersal. A person speaking could be heard by only a relatively few persons, especially in the days before radio and television, but a printing press could turn out hundreds, even thousands, of copies of rebellious or blasphemous publications for wide distribution. Also, while the spoken word can be heard only once and by those present, printing has permanence in that it can be read over and over and passed from person to person. Officials saw that as a real danger.

In 1476, not many years after Gutenberg's invention, a printing press was set up in England by William Caxton; and printing there was quickly declared a prerogative of the Crown. Two kinds of controls were established. One was censorship, which meant that all material to be printed had to be approved in advance by the government. The other was licensing, which meant that no press was permitted to operate without first obtaining a license from the government.

License means permission to act, to carry on a particular kind of work or activity. It also means that the government that issues the licenses can say who may engage in a particular kind of activity or business and who may not do so.

When the state requires a license for driving a car, it dictates who may legally drive. A person who drives without a driver's license is breaking the law. Numerous professions, occupations, and businesses are licensed. Doctors, nurses, lawyers, teachers, real estate brokers, and many others cannot legally engage in their kind of work without being licensed to do so. Licensing is primarily done to protect the public against incompetent treatment and workmanship, but it incidentally provides income for the state plus control.

It should be noted that in recent years the word "certificate" has replaced "license" in some kinds of occupations, but the meaning is the same. A certificate is a document that certifies that the person it is issued to has fulfilled requirements set by the state and thus may legally engage in a specific kind of profession or occupation.

The licensing of printing was required for many years in England and in the American colonies governed by England. Henry VIII, King of England from 1509 to 1547, issued a proclamation in 1534 requiring the licensing of books before they were printed, and that requirement was later extended to include all publications.

The notorious Star Chamber was established as a court in 1487 especially to handle cases of publication without government approval and cases of treasonable speech — and speaking or writing critically of the king was considered an act of treason. The Star Chamber, noted for severity of punishment and trial without jury, continued for more than 150 years until it was abolished in 1641.

Even then, government control of printing continued. The prevailing legal attitude at that time is revealed in an opinion of an English court in 1680, which read in part:

■ We did subscribe, that to print or publish any newspaper or pamphlet of news whatsoever is illegal; that it is a manifest intent to the breach of peace, and they may be proceeded against the law for an illegal thing.

The court opinion further stated that "even though the publication is not scandalous, it is still illegal and the author ought to be punished." The opinion further added that "this is a public notice to all people, and especially to printers and booksellers, that they ought to print no book or pamphlet whatsoever, without authority."

One of the most eloquent, thoughtful arguments in opposition to such restraint was made by John Milton, English poet and author, after the Parliament reestablished censorship of the press in June 1643. Titled *Areopagitica*,[1] it is a plea for reason and for liberty of unlicensed printing.

In it, Milton says, "Who kills man kills a reasonable creature, God's image; but he who destroys a good book, kills reason itself."

He placed freedom of thought first among freedoms. "Give me liberty to know, to utter, and to argue freely according to conscience, above all liberties."

The publication of falsehoods should not be feared, he wrote, because truth given a fair chance would always triumph. "Though all the winds of doctrine were let loose to play upon the earth, so Truth be in the field, we do injuriously, by licensing and prohibiting, to misdoubt her strength. Let her and Falsehood grapple; who ever knew Truth put to the worse, in a free and open encounter."

The *Aeropagitica* was published in November 1644; but about 50 years would pass before Parliament refused in 1695

---

1. Subtitle: A Speech for the Liberty of Unlicensed Printing to the Parliament of England.

to reenact the law requiring licensing of the press. Even then, government control of the press continued for about a third of a century longer in the American colonies. Instructions to governors sent to the colonies included this statement regarding printing:

> ■ As great inconvenience may arise by liberty of printing within our said territory under your government you are to provide by all necessary orders that no person keep any printing-press for printing, nor that any book, pamphlet, or other matter whatsoever be printed without your especial leave and license first obtained.

Those instructions were strictly followed. The first newspaper ever published in the American colonies lasted just one day. It was called *Public Occurrences* and was published in Boston on September 25, 1690. It was immediately suppressed because it was not licensed and because it "contained reflections of a high nature," whatever that means. Fourteen years would pass before another attempt was made to publish a newspaper in the colonies and that time it succeeded. The *Boston News-Letter* published its first issue on April 24, 1704, and continued publication for the next 72 years.

As the framers of the U.S. Constitution were well aware of the evils of censorship and thought control, it is not surprising that they placed freedom of speech as The First Freedom in the Bill of Rights. Although the First Amendment prohibits licensing of printing, it does not prohibit licensing of occupations and businesses, with one notable exception: It would be a violation of the guarantee of free speech for the state to set qualifications and issue licenses for reporters, writers, editors, and speakers. In other words, there can be no such thing in this country as a certified or licensed reporter or editor or broadcast announcer or public speaker.

A printing company or a newspaper plant, however, has a dual nature. It is free from being licensed insofar as the content of its publications is concerned, but it is subject to being licensed to operate as a business, just as any other business can be licensed.

CHAPTER
25

❀

*BROADCASTING
IS LICENSED
COMMUNICATION*

BROADCASTING IS LICENSED COMMUNICATION

❧

Although a license by the government is not required to publish a newspaper, a magazine, or a book, it is required to operate a radio or television station, even an amateur station. The difference lies in the nature of the world in which we live.

There is really no physical limit to the number of publishing offices that can exist. They can be side by side, on top of one another, and all over town; but there is an absolute limit to the number of frequencies over which radio and television signals can be sent. Although the electronic spectrum has an enormous range of frequencies or wave lengths, only a portion can be used for broadcasting; and as the spectrum is a part of nature, it cannot be changed by any means. That being true, it was decided early on that broadcast frequencies are such a valuable natural resource that ownership by individuals and companies would not be permitted. Rather, they would belong to the people and be governed for their benefit by the federal government.

To use a frequency for broadcasting, a person or a company must obtain a license from the Federal Communications Commission, and the station for which the license is issued must "serve the public interest, convenience, and necessity." To make sure that a licensee understands that he does not own the frequency but is only licensed to use it, Section 304 of the Communications Act of 1934 states in part:

■ No station license shall be granted . . . until the

312

applicant therefor shall have signed a waiver of any claim
to the use of any particular frequency . . .

Only citizens of the United States are eligible for broadcast licenses. The law states that licenses "shall not be granted
to or held by any alien or the representative of any alien, any
foreign government or the representative thereof, or to any
corporation organized under the laws of any foreign government."

Government licensing of broadcasting extends only to
stations, including the assigning to each station the frequency
it must use in broadcasting. The licensing of broadcast
engineers, formerly required to assure that they were qualified to operate the transmitters, has been discontinued so that
now the FCC checks only to see that stations are broadcasting
on their assigned frequencies. Amateur radio operators are
still required to pass an examination to qualify for licensing.
No licenses are required for actors, writers, and directors, or
for anyone who speaks on radio or television.

That radio and television stations are licensed "to serve the
public interest, convenience, and necessity" rings hollow at
times in view of the enormous profits they have made over the
years and in view of much programming designed to attract
the largest audiences possible; but government steered toward that goal, although erratically at times, while allowing
broadcasting to operate as a profit-making industry. As early
as 1924, Herbert Hoover, as Secretary of Commerce,[1] said:

■ The Commission is convinced that the interest of the
broadcast listener is of superior importance to that of the
broadcaster . . . While it is true that broadcasting stations

---

1. Broadcasting was under control of the Department of Commerce in
those years; it is now an independent agency. Hoover served as
Secretary of the Department from 1921 to 1929. On March 4, 1929,
he was inaugurated President of the United States.

in this country are for the most part supported or partially supported by advertisers, broadcasting stations are not given these great privileges by the U.S. Government for the primary benefit of advertisers. Such benefit as is derived by advertisers must be incidental and entirely secondary to the interest of the public. The emphasis must be first and foremost on the interest, the convenience, and the necessity of the listening public, and not on the interest, convenience or necessity of the individual broadcaster or the advertiser.

Serving the public interest is laudable, but requiring a government license to communicate creates problems. Inherent in the power to license is the power to control, so government licensing of a medium of communication can infringe on the right of free speech guaranteed by the Constitution. To reconcile the necessity of licensing broadcast stations with the right of free speech, the Communications Act of 1934 includes a guarantee of freedom from government censorship. Section 326 reads:

■ Nothing in this Act shall be understood or construed to give the Commission the power of censorship over the radio communications or signals transmitted by any radio station, and no regulation or condition shall be promulgated or fixed by the Commission which shall interfere with the right of free speech by means of radio communication.

That guarantee of free speech is limited, however, by this clause:

■ No person within the jurisdiction of the United States shall utter any obscene, indecent, or profane language by means of radio communication.

Although 1920 is credited with being the year in which radio broadcasting to the public began, electromagnetic radiation which makes broadcasting possible was unknown to science until 1864 when its existence was predicted by James Clark Maxwell, a Scottish physicist. His theory was proven experimentally a few years later by Heinrich Rudolph Hertz, a German scientist who lived from 1857 to 1894 and in the 1890's demonstrated that electrical energy could be sent through the air in the form of waves.[2]

---

2. Broadcast signals, which become words, sounds, and pictures when they are received, are conveyed on electromagnetic waves that have length and frequency. The length of a wave is the distance from one crest to the next. The shorter the wave the higher the frequency, and the longer the wave the lower the frequency. When a wave goes from one crest to the next it completes a cycle. In broadcasting, frequencies are measured in cycles per second, and they range from thousands to millions and even to billions of cycles per seconds (cps).

Windblown waves on water are irregular; but electromagnetic waves remain constant at the length at which they are transmitted. All travel at the same velocity, which is the speed of light or about 186,282 miles per second.

The distance broadcast signals travel depends upon the power with which they are sent and the length of the waves. Shortwave signals or frequencies, for example, can reflect from the ionosphere back to earth and be received thousands of miles from the transmitter. FM and TV signals, on the other hand, are long and travel only in a line of sight, unable to cross mountains or follow the curvature of the earth.

The electromagnetic spectrum includes all kinds of electric and magnetic radiation, ranging from gamma rays, which have the shortest wave lengths, through X-rays, ultraviolet light, visible light which enables us to see things, infrared light, microwaves, and radio and television waves.

A spectrum is a continuum or range of entities. An example is the band of colors in a rainbow, or those produced when sunlight is passed through a prism, showing colors ranging from violet to deep red with blue, blue-green, green, yellow-green, yellow, orange, and red in that order between. Each color, it may be noted, has its own wave length, with violet the shortest and red the longest among the colors. Sunlight, as is well known, is a blend of "all the colors of

By that time electricity had been in use in communication for twenty years but only over metal lines, not through the air. Samuel F.B. Morse, inventor of the telegraph, had succeeded in sending a message 1,700 feet on September 2, 1837, and spent the next seven years improving his invention, financed in part by an appropriation by Congress. On May 24, 1844, the first message was sent by telegraph over a line from the Supreme Court chamber in the Capitol in Washington, D. C., to Baltimore. It read "What hath God wrought?" It wasn't until 1876 that the first complete sentence was transmitted by telephone, the invention of Alexander Graham Bell. Those were years of "firsts," with radio and television soon to follow.

It would be difficult if not impossible to list the names of all the hundreds, probably thousands, of persons who contributed to the development of electronic communication.

---

the rainbow." All other forms of radiation, including ultraviolet, infrared, and x-rays, gamma rays, and radio waves, are invisible.

Wave lengths, particularly those of light, are measured in angstrom units, with each unit equal to one ten-millionth of a meter. In the early days of radio, broadcast waves were measured in kilocycles, not angstroms, with the word "kilo" meaning one thousand. Thus, one kilocycle indicated 1,000 cycles. That has been changed so that today frequency or cycles-per-second are written in Hertz, usually abbreviated to Hz. The number accompanying the abbreviation indicates the position in the electromagnetic spectrum. A radio station listed as 820 on the AM dial, for example, is located at 820 Hz in the spectrum. Television broadcasting occupies a much larger part of the spectrum than does radio, so the word "channel" is used to indicate a wider band than that of a radio frequency.

Besides kHz indicating thousands of cps, higher frequencies are indicated by MHz, with M in the abbreviation for million; GHz, with G the abbreviation for Giga indicating a thousand million (a billion); and THz, with T the abbreviation for Tera indicating a million (a trillion) cps. Frequencies for broadcasting range from below 3 kHz to 300 GHz.

Guglielmo Marconi, an Italian electrical engineer, is credited with inventing the wireless telegraph and with sending and receiving the first wireless signals in 1895. By 1899 wireless telegraphy had advanced so far that Marconi was sending messages across the English Channel from England, and by 1901 the first telegraphy messages were sent across the Atlantic Ocean.

An Englishman, Sir John Fleming, invented the diode rectifier tube in 1905; and an American, Lee de Forest, the triode amplifier vacuum tube in 1906 and the radio tube oscillator in 1915, inventions essential in broadcasting.

In the early part of this century wireless messages were sent only as telegraph signals, as Morse code dots and dashes. When radio broadcasting began, it was called "radiotelegraphy" and later shortened to "radio."[3] The word "wireless" is still used by some in England.

Dramatic use of the wireless telegraph came with the sinking of the S.S. Titanic on April 14-15, 1912, after striking an iceberg in the North Atlantic. Wireless operators sent messages in Morse code, directing nearby ships to rescue passengers from the Titanic and relaying news of rescue operations to the world. Their actions contributed to saving 705 lives, and it demonstrated the usefulness of ship-to-ship and ship-to-shore wireless telegraphy.

Among the operators was a young man named David Sarnoff, who received wide publicity for his part. He had learned Morse code at age 17, and he was on duty at the American Marconi Company office in New York City when the SOS call came in. For the next 72 hours he sat at his set sending and receiving messages regarding the disaster.

Sarnoff, who was born in Minsk, Russia, in 1891, and

---

3. The word "radio" referring to radiant energy was first used in or about 1887. In 1903 it was first used to mean broadcasting. The word "television" first appeared in print in 1907.

came to the U.S. when he was nine years of age, became an outstanding leader in the development of broadcasting, serving as president of RCA beginning in 1930 and as chairman of the Board from 1947 until his retirement in 1969.

The use of the broadcast media for public benefit in time of emergency was recognized early on and is protected by Section 606 of the Communications Act by giving the President of the United States the power virtually to take over any or all stations. The Section reads:

■ Upon proclamation by the President that there exists war or a threat of war or a state of public peril or disaster or other national emergency, or in order to preserve the neutrality of the United States, the President may suspend or amend, for such time as he may see fit, the rules and regulations applicable to any or all stations . . . and may cause the closing of any station. . .

The first two decades of this century saw a number of firsts in scientific development, including the first transcontinental airplane flight in September-October 1911 and the first transcontinental telephone conversation on January 25, 1915, between New York and Pasadena. Transmission of voice by radio developed gradually during those years, so that by 1915 the Bell Telephone Company of Arlington, Virginia, was conducting voice experiments across the Atlantic Ocean. An experimental radio station was established at the University of Wisconsin in 1915 and in Pittsburgh in 1916.

There is disagreement as to which radio station was first to begin broadcasting to the public on a regular basis. Westinghouse station KDKA in Pittsburgh received a commercial license for code transmission on October 27, 1920, and authority to experiment with voice for one year. On November 2 that year it made history by broadcasting the returns of the Harding-Cox presidential election returns. WBZ in Springfield, Mass., was issued the first regular broadcast license on September 15, 1921, and KDKA received a regular license later that year.

The growth of radio was explosive. By 1924 the listening audience numbered 20 million; and by the next year there were more than 500 stations on the air, with a backlog of license applications pending.[4] The exact number broadcasting in those days is unknown, for two reasons. One lay in determining what constituted a bona fide radio station, as all kinds were on the air. Numerous broadcasters operated small stations on an amateur basis, with programs planned only a few minutes before going on the air and on no regular schedule. The other reason is that many broadcasters went on the air without obtaining a license, so the government had no accurate count.

Being able to hear music and voices out of the air from distant points was a phenomenon that fascinated virtually everyone. In the 1920s youngsters all over the country were building crystal receiving sets, and in rural homes without electricity listeners gathered around receiving sets powered by wet-cell batteries. The invention by Edwin A. Armstrong of the superheterodyne receiver, first demonstrated in 1922, was a giant step in making radio receiving sets popular.

Listeners in those days often were more interested in the

---

4. All were using the AM (amplitude modulation) system of broad casting. It wasn't until 1933 that static-free FM (frequency modulation) broadcasting was demonstrated by its inventor, Edwin Armstrong. On May 20, 1940, the FCC authorized FM broadcasting on a limited basis and on January 1, 1941, on a full basis. When the U.S. entered World War II in December that year, civilian use of FM radio was frozen, but FM was used extensively by the Armed Forces. After the war ended in 1945, its use was again authorized. In fact, the government gave some of its surplus equipment to colleges and universities that applied for it.

stations and their locations than in what was being broadcast.[5] Keeping a log of the stations they could hear was common, and some stations actually went off the air occasionally to enable people in their localities to tune in to distant stations and thus add more call letters to their lists.

Some of the first broadcast stations were operated by colleges and universities, some by newspapers to increase circulation and advertising, others by department stores and other outlets that sold radios, and, of course, by such manufacturers of radio receiving sets as Westinghouse and General Electric.

A fascinating example of the establishment of a radio station to promote the sale of radios was that of Roy H. Thomson in Canada. As a young man he had the rather discouraging job in the late 1920s of trying to sell De Forest Crosley radios in and around North Bay, Ontario, to farmers and miners who could hear little but static because they were so distant from any radio station.

Thomson obtained a broadcast license, borrowed about $600, and with makeshift equipment started a small broadcast station in North Bay. With the call letters CFCH, it went on the air in 1931. With it he was able to promote the sale of radios and also to sell advertising time to other businesses. Within three years he had two more stations in operation in Ontario, CKGB in Timmins and CJKL in Kirkland Lake; and in 1934 with a down payment of $200 he took possession of *The Press*, a weekly newspaper in Timmins.

Those four acquisitions marked the beginning of a world-wide communications empire. Within the next 30 years Thomson had parlayed his holdings to become owner of more newspapers than anyone else in the world and had been made

---

5. A parallel was the early motion pictures. The phenomenon of pictures actually moving was entrancing; the scene or film content was incidental and of much less interest.

a Baron by the Queen of England before his death on August 4, 1976. By 1967 there were 138 Thomson newspapers in seven countries, including 41 in Canada, 27 in the United States, and 55 in Great Britain.[6] His holdings also included eight radio stations and seven television stations; 138 magazines, including 62 in Britain and 76 in South Africa; six book publishing companies and 19 printing companies; and various other businesses.

Although broadcasting eventually became of age and a powerful force in American life, in its infancy in the early 1920s it was so freewheeling under lax government control that by the middle of the decade chaos ruled the airwaves. Stations changed frequencies, went on and off the air, and increased or decreased power as they chose. The major reason for that condition lay in two court decisions that diminished the authority of the government to regulate the industry.

The first law Congress passed to regulate broadcasting was designed to protect passengers at sea rather than controlling domestic radio. The Wireless Act of 1910 forbade all ships of U.S. registry carrying 50 or more passengers to leave a port in this country without "efficient apparatus for radiocommunications, in good working order," capable of transmitting and receiving code for 100 miles.

Two years later Congress passed the Radio Act of 1912, which placed the licensing of radio stations and radio operators under the Department of Commerce and Labor.[7] The law gave the Department the responsibility of assigning frequencies, but it provided only minimum authority to govern

---

6. By November 1991 the number had grown to 123 daily newspapers in the United States and 38 in Canada, with a total daily circulation of 3.5 million, plus numerous community weeklies and shoppers. The story of Thomson's life is told in *Roy Thomson of Fleet Street* by Russell Braddon, Walker, New York, 1966, 396 pages.
7. Labor became a separate Department on March 4, 1913.

broadcasting.

The weakness of the law was revealed when broadcasting showed promise of becoming a major industry. In 1923 in the case of *Hoover v. Intercity Radio Company, Inc.*, the U.S. District Court in Washington, D.C., ruled that the Department of Commerce must issue a broadcast license to a qualified applicant, even though that would probably lead to interference with the signals of other stations.

Three years later a decision by a U.S. District Court in Illinois virtually ended regulation the Radio Act of 1912 was supposed to provide. The case, *United States v. Zenith Radio Corporation et al*, had its origins in an action by the Department of Commerce limiting the Zenith Radio Corporation to two hours of broadcast time per week from its Chicago station. The Corporation was assigned a specific frequency for use only from 10 p.m. to midnight on Thursdays and then only when the use of that frequency was not desired at that time by a station in Denver owned by the General Electric Company.

When Zenith ignored the assignment and broadcast whenever it chose, the Department of Commerce brought criminal court action against the Corporation. The U.S. District Court for the Northern District of Illinois dismissed the case on July 9, 1926, holding that "the Secretary of Commerce has no power to impose restrictions as to frequency, power, or hours of operation" and that "a station's use of a frequency not assigned to it is not a violation of the Radio Act of 1912."

In the meantime the government was attempting to establish guidelines for this new industry by holding National Radio Conferences in 1922, 1923, 1924, and 1925; and out of those conferences came recommendations for legislation. Two years later the Radio Act of 1927 was passed by Congress requiring that an applicant must not only be able to satisfy the express conditions of the law regarding the issuance of licenses but also prove to the satisfaction of the Federal Radio Commission that present, or contemplated, operation would serve "the public interest, convenience, and necessity." The Act established a Federal Radio Commission to determine policy.

The need for effective government regulation is illustrated by the use, or misuse, of radio in its early days by a certain Dr. John Richard Brinkley, a medical quack who became nationally known for his "goat-gland implants" to rejuvenate the sexual powers of men.

With mail-order medical school degrees, he set up a small hospital in 1918 in Milford, Kansas, in which to perform the surgery. In 1923 he obtained one of the two most powerful radio transmitters in the United States for his station, KFKB, which he used to promote his "medical cures" and became rich in the process. Men came from all parts of the country for the "cure," and at one time he was performing about 50 goat-gland operations a week, at $750 each.

In 1928 he began a Medical Question Box on his radio station to peddle prescriptions by mail. For a half hour three times a day he would read letters over the air from listeners who wrote to him describing their symptoms. His secretary would choose as many letters as she thought he needed for a broadcast; and the doctor would pick them up on his way to the microphone, read them on the air, and make instant diagnoses. His response to a letter might read:[8]

■ Now here is a letter from a dear mother — a dear little mother who holds to her breast a babe of nine months. She should take Number 2 and Number 16 and — yes — Number 17, and she will be helped. If her druggist hasn't got them, she should write and order them from the Milford Drug Company, Milford, Kansas, and they will be sent to you, Mother, collect. May the Lord guard and

---

8. Gerald Carson, *The Roguish World of Dr. Brinkley,* Rinehard & Co., 1960. See also *Medical Economics* magazine, December 5, 1960, pages 239-292.

protect you, Mother. The postage will be prepaid.

Dr. Brinkley enlarged his business by placing his medicines in drugstores across the country, rather than handling all orders through his own in Milford, with each druggist receiving $1 for each prescription of his that was sold. The business was indeed lucrative, with income from drugs averaging about $10,000 a week.

At the time he was "on a roll." So many people were listening to his broadcasts that *Radio Digest* magazine awarded KFKB its Gold Cup for being the most popular station in the United States. But it was not to last. In 1930 the Federal Radio Commission revoked his broadcast license on the grounds that his programming was "not in the public interest"; and in the same year the Kansas State Board of Medical Registration revoked his license to practice medicine.

Although those were setbacks, Dr. Brinkley was ingenious. He handed his scalpels over to his assistants; and he was able to establish a radio station, XERF, in Mexico across the Rio Grande river from Del Rio, Texas, where he continued his broadcasts by telephone line from Milford. The radio station, broadcasting with 180,000 watts could be heard throughout most of the United States and was reputed to be the most powerful radio station in the world.

He continued in business for the next ten years, but gradually his practice declined, he lost his Mexican broadcast license, and went bankrupt in 1941. He suffered a heart attack that year, and on May 26, 1942, he died at the age of 56.

The Radio Act of 1927, inadequate for the rapidly expanding world of electronic communication, was replaced seven years later by the Federal Communications Act of 1934. That Act established the Federal Communications Commission as a permanent independent Federal agency governed by seven members, or commissioners, appointed by the President of the United States with staggered terms of seven years each. Although amended a number of times, the Act continues to govern broadcasting today.

The Act gives the FCC authority over all aspects of electronic communication, including not only radio and television but also telephone, telegraph, cable, satellite, and facsimile transmission. It gives the FCC such powers over radio and television broadcasting as authority to issue station licenses, assign frequencies, set the power a station may use and the hours it may be on the air daily, monitor broadcasts, levy fines for violations, and limit the minutes for commercials per hour. The power to grant licenses carries with it the power to revoke or refuse to renew them; and although that power has seldom been used, broadcasters are well aware that it exists.

Despite strictures exercised by the FCC, or perhaps because of them, radio enjoyed a Golden Age during the 1930s and 1940s, becoming America's first universal medium of communication and an extremely popular method of entertainment. The entire country became accustomed to listening to the news, and practically all activity stopped while the 15-minute *Fresh Air Taxicab Company* comedy sketches by Amos and Andy were on the air at noon and in the evening. They began broadcasting the sketches on the NBC network in 1929 to an audience that soon reached an estimated 40 million.[9] The country became a land of listeners.

Children everywhere knew theme songs, commercials, and characters in such programs as *The Singing Lady, Little Orphan Annie, Jack Armstrong, Uncle Don,* and *Chandu the Magician.* Soap operas were born with *Ma Perkins, Backstage Wife,* and *Young Dr. Malone;* and such programs as *The Shadow, The Lone Ranger, The Mercury Theater, The Lux Radio Theater,* and the *Dupont Cavalcade of America* con-

---

9. Enormous when one remembers that the population of the United States in 1930 was only about 123 million, less than half of what it is now.

sistently drew large audiences.

Among radio performers who achieved fame were Rudy Vallee, Eddie Cantor, George Burns and Gracie Allen, Fibber McGee and Mollie, Jack Benny and Mary Livingstone, Edgar Bergan and Charlie McCarthy, Bob Hope, Ed Wynne, and Fred Allen. Announcers who became household names included Edward R. Murrow, Arthur Godfrey, Gabriel Heatter, Lowell Thomas, Elmer Davis, H.V. Kaltenborn, Graham McNamee, Fulton Lewis, Jr., and Douglas Edwards; and music by Paul Whiteman, Vincent Lopez, Rudy Vallee, and Wayne King became enormously popular.

CHAPTER
26

❀

TO OPERATE IN THE PUBLIC INTEREST

TO OPERATE IN THE PUBLIC INTEREST

❧

The United States is virtually the only country to license broadcasting to operate for profit and at the same time to serve the public interest. Aside from the Postal Service, communication in this country began as and continues to be private commercial enterprises. Telephone, telegraph, cable, radio, television, facsimile transmission, and, for the most part, satellite communication are all operated for profit in the United States, in contrast to countries where most or all communications media are government monopolies or are government controlled. Broadcasting in Great Britain,[1] Canada, West Germany, and Japan, as examples, began as

---

1. The British Broadcasting Corporation (BBC), which has served as a standard for Western television, is still supported by viewers, except for BBC World Service, which is supported by the Ministry of Foreign and Commonwealth Affairs. A license fee of £77 for color and £ 25.5 for black and white is charged each household with television annually.

   BBC is not a monopoly, however. The Independent Television (ITV) network, supported by advertising, has been the chief competitor of BBC since 1955. This is Channel 3, which is divided among 10 companies on a regional basis. Channel 4 is also commercial and broadcasts nationally.

   In 1986 France granted private status to one of the three government controlled television channels in that country, but limited the amount of advertising they may carry.

government operations. Advertising-supported broadcasting was introduced later, but from the start the people in those countries became accustomed to paying a fee for owning radio and television sets.

Advertising as a means of support and source of profit for broadcasting was not immediately recognized or even favored in America when radio first went on the air. In its infancy the industry had serious doubts about advertising of any kind in the belief that radio should not be used for that purpose. A program on August 22, 1922, however, changed that by revealing the potential of advertising. The program was a paid commercial announcement, probably the first on radio, consisting of a 10-minute talk on Station WEAF in New York City on behalf of the Queensborough Corporation, a real estate firm. The station charged $50 for the time. As a result of that "commercial," the Corporation sold two buildings in the Borough of Queens. Within a few years commercials and sponsored programs had become the primary source of income in broadcasting.

While radio broadcasting was still in its infancy in the 1920s, experimentation had already begun in television, with numerous scientists and inventors contributing to its development. References disagree on the date of the first successful transmission of images by electromagnetic waves; but Charles Francis Jenkins, an inventor, is credited with sending a still picture from one room to another in 1922.[2] The next year he sent a recognizable picture of President Harding from Wash-

Noncommercial public broadcasting in the United States (PBS and NPR) is partially supported by public contributions and the government through the Corporation for Public Broadcasting. Also available on a fee basis are such entertainment cable networks as Home Box Office, the Disney Channel, Cinemax, Showtime, and the Movie Channel.

2. David Lachenbruch, "They Called It Radiomovies," *TV Guide*, July 3, 1971 .

ington, D.C., to Philadelphia; and on July 2, 1928, he began telecasting animated films showing silhouettes of children, dolls, and fairies one hour a day three days a week in Washington. He insisted on calling the process "radiovision," claiming that "television" meant sending signals by wire while radiovision meant sending signals by radio waves.

Jenkins and other experimenters used an invention by Paul Nipkow, which consisted of a spinning disk with 48 spiral holes near its outer edge to disassemble a scene into dots and a similar spinning disk at the receiving end to reassemble the scene. That was superseded by the invention of the iconoscope by Vladimir Zworykin, a Russian émigré who worked at Westinghouse.[3] His invention, patented in 1923, was the forerunner of the television camera and made possible the cathode ray tube which reproduces images on television receivers.

---

3. Television cameras and receivers, based on Sworykin's invention and on developments by Philo Farnsworth, record and display pictures by means of streams of electronic particles called electrons. The viewing screen of a television receiving set is coated with phosphor dots which glow when struck by electrons propelled by a cathode ray tube called an electron gun. The electron beam sweeps the 525 lines on the screen (625 lines in European television sets) 30 times a second, scanning from left to right and top to bottom so rapidly that the movement appears smooth. A color receiving set has three electron guns, one for each of the primary colors, red, blue, and yellow. The dots on the screen glow with their respective colors when struck by electron beams.

   High definition television (HDTV) is currently under development with promise to equal, or at least closely approach, the quality of wide-screen movies and sound of compact disks. One system under study transmits analog signals as waves, with 1,125 lines on the television screen. The other employs digital technology in transmitting signals. High definition television has potential use in screens for personal computers, medical imaging systems, and in future military systems such as radar screens. Zenith and A.T. & T. successfully transmitted HDTV signals from Milwaukee to

By 1931 the Federal Radio Commission had issued licenses for 26 experimental television stations, few if any of which broadcasted with any regularity. Among them was one operated by NBC with an antenna atop the Empire State Building, broadcasting the cartoon "Felix the Cat" as its first program on the air. CBS soon had an experimental station in operation with the antenna atop the Chrysler Building. Television screens were tiny in those days, and pictures were gray and flickering, in contrast to the large screens and clear images that came later.

In Germany in 1936 Reichrundfunkgesellschaft (national broadcasting company) set up television sets in public rooms throughout Berlin so people could watch the ongoing Olympic Games at the time. By the next year BBC in London began offering regular television programming to about 14,000 subscribers.[4]

Interest in television increased dramatically with the broadcast of President Franklin D. Roosevelt speaking at the opening of the New York World's Fair on April 30, 1939. More than a thousand sets were sold in the next few weeks, presaging a bright future for the industry. In 1940 the 22nd Republican National Convention in Philadelphia was covered by television cameras, with Wendell Wilkie the first presidential candidate whose nomination was televised.

Television development, however, was suspended during World War II, which the United States entered immediately after the Japanese bombing of Pearl Harbor on December 7, 1941. On April 27, 1942, less than four months later, the FCC announced that because of wartime restrictions on labor and

---

Glenview, Illinois, on May 28, 1993, a distance of 75 miles, marking an important step in the development of high definition television.

4. Hans Fantel, "Television in the Beginning." *The New York Times*, May 7, 1989.

materials, it would grant no new television licenses or construction permits during the war. Broadcasting was limited, with only six commercial stations on the air for about four hours a week until after the war ended in 1945.

After that dormancy, television experienced astonishing growth. In 1946, a year after the war had ended, six stations were on the air. Two years later in 1948 there were 19 stations on the air at the beginning of the year with about 186,000 sets in use; by the end of the year almost 40 stations were broadcasting to more than a million sets. By 1950, the number of stations had reached 107, broadcasting in 61 markets. The number of stations grew from 422 in 1955 to 668 in 1965, to 862 in 1970, 941 in 1974, and continued to grow. In 1950, 3.8 million homes had television sets; by 1970 the number had reached 60.1 million; and by January 1, 1980, ninety eight percent of all households had at least one television set.

Broadcasting in color began in the early 1960s. By the 1965-66 season most programming by the three networks was in color, and within another year black-and-white programs had almost disappeared.

By the middle of 1993, according to *Broadcasting* magazine,[5] there were 11,397 radio and 1,541 television stations on the air in the United States, as follows:

Commercial AM Radio Stations	4,956
Commercial FM Radio Stations	4,836
Educational FM Radio Stations	1,605
Commercial VHF Television Stations	558
Commercial UHF Television Stations	592
Educational VHF Television Stations	124
Educational UHF Television Stations	240

In 1944 the FCC set aside 12 VHF and 70 UHF channels

---

5. *Broadcasting*, May 10, 1993, page 55.

for television, the number still available for broadcasting signals along the surface of the Earth. In addition, cable companies such as CNN and HBO broadcast via geostationary satellites 22,300 miles above the Earth, with signals that do not interfere with ground-level transmission. Cable has become a thriving business. By 1990 a total of 50,897,000 homes, 56.5 percent, in this country were subscribers. Cable reception, of course, includes stations of all kinds, not just those broadcasting by satellite. Technology is becoming available for cable systems to expand up to 150 channels by 1996.[6]

The number of television stations is expected to increase considerably with the addition of more with low power, perhaps an increase of as many as 4,000 by the end of this decade. Low-power stations are like other television stations, except that they are limited to a few thousand watts with signals that do not reach more than 25 miles. In contrast, full-power stations transmit at millions of watts of power, generating signals that reach as far as 70 miles.

By 1990 there were 809 low-power stations on the air, and the FCC had granted permits for 1,237 more. Low-power stations provide opportunity for more local programming, and they are advantageous to local advertisers because of low rates in contrast to the higher rates charged by full-power stations.

As television burgeoned after World War II, many people saw in that miracle of communication the potential for great beneficence for all mankind. E.B. White aptly expressed that hope in 1966 when he wrote that "television should be the visual counterpart of the literary essay."

Envisioning its potential, Mr. White said, "Television should arouse our dreams, satisfy our hunger for beauty, take

---

6. *The New York Times*, November 18, 1991.

us on journeys, enable us to participate in events, present great drama and music, and explore the sea and the sky and the woods and the hills. It should be our Lyceum, our Chautauqua, our Minsky's, and our Camelot."[7]

That television never fully fulfilled that kind of dream has been a disappointment to many. By programming light entertainment such as game shows, soap operas, situation comedies, and motion pictures, broadcasters have attracted larger audiences and thus more advertising income than possible by steady cultural programming. The emphasis on popular programming rather than on social uplift and community betterment has been widely criticized, even by some members of the Federal Communications Commission itself. Newton Minow, Chairman of the FCC during the Kennedy administration, in a speech at the annual convention of the National Association of Broadcasters in 1961 characterized television as "a vast wasteland."

Nicholas Johnson, member of the Federal Communications Commission, said in an address before the New York Consumers Assembly on March 4, 1972, that commercial television was the foremost enemy of intelligent consumerism.[8]

He described television as a "social disaster area," saying that the medium ducked controversial issues in its programming, promoted unhealthy diets with its advertising, and was "the number one pusher of the drug life" with its commercials for tranquilizers, sleeping pills and the like.

"For a medium that is so powerful to abuse its power is sad," Johnson said. "For a medium that is statutorily required to operate in the public interest, it is close to criminal."

One of the most effective critics of television in the public sector was Action for Children's Television. For almost a

---

7. Lawrence W. Lichty, *The Wilson Quarterly*, Winter 1981.
8. *The New York Times*, March 5, 1972, page 58L.

quarter of a century its thrust was promotion of better television for children rather than censorship. The organization was founded in 1968 in Newton, Massachusettes, by Peggy Charren in response to concern over possible negative effects of television on children and in recognition of the potential of television for child development.[9]

In monitoring television, ACT was dismayed to find how much time children were spending watching television and appalled by the prevalence of violence and the amount of advertising in children's programs.

A study reported in 1973 showed that the average child was watching television 3 hours each weekday, 3.5 hours on Saturday, and 2.3 hours on Sunday, for about 21 hours a week.[10] That apparently has not decreased over the years, as a study in 1990 reported, "Children in the United States spend 4 hours a day watching television, more than they spend in the classroom or in any activity except sleep."[11]

While applauding such programs as *Sesame Street, Mr. Roger's Neighborhood, Captain Kangaroo,* and *Walt Disney Presents,* shown primarily but not exclusively on noncommercial stations, members of ACT found an excessive amount of violence in much of television and especially in the cartoon programs that dominate Saturday morning viewing on commercial channels and are watched so avidly by children. They found that 71 percent of children's programs on commercial television included at least one instance of human violence. Over half of all program time was devoted to crime, the supernatural, or strife among the characters, and less than 3 percent devoted to such topics as family life, religion, business, government, literature and art.[12] ACT seriously ques-

---

9. ACT discontinued operations in 1992.
10. *Parade*, March 4, 1973.
11. *World Monitor*, December 1990.
12. *Parade*, January 30, 1972.

tioned whether children were being taught the wrong values by such programming.

Although *Sesame Street* was the most watched, as an earlier report stated, "half of the nation's children aged 2 to 11 are sitting before their television sets every Saturday morning watching cartoon-filled screens," a condition that apparently continues.[13] The programming is a change from the early years of television when Saturday morning offerings consisted mostly of adventure series such as *The Lone Ranger* and *Captain Video*. Cartoons began to replace those shows in the 1960's because they proved to be enormously profitable, and they continue to dominate "kidvid" programming on commercial television.

ACT found cartoon programming to be extremely heavy with advertising, with an average of one commercial being shown every 2.8 minutes — far more than on adult programs.[14] As many as 24 commercials an hour for cereals and toys were logged during children's favorite programs. With even a moderate young television viewer being exposed to more than 25,000 commercials a year, ACT felt that advertisers were taking advantage of the innocence of children to promote their products, often at the expense of good healthy habits and even physical safety.[15]

With advertising to children so lucrative, the quantity has not diminished noticeably in recent years, despite protests. In the summer of 1991 the American Academy of Pediatrics recommended a total ban on food advertising on children's television after a study showing that one Saturday morning of cartoon programs contained 202 junk-food commercials.

ACT questioned whether some advertising was in violation of Section 317 of the Communications Act, which

---

13. *TV Guide*, October 11, 1969.
14. *Parade*, January 30, 1972.
15. *The New York Times*, May 12, 1974.

requires identification of sponsors of programs so listeners and viewers will not be deceived. It reads:

■ Section 317: All matter broadcast by any radio station for which service, money, or any other valuable consideration is directly or indirectly paid, or promised to or charged or accepted by, the station so broadcasting, from any person, shall, at the time the same is so broadcast, be announced as paid for or furnished, as the case may be, by such person.

The ACT study resulted in widespread discussion, numerous magazine articles, and several studies on the effects of television on viewers, some financed by the U.S. government. One study of Saturday morning cartoons found of 95 cartoon plays analyzed, only two in 1967 and one each in 1968 and 1969 did not contain violence. A series on government-sponsored studies produced evidence linking violence on television to aggressive behavior of children.[16] A study by the Office of the Surgeon General of the U.S. Public Health Service concluded that "present television entertainment may be contributing to the aggressive behavior of many normal children." A report by the National Institute for Mental Health was more positive, stating that "there is a direct, causal link between exposure to television violence and the observer's subsequent aggressive behavior."

Time spent by children in watching television and the amount of violence they see did not abate despite citizen protests. A study by the American Psychological Association released in March 1992 stated that "the average child watches television about three hours a day and sees at least 8,000 television murders by the seventh grade and more than 100,000 other acts of violence."

Apparently many people believe that the prevalence of

---

16. *Washington Post*, September 4, 1971.

violence on television has a negative effect on children and is a contributing factor in the increasing crime rate in America. As protests multiplied, Congress began to talk of enacting legislation to regulate television.

Attorney General Janet Reno openly warned television executives that they must reduce violence on television or expect Congress to enact legislation requiring them to do so. The discussion raises an unanswered question: So far, legislators and the courts have been unable to fashion a satisfactory definition of pornography. Would defining television violence be any less difficult?

One writer has asked:[17] Is violence on television –

■ Threatening words? Or a pie in the face? Or Elmer Fudd firing a shotgun at Daffy Duck? Is it professional wrestling? Or a barroom brawl on the CBS sitcom *Love and War*?

Some bills have already been introduced in Congress, but few attempt to define violence. Rather, they leave that to the Federal Communications Commission.

Also, these events occurred in the summer of 1993:

1. On June 30, executives of four television networks, ABC, CBS, NBC, and Fox, announced that those networks were adopting a system of rating, to begin in September, to indicate the degree of violence in programs to be broadcast. The ratings would be put on the air, they said, just before shows heavy with violence are broadcast, to help parents decide whether the shows would be suitable for their children.

The rating as first proposed would be an eight-word warning "Due to violent content, parental discretion advised."

---

17. Marc Gunther, Knight-Ridder Washington Bureau, *The Bradenton Herald*, October 29, 1993, page 1.

The announcement was made one day before Congress began hearings on proposed legislation to curb television violence.

2. On July 29, 15 cable channels, including HBO, USA, MTV, and Nickelodeon, announced that they would join the networks in using a rating system to indicate degrees of violence on programs they carry.

3. Four days later, on August 2, a conference on television violence was held in Los Angeles, attended by more than 600 television executives, writers, and producers, plus social scientists and members of interested citizens organization. Sponsored by the National Council for Families and Television, the conference was an indication of how significant the matter of television violence had become.

By the end of 1993, the question of violence on television remained unanswered. With a lack of agreement and the failure of the television industry to act, Congress seemed determined to curb excesses of violence. Ten bills had already been introduced to require such curbs.

In January 1994, cable television executives released information about a plan which calls for an independent committee to monitor violence on television plus rating codes to allow viewers to block out violent programs on specially equipped television sets.[18]

In the meantime, the four networks changed their positions to become strongly opposed to ratings of television programs in regard to violence although they are using parental advisories.

Before the end of January, however, the networks had agreed to establish an independent system for monitoring violence on television.

18. Associated Press, as reported in *The Bradenton Herald*, January 22, 1994.

Standing out starkly in the discussions at the conference in Los Angeles and in the Congressional hearings were substantial differences between the television industry on the one hand and citizen groups and social scientists on the other. The question raised by the industry was whether television should have to continue in the role as the nation's babysitter which it had done extensively in past years.

In 1970 ACT had petitioned the FCC to rule that children's programs be broadcast without commercials, that performers not be permitted to sell products during their programs, and that all television stations be required to broadcast no fewer than 14 hours a week of programs designed for children of different age groups. The request was not granted; but the FCC did call on broadcasters to be more sensitive regarding programs for children and to the possibility of children being exploited by advertisers. It recommended that stations observe a new code of the National Association of Broadcasters (NAB), which placed a limit on time for advertising, called for a reasonable amount of educational programming for children, and asked that broadcasters make clear the distinction between programming and advertising and not permit host selling.

Then during the Reagan administration in the 1980s while Mark S. Fowler was chairman, the FCC struck down rules against program-length cartoon shows such as *He-Man* and *Masters of the Universe* that had been developed by toy companies as marketing devices. It also relaxed rules to permit more commercials during hours when children watch most television.

Disappointed, ACT continued the battle; and it was not alone. Over the years it was joined by the Council on Children, Media and Merchandising, and by other organizations in testifying at Congressional hearings, in making appeals to the NAB, and in presenting petitions to the Federal Trade Commission and the Federal Communications Commission.

In October 1983 ACT filed complaints against five television stations, stating that they were broadcasting programs based exclusively on toy products or characters which, in turn, are depicted on the screen for virtually the entire program. Such programs, ACT contended, are designed to promote the sales of such products under the guise of entertainment, and it requested the FCC to order those licensees to compute those program-length commercials (PLCs) as commercial time and to log them as commercial matter.

The FCC denied the request on April 11, 1985, stating that there was no evidence demonstrating that exposure to programming based on products harms the child audience and that there was no evidence of intermingling commercial and programming material.

The National Association for Better Broadcasting (NABB) then joined in by appealing the FCC denial on May 30, 1985; and on September 25, 1987, the U.S. Court of Appeals for the district of Columbia reversed the FCC decision and sent the case back to the FCC for further consideration. On June 1, 1989, the FCC denied the NABB's complaint. The NABB again appealed, contending that toy-based barter shows should carry sponsor identification.

Another route taken by ACT in cooperation with other consumer and children's rights advocate groups was an attempt to obtain legislation to curb excessive advertising on children's television programs. Congress passed a bill in 1988 to meet that objective, but it was vetoed by President Reagan. Advocates persisted, however, and in early fall of 1990 Congress approved the Children's Television Act, which President Bush allowed to become law without his signature and which became effective on October 18 of that year.

The law gave broadcasters 180 days in which to limit commercials on children's programming to 12 minutes per hour on weekdays and to 10.5 minutes an hour on weekends. Since 1984 there had been no limits on the time stations may use for advertising, with the result that advertising during children's shows had increased to 12 minutes an hour on weekends and up to 14 minutes an hour on weekdays. That is considerably more than the average of fewer than 8 minutes an hour on prime time shows.

The law also required the FCC to study the role of "program-length commercials" that feature characters that are also popular toys and which ACT and other children's rights advocates object to. In addition, the law directed the FCC to take into consideration how well each broadcast station is serving the educational needs of children as a condition for license renewal.

The law provided for easing restrictions by stating that after January 1, 1993, the FCC "may review and evaluate the advertising duration limitations and may modify (other) such limitations in accordance with the public interest."

Enactment of the law was widely applauded by individuals and by the coalition of 35 national educational, professional, and religious organizations that had joined the ACT in urging its passage. Although the broadcast industry itself praised the law when it became effective, less than four months later the NAB in speaking for the industry urged the FCC to ease requirements mandated by the law.

Specifically, the NAB requested that (1) cartoon and reruns of prime-time programs be permitted to qualify as "educational and informational programming" for children, (2) limits on time allowed for commercials be placed only on programs for children under eight years of age rather than on all children's programming, (3) broadcasters not be required to document compliance with the law, and (4) stations be permitted to continue broadcasting programs based on popular children's toys such as *G.I. Joe, He-Man,* and *ThunderCats.*

The FCC subsequently ruled that only those program-length shows based on toys such as *G.I. Joe* and *He-Man* that included paid advertisements for the same toys could be classified as program-length commercials, but it ruled that advertising for the toy may appear in the next time slot.

The FCC, under pressure from the public, from the broadcast industry, and from Congress, adopted rules on April 9, 1991, setting limits on advertising in children's programs as specified by the Children's Television Act of 1990, and set standards aimed at improving the quality of children's programs on television. The rules, which became effective on October 1, 1991, require commercial broadcast stations and cable television operators to maintain records that summarize their efforts to provide educational and informational programming for children under age 16 as a condition for license renewal, with public noncommercial television exempt.

Critics contend that the law is vague in defining what constitutes educational television, a criticism supported by a study in 1992 by the Center for Media Education which found that some stations were actually listing such cartoon shows as *The Jetsons, Super Mario Brothers,* and even *G.I. Joe*, as educational. Also the law does not stipulate when educational programs must be broadcast, with the result that some stations are running them before 6:30 a.m. or during school hours.

The law governing broadcast content would be unconstitutional if applied to print media. In fact, President Bush's refusal to sign the Children's Television Act into law was based on his contention that its provisions would infringe on broadcasters' right of free speech. The law and FCC rules are illustrative of the pressures by both government and the public under which broadcasters operate.

The balance between freedom for broadcasters on one hand and the desires of and the pressures applied by the listening and viewing audience is a constantly shifting one. Both locally and nationally, various groups have lobbied for and against particular kinds of programs. They include such diverse organizations as the U.S. Catholic Conference, Morality in Media, The Foundation to Improve Television, Accuracy in Media, People for the American Way, Moral Majority, Gay Activist Alliance, National Organization for Women, and other religious, racial and ethnic groups. In general, pressure groups have been more successful in obtaining concessions from local stations than from the networks because local broadcasters are more vulnerable to economic and social pressures than are the networks.

CHAPTER
27

❁

UNDER PRESSURE BY
GOVERNMENT AND THE PUBLIC

UNDER PRESSURE BY GOVERNMENT AND THE PUBLIC

❧

A significant leverage on broadcasters became available to the public in 1969 as a result of a protest to the renewal of the license of Station WLBT-TV, Channel 3, operated by the Lamar Life Broadcasting Company in Jackson, Mississippi. The case dates back to the time of civil rights protests, marches, and sit-ins in the early 1960s.

As the movement spread, some television broadcasters in the South began trying to discredit civil rights leaders by portraying them as criminals, sex perverts, and Communists. An ordained minister named Everett Parker found a way to strike back. As Director of the Office of Communication of the United Church of Christ, he established a network of church members, students, and civil rights workers to monitor local broadcasters. With the evidence thus obtained, he met with LeRoy Collins, former governor of Florida who at the time was head of the National Association of Broadcasters, and he asked Collins to issue a policy statement calling for broadcast members of the Association to give blacks fair treatment in programming and in employment.

When the NAB failed to issue the statement, Parker decided on another tack. He and attorneys working with the church persuaded the OCUCC in cooperation with individuals and a church in the Jackson area to petition the FCC to be allowed to intervene in the hearings in 1965 on renewal of the license of WLBT, which they considered one of the worst station offenders. They had ample evidence that the station had not served the needs of black residents, although blacks numbered about half of the city's population, and had broadcast no programs stating views of blacks on segregation.

Their petition broke precedent. Never before had anyone or any group except other broadcasters intervened in license renewal hearings. Generally licenses were renewed more or less automatically, without a hearing unless some broadcaster believed that the signal of a station being considered for licensing would interfere with his signal.

Arguing that allowing the group from Jackson to take part in the hearings would take time and involve additional expense for both the FCC and WLBT, the FCC denied their petition on the grounds that the petitioners lacked standing since they had no financial interest in the broadcast station. The petitioners then appealed to the Court of Appeals for the District of Columbia, the court designated in Section 402 of the Communications Act of 1934 to hear all appeals from FCC decisions.

The Court in 1966 ordered the FCC to hold hearings on the petition; and at those hearings Parker and the Church attorney, Earle K. (Dick) Moore, presented evidence of the failure of the station to broadcast favorable comments on the civil rights movement.[1] Despite that evidence, the FCC decided to renew the station's license. Parker and his colleagues again appealed; and in 1969 the Court with Judge Warren E. Burger presiding ordered the FCC to find a new licensee for WLBT.[2]

---

1. Office of Communication of the United Church of Christ v. Federal Communications Commission, 359 F 2d 994 (D.C. Cir. March 25, 1966).
2. Office of Communication of the United Church of Christ v. Federal Communications Commission 425 F 2d 543 (D.C. Cir. June 20, 1969).

That was, incidentally, the last case in which Judge Burger participated before he was appointed that year as Chief Justice of the U.S. Supreme Court by President Nixon.

The case pointed to a method for individuals or pressure groups to enter protests and make demands on broadcasters; namely, by opposing license renewal or attempting to block the sale or purchase of a station. That was made possible by a court ruling in the mid-1960s that the FCC must consider complaints from viewers in deciding whether a station license warrants being renewed. Although a number of attempts have been made to persuade the FCC to deny license renewal, few have succeeded. The WLBT license was revoked as a result of court action rather than by a FCC decision.

Complainants have been more successful in obtaining concessions from broadcasters than they have been in bringing about license transfers, especially in attempts to block sales or purchases of stations because such attempts can force a hearing before the Federal Communications Commission, which is both time-consuming and expensive. Some stations have thus found it quicker and easier to submit to citizen demands than to fight.

A case in Texarkana, Arkansas-Texas, in 1969 provided an example. There 12 community organizations accused KTAL-TV in that city of failing to meet the needs and interests of the black population and opposed renewal of its license. To protect its license, the station owner agreed "to begin presenting regular programs for the discussion of controversial issues, including both black and white participants and to encourage "the airing of all sides of these issues."

The owners also pledged to discuss programming regularly with all segments of the public, consult with substantial groups in the community, and "make no unessential reference to the race of a person." In addition, they promised to recruit and train a staff "broadly representative of all groups in the community" and to employ a minimum of two full-time black reporters.[3]

Administrators and executives, both governmental and business, try to manage the news so that their actions and decisions are presented favorably. President Franklin D. Roosevelt was especially adroit in managing the news during his administration.[4]   Others have not been as successful. During the Vietnam war, when the country was beset by violent protests, tension between the media and the White House became particularly intense, with the media often critical of the policies of President Johnson, who served from 1963 to 1969, and President Nixon, 1969 to 1974.   Both presidents tried to exert pressure on the news media; but it was during the Nixon administration that harassment and veiled threats against the media and especially against television by the White House reached new heights.

Highlighting the conflict were two particularly critical speeches by Vice President Spiro Agnew late in 1969, one in Des Moines, Iowa, on November 13, and the other in Montgomery, Alabama, on November 20.[5] The White House had been incensed by the negative analysis made by commentators on the three dominant networks of an address that had been presented on network television on November 3 in support of the government's policy on the war in Vietnam. In response, Agnew lashed out at the networks in speeches prepared by the White House staff. In Des Moines, he said in part:

■   Monday night a week ago, President Nixon delivered the most important address of his Administration, one of

3. *Editor & Publisher*, August 30, 1969.
4. His methods of dealing with the press are described by Betty Houchin Winfield in *FDR and the News Media*, University of Illinois Press, 276 pages, 1990.
5. Agnew was inaugurated vice president on January 20, 1969, and resigned under pressure on October 10, 1973.

the most important of our decade. His subject was Vietnam. His hope was to rally the American people to see the conflict through to a lasting and just peace in the Pacific. For 32 minutes, he reasoned with a nation that has suffered almost a third of a million casualties in the longest war in its history.

When the President completed his address—an address, incidentally, that he spent weeks in the preparation of—his words and policies were subjected to instant analysis and querulous criticism. The audience of 70 million Americans gathered to hear the President of the United States was inherited by a small band of network commentators and self-appointed analysts, the majority of whom expressed in one way or another their hostility to what he had to say. It was obvious that their minds were made up in advance.

The purpose of my remarks is to focus your attention on this little group of men who not only enjoy the right of instant rebuttal to every Presidential address, but, more importantly, wield a free hand in selecting, presenting, and interpreting the great issues of our nation.

Now how is the network news determined? A small group of men, numbering perhaps no more than a dozen anchormen, commentators and executive producers, settle upon the 20 minutes or so of film and commentary that's to reach the public. They decide what 40 to 50 million Americans will learn of the day's events in the nation and in the world.

He implied that the news media should reflect the views of the administration, and he reminded broadcasters that broadcasting is licensed by the government.

Agnew's criticisms of the media were endorsed by President Nixon; but broadcasters in general felt that the attacks were unfair, that they were an attempt by government to suppress responsible discussion of the Vietnam war, and they felt threatened. In regard to monopoly by network commentators, which Agnew spoke of, broadcasters pointed out that the President of the United States has at his request the use of the networks at virtually any time he wishes to speak to the nation, which is in itself a kind of monopoly. And in fact, President Nixon had had more prime time exposure on network television in his first 18 months in office than his three predecessors, having appeared on television as often as Presidents Eisenhower, Kennedy, and Johnson combined during comparable time periods in their administrations.

Broadcasters are subject to pressure by government as well as by citizens' organizations, and that can come from various sources. The Federal Trade Commission has authority to police advertising to prevent fraud and deception. The Department of Justice enforces antitrust laws that govern the sales and purchases of broadcast stations; and Congress has the power to hold hearings and to amend laws governing broadcasting.

In view of the sensitivity of politicians to television, broadcasters are vulnerable to pressure and control by various executive agencies as well as by Congress. Since members of the Federal Communications Commission are appointed by the President, it is to be expected that they are sympathetic to his views. The Office of Management and Budget (OMB) is a White House operation established to coordinate budget requests from agencies of the executive branch of government, which include the FCC. It thus controls the kinds and amounts of financial requests that are sent to Congress. Further pressure can be applied by the National Telecommunications and Information Administration (NTIA), established in 1978 as successor to the Office of Telecommunications Policy which was established in 1970 under White House control.

The potential for government interference in broadcasting, both commercial and noncommercial, is always present through licensing and FCC regulations, but noncommercial broadcasting is even more vulnerable in that a portion of its financing, about 16 percent, is by the federal government.

The only time that PBS has been threatened by pressure from government in regard to program content, however, was during the Nixon administration.

Clay T. Whitehead, director of the Office of Telecommunications policy at the time, objected to some news and public affairs programming by PBS because it was critical of Nixon policies, and he implied that public broadcasting would be without permanent funding if programming continued in that vein. He said he felt that too much authority was centralized in the Corporation for Public Broadcasting, that public funds appropriated by Congress for the Corporation should not be spent on discussion of controversial matters, and that such programs as *Buckley's Firing Line*, *Bill Moyer's Journal* and *Washington Week in Review* were too controversial.

Network news was also warned by Mr. Whitehead for what he perceived as bias against the Nixon administration. In a speech at a luncheon meeting of Sigma Delta Chi, professional journalism society, in Indianapolis on December 12, 1972, Mr. Whitehead said that "station managers and network officials who fail to correct imbalance or constant bias in network news, or who acquiesce by silence, can only be considered willing participants, to be held fully accountable at license renewal time."

The pressure abated after Nixon resigned the presidency on August 9, 1974, and was succeeded by Gerald R. Ford. Since then there has been less effort by government to influence the content of either commercial or public broadcasting. In fact, government control of the broadcast industry has been relaxed rather than strengthened in recent years, starting with the Carter administration which began on January 20, 1977. Widespread deregulation was instituted by the FCC while Charles Ferris was chairman in 1978-81, and it gained impetus during the Reagan administration.

The FCC increased the time required for station license renewal from three to five years for television and to seven years for radio, and it abolished much of the burdensome paper work required for license renewal.

The limit on time permitted for commercial advertising was lifted, except in programs for children. Originally the FCC had set a limit of 18 minutes of commercials per hour for television and 16 minutes for radio. Now stations may run as many commercials as they wish and believe appropriate.

Several rules governing nonentertainment programming were dropped, giving stations greater freedom to decide the number and kinds of news and public affairs programs they wished to broadcast. Also broadcasters are no longer required to devote a small portion of their time to public affairs and to programs for children.

Deregulation reached into cable transmission with the enactment of the Cable Communications Policy Act of 1984, which freed most cable systems from local control over their rates and services.

Although deregulation was generally approved by broadcasters, it was not of unmixed benefit. The discontinuance of rules limiting entry into broadcasting plus the willingness of the FCC to assign new broadcast frequencies and channels to existing markets often led to intense competition for audiences and advertising dollars.

Of all deregulation changes, the one that probably pleased broadcasters most concerned the Fairness Doctrine, which is discussed in detail in Chapter 29. Instituted in 1949, it required broadcast stations to devote a reasonable percentage of time to discussion of public issues in their own communities and to provide for response to programming that touched on controversial subjects. Its modification in 1987 relieved broadcasters of the responsibility of arranging for responses and providing air time to meet the requirement — a requirement that many broadcasters believed to be unconstitutional.

Deregulation also included liberalizing station ownership rules. To insure diversity, the FCC had limited ownership as early as 1940 when it ruled that no one person or company could own more than six FM radio stations. The next year, when television was in its infancy, the FCC set a limit of three for television stations. In 1946 the limit on single ownership of AM radio stations was raised from six to seven; and in 1953 the FCC adopted the 7-AM, 7-FM, and 5-TV station limit. The next year it raised the limit on single ownership to five VHF and two UHF television stations.

In 1984, as part of the deregulation of broadcasting, the FCC set the limit on single or common control of broadcast stations at 12 AM, 12 FM, and 12 TV stations. Ownership rules, however, are much more complex than the 12-station rule appears. It includes pages of provisions with exceptions and conditions regarding market location, signal overlap, coverage limits, assignment of frequencies and power, and rules to encourage ownership by minorities and women. Excerpts from Title 27, Section 73.3555 of the U.S. Code of Federal Regulations as revised October 1, 1990, illustrate:

■ No license for a commercial AM, FM, or TV broadcast station shall be granted, transferred or assigned to any party . . . if (it) would result in such party or any of its stockholders, partners, members, officers or directors, directly or indirectly, owning, operating or controlling, or having a cognizable interest in, either:

(i) More than 14 stations in the same service,

or

(ii) More than 12 stations in the same service which are not minority controlled.

The Section continues by stating that:

■ . . . no license will be granted for a commercial TV station that would result in anyone having a cognizable interest in, either:

(i) TV stations which have an aggregate national audience reach exceeding 30 per cent,

or

(ii) TV stations which have an aggregate national audience reach exceeding 25 per cent and which are not minority controlled.

Regulations on ownership of radio stations were further liberalized in 1992, effective on August 1 of that year, to permit a single person or a company to own as many as 30 AM and 30 FM stations nationwide, replacing the limit of 12 of each. At the same time the so-called duopoly rule that prohibited ownership of more than one AM and one FM station in a single city was changed to permit multiple ownership, with the number dependent upon the number of stations in a city. For example, in a city with fewer than 15 radio stations, a person or a company may own three stations of which only two may be FM stations. Companies are permitted to own two AM and two FM stations in cities that have between 15 and 29 stations; three AM and two FM stations in cities with 30 to 39 stations; and three of each in cities that have 40 or more stations.

News, once an important part of radio programming, declined sharply after the deregulation of radio. Full-time news staffs were reduced sharply. Before deregulation, radio stations were required to devote at least 8 percent of their broadcast time to non-entertainment programming. But programming had changed over the years, so that outside of morning drive time, news no longer had high priority on many stations and still don't.

Loosening the restrictions on broadcast station ownership, accompanied by the trend in recent years toward consolidation of the media into huge conglomerates, is seen by some as a threat to the diversity of news and information sources vital to a democracy. Consolidation has been taking place in all the media. Among newspapers, for example, all but about 300 of the nation's 1,600 dailies are owned by groups and conglomerates.

Before the most recent ownership restrictions were

loosened, one observer warned that "further consolidation of the electronic media threatens to seriously undermine the diversity of sources vital to a healthy democracy."[6]

"Instead of promoting competition among the electronic media industries," he continued, "the FCC plans would remove the few remaining safeguards that now prevent a handful of huge conglomerates from owning and controlling all the means of mass communication in this country."

Cross-ownership was for many years a matter of concern for the FCC in its efforts to assure diversified control of the media, and ownership of two major media outlets is still prohibited in the same market, except in a sale when a suitable owner cannot be found. A city or community with one daily newspaper that owned the dominant broadcast station in the area was the kind of monopoly of "voices" it wished to prohibit. As early as 1941 the FCC held hearings on a proposed rule to prohibit newspapers from owning broadcast stations. However, in 1944 the Commission voted unanimously not to adopt general rules against newspaper/broadcast cross-ownership.

Again in 1970 the FCC raised the issue by proposing rules that would prohibit ownership by newspapers of broadcast stations and cable television systems, and force the breakup of such cross-ownership wherever it existed. The proposal was not implemented, however; its adoption would have meant the forced sale of 380 radio stations and 96 television stations in 155 communities over a five-year period. The need for such divestitures was hardly necessary anyway to attain diversity because of the great increase in the number of broadcast stations across the country.

Deregulation was, in part, a response to changes that were

---

6. Jeff Chester, "The FCC," *Columbia Journalism Review*, Nov. - Dec., 1991, page 50. Mr. Chester is Director of the Teledemocracy Project, a media policy watchdog group sponsored by Ralph Nader.

providing the public with a multitude of viewing and listening options previously unavailable, including an increasing number of broadcast stations, cable transmission, satellite communication, and widespread use of VCRs. It also reflected a growing belief by the FCC that market forces were generally more effective than government regulations in insuring that broadcasters meet the needs of their viewing and listening audiences. Competition, not government control, was the better regulator.

That viewpoint has been hotly debated, with critics contending that the FCC no longer considered broadcasters as stewards of a valuable natural resource to be managed in the public interest but rather as business men and women with the primary responsibility of increasing profits through attracting larger audiences. In response, defenders of FCC action argued that profitability is not inconsistent with serving the public interest.

In a related area, critics deplored discontinuance of the anti-trafficking rule, which required an owner to operate a station for at least three years after its construction or acquisition before being permitted to sell it. The rule still applies to "unbuilt" stations but not to existing ones, so they can go on the market at any time. Critics pointed to the surge of buying and selling that followed cancellation of the rule as evidence that the FCC had opened the way for investors to make more money in trading in broadcast stations than in operating them. In effect, they contended, abolition of the rule resulted in stations becoming real estate properties to be bought and sold for profit rather than as media to serve the public interest.

In response, defenders of the FCC held that the rule was abolished to encourage the sale of underdeveloped properties to owners interested in improving them. As increasing the value of a station depends almost entirely on increasing its listening or viewing audience, the new owners would give the public what it wanted rather than what the FCC decided it should have. The public interest would actually be better served in that manner, they contended. That, of course, revolved around the argument of seeking higher profits by appealing to the lowest common denominator versus providing programs of cultural and social uplift.

Despite all deregulation in recent years, the FCC still has authority granted by Congress to regulate broadcasting. It has the power not only to grant, revoke, or refuse to renew broadcast licenses but also to issue cease and desist orders, to warn stations, and to levy fines on stations that do not operate in conformity with their licenses, that fail to comply with the provisions of the Communications Act, and that violate rules and regulations of the Commission.

The most intractable problems faced by the FCC undoubtedly have arisen over programs that test the limits on broadcasting indecent, obscene, and profane material. It is not that the Commission is without authority. Section 326 of the Communications Act, which prohibits utterances of any obscene, indecent, or profane language on the air, is reinforced by Title 18, Section 1464, of the U.S. Code, which provides criminal penalties for the use of such language in broadcasting. Also the U.S. Supreme Court ruled in 1978 that the FCC could ban as indecent the daytime broadcasting of a monologue by the comedian George Carlin titled "Seven Dirty Words" in order to shield children from hearing such material.[7]

After "shock radio" came into use in the middle 1980s, the FCC issued new guidelines in 1987 which in essence banned the broadcasting of "indecent" material before midnight, or at any time when there is reasonable risk that children may be in the audience. The Commission defined indecent language or material as that which describes or depicts, "in terms patently offensive as measured by contemporary community stan-

---

7. FCC v. Pacifica Foundation, 438 U.S. 726 (1978).

dards for the broadcast medium, sexual or excretory activities or organs." Broadcasts that fit within that definition, not just those using the "seven dirty words," are subject to the FCC indecency enforcement standards.

Enforcing standards for broadcast content is at times complex because of possible conflict with the right of free speech. A case in point involved Station KZKC-TV in Kansas City. In apparent violation of the FCC prohibition, the Station showed the movie, *Private Lessons*, at 8 p.m. on May 26, 1987, a time when children were likely to be watching. The movie is about a 15-year-old boy who is seduced by the housekeeper. A year later on June 23 the FCC voted to levy a fine of $2000 for violation of Title 18, Section 1464, of the U.S. Code, mentioned above.

In October 1992, the FCC imposed a fine of $105,000 on KLSK-FM, Los Angeles, for raunchy morning broadcasts by Howard Stern and later voted to fine Infinity Broadcast Co., which employs Stern and owns his New York radio base, WXRK-FM, $600,000. The company and the stations have appealed.

Before the Notice of Apparent Liability regarding KZKC-TV was issued, the U.S. Court of Appeals for the District of Columbia Circuit ruled that the FCC ban on broadcasting "indecent" language during evening hours violated the right of free speech. The three judges held that the ban would not necessarily prevent substantial numbers of unsupervised children from seeing or hearing such material. In the opinion of Judge Ruth Bader Ginsburg, concurred in by the two other judges, "broadcast material that is indecent but not obscene is protected by the First Amendment."[8]

The Court upheld the FCC's definition of "indecent" material and its ban on the broadcasting of such material between 6 and 10 p.m., but it stated that the FCC's only basis

---

8. Action for Children's Television v. FCC, 852 F 2d 1332 (D.C. Cir. 1988).

for regulating such material "is not to establish itself as a censor but to assist parents in controlling what young children will hear.[9]

In its decision, the Court upheld the FCC's warning to a New York radio talk show not to use indecent language in its morning air times, but it overturned warnings to the student-operated radio station KCSB-FM in Santa Barbara, Calif., and to a Pacifica Foundation, Inc., radio station in Los Angeles for broadcasts that took place after 10 p.m. but before midnight.

In an order released September 6, 1988, vacating the Notice of Apparent Liability against KZKC-TV, the FCC stated:[10]

■ The Court decision precludes evening enforcement until the Commission has sufficiently justified an hour after which parents can be expected to supervise their children's viewing and listening habits . . . We take this opportunity to reiterate that we take seriously our obligation to enforce 18 U.S.C. Section 1464. Nonetheless, we can fulfill this responsibility only to the extent permissible under existing law . . .

Under such time as further rulings from the courts permit us to conclude otherwise, we will take enforcement action only against daytime indecent broadcasts . . . Obscene broadcasts continue, of course, to be prohibited at all times of day and night.

Regulations that prohibit the broadcast of sexually oriented indecent programs on radio and television between 6 a.m. and 10 p.m. were upheld in a decision on June 30, 1995, by the U.S. Court of Appeals for the District of Columbia Circuit.

---

9. Ibid
10. Ibid

CHAPTER

28

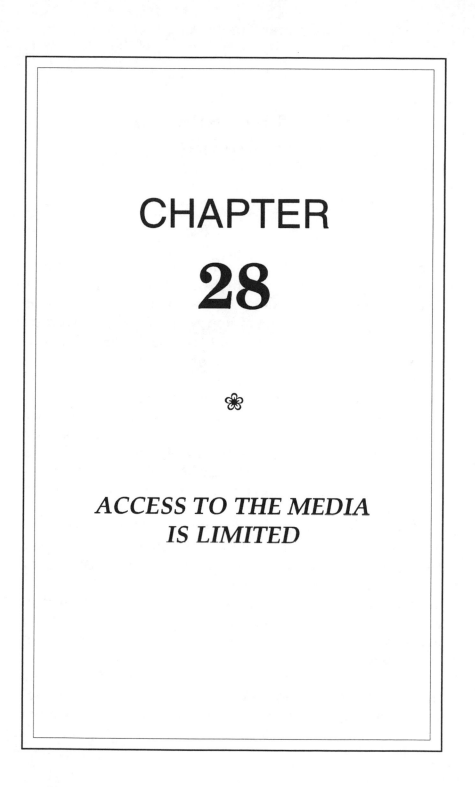

ACCESS TO THE MEDIA
IS LIMITED

ACCESS TO THE MEDIA
IS LIMITED

❧

Suppose you read about a proposal to alleviate traffic congestion by constructing a superhighway that would run right
through your city, virtually dividing it into halves. You
strongly oppose the plan and immediately write a vigorous
protest, stating your reasons; but the newspaper refuses to
publish it. What recourse do you have? Almost none.

There is no way that you as a citizen, or that any government official or government agency, can force a newspaper to
publish anything it does not choose to publish. You could buy
advertising space for your message, provided the newspaper
will sell the space to you; but just as newspapers can refuse
news and editorial copy, so also can they refuse advertising —
except when such refusal of advertising is in restraint of trade
or is discriminatory.

Unfair? Perhaps so, but that's the way it is. You could
argue that the only daily newspaper in your community
should be required to accept your advertisement because (a)
it is a common carrier, or (b) it is a public utility, or (c) it is a
public place of accommodation. Businesses and services in
any one of those classifications must accept business from
everyone who requests it and is able to pay for it. A common
carrier is a company, such as a bus line or a railroad, engaged
in transporting passengers and goods for profit; a public
utility is one that provides such essential services as electricity, gas, and telephone; and a place of public accommodation

is a business office, store, restaurant, amusement park, or other such place open to the public.

As a place of business, a newspaper is open to the public just as other businesses are, by law and by custom; but access stops with the content of the newspaper. That principle has been upheld by the courts in a number of cases. As recently as 1990 the Third District Federal Court of Appeals in Wisconsin upheld the principle that newspapers are not common carriers and do not have to accept all advertising offered them. The case arose when the Green Bay *Press-Gazette* refused two classified advertisements in 1986, one from a gay organization and one from a lesbian organization. The organizations sued, contending that the newspaper was subject to the Wisconsin public accommodation law; but the Court held that it is not — ruling in effect that a newspaper cannot be legally compelled to accept advertising which it considers unacceptable.

The same principle applies to commercial broadcast stations. Section 3(h) of the Federal Communications Act of 1934 stipulates that a broadcaster shall not be deemed a common carrier and therefore not required to accept all matter offered for broadcast.

Cogent arguments for greater access to the press have been made in the past. In the late 1960s, for example, during a time when the country was racked by protests against the war in Vietnam, a man named Jerome A. Barron stimulated considerable discussion of this subject by speaking for a new interpretation of the First Amendment. Then associate professor of law at George Washington University in Washington, D.C., Barron explained his ideas in several articles, including one in the *Harvard Law Review* in June 1967 and one in *Seminar* in March 1969.[1]

---

1. Jerome A. Barron, "Access to the Press: A New Concept of the First Amendment," *Seminar*, March 1969, pages 23-26.

He argued that "forbidding government restrictions on expression is quite useless if the power to prevent access to the channels of communication may be exercised at the pleasure of those who control them."

Worded another way, he said, "The difficulty of doing anything about this situation is that the First Amendment has conventionally been thought of as prohibiting *governmental* restraints on expression. But what about private restraints on expression?"

Barron pointed to two conditions that he insisted indicated a need for more access to the press. One was the failure of established newspapers to publish "divergent opinions and ideas." He contended that the unwillingness of existing mass communications to present unpopular and controversial ideas had contributed to the civil rights marches and sit-ins in the South, to the riots in Detroit and the Watts district in Los Angeles, and to Vietnam war protests.

"For those who are able to obtain access to the media, our law is a source of considerable strength. But what about those whose ideas are too unacceptable to gain entrance to the media?" he asked.

"The horror of upsetting the community apple cart which dominates the press in this country . . . drives the dissenter to look for novel, even violent, techniques to capture attention of the public."

The other condition Barron cited is the concentration of ownership of newspapers. "The lack of any obligation on newspapers to publish minority viewpoints is particularly aggravated by the rise of the one-newspaper city," he said, and he cited figures showing that the number of cities with competing daily newspapers had declined from 689 to only 87 in the years between 1910 and 1954.[2]

---

2. The number of daily newspapers of general circulation in the U.S. continues to decrease. The number in November 1990 was 1,611,

Professor Barron's ideas caused considerable comment at the time. In its biennial conference in 1968, the American Civil Liberties Union adopted a resolution urging its National Board of Directors to file suits to establish the legal right of access to the press. The section on Individual Rights and Responsibilities of the American Bar Association held a session on "Mass Media: Rights of Access and Reply" at the ABA's national convention in 1969. The Freedom of Information Committee of the American Society of Newspaper Editors included a special section on this topic in its report in 1970.

Some legal action regarding access has centered on editorial advertising; that is, on noncommercial messages relating to issues and controversy. In one such case, for example, an advertisement of that kind prepared by the Chicago Joint Board of Amalgamated Clothing Workers of America Union in 1969 was refused by the four daily newspapers in Chicago. The reason, the advertising manager of *The Chicago Tribune* said, was that the advertisement was "unfair and would be misleading" in that "it singled out Marshall Field as selling foreign-made merchandise and urged readers not to buy from that retailer."

The Union filed suit in federal court, contending that its right of free speech and its right to equal protection under the laws had been violated by the newspapers' rejection of the advertisement, but Judge Abraham L. Marovitz in a summary judgment in favor of the newspapers said in part:

---

which contrasts with about 2,600 being published at the turn of the century and 161 fewer than were being published 40 years earlier in 1950. A total of 19 went out of business in 1991.

Only 83 cities had competing (two or more) daily newspapers as of November 1990, and in 42 of those cities the newspapers had the same ownership. Stated another way, each of 1,528 cities in the U.S. had only one daily newspaper.

■ We are not insensitive to the problems that have developed or may arise because of a lack of access to the market place of ideas ... the failures to communicate effectively through conventional means have led some to attempt to persuade unconventionally and often violently ...

To the extent that the market mechanism is impaired ... we think that the public is done a disservice. Yet, if, in many respects, private censorship is no better than public censorship, the fact remains that the right to free speech was never intended to include the right to use the other fellow's presses, that the Constitution relates only to government and not to private action.

In another decision, in 1937, a court ruled that "a publisher of a newspaper has the same rights, no more or less than individuals, to speak, write or publish his views and sentiments, and is subject to the same restrictions."[3]

Political candidates have been given special consideration in much of the discussion on access to the media. In broadcasting, since 1927 with the enactment of the Federal Radio Act at that time, they have had by law the right of reply. The Equal Time provision is explained in the next chapter.

Access to print and broadcast media by candidates for federal offices (Presidential and Congressional) was limited when Congress put a cap on campaign expenditures by enacting the Federal Elections Campaign Act of 1972, which created the Federal Elections Commission and became effective on April 17, 1972.

Although a cap remains, the U.S. Supreme Court ruled that the limitations placed by the law on expenditures by candidates on their own behalf violated the candidates' right to freedom of speech.[4]

---

3. Curry v. Journal Publishing Co., 41 N. M. 318, 68 P.2d 168, 175 (1937).
4. James L. Buckley et al, v. Frank R. Valeo, Secretary of the U.S. Senate, 424 U.S. 1(January 30, 1976).

Expenditure limitations are stated in Title 11, Code of Federal Regulations, 9035 and 9035.2 (1-1-92 Edition).

Attempts have been made to grant political candidates the right of reply in the print media, but that has never succeeded. As long ago as 1913 the State Legislature of Florida enacted Statute 104.38 requiring newspapers in that state to give free space to candidates for reply to articles and editorials opposing them. The law stated:

■ If any newspaper assails the personal character of any candidate or attacks his official record . . . or charges said candidate with malfeasance in office . . . or gives to another free space for such purpose, such newspaper shall upon request immediately publish free of any cost any reply he may make thereto in as conspicuous a place and in the same kind of type . . . provided such reply does not take up more space than the matter replied to.

Rarely used, the law was eventually declared unconstitutional. One instance of its use was the arrest of Herbert M. Davidson, editor of *The Daytona Beach News-Journal* just prior to the primary election in 1952 on a complaint by Joseph Ginsberg, one of seven candidates for the City Commission. Ginsberg charged that the editor had refused to publish his reply to an editorial, which he had; but the case was dismissed nolle prosequi[5] by the County Judge, Robert Wingfield, after the county prosecutor had filed a motion stating that the affidavit and warrant were legally insufficient.

Nineteen years later on October 1, 1971, Davidson, then president of *The News-Journal*, was again arrested on a charge of violating the same law. That complaint was sworn out by the mayor, Richard Kane. Curiously, the warrant signed by County Judge Robert Durden ordered the sheriff to

---

5. To be unwilling to prosecute.

arrest "the said News Journal Corporation and bring it before me at the County Judge's Court." As that was impossible, the arresting officer escorted Davidson to the Sheriff's office where he signed an appearance bond and was released.

The newspaper had published one reply by the Mayor to an editorial, but the Mayor demanded space for a second reply which the editor refused to grant because "it wasn't a reply." In a hearing on the case on January 21, the defense attorneys argued that the political column to which the Mayor wanted to reply didn't come within the provisions of the law. "At no time was Mayor Kane's personal character assailed," they stated. "The column did not at any time accuse the Mayor of evil deeds. It did not attack his official record. It did not attack his voting record. It dealt with a difference in political philosophy."

Three weeks later on February 14, 1972, Judge Durden dismissed the charges against the News-Journal Corporation and ruled that the law under which they had been brought was unconstitutional. He stated that "the language of the statute is too vague, indefinite and uncertain to constitute notice of what language may fall within the purview of the statute and what constitutes a reply which must be printed at the request of a candidate."

A test case that settled the matter permanently arose the same year when Pat L. Tornillo Jr. sued the *Miami Herald* for refusing to give him free and equal space to reply to two editorials that were critical of his candidacy for the Florida House of Representatives.

Judge Francis Christie of the Dade County Circuit Court also ruled that the law was unconstitutional. "Clearly," the Judge said, "if the State may not prohibit what a newspaper may print, it cannot assume the editorial function and direct the newspaper what to print."

The State Supreme Court, however, reversed the decision on July 18, 1973, by a 6-to-1 vote, holding that the law was constitutional. The Court said that the law is "designed to add to the flow of information and ideas and does not constitute an incursion upon First Amendment rights or a prior restraint since no specified newspaper content is excluded." The decision reads in part:

■ The mandate of the statute refers to any reply which is wholly responsible to the charge made in the editorial or other article being replied to, and that is neither libelous nor slanderous of the publication, nor of anyone else, nor vulgar or profane.

The right of the public to know all sides of a controversy . . . is being jeopardized by the growing concentration of ownership of the mass media into fewer and fewer hands, resulting ultimately in private censorship.

By this tendency toward monopolization, the voice of the press tends to become exclusive in its observation and its wisdom, which in turn deprives the public of their right to know both sides of the controversy.

(This decision upholding the law) will encourage rather than impede the wide-open and robust dissemination of ideas and counterthought which is essential to intelligent self-government.

The case was appealed to the U.S. Supreme Court, which ruled unanimously in 1974 in favor of the *Miami Herald,* stating that "for better or worse, it is fundamental to the First Amendment that editors be free to do their own editing rather than to have the government do it for them."[6]

Professor Barron, advocate for greater access to the press, represented the plaintiff, Mr. Tornillo, in the case, and in so doing, argued that "government has an obligation to ensure that a wide variety of views reach the public." He pointed out that the newspaper industry has changed since the time of the adoption of the Bill of Rights in 1791, stating in part:

---

6. Miami Herald Publishing Company v. Tornillo, 418 U.S. 241 (1974).

■ The elimination of competing newspapers in most of our large cities, and the concentration of control of media that results from the only newspaper being owned by the same interests which own a television station and a radio station, are important components of this trend toward concentration of control of outlets to inform the people.

The result of these vast changes has been to place in a few hands the power to inform the American people and shape public opinion . . . (The effect has been that) the public has lost any ability to respond or to contribute in a meaningful way to the debate on issues . . .

In the opinion of the Court, Chief Justice Warren Burger stated in part:

■ A responsible press is an undoubtedly desirable goal, but press responsibility is not mandated by the Constitution and like many other virtues it cannot be legislated.

Faced with the penalties that would accrue to any newspaper that published news or commentary arguably within the reach of the right of access statute, editors might well conclude that the safe course is to avoid controversy and that, under the operation of the Florida statute, political and electoral coverage would be blunted or reduced . . . the Florida statute fails to clear the barriers of the First Amendment because of its intrusion into the function of editors . . . It has yet to be demonstrated how governmental regulation of this crucial process can be exercised consistent with First Amendment guarantees of a free press . . .

In another case in 1974 a political candidate was denied access to advertising space in public transportation.[7] In 1970 Harry J. Lehman was a candidate for the office of State

---

7. Lehman v. Shaker Heights, 418 U.S. 298 (1974).

Representative to the Ohio General Assembly for District 56, which includes the city of Shaker Heights. On July 3 he applied to purchase car card space on the Shaker Heights Rapid Transit System, but was refused because the management agreement with the city did not permit political advertising. It carried car cards advertising various products and companies but never any political or public issue advertising.

Lehman sued, contending that the car cards "constituted a public forum protected by the First Amendment and that there is a guarantee of nondiscriminatory access to such publicly owned and controlled areas of communication ..."

The case went all the way to the U.S. Supreme Court where by a vote of 5 to 4 the Court upheld the transit system. In the majority opinion, Justice Harry A. Blackmun stated:

■ The card space, although incidental to the provision of public transportation, is part of the commercial venture. In much the same way that a newspaper or periodical, or even a radio or television station, need not accept every proffer of advertising from the general public, a city transit system has discretion to develop and make reasonable choices concerning the type of advertising that may be displayed in its vehicles ... No First Amendment forum is here to be found ... (and) there is no First or Fourteenth Amendment violation.

That corporations are guaranteed freedom of speech by the First Amendment was affirmed in a case that arose in Massachusetts regarding a proposed law to institute a graduated state income tax.

Five corporations headquartered in Massachusetts decided they would publicly oppose passage of the law. The state attorney warned them that state law prohibited corporations from spending money on advertising and other methods of opposing the proposed law.

371

The U.S. Supreme Court ruled otherwise in a 5-to-4 decision.[8] In the majority opinion, Justice Lewis F. Powell, Jr. said, "There is no support in the Constitution for the proposition that expression of views on issues of public importance loses First Amendment protection simply because its source is a corporation."

"For determining whether proposed speech," he continued, "is within the protection of the First Amendment, the inherent worth of the speech in terms of its capacity for informing the public does not depend on the identity of the source, whether corporation, association, union or individual."

---

8. First National Bank of Boston v. Francis X. Bellotti etc., 435 U.S. 765, (April 26, 1978).

CHAPTER
29

*IN FAIRNESS, CANDIDATES ARE
GUARANTEED EQUAL TIME*

IN FAIRNESS, CANDIDATES ARE GUARANTEED EQUAL TIME

✤

Within certain limits, access to radio and television by political candidates (and the general public) is mandated by law. This policy, known as the *Fairness Doctrine*, prevents a station from giving one candidate unfair advantage over another candidate. Fairness to candidates was thus guaranteed by Section 18 of the Radio Act of 1927 and incorporated as Section 315 of the Communications Act of 1934, which reads:

■ If any licensee shall permit any person who is a legally qualified candidate for any public office to use a broadcasting station, he shall afford equal opportunities to all other such candidates for that office in the use of such broadcasting station . . . Provided that such licensee shall have no power of censorship over the material broadcast under the provisions of this section. No obligation is hereby imposed upon any licensee to allow the use of its station by any such candidates.

The law was later extended to include editorials that favor or oppose a candidate, as specified in Section 73.1930 of the Code of Federal Regulations:

■ Where a licensee (radio or television station), in an editorial, endorses or opposes a legally qualified candidate or candidates, the licensee shall, within 24 hours after the editorial, transmit to, respectively, the other qualified candidate or candidates for the same office of the candidate opposed in the editorial, notification of the date and the time of the editorial, a script or tape of the editorial, and an offer of reasonable opportunity for the candidate or a spokesman of the candidate to respond over the licensee's facilities.

These regulations refer not only to over-the air broadcasts on radio and television stations but also to cablecasts over cable television systems.

Now, when a radio or television station or a cable system gives or sells time to a political candidate for use in promoting his candidacy, the station or the system must permit all other candidates for the same office equal opportunities to use the station or the system.

Also, when a radio or television station broadcasts an editorial opposing a political candidate, it must give that candidate reasonable opportunity to reply. Further, when a station broadcasts an editorial favoring or endorsing a candidate, it must give that candidate's opponents for that office equal opportunity in the use of the station.

Although access requirement for political candidates has commonly been called the "Equal Time" provision, the law actually requires "Equal Opportunities" and not necessarily precise equal time measured in minutes. Thus if one candidate is given the time free, opponents must be given free time to respond; and if a candidate is charged for the time, opponents must be charged at the same rate. The rate for political candidates "shall not exceed the charges made for comparable use of such station for other purposes." If a candidate buys time for his broadcast or broadcasts and his opponent is financially unable to buy time for responding, the station is under no obligation to give the opponent the time free or at a lower rate. Equal opportunities also mean approximately the same time of day. If one candidate broadcasts at 7 o'clock in the evening, his opponent cannot be shunted off to, say, 2 o'clock in the morning.

The law states that no broadcast station is obligated to allow a political candidate to use its facilities, but it may do so under certain conditions. The word "use" in that provision of the law was not agreed upon for several years after the law was enacted.

A complication regarding use by political candidates can arise in some elections when there are several candidates representing minority parties as well as those from the two major parties, all running for the same office. A station would not necessarily find it inconvenient or costly to provide equal opportunities for one or two opposing candidates, but several could constitute an overload on broadcast time. Stations therefore permit use with care.

Another problem can arise in regard to a candidate who is in office and is running for reelection. Is it considered *use* if the incumbent is given time on radio or television to report to the public on the activities of his office or is interviewed on the air on matters relating to that office? Is either considered *use* of broadcast facilities in terms of Section 315?

The question came up in 1956, for example, when President Eisenhower asked for and received 15 minutes of free time on the networks to report to the public on a crisis that had arisen in the Middle East. He was at the time a candidate for reelection; and his major opponent, Adlai Stevenson, and a minority party candidate both asked for equal time. The FCC ruled that the President's broadcast was exempt from the Section 315 requirement for equal time because he was using the broadcast facilities to report to the people on an international crisis.

The question of use was finally settled three years later in connection with a race for the office of mayor in Chicago where the incumbent was Richard Daley and one of his opponents was a perennial candidate named Lar Daly. As would be expected, the Mayor was frequently in the news on radio and television in his official capacity, so Lar Daly protested to the FCC that the Mayor was getting unfair advantage and asked that the Chicago broadcast stations be required to report equally on his, Daly's, activities. Much to the consternation of the broadcast industry, and to politicians, the FCC by a vote of 4-to-3 agreed with Daly that the appearance of a candidate in newscasts constituted use under Section 315 and therefore the Chicago stations must give Daly news coverage equal that given the Mayor.

If that ruling had been allowed to stand, broadcasters would have been highly restricted in reporting news not only of candidates but also of office holders by becoming liable to unreasonable equal-time requirements. Congress took note and immediately passed a bill, signed into law by President Eisenhower on September 14, 1959, stating that the appearance of a legally qualified candidate on any bona fide newscast, on-the-spot coverage of a news event, on a news documentary, and on regularly scheduled news interviews (such as "Meet the Press" and "Face the Nation") "shall not be deemed to be *use* of a broadcasting station" within the meaning of Section 315.

The law means, in effect, that broadcasters are free to pick and choose which candidates they feel are more newsworthy and can report on them without the risk of having to give others "equal opportunity."

The FCC has found it necessary to rule on other questions regarding use over the years. It has ruled that Section 315 does not apply in regard to a person speaking for or on behalf of a candidate, but it does apply, as examples, when a candidate broadcasts in some capacity other than as a candidate, when he appears on a variety show for a brief bow or statement, when as a Congressman he gives a weekly report to his constituents, when a candidate gives a victory or acceptance speech upon being nominated by his party, or when a candidate delivers a nonpolitical lecture as part of a regularly scheduled series broadcast on an educational station.

Among other questions pertaining to use that have arisen in past years was one regarding press conferences and another regarding political debates. In September 1975 the FCC ruled that broadcasting presidential press conferences is bona fide news coverage, thus exempt from Section 315, and later the Commission added that all press conferences by candidates for all offices are subject to the judgment of the broadcasters as to whether the conferences come under the rubric of news and thus are exempt.

The first televised political debates of national significance were the four in 1960 between John F. Kennedy, the Democratic presidential candidate, and Richard M. Nixon, the Republican presidential candidate. Those debates were exempted from the Section 315 requirement of equal time for opponents by a special Congressional resolution. The exemption was necessary because there were more than a score of qualified candidates in that election, as there are in all presidential elections. In 1975 the FCC ended that cumbersome method of exemption by ruling that debates between candidates of major political parties are exempt from the equal-time provision if the debates are arranged by someone or some organization other than the candidates or the broadcasters. For that reason, the debates were sponsored by the League of Women Voters, which had had years of experience in sponsoring political debates. The debates during presidential election years are now sponsored by the Commission on Presidential Debates, a nonpartisan group founded in 1987 with headquarters in Washington, D. C.

When a broadcast station permits a candidate to use its facilities to promote his candidacy, it cannot control what the candidate says in his broadcast. Since Section 315 states that the licensee "shall have no power of censorship over the material broadcast under the provisions of this section," candidates have freedom to speak uncensored by broadcast stations and the stations are not liable for any libelous or slanderous statements made by candidates.

That immunity for broadcasters, however, took about thirty years to achieve. The general principle of law is that anyone or any organization that assists in any way in the dissemination of slander or libel is liable for damages as is the person who said or published it. The laws in several states held broadcasters responsible for everything that went on the air, thus creating a dilemma in regard to political broadcasts. Section 315 said they were not responsible; state law said they were. Generally this conflict in law did not create a problem because it was common practice for station attorneys to read candidates' scripts in advance and advise them of words or sentences that could lead to lawsuits. In fact, some radio stations required scripts to be submitted two days in advance, and candidates could not deviate from changes made by the station. Occasionally, when the candidate refused to submit to the station requirements, the engineer would be provided with a script and "accidentally" bleep out libelous words through a "malfunction" of the broadcasting equipment.

The problem was resolved when broadcasters were given permanent immunity through a decision of the U.S. Supreme Court on June 29, 1959, in a case that arose on October 29, 1956, when A. C. Townley, an independent candidate in North Dakota for the U.S. Senate, demanded equal time on Station WDAY-TV in Fargo.[1] The station granted him the time; but when it examined his script, it warned him that the script contained a libelous statement. In that statement, Townley accused his opponent of "conspiring to establish a Communist Farmers Union Soviet right here in North Dakota," and said the Farmers Union was "Communist controlled."

The Farmers Union filed suit against Townley and WDAY-TV, asking for $100,000 in damages. The District Court dismissed the case against the station on the ground that it was protected by Section 315. The case was then appealed to the

---

1. Farmers Educational and Cooperative Union of America v. WDAY, Inc., 360 U.S. 525 (1959).

North Dakota Supreme Court, which ruled by a vote of 4-to-1 that radio and television broadcasters are not liable for libelous statements made by political candidates over their facilities. "We cannot believe," the Court sated, " that it was the intent of Congress to compel a station to broadcast libelous statements and at the same time subject it to the risk of defending actions for damages."

The case was then appealed to the U.S. Supreme Court, which agreed, although not unanimously, with the North Dakota courts that Section 315 grants radio and television stations an immunity for libelous statements made in broadcasts by political candidates. The decision set a precedent that forestalled any more such suits.

The majority opinion in that case delivered by Justice Hugo Black contains some background on Section 315: It reads in part:

■ Although the first, and for years the only judicial decision dealing with the censorship provision, did hold that a station may remove defamatory statements from political broadcasts, subsequent judicial interpretations of Section 315 have with considerable uniformity recognized that an individual licensee has no such power. And while for some years that Federal Communications Commission's views on this matter were not clearly articulated, since 1948 it has continuously held that licensees cannot remove libelous matter from speeches by candidates . . . permitting a broadcasting station to censor allegedly libelous remarks would undermine the basic purpose for which Section 315 was passed — full and unrestricted discussion of political issues by legally qualified candidates.

That section dates back to, and was adopted verbatim from the Radio Act of 1927 . . . Recognizing radio's potential importance as a medium of communication of political ideas, Congress sought to foster its broadest possible utilization by encouraging broadcast stations to make their facilities available to candidates for office without discrimination, and by insuring that these candidates when broadcasting were not to be hampered by censorship of the issues they could discuss . . . allowing censorship . . . would almost inevitably force a candidate to avoid controversial issue during political debates over radio and television, and hence restrict the coverage of consideration relevant to intelligent political decision.

The Fairness Doctrine goes beyond the right of reply by political candidates as mandated in Section 315 to include personal attacks. Title 47, Section 73.1910 of the Code of Federal Regulations, Revised Edition dated October 1, 1990, reads:

■   The Fairness Doctrine is contained in section 315(a) of the Communications Act of 1934, as amended, which provides that broadcasters have certain obligations to afford reasonable opportunities for the discussion of conflicting views on issues of public importance.

The right of reply is mandated as follows:

■   When, during the presentation of views on a controversial issue of public importance, an attack is made upon the honesty, character, integrity or like personal qualities of an identified person or group, the licensee shall . . . offer a reasonable opportunity to respond over the licensee's facilities.

The law requires the station to notify the person or the group attacked within a week and send a script or tape or an accurate summary of the broadcast with the notification. Personal attacks exempted from this requirement are those made on foreign groups or foreign public figures, those occurring during uses by legally qualified candidates or by their authorized spokespersons, and those that occur in news interviews and on-the-spot news coverage; but the requirement does apply to personal attacks made in editorials broadcast by the station.

The right of reply to a personal attack was upheld by the U.S. Supreme Court in 1969 in its landmark decision in the Red Lion case, which had its origin in the presidential campaign in 1964.

At issue was a portion of a broadcast over Radio Station WGCB in Red Lion, Pennsylvania, on November 25,[2] 1964, of a tape recording made by the Rev. Billy James Hargis in the studio of the Christian Crusade in Tulsa, Oklahoma. The Rev. Mr. Hargis was a conservative, strongly anticommunist radio evangelist who preached the "infallible word of God" and believed that the election of Barry M. Goldwater was essential to the survival of America as a free nation. In the presidential election on November 3 that year, however, Lyndon B. Johnson, Democratic candidate, defeated Goldwater, Republican candidate, by 486 to 52 electoral votes.

In his evangelical work, the Rev. Mr. Hargis recorded his sermons in Tulsa and sent them on a regular basis to numerous radio stations across the country, paying for the time with contributions from listeners. He had been incensed by the publication during the campaign that summer of a highly critical biography titled *Barry Goldwater: Extremist on the Right* by Fred J. Cook. About three weeks after the election, Hargis devoted a portion, less than two minutes, of one of his taped sermons to an attack on Cook that led to litigation. He said that "Cook had been fired by *The New York World Telegram* for making a false charge publicly on television against an unnamed official of the New York City government;" that Cook had then worked for a Communist-affiliated publication; that he had defended Alger Hiss (U.S. official

---

2. Records differ on the date. In the U.S. Supreme Court opinion, 395 U.S. 367 (1969), the date is given as November 27. Fred W. Friendly in "What's Fair on the Air?" *The New York Times Magazine*, March 30, 1975, gives the date as November 25.

convicted in 1950 for perjury regarding Communist conspiracy); that he had attacked J. Edgar Hoover and the Central Intelligence Agency; and that he had written this book to smear and destroy Barry Goldwater.

Hargis had more reason to attack Cook then merely his displeasure with the biography of Goldwater. Cook had also written an article for *The Nation* magazine titled "Hate Groups of the Air" in which Hargis figured prominently.

The Democratic National Committee encouraged anti-conservative publicity during the campaign as a means of helping to defeat Goldwater, and, according to Fred Friendly, indirectly sponsored publication of the Goldwater biography through The National Council for Civic Responsibility. Lawyers working with the Committee helped Cook draft a letter demanding free time to reply to the "scandalous and libelous attack" on him by Hargis. The letter was mailed in mimeographed form to about 200 stations that had carried the Hargis broadcast. About fifty stations replied with an offer of time for reply, but WGCB in Red Lion replied, "Our rate card is enclosed. Your prompt reply will enable us to arrange for the time you may wish to purchase."

In response, Cook petitioned the FCC to direct the station in Red Lion to give him the time free, which the FCC did; but the station owner, the Rev. John M. Norris, refused the FCC order and brought suit against the FCC in the Court of Appeals in Washington, D. C. The Court upheld the FCC, which then proceeded to publish a new set of rules "to clarify and make more precise the obligations of broadcast licensees where they have aired personal attacks and editorials regarding political candidates."

While Red Lion litigation was under way, the Radio-Television News Directors Association (RTNDA) became concerned that the rights of broadcasters were being endangered. In an effort to protect their freedom, the RTNDA brought suit in the Seventh Circuit Court of Appeals in Chicago, contesting the authority of the FCC to impose the fairness doctrine personal-attack rules.[3]   The Association, contending that the rules abridged freedom of speech and of the press, retained Archibald Cox, Harvard Law Professor and former U.S. Solicitor General,[4] as its representative in the case. In a unanimous decision, the Court in Chicago struck down the FCC rules "as colliding with free-speech and free-press guarantees in the First Amendment."

With the Court of Appeals in Washington upholding the authority of the FCC, and the Court of Appeals in Chicago denying the FCC such authority, the cases were then certain to be appealed to the U.S. Supreme Court, as they were, and there they were considered together. In a unanimous decision handed down on June 9, 1969, the Supreme Court upheld the authority of the FCC to establish and enforce the rules.[5]

Excerpts from the opinion of the Court, written by Justice Byron R. White, follow:[6]

■   Before 1927, the allocation of frequencies was left entirely to the private sector, and the result was chaos. It quickly became apparent that broadcast frequencies constituted a scarce resource whose use could be regulated and rationalized only by the government . . . Consequently, the Federal Radio Commission was established to allocate frequencies among competing applicants in a manner responsive to the public "convenience, interest, or necessity."

Because of the scarcity of radio frequencies, the Government is permitted to put restraints on licensees in

---

3. The RTNDA was joined in the suit by CBS, NBC, et al.
4. He later became Chairman of Common Cause.
5. Red Lion Broadcasting Co. v. FCC, 395 U.S. 367 (June 9, 1969).
6. Only seven justices participated in the decision. Justice Fortas had resigned earlier that spring and that seat was vacant. Justice Douglas abstained because he had been absent during the oral arguments recovering from an appendix operation.

favor of others whose views should be expressed on this unique medium . . . It is the right of the viewers and listeners, not the right of the broadcasters, which is paramount.

Where there are substantially more individuals who want to broadcast than there are frequencies to allocate, it is idle to posit an unbridgeable First Amendment right to broadcast comparable to the right of every individual to speak, write, or publish.

Although broadcasting is clearly a medium affected by a First Amendment interest, differences in the characteristics of new media justify differences in the First Amendment standards applied to them . . .

Nor can we say that it is inconsistent with the First Amendment goal of producing an informed public capable of conducting its own affairs to require a broadcaster to permit answers to personal attacks occurring in the course of discussing controversial issues, or to require that the political opponents of those endorsed by the station be given a chance to communicate with the public. Otherwise, station owners and a few networks would have unfettered power to make time available only to the highest bidders, to communicate only their views on public issues, people and candidates, and to permit on the air only those with whom they agreed. There is no sanctuary in the First Amendment for unlimited private censorship operating in a medium not open to all . . . we hold that the regulations and ruling at issue here are both authorized by statute and constitutional.

In that decision, the Court set forth two significant principles:

■ The FCC requirement that broadcasters allow answers to personal attacks is not an abridgment of the right of free speech and press guaranteed by the First Amendment.

■ The First Amendment may be applied differently to broadcasting from that applied to the print media because of the unique characteristics of broadcasting.

The decision stunned broadcasters, who had always believed that radio and television should have the same freedom as the press; and they had been insisting on that equality since the Fairness Doctrine was instituted in 1949. Their rationale for opposing government control of broadcast content explicit in the Fairness Doctrine was clearly stated by Frank Stanton, president of CBS, in a talk at a meeting of Sigma Delta Chi[7] in Chicago on May 24, 1961, in which he said in part:

■ A free society cannot say of one medium that it shall have less freedom than another . . . If the freedom of any medium is restricted, the foundation for the freedom of all media is gone, and freedom eventually becomes a government handout.

Nor can a free society give governmental agencies the power to roam around the substance of publications or of broadcasts, choosing what matter shall be free and what subject to government restraints and reprisals, except in the case of clearly and publicly defined security matters.

Despite protests, however, the Supreme Court has upheld distinctions among press, broadcast, motion picture, and commercial (advertising) speech.

In *Joseph Burstyn, Inc. v. Wilson* in 1952 the Court held that "motion pictures are (not) necessarily subject to the precise rules governing any other particular method of expression," and in *Virginia State Board of Pharmacy v. Virginia Citizens Consumer Council* in 1976 it held that commercial speech (advertising) can be regulated by the government.

Most discussion and contention over government control of broadcasting arose over the Fairness Doctrine, in which the FCC sought to determine the role of broadcasters in public

---

7. Later renamed Society of Professional Journalists, SDX.

service. As early as 1929 the Federal Radio Commission, in considering how this new medium of communication should function, issued a statement that said in part that "the public interest requires ample play for the free and fair competition of opposing views."

The matter remained dormant until 1939 when Station WAAB of the Yankee Network, Inc., applied for renewal of its license. The Mayflower Broadcasting Company filed an objection on the ground that the station had been broadcasting editorials and therefore should be denied license renewal and that the license should be transferred to itself. The FCC denied the petition because WAAB had stopped editorializing on the air and did not plan to resume doing so, and also because the FCC believed that the Mayflower Broadcasting Company did not have the financial resources to construct and operate a station.

In renewing the WAAB license, the FCC issued what came to be known as the Mayflower Decision, which forbade broadcasting of editorials. Dated January 16, 1941, it states:

■ A truly free radio cannot be used to advocate the cause of a licensee. It cannot be devoted to support the candidates of his friends. It cannot be devoted to principles he happens to regard most favorably. In brief, the broadcaster cannot be an advocate.

Then eight years later in 1949 the FCC reversed itself, largely in response to complaints by broadcasters that denial of the right to editorialize was an infringement on freedom of speech. After hearings titled, "In the Matter of Editorializing by Broadcast Licensees," the FCC issued the "Revised Mayflower Decision" ruling that editorials are permissible and it stipulated that a reasonable amount of time must be given to discussion of controversial issues. Guidelines stated that such discussion must not be one-sided and that broadcasters must see to it that opposing views are presented.

In a document titled, "Report on Editorializing by Broadcast Licensee," which became known as the Fairness Doctrine, the FCC stated the "necessity" for broadcasters to devote "a consideration and discussion of public issues in the community." With respect to such programs, the FCC stated, stations should give attention "to the different attitudes and viewpoints concerning those vital and often controversial issues which are held by the various groups that make up the community."

Broadcasters found compliance with the Fairness Doctrine costly in terms of broadcast time for which compensation was not possible, and they found it burdensome in that stations were required to seek out persons to make replies to controversial issues discussed on the air. The ruling had a negative effect in that, in many instances, it resulted in broadcasters' refusing to program anything controversial in order to avoid the hassle of obtaining and broadcasting replies. Also, broadcasters felt that the Doctrine was a denial of their freedom under the First Amendment.

Although the Fairness Doctrine was a noble idea, its flaws were sufficient to cause it to self-destruct. Government requirements on broadcast content were one such flaw, although not the fatal one. The greater flaw was the virtual impossibility of determining precisely what constitutes "a controversial issue." One example of what the FCC faced was a request in 1966 by John F. Banzhaf III, a lawyer in New York, for free time for responsible groups opposed to smoking to respond to cigarette commercials. The FCC agreed, and issued a ruling that stations presenting cigarette commercials must also allow opportunity for the other side, that is, that smoking may be hazardous to your health, as stated in the Surgeon General's Report.

That ruling brought protests from some stations as well as from the National Association of Broadcasters (the NAB) which feared that if the FCC can make that rule regarding cigarettes, can it also do the same with other products? The

FCC answered that the cigarette issue was unique, so there would be no Fairness Doctrine application to any other products.

The FCC struggled valiantly to handle Fairness questions, issuing an Advisory in 1963 to clarify the Doctrine and a Fairness Primer the next year. It was in 1964 that the Red Lion case originated, with the Supreme Court decision in 1969 leading to more confusion than clarification concerning the meaning of "controversial issues." By 1971 the FCC was receiving more than 2,000 requests and petitions annually for free time to reply to controversial issues. They arose from all sorts of programs, including documentaries, news broadcasts, talk shows, commercials, and dramatic programs on radio and television.

With the end of the war in Vietnam and the end of the military draft in 1973, the mood of the country changed, resulting in fewer protests and fewer "demands for equal opportunity" on broadcast stations. The FCC still continued enforcing the Fairness Doctrine, repeating its policy in a bulletin in March 1975, which stated in part:

> ■ The purpose of the Fairness Doctrine is to protect the right of the public to be informed, not to provide broadcast time to any particular person or group.
>
> The Commission believes that licensees are obligated to give the public more than one viewpoint on a controversial issue of public importance. The policy requires a licensee who presents one side of a controversial issue of public importance to afford reasonable opportunity for presentation of opposing viewpoints on that issue.
>
> Opposing views need not be presented on the same program or even in the same series of programs, so long as an effort is made in good faith to present contrasting views . . .

It was not to be. The end of that concept of fairness on the air was signaled by the election of Ronald Reagan as president on November 4, 1980. He had run on a platform of "less government," and much deregulation of industry took place during his tenure.

The Commission recognized by 1984 that conditions had changed drastically, and it questioned whether, in the market place at that time, the Fairness Doctrine was needed to foster the First Amendment goal of "the widest possible dissemination of information from diverse and antagonistic sources." It also questioned whether the Fairness Doctrine was not in fact counterproductive, actually "chilling" in its effect on the free expression of ideas.

The NAB presented data showing that there was no scarcity of media voices, noting that more than 7,000 new broadcast stations had gone on the air since the 1949 Report; and it also cited a number of case studies documenting the existence of a "chilling effect" on free expression resulting from the complexity and vagueness of the Fairness Doctrine and the economic burdens it imposed on broadcasters.

To forestall abolition of the Fairness Doctrine, Congress passed a bill in the summer of 1987 that would write the Doctrine into law; but President Reagan vetoed the bill on June 20 as "antagonistic to the freedom of expression guaranteed by the Constitution." About six weeks later the FCC, whose composition had been changed by Reagan appointments, voted unanimously on August 4 to discontinue the Fairness Doctrine. In doing so, it contended that the Doctrine "had resulted in excessive and unnecessary government intervention into the editorial processes of broadcast journalism" and that it "had the net effect of reducing rather than enhancing the discussion of controversial issues of public importance."

That is what broadcasters had been saying for years. They had insisted that the Fairness Doctrine not only infringed on their freedom of speech but actually hindered discussion through fear that if they covered a controversial topic, they would be deluged with requests for free time. Often they refused to broadcast any sort of program that could be considered controversial in order to avoid providing "reasonable opportunity for reply." As one critic pointed out, "If neither side of a controversy receives any air time, then coverage has been equal."

Repeal of the Fairness Doctrine, however, was not total. Still in effect are Section 315 regarding equal opportunity for political candidates and, although rarely used, the right of reply to personal attacks on the air. Abolished was the requirement that a broadcaster must afford reasonable opportunity for the presentation of opposing viewpoints on controversial issues of public importance.

Another plan adopted by the FCC for public access to television besides that of the Fairness Doctrine which appeared to be desirable but proved to be virtually useless is the Prime Time Access Rule. In 1970, with the three networks dominating television broadcasting, the FCC decided that for television to operate in the public interest some of prime time should be reserved for programs by community leaders and civic groups on matters of local interest. To this end it adopted a regulation which, as amended, reads:

> ■ Effective September 8, 1975, commercial television stations owned by or affiliated with a national television network in the 50 largest television markets shall devote, during the four hours of prime time, no more than three hours to the presentation of programs from a national network, programs formerly on a national network (off-network programs) other than feature films, or, on Saturdays, feature films.

The regulation explained that "the top 50 markets are the 50 largest markets in terms of average prime time television audience for all stations in the market," and it made exceptions for fast-breaking news, political broadcasts, runover of live network broadcasts of sporting events, and various other live broadcasts. Prime time is listed as being from 7 to 11 p.m.

Eastern and Pacific time and from 6 to 10 p.m. Central and Mountain time.[8]

Two factors made it impractical for the prime time hour to be used as visualized. One was the escalating costs of television programming, which was far beyond what most local groups could afford; the other was the lack of organized talent at the community level that could produce programs of sufficient professional quality to attract and hold audiences. In the absence of local programs, the stations began filling the hour with game shows such as *Family Feud* and *Wheel of Fortune* and syndicated programs such as *Mash* and *Growing Pains*. While stations like the arrangement because the shows are popular and highly profitable, the local community utilization of the time has been largely forgotten.

Still another effort by the FCC to provide local access to television broadcasting has been in the area of cable transmission. In the early 1950s cable transmission began as community antenna television (CATV) in communities unfavorably located for receiving signals from the nearest television stations. Because signals travel in a straight line, towns and villages in valleys and beyond mountains were handicapped in receiving clear signals. To overcome the handicap, a community would organize a company to erect a large antenna atop a hill or a nearby high point, run cables to subscribing homes below, and charge each home a fee to cover costs.

That system brought in one station, or possibly two or three; but soon the establishment of microwave transmission capable of bringing in multiple stations gave television reception a new dimension. It raised such questions as these: Does a cable company have a right to pick up signals from a television station and charge customers for its transmission? Is some of the transmission violating copyright laws? What

---

8. Time of day for largest number of radio listeners is called Drive Time and runs from 6 to 9 a.m. and 4 to 7 p.m.

government agency has the authority to regulate cable television?

Authority of the FCC to regulate cable television was affirmed by the U.S. Supreme Court when it ruled on June 10, 1968, that CATV is interstate communication and therefore subject to Federal regulation and that the authority of the FCC to regulate cable television "is ancillary to the effective performance of the Commission's various responsibilities for the regulation of television broadcasting."[9]

Applying to cable transmission the principle that broadcasting is to operate in the pubic interest, at least in some respects, the FCC in 1969 ruled that any cable system having 3,500 or more subscribers must provide original, nonbroadcast material to a significant extent. As the word "significant" was not defined, some cable systems complied merely by focusing a camera on a clock so viewers could always know the correct time by tuning to that channel. Other cable companies did bring in significant nonbroadcast programs.

That requirement, eventually dropped, was retained in a set of rules the FCC issued in 1972 which required the cable systems in the top 100 markets to make some nonbroadcast access channels available to provide for local interest. The channels included:

■ Public Access Channel, available to the public on a first-come first-served basis where individuals can communicate whatever they wish, without censorship by the system and without having to pay for the time.

■ Educational Access Channel, assigned full-time for use by educational authorities and institutions.

■ Local Government Access Channel, for use by local government.

---

9. United States v. Southwestern Cable Co. and Midwest Television Inc. v. Southwestern Cable Co., 392 U.S. 157 (1968).

■ Leased Access Channels, for use by individuals, companies, and organizations, with no advertising restrictions, on a lease basis. Under that plan, which is still in effect, cable channels are open to local entrepreneurs to operate on a profit or nonprofit basis.

These requirements were in harmony with the FCC's belief that cable operators have an obligation to provide public access channels; and in fact it ruled that in return for the privilege of using the air, cable systems must provide a public forum "for the enrichment of the lives of the people." The U.S. Supreme Court, however, ruled in April 1978 that the FCC did not have the right to require access channels. Although then no longer compulsory, some cable systems continued to provide access channels as they still do today.

Further changes in cable regulations were made by the Cable Communications Policy Act of 1984, reflecting deregulation which took place from 1981 to 1989 during the Reagan administration. This Act, which became Title VI of the Communications Act of 1934 as amended, does not classify cable systems on the basis of the top 100 markets in regard to access channels for community use. Rather, all cable systems are on the same basis in this regard, but none are required by FCC regulations to provide public, educational, or local government access channels. Now, under the present law, a community may have one or more access channels in its cable system in one of two ways. One is for the cable company to provide an access channel as a good-will gesture; the other is for the local governing body to require in the franchise agreement that the cable system provide one or more access channels.

Section 611 of the Cable Communication Policy Act of 1984 states:

■ A franchising authority may establish requirements in a franchise with respect to the designation or use of channel capacity for public, educational, or governmental use . . . A cable operator shall not exercise any editorial control over any public, educational, or governmental use . . .

The provision regarding leasing of some unused channels is retained in the Act to "assure that the widest possible diversity of information sources are made available to the public from cable systems." Such channels are to be designated on a percentage of the total number of channels, so that a cable system with 36 to 45 activated channels must designate 10 per cent of them as available for lease; those with 55 or more channels, 15 percent; but systems with fewer than 36 channels are exempt from this requirement.

The Communications Policy Act of 1984 was modified by the 1992 Cable Act primarily in regard to rates and the content of leased channels.

Since December 29, 1986, most cable systems have been free to set the amount they charge without local government approval. The 1992 Cable Act requires the FCC to set maximum rates that can be charged for such services as basic service, leased channels, and premium and pay-per-view channels. Other services may be reviewed by the FCC after receipt of price complaint.

The 1992 Cable Act requires the FCC to establish rules that will curb the presentation of indecent and obscene programming on leased access channels; and it requires cable operators to place all "indecent" leased programming on a single channel, available only to subscribers who specifically request it, or to adopt guidelines to protect viewers from indecent and obscene programming.

The 1992 law prohibits cable operators from having any editorial control over the content of public, educational, and government channels; but it does allow them the right to prohibit obscene or sexually explicit material, or material soliciting or promoting unlawful conduct, on any public, educational, or governmental channel; with the provision that cable operators will be held accountable for the transmission of such material.

The Act also makes commercial theft of cable television signals a felony, with penalties of $50,000 and 2 years imprisonment for the first offense and $100,000 and 5 years imprisonment for any subsequent offense.

Cable television continues to play an increasingly important role in American society. It now provides about 60 percent of the viewing public with all their television news, information, and entertainment. The future promises further advances, with scientific development making it possible for cable systems to expand up to 150 channels within a few years.

CHAPTER
30

✾

YOU HAVE A RIGHT TO READ

YOU HAVE A RIGHT TO READ

❦

"The essence of the First Amendment right to freedom of the press is not so much the right to print as it is the right to read."

Few will disagree with that statement, made by a Federal District Court judge in a decision in 1964.[1] Yet, is the right to read unlimited? Does the government not have a duty to protect its people from degrading pornography that is immoral and serves no useful purpose? Certainly many people think so and favor restrictions on all forms of obscenity and other kinds of harmful materials.

So have two government agencies that for years vigorously censored reading and viewing matter. They are the U.S. Postal Service (formerly the Post Office Department) and the U.S. Customs Service (formerly the Bureau of Customs). The Customs Service is responsible for preventing pornographic materials from entering the country, and the Postal Service is responsible for keeping such materials from being delivered by mail anywhere in the country.

Was that kind of control of reading matter unconstitutional? No, the Bureau of Customs argued. The First Amendment guarantee of a free press does not include the foreign press, the Bureau said; and as the Amendment has no relation to international trade, it does not prohibit Congress from giving Customs the right to seize and hold in custody

---

1. United States v. 18 Packages of Magazines, 238 F. Supp. 846, 847-8 (N.D.Cal. 1964).

obscene books and magazines shipped to this country from abroad.

The Post Office Department also held that its actions were exempt from any restrictions that might be imposed by the First Amendment. As a collection and delivery service, it contended that it has the right to decide what it will collect and deliver. That argument was upheld by Stephen J. Field, a justice of the U.S. Supreme Court from 1863 to 1897. He stated in an ex parte opinion that the government as owner of the mail service has the right to set rates and provide facilities for carrying the mail; and because the Department is a government entity, Congress has the right to name what kinds of communications and materials are acceptable for collection and delivery.

Such restrictions as Congress chose to set would not be a violation of the First Amendment guarantee of freedom of speech and the press, Justice Field stated, because there were other channels of communication open to the public, so no one could rightly complain if the mails were closed to forms of expression that Congress deemed noxious. He did say, however, that the Fourth Amendment, which prohibits unreasonable searches and seizures, was applicable, so postal officials had no right to open sealed mail without first obtaining a search warrant.

Both arguments, that of the Bureau of Customs and that of the Post Office Department, were specious, of course. Few in authority, however, seemed to question them. As a result, for many years the American people were strictly protected from the evils of pornography, from printed matter, pictures, and art objects that were considered prurient or obscene or morally objectionable by both Customs and Post Office officials.

Legal prohibition of the obscene began early in this country, with Vermont passing a law in 1821 against indecent literature, the first state to do so. Other states followed, with Connecticut passing a similar law in 1834 and Massachusetts in 1835.

In 1842 Congress made the Bureau of Customs a guardian of purity by enacting a law, part of which prohibited "the importation of all indecent and obscene prints, paintings, lithographs, engravings, and transparencies," and it stated that "all invoices and packages whereof any such articles shall compose a part, are hereby declared liable to be proceeded against, seized, and forfeited by due course of law, and the said articles shall be forthwith destroyed."

The law was amended in 1857 to include such articles as images, statues, figures and indecent photographs, including "dirty" postcards from France. It covered any indecent articles that foreign travelers attempted to bring into the country as well as commercial imports.

In 1873 the original law was redrafted to provide for the seizure of obscene printed publications. The original law had prohibited only obscene pictorial matter from entering the country. From then on for the next sixty years, until the Supreme Court decision in the Ulysses case in 1933 (*United States v. One Book*), Customs prevented anything from entry that it considered "off color."

In judging literature, Customs officials applied the Hicklin test, which meant that any book or magazine that contained even one obscene word or sentence could be denied entry. On that basis, numerous literary works of merit were kept out; and books by noted authors such as Aristophanes and Voltaire were seized. A 17-volume limited edition of *Arabian Nights* by Sir Richard Francis Burton, for example, could not be imported.

One Customs official told a newspaper reporter in 1930 that he had read and barred 272 titles involving thousands of volumes from entering the country. Among books seized by Customs as late as 1929 were Giovanni Boccaccio's *Decameron*, Rabelais' *Gargantua,* and Daniel Defoe's *Foxana* and *Moll Flanders.* There was no provision for department review. Publishers could go to court, but that was time-consuming and expensive. In one important respect,

Customs was saddled with a task it was not designed to perform. Its primary work was valuation of merchandise, not literary judgment.

Books considered obscene could be admitted if they were expurgated; that is, if they were published in editions that omitted the offending words and passages. Numerous books were reprinted to meet that requirement. Among them, as an example, was *All Quiet On The Western Front* by Eric Remarque, a best-selling antiwar work published after the end of World War I.

Movies from abroad were reviewed by a customs official designated as a "reviewer." If he found something he considered obscene in a film, he would recommend to the Deputy Collector that the film be retained. The recommendation would then be sent to Washington for approval, which was almost always routine; and the importer would be notified that the film had been seized as contraband. The Bureau of Customs, not the courts, decided what was obscene and what was not.

The Post Office Department was equally vigorous in censorship of the obscene. One of the oldest institutions in the country, the Post Office dates back to 1619 when Massachusetts enacted a law establishing the first in the American colonies. In 1753 Benjamin Franklin was appointed deputy postmaster for the North British Colonies in American, but he was dismissed from the position in 1774 because of his support for independence from England. The next year the Continental Congress, which was organized in 1774, appointed him Postmaster General and reappointed him to the position in 1776. That was while the Revolutionary War was being fought to obtain freedom from England and before the present Constitution had been adopted.

In the more than two centuries since that time, a number of significant changes have been made in the postal service. In 1819 the Post Office Department was given cabinet rank; in 1847 Congress authorized the use of postage stamps; and on July 1, 1971, the Department became the U.S. Postal Service (USPS) as it is today.

The first comprehensive law providing for the classification of mail was enacted by Congress on March 3, 1879. Then there were three major classes of mail; today there are four. They are First Class, for sealed mail; Second Class, for newspapers, magazines, and other periodicals; Third Class, for bulk mail; and Fourth Class, for parcel post packages.

The Postal Service with a work force of 800,000 and delivering billions of pieces of mail a year (62.8 billion in 1989) provides a means of communication vital to virtually every aspect of American society. Two facets of its operation, however, led to litigation in the past. One was its arbitrary censorship of materials it considered obscene; the other was the interpretation of its authority to grant and to withhold second-class mailing permits.

Second class provides a low rate of postage for newspapers, magazines, and other periodicals that qualify, to encourage "the widest dissemination of news, information, and opinion to the public at the lowest possible cost." As stated by the Postal Commission of 1911, "the original object in placing the second class matter at a rate far below that of any other class of mail was to encourage the dissemination of news and current literature of educational value." That is in keeping with the principle applied at the very beginning of the present government. A favorable rate of postage was granted newspapers by the Act of February 20, 1792, and the rate was extended to magazines and pamphlets by the Act of May 8, 1794.

To be eligible for a second-class permit, a periodical must be printed, not mimeographed or duplicated; it must be issued at regular intervals and not less than four times a year; it must contain information besides advertising; and it must have a legitimate list of subscribers.

Determining whether a publication meets those requirements is relatively simple, but another requirement which pertains to content calls for judgment. The law states that "the publication must be originated and published for the dissemination of information of a public character, or devoted to literature, the sciences, arts, or some special industry." Disagreements over that requirement eventually reached the courts.

A second-class permit is vital for newspapers, magazines, and other periodicals that use the mail for all or most of their circulation, for without the permit circulation costs by any other class would be prohibitive. The Postal Service can thus stop circulation of a publication dependent upon a second-class permit merely be revoking the permit. What authority the Postal Service has to revoke such permits and under what conditions it may legally do so has been tested in two cases that reached the U.S. Supreme Court, both on the basis of content but with opposite results.

In a decision in 1921 the Supreme Court upheld the authority of the Postmaster General to revoke a second-class mailing permit.[2] The case began when the Third Assistant Postmaster General, after holding a hearing on September 22, 1917, withdrew the second-class privilege of the *Milwaukee Leader* for violating the Espionage Act of 1917.

The Act provided that when the United States was at war (and it was at the time of the hearing in 1917), any newspaper published in violation of any provision of the Act becomes "nonmailable" and may not be "conveyed in the mails or delivered from any post office or by any letter carrier."

Between April 14 and September 13, 1917, the first five months after the United States had entered World War I, the *Milwaukee Leader* published numerous articles opposing the war, stating that the war was unjustified and dishonorable on the part of the United States and that it was a capitalistic war

---

2. Milwaukee Social Democrat Publishing Company v. Burleson, 255 U. S. 407 (1921).

forced upon the people to serve selfish ends. Other articles called the military draft unconstitutional, arbitrary, and oppressive; and it urged that the draft law not be obeyed. The newspaper stated further that the United States was waging a war of conquest and fighting for commercial supremacy and world domination.

When the case went to court, both the trial court and the appeals court upheld the right of the Post Office to revoke the second-class permit. The case then went to the U.S. Supreme Court where the decision to deny the *Milwaukee Leader* a second-class mailing privilege was upheld. The decision was not unanimous, however. Both Justices Oliver Wendell Holmes and Louis D. Brandeis wrote dissenting opinions that were influential in a future court decision on this subject.

In the majority opinion, Justice John H. Clarke stated that the articles in the *Leader* "prove clearly that the publisher ... was deliberately and persistently doing all in his power to deter readers from supporting the war ... and to induce them to lend aid and comfort to the enemies. The order of the Postmaster General not only finds reasonable support ... but is amply justified."

He held that the power to suspend or revoke a second-class privilege accompanies the power to grant the privilege, a rule, he wrote, that "has been recognized by statute and by many decisions of this court."

Justice Brandeis, in dissent, questioned whether Congress had conferred on the Postmaster General the authority which he had exercised in this case, or whether the authority had been illegally exercised. In this regard, he wrote, "The trial and punishment of the crime is a function which the Constitution intrusts to the judiciary. I am not aware that any other civil administrative officer has assumed . . . the power to inflict upon a citizen severe punishment . . ."

Justice Holmes in his dissent agreed, stating that "the only power given to the Postmaster is to refrain from forwarding the papers when received and to return them to the senders."

He stated further:

> ■ ... the use of the mails is almost as much a part of free speech as the right to use our tongues, and it would take very strong language to convince me that Congress ever intended to give such a practically despotic power to any one man.

The question of whether the Postal Service had the authority to deny second-class mailing privileges on the basis of the contents of publications was the key question in the decision by the U.S. Supreme Court in 1946.[3] The case arose when Postmaster General Hannegan revoked the second-class permit of *Esquire, Magazine for Men,* in 1943 because of the contents of issues from January to November that year. That order, if enforced, would virtually put the magazine out of business as its second-class mail permit was worth about a half million dollars a year.

Hannegan looked upon the low mail rates provided by the Post Office as a government subsidy, and he believed that a government subsidy should not be used to benefit any publication that was not pro bono publico. To enjoy the second-class mailing privilege, Hannegan said, "A publication is bound to do more than refrain from disseminating material which is obscene or bordering on the obscene. It is under a positive duty to contribute to the public good and the public welfare."

Postal officials recognized the impossibility of judging the literary and educational qualities of periodicals, so the granting of a second-class permit has never depended on whether the periodical is well written or poorly written, or whether its contents have literary merit. At the same time, however, they held that to be eligible, a publication must

---

3. Hannegan v. Esquire, 327 U.S. 146 (1946).

contribute positively to society. "A second-class mail privilege is a publication's certificate of good moral character," declared Postmaster General Walker in the annual report of the Post Office Department in 1942. In the opinion of postal officials, *Esquire* magazine did not meet that criterion.

Esquire had begun publication ten years earlier in 1933, at which time it had been granted a second-class permit. The magazine was considered somewhat sexy, but certainly it did not contain the erotic overtones of *Playboy* and *Penthouse*, which began publication some years later. The revocation order, or rather, a citation to show cause why the magazine's second-class permit should not be revoked, was not based on allegations of obscenity but instead on the failure of the magazine to contribute to the public good. Mr. Hannegan stated:

■ Writings and pictures may be indecent, vulgar, and risqué and still not be obscene in a technical sense . . . When, however, they become a dominant and systematic feature they most certainly cannot be said to be for the public good, and a publication which uses them in that manner is not making the "special contribution to the public welfare" which Congress intended in the Fourth condition.

When the case reached the U.S. Supreme Court, the Court upheld the right of *Esquire* to a second-class mailing permit in a unanimous decision. Although the decision restated that the Court has held that Congress can constitutionally make it a crime to send fraudulent or obscene materials through the mail, it has not left the Postmaster General with power "to prescribe standards for literature or the art which a mailable periodical disseminates."

The Court opinion, written by Justice William O. Douglas, reads in part:

■ . . . the favorable second-class rates were granted . . . so that the public good might be served . . . But that is a far cry from assuming that Congress had any idea that each applicant for the second class rate must convince the Postmaster General that his publication contributes to the public good or to the public welfare . . .

To uphold the order of revocation would . . . grant the Postmaster General a power of censorship. Such a power is so abhorrent to our traditions that a purpose to grant it should not be easily inferred.

CHAPTER
31

❀

*CENSORSHIP KEPT THE
MAIL CLEAN*

CENSORSHIP KEPT THE
MAIL CLEAN

❦

As early as 1835 an attempt was made to give the Post Office authority to censor the mail as a result of the Abolition movement. President Jackson felt that antislavery tracts and pamphlets being mailed to addresses in slave states could stir up trouble there, so he urged Congress to give the Post Office power to stop that kind of mail.

Nothing came of that; but censorship of the obscene began with the Congressional Act of March 3, 1865, which stated that "no obscene book shall be admitted to the mails . . . (and all such publications deposited in or received at any Post Office or discovered in the mails shall be seized and destroyed or otherwise disposed of." The Act imposed criminal penalties for knowingly mailing obscenity.

The codification of laws in 1872 extended the obscenity law by stating that "no letter upon the envelope of which, or postal card upon which, scurrilous epithets have been written should be carried in the mail."

Postal censorship of the obscene began in earnest after Congress passed what is commonly known as the Comstock Act of 1873. The Act read in part:

■ Section 1461. Mailing Obscene or Crime-Inciting Matter.

■ Declared to be unmailable matter and shall not be conveyed in the mails or delivered by any post office or by any letter carrier:

■ Every obscene, lewd, lascivious, or filthy book, pamphlet, picture, paper, letter, writing, print, or other publication of an indecent character; and

■ Every article or thing designed, adapted, or intended for preventing conception or producing abortion, or for any indecent or immoral use; and

■ Every article, instrument, substance, drug, medicine, or thing which is advertised or described in a manner calculated to lead another to use or apply it for preventing conception or producing abortion, or for any indecent or immoral purposes; and

■ Every written or printed card, letter, circular, book, pamphlet, advertisement, or notice of any kind giving information, directly or indirectly, where, or how, or from whom, or by what means any of such mentioned matters, articles, or things may be obtained or made, or where or by whom any act or operation of any kind for the procuring or producing of abortion will be done or performed, or how or by what means conception may be prevented or abortion produced, whether sealed or unsealed; and

■ Every paper, writing, advertisement, or representation that any article, instrument, substance, drug, medicine, or thing may, or can, be used or applied for preventing conception or producing abortion, or for any indecent or immoral purpose; and

■ Every description calculated to induce or incite a person to so use or apply any such article , instrument, substance, drug, medicine, or thing.

■ The term "indecent" as used in this section (of the law) includes matter of a character tending to incite arson, murder, or assassination.

■ Violation of this Act is punishable by a fine of not more than $5,000 and imprisonment of not more than 5 years or both for the first offense and double for each offense thereafter.

In brief, the Act made it illegal to mail or attempt to mail any material that was considered obscene or that promoted fraudulent banking practices, swindles by mail, medical quackery, birth control, and abortion.

The Act is named for Anthony Comstock, who was instrumental in getting it enacted. He was born in 1844 in Connecticut, enlisted for a short time as a soldier in the Civil War, and moved to New York City in 1867 where he worked as a store clerk. There he became appalled by the "shocking" books and pictures he saw being passed around by employees, and as a result he made fighting obscenity and immorality his life's work.

Comstock spent much of his spare time searching newsstands and bookstores for "offensive" publications. The New York State Legislature had passed a law in 1868 against obscene literature, and Comstock took advantage of the law to enter legal complaints against dealers he found offering "immoral and obscene" books and magazines for sale.

He wanted a Federal law, however, so he could go after the publishers nationwide, not only dealers, so in 1872 in cooperation with the YMCA he organized the New York Committee for the Suppression of Vice to aid in the enforcement of the state law against obscenity and also in obtaining the federal legislation he wanted. (The word Committee was later changed to Society.)

At age 28, Comstock moved to Washington, D.C., to lobby for a law against pornography and vice. Because of his intense interest, he was well prepared to persuade Congress to enact an obscenity law as he was reported to have known more than anyone else in government about the law of 1865 that prohibited sending obscene material by mail. He was successful as the bill he wished to have passed was approved by both the House and the Senate with less than an hour of debate in a flurry of last-minute legislation in the closing session of Congress. The final vote came at 2 a.m. on a Sunday morning, in 1873, with the clock stopped at midnight.

After the law passed, Comstock gave up his work as a store clerk and went into the business of censorship full time. He was able to get himself appointed as a special agent of the Post Office Department with police powers; and he served in that position for 42 years with great zeal without salary but receiving a part of the fines collected on convictions until his death in 1915. By the time the first full year had passed under the Federal obscenity act, Comstock reported that he had seized 194,000 obscene pictures and photographs, 134,000 pounds of books, 60,300 rubber articles, 5,500 sets of playing cards, and 31,150 boxes of pills and powders.

Within three years he was able to get Congress to pass another law, this in 1876, which expanded the law of 1873 to make it illegal to mail obscene literature, contraceptive devices, and information on contraception and abortion and strengthened the prohibition against lotteries.

Comstock has been described as outlandish in appearance, with potbelly, mutton-chop whiskers, thick neck, jutting jaw, ignorant, and devoid of humor. Regardless, he kept the mails "clean" through confiscation of thousands of articles and innumerable publications. As a result of his fanaticism, Comstockery became a word in the English language meaning "overzealous moral censorship of fine arts and literature."

What is surprising is that there was so little opposition to the obscenity laws enacted by Congress in the 19th century and enforced for years by the Post Office and the Bureau of Customs.[1] There was some opposition by liberal individuals and free-thinking groups, the National Liberty League as one such organization; but censorship was supported in the main by many leading citizens, for how could any right-thinking person not be against obscenity and vice?

---

1. *Purity in Print* by Paul S. Boyer, Scribners, 1968, is a history of book censorship during this period in the United States.

The broad powers assumed by the Post Office and the Bureau of Customs were supported for many years by the courts and the Congress. In 1878 Judge Orlando Jackson held in an ex parte opinion that Congress has the power under the Constitution to determine what could and what could not be sent through the mails. In 1890 the Attorney General ruled that the Post Office had the right to stop the mailing of "any publication that printed obscene passages from any book or magazine." In 1892 the Rapier ex parte opinion held that the act of mailing obscene material does not prevent its publication and therefore barring it from the mail is not a form of censorship.

In 1895 Congress refused to broaden the already existing obscenity laws; but in 1908 it did pass legislation making unmailable "all matter tending to incite arson, murder, and assassination." In the same year the U.S. Supreme Court ruled that it was constitutional for the Post Office to seize mail addressed to a person or to a company believed to be using the mail to defraud.

The power of the Post Office was increased by provisions of the Espionage Act of 1917 which added treasonable and seditious material to the list of matter that had already been declared unmailable. By this action, disloyalty to the government was added to obscenity as a reason for unmailability. It was that Act that led to the revoking of a second-class permit for the *Milwaukee Leader*, mentioned in the previous chapter.

Thus, in the latter part of the 19th century and the first half of the 20th century, a variety of articles and publications were illegal to mail. They included publications containing vulgar and filthy words or expressions considered obscene; pictures of prize fights; lottery tickets and information about lotteries; envelopes and postcards with defamatory statements written on them; seditious and disloyal statements about the U.S. government; materials on sex education, family planning, and contraception; and contraceptive devices and information about abortion.

This search for the obscene led to declaring as unmailable numerous well-known books and other publications. The best-selling novel *Forever Amber* by Kathleen Winsor, for example, was declared unmailable after its publication in 1944. So was *Playboy* magazine in 1954. On one occasion a cover for *Natural History* magazine bearing the picture of an American Indian girl with the upper part of her body unclothed was refused clearance by the Post Office, forcing the publisher to use a substitute cover. A case almost as extreme occurred in 1907 when an issue of the *American Journal of Eugenics* was declared unmailable because it contained an advertisement for a book called *The History of Prostitution*.

One result of those prohibitions was the curious situation in which books deemed obscene by the Post Office and thus unmailable could be bought openly in bookstores. Examples at times over the years included *Tobacco Road* and *God's Little Acre* by Erskine Caldwell; *Strange Fruit* by Lillian Smith; *Appointment in Samarra* by John O'Hara; *The Cautious Amorist* by Norman Lindsay; *Thirteen Woman* by Tiffany Thayer; and *For Whom the Bell Tolls* by Ernest Hemingway. Such books could be bought in bookstores, but they could not be ordered by mail. Even catalogues listing such books could not be mailed.

The system of censorship developed by the Post Office and the Customs Bureau operated independently from the criminal enforcement of obscenity laws. The system was arbitrary, with officials, not courts, deciding what kinds of printed materials could be admitted into the country and what kinds could be delivered by mail. That kind of censorship was carried on under the Comstock Act with vigor during the first part of this century, with referrals numbering up to 3,000 a year as late as from 1950 to 1956. During the decade from 1946 to 1956, for example, two to three hundred cases were referred for mail blocks annually.

As none of the anti-obscenity laws of 1865, 1873, and 1876 defined obscenity or prescribed methods for enforcing the acts, postal officials were free to decide for themselves what was obscene and how to dispose of such matter. A postal worker could refer a publication to the local postmaster to send on to the Fraud and Mailability Division of the Post Office Department in Washington, D.C., for action. One method of policing the mails was confiscation of copies of an offending publication. Another was placing a mail block, which simply stopped the mail from going on to the addressee.

Under law, authority to refuse mailing privileges rested with the Postmaster General and a few of his subordinates. As self-appointed guardians who kept the mails clean, their decisions were final — except that the sender or addressee could file suit. Since court trials are time-consuming and expensive, most decisions were accepted without legal protest.

The same condition existed with the Bureau of Customs. As a result, every postmaster and every Customs official became a censor, each using his own judgment as to whether a particular book or magazine or art object was obscene. With no generally accepted test for obscenity, there were instances in which a publication or article passed by Customs would be declared unmailable by the Post Office Department, and instances in which a publication or article denied entry by Customs would be approved by the Post Office Department for mailing.

After the passage of the Comstock Act in 1873, a fervor gripped the country in an intense battle against obscenity and immorality, with state legislatures passing laws and city councils enacting ordinances to protect the public from such evil influences. By the late 1920s every state except New Mexico had enacted legislation against obscenity. Thus the fight against obscenity was not limited to agencies of the Federal government.

Efforts at suppression of obscene literature were carried on by civic and church organizations as well as by government officials, often with cooperation between them. Among active national organizations taking part were the Roman Catholic National Office for Decent Literature, the Board for Christian Social Action of the American Lutheran Church, the Commission on Christian Social Concerns of the Methodist Church, and the Churchmen's Commission for Decent Publications. Among secular organizations was the Citizens for Décent Literature.

Locally both individuals and organizations got into the act. Officers of the anti-obscenity organizations as well as members worked closely with police departments and prosecuting attorneys in suppressing what they considered to be obscene literature and motion pictures. Among organizations was the New England Watch and Ward Society, which was widely publicized. "Banned in Boston" became a national catch phrase,characterizing a city in which regulations were strict. Among books banned were a number of highly acclaimed titles including Theordore Dreiser's *An American Tragedy*. A book banned in Boston could be purchased elsewhere, and generally the banning led to a large increase in sales. The book, *Oil,* by Upton Sinclair was suppressed without a court order, as was *Elmer Gantry* by Sinclair Lewis. H. S. Mencken was tried in Boston for selling a copy of the *American Mercury*, a magazine he edited in New York, but was acquitted.

Although the Postal Service and city governments have discontinued censorship, except for materials that are clearly pornographic, individual citizens and pressure groups still continue trying to keep school and public libraries "clean."

Over the years numerous well-known books have been attacked by citizen pressure groups. Among them, and the places of protest, are *1984* by George Orwell, in Minnesota; *The Scarlet Letter* by Nathaniel Hawthorne, *The Good Earth* by Pearl Buck, and *Drums Along the Mohawk* by Walter Edmond, in Michigan; *Brave New World* by Aldous Huxley and *The Magic Mountain* by Thomas Mann, in Arizona; plays by George Bernard Shaw and Tennessee Williams, *Catcher in the Rye* by J.D. Salinger, and *J.B.* by Archibald MacLeish, in California.

In 1961 a pressure group was able to have Tarzan books by Edgar Rice Borroughs removed from elementary school libraries in one city because Tarzan and his mate Jane had never married.

Among other well-known titles that have been challenged are *Huckleberry Finn* by Mark Twain, *The Wizard of Oz* by Frank Baum, *Of Mice and Men* by John Steinbeck, *Slaughterhouse Five* by Kurt Vonnegut, and *Exodus* by Leon M. Uris.

School and public libraries were and continue to be prime targets of individuals and of organizations such as the religiously oriented American Family Association, formerly known as the National Federation for Decency, based in Tupelo, Mississippi. Still commonplace is pressure on administrators and directors of libraries to remove "obscene" books from the shelves and in schools so they won't be available to children. For example, People for the American Way reported that in the 1986-87 academic year 153 attempts were made by persons and organizations to get books removed from school and public libraries in 41 states, with more than a third of the attempts successful.

In the year ending in May 1989, attempts were made to remove more than a hundred books, including the seemingly innocuous *Garfield Has Nine Lives* by Jim Davis. A parent in Saginaw, Michigan, found some of the language and the drawings offensive.

In 1990-91 such innocent-sounding titles as *Little Red Riding Hood* and *My Friend Flika* were among stories and books challenged along with such traditional censorship targets as *The Adventures of Huckleberry Finn* and the *American Heritage Dictionary*.

A survey by the University of Wisconsin revealed 739 attempts to ban or restrict circulation of books and magazines in high schools across the country between 1987 and 1990, with about 48 per cent of the attempts successful. The book most objected to was *Forever* by Judy Blume, which tells about an adolescent girl who loses her virginity. Magazines most objected to were *Rolling Stone* and the swimsuit edition of *Sports Illustrated.* Two thirds of the protests were by parents, about a fifth by school teachers and administrators, and the others from various organizations and individuals. The American Library Association, headquarters in Chicago, reports bimonthly in its Newsletter on Intellectual Freedom on attempts in the United States to suppress books and other intellectual materials. The number of such cases rises every year, the Association states.

Far-reaching changes, however, have taken place in the last half of this century.

One significant change was society's increasingly liberal view after World War II of what constitutes obscenity and immorality. People generally adopted a more tolerant view and willingness to allow greater freedom of expression.

Another was the development and acceptance of a more precise definition of obscenity. The U.S. Supreme Court established an official test for obscenity in its decision in the Roth case in 1957, discussed in Chapter 32, and refined and amended the test in a number of decisions in following years.

Procedure for censorship in the Bureau of Customs began to change in 1930 with the passage of the Smoot-Hawley Tariff Act on June 17 of that year. The Act contained an amendment that retained the ban on the importation of "obscene" books but stipulated that books must be judged in their entirety, not on isolated passages as the Hicklin test called for. The amendment shifted final authority from anonymous Customs officials to the courts where books cited as obscene would be given judicial review. It also gave discretionary power to the Secretary of the Treasury to admit "so-called classics" and books of "literary and scientific merit."

A real turning point came three years later in 1933 in the court decision in the *Ulysses* case. This was in regard to James

Joyce's novel *Ulysses* which had been declared obscene and thus denied entry into the United States. In it, Joyce, an Irish writer, used the stream-of-consciousness technique to follow three persons through one day, June 16, 1904, in Dublin, Ireland. The book is so difficult to read that a printed guide is needed to explain the many allusions and devices the author uses. Upon publication it could not pass standards of censorship at that time in England and the United States as it is heavy on sex and scatology. It contains numerous four-letter Anglo-Saxon words that are taboo in polite society and frank descriptions of erotic dreams of some of the characters, especially those of a woman named Mollie Bloom.

Joyce had difficulty in finding a publisher, so his friend Ezra Pound suggested that he send some early chapters to *Little Review,* an avant-garde magazine being edited and published in New York by two women, Margaret Anderson and Jane Heap. They agreed to publish the chapters in serial form and later chapters as they were ready; but the U.S. Post Office seized and burned four issues of the magazine. The two women editors were then tried before a panel of three judges in 1921, found guilty of publishing obscenity, and fined $50 each.

The next year, 1922, the book was published in Paris, where Joyce was living and working; but it was soon banned in both Great Britain and the United States as obscene. A shipment to England was seized by customs officials; and in the United States Post Office officials began confiscating copies as they entered the country by mail. Customs also prevented shipments of the book from coming into the country.

Ten years later Random House publishers in New York decided to challenge the obscenity ruling on *Ulysses*, so a representative of the firm deliberately brought a copy through customs and pointed out that its entry into the country was unlawful. The government had no choice but to prosecute, in what was in effect a test case, and did so under a provision of the Tariff Act of 1930 that permitted legal action against a book rather than against the person who published, bought, or sold it.

The case was tried in the Federal Court in New York City in 1933 where Judge John M. Woolsey ruled that "nowhere does the book tend to be aphrodisiac, and may, therefore, be admitted into the United States."[2] The next year the decision was upheld in the Circuit Court of Appeals by a vote of two of three judges who heard the appeal.

In his decision, Judge Woolsey of the District Court stated in part:

■ ... in spite of its unusual frankness I do not detect the leer of the sensualist. I hold, therefore, that the book is not pornographic ...

The words which are criticized as dirty are old Saxon words known to almost all men, and, I venture, to many women, and are such words as would be naturally and habitually used, I believe, by the types of folks whose life, physical and mental, Joyce is seeking to describe ...

The meaning of the word "obscene" is legally defined by this court as: tending to stir the sex impulses or to lead to sexually impure and lustful thoughts.

Whether a particular book would tend to excite such impulses and thoughts must be tested by the Court's opinion as to its effect on a person with average sex instincts ...

The two judges in the three-judge panel in the Court of Appeals who upheld Judge Woolsey's decision were Learned Hand and Augustus N. Hand. In their decision, they stated:

■ We do not think that "Ulysses," taken as a whole, tends to promote lust and its criticized passages do this no

---

2. United States v. One Book Called "Ulysses," 5 F. Supp. 182 (S.D.N.Y. 1933)

more than scores of standard books that are constantly being bought and sold. Indeed a book of physiology in the hands of adolescents may be more objectionable on this ground than almost anything else.

We believe that the proper test of whether a given book is obscene is its dominant effect. In applying this test, relevancy of the objectionable parts to the theme, the established reputation of the work in the estimation of approved critics . . . are persuasive pieces of evidence.

The Smoot-Hawley Act and the decision in the *Ulysses* case resulted in authority being taken from Customs collectors by 1937 and placed with an "expert" in the Customs office in Washington, D.C. A series of cases in following years also limited the power of postal officials to censor the mail.

Twelve years after Ulysses came the case of *Walker v. Popenoe*,[3] which began when the Post Office seized copies of the booklet, *Preparing for Marriage*, by Paul Popenoe as obscene and therefore unmailable. The U.S. Court of Appeals ruled in 1945 that the booklet was not an unmailable obscenity. Judge Thurman Arnold in announcing the decision condemned the seizure of the booklet as a violation of the rights guaranteed by the Fifth Amendment to life, liberty, or property, without due process of law.

The Post Office Department ignored that decision and continued its usual procedure of seizing publications it deemed obscene until Congress passed the Administrative Procedures Act the next year. The Act requires government agencies that make decisions affecting the rights of citizens to hold hearings with ample advance notice and opportunity to present evidence and to cross-examine adverse witnesses before decisions become final. The Act also prevents government officials from arbitrating or judging cases they have already investigated and prosecuted. That legislation plus the Su-

---

3. Walker v. Popenoe, 149 F. 2d. 511 (D.C. Cir. 1945).

preme Court decision that same year, 1946, in the *Esquire* magazine case put a sizable dent in the power the Post Office Department had assumed to censor the mails.

In 1960 the Post Office Department was denied censorship in a case that arose when the New York Postmaster held up delivery of copies of the book, *Lady Chatterley's Lover* by D.H. Lawrence, a noted author.[4] After a hearing, the Postmaster General ruled that the book was obscene and thus not mailable. The case reached the Second Circuit Court of Appeals in 1960 where statements by a number of distinguished literary figures were heard as part of the arguments. The Court ruled that the book, taken as a whole, was not obscene and therefore was mailable.

Lady Chatterley's Lover was first published in England in 1928 and banned there until 1960, and published in the United States in 1959 and banned here. The book tells the story of an aristocratic woman whose husband is impotent as the result of a war wound. She has an affair with her husband's gamekeeper, becomes pregnant, divorces her husband, and chooses to leave the class of society in which she has been living to live with the gamekeeper. Although the book contains some explicitly sexual language and taboo words, the author's thrust is not so much to titillate as to express opposition to the industrialization of the English Midlands, the British caste system, and inhibitions regarding sex.

The Court decision had the effect of further diminishing the authority of the Post Office as a censoring agency and in extending freedom of expression. In his written opinion, Judge Frederick van Pelt Bryan stated in part:

■ The Postmaster General's finding that the book is nonmailable because it offends contemporary standards

---

4. Grove Press v. Christenberry, Second Circuit Court of Appeals, 276 F 2d 443 (2d Civ N.Y. 1960).

bears some discussion (In this case, *Grove Press v. Christenberry*, Grove Press was the publisher and Christenberry the Postmaster General.)

I am unable to ascertain upon what the Postmaster General based this conclusion. The record before him indicates general acceptance of the book throughout the country and nothing was shown to the contrary. The critics were unanimous. Editorial comment by leading journals of opinion welcomed the publication and decried any attempt to ban it . . .

The contemporary standards of the community and the limits of its tolerance cannot be measured or ascertained accurately . . .

I hold that at this state in the development of our society, this major English novel does not exceed the outer limits of the tolerance which the community as a whole gives to writing about sex and sex relations.

The decision was upheld by the Circuit Court of Appeals, and the case was not appealed to the U.S. Supreme Court.[5]

Another case arose when the postmaster in Alexandria, Virginia, stopped delivery on March 25, 1960, of 405 copies of some magazines he considered unmailable. The magazines, titled *M A Naul, Trim,* and *Grecian Guild Pictorial*, pictured numerous nude or nearly nude male models and carried some advertisements for nudists' photographs. The postmaster notified Washington that he was holding the copies pending their decision. After examining the copies, Postmaster General J. Edward Day ruled that the magazines were obscene, that they had been published primarily for homosexuals, and that they contained information regarding places where obscene material could be obtained.

---

5. The publication of *Lady Chatterley's Lover* in 1958 and the court decision that legally it was not obscene was followed by an explosion in the pulp sex novel market.

This case reached the U.S. Supreme court which ruled in 1962 by a vote of 6-to-1 that although the material in the magazines was undoubtedly "patently offensive" to some persons and that the pictures might be considered unpleasant and uncouth, the magazines were not obscene and thus were eligible to be mailed.[6]

Although there was no clear-cut consensus among the justices for this decision, it tended in the main to extend freedom of the press and to limit the powers the Post Office Department had arbitrarily assumed to decide which publications were obscene and thus unmailable.

Keeping the mail clean meant not only sanitizing it in regard to obscenity but also in regard to such evil as Communism. Congress passed a law in 1962 that authorized the Post Office to hold unsealed publications, primarily those from Communist countries, and to notify the persons to whom such mail was addressed that the mail was being withheld from delivery. To implement the law, the Post Office set up 10 or 11 screening points through which all unsealed mail from designated foreign countries was routed. The law exempted that kind of mail addressed to government offices and educational institutions, or officials thereof, and for mail send pursuant to a reciprocal cultural international agreement.

At the screening points, the nonexempt mail was examincd by Customs authorities. When those authorities determined that a piece of mail was "communist political propaganda," the addressee was mailed a notice identifying the mail being detained and advising the mail would be destroyed unless the addressee requested delivery by returning an attached reply card within 20 days. Under that system the Post Office could, and did, maintain a list of all persons receiving mail of that kind; and then it turned the names over to other government agencies including the House Committee on Un-

---

6. Manuel Enterprises, Inc. v. Day, 370 U.S. 478 (1962).

American Activities.

In two cases heard together, the U.S. Supreme Court in 1965 struck down the law, ruling that the First Amendment guarantees the right to hear and to read as well as the right to speak and to print. In the opinion of the Court, concurred in by seven of the justices, Justice Douglas stated that "the statute, Section 305 (a) of the Postal Service and Federal Employees Salary Act or 1962, as applied, placed an unconstitutional limitation on the addressee's right of free speech as guaranteed by the First Amendment."[7]

In the Court opinion, Justice Douglas stated, "We conclude that the Act as construed and applied is unconstitutional because it requires an official act (viz., returning the reply card) as a limitation on the unfettered exercise of the addressee's First Amendment rights."

In concurring, Justice Brennan said, "The dissemination of ideas can accomplish nothing if otherwise willing addressees are not free to receive and consider them."

Censorship power of the Postal Service was further restricted as the result of a case that arose when Postmaster General Winton Blount ruled that two magazines were obscene and ordered them withheld from the mail. In doing so, he was acting under authority granted by the Postal Reorganization Act of 1970. One of the magazines was titled *The Mail Box* and was run by Tony Rizzi in Los Angeles; the other was *Book Bin*, published by a firm in Atlanta.

The Supreme Court heard the two cases together, and in 1971 unanimously declared as unconstitutional two provisions of law that the Post Office had been using to stop obscenity from going through the mail.[8] One provision per-

---

7. Corliss Lamont v. Postmaster General of the United States and John F. Fixa, Individually and as Postmaster, San Francisco, California et al v. Leif Heilberg, 381 U.S. 301 (May 24, 1965).
8. Winton M. Blount v. Tony Rizzi and U. S. v. The Book Bin, 400 U.S. 410 (January 14, 1971).

mitted the Post Office to refuse to accept mail and to refuse to sell money orders to persons or companies who were deemed, through administrative hearings, to be dealing in obscene materials. The other permitted the Post Office to discontinue mail delivery to such persons or companies until hearings were completed.

In the decision the Court also held as unconstitutional a provision of law that required the owner of alleged obscene materials, not the Post Office, to initiate judicial proceedings to determine whether the materials could properly be ruled as obscene. In other words, the Court held that the censor, not the person or company whose materials were being challenged, must initiate proceedings. "In order to avoid constitutional infirmity, a scheme of administrative censorship (1) must place the burden of initiating judicial review . . . on the censor" and (2) the judicial review must be prompt, the Court opinion stated.

This was in keeping with an earlier decision, one in 1965, involving failure to submit a film to the State Board of Censors in Maryland before showing it to the public.[9] In that case, the Court held that it was the responsibility of the censoring agency to prove that the film was unacceptable, and not the responsibility of the exhibitor to prove that it was acceptable.

Although the Supreme Court placed restrictions on procedures used by the Postal Service and the Customs Service in their control of the flow of what they considered to be obscenity, the Court in two cases decided in 1971 reinforced their right, in fact, their authority, to refuse to be distributing agencies for obscene matter.

One of those cases arose when Milton Luros, a publisher, was stopped by U.S. Customs officials from bringing allegedly obscene photographs into the country from Europe. He

---

9. Freedman v. Maryland, 380 U.S. 51 (1965) Discussed further in the next chapter.

claimed at a trial that he wanted to use the pictures to illustrate a book showing sexual positions for sale commercially. The District Court ruled that the law prohibiting him from importing the photographs was unconstitutional, but the U.S. Supreme Court reversed that decision by a vote of 6-to-3 and remanded the case.[10] In the majority opinion, Justice Byron R. White stated, "The First Amendment does not preclude the government from prohibiting the importation of obscene materials for commercial distribution."

The District Court had based its decision in favor of Luros largely on the U.S. Supreme Court decision two years earlier in the case of *Stanley v. Georgia*, discussed in Chapter 33, in which the Court had held that a person has a right to have pornographic materials in the privacy of his own home. Justice White, however, stated, "Regardless of the right to receive and possess obscene material for private use in one's home, the government can properly prevent importation of obscene materials, even when intended for private use."

A case similar in one respect had arisen in the 1950s when Dr. Alfred Kinsey, faculty member at Indiana University specializing in the study of human sexual behavior, collected books and pictures from around the world depicting and describing sexual attitudes and practices but was denied their entry into the United States as some were obviously obscene. Dr. Kinsey took the case to court.

The Federal Court in New York decided in 1957 in his favor.[11] The U.S. Supreme Court had shortly before that defined obscenity in the Roth case, so Judge Edmund L. Palmieri in ruling for Dr. Kinsey was required to follow the Roth guidelines in making his decision. In so doing, he said in part:

---

10. United States v. Thirty-Seven Photographs, 402 U.S. 363 (1971).
11. United States v. Thirty-One Photographs, 156 F. Supp 350 (S. D. N. Y. 1957).

428

■ The Tariff Act of 1930 provides no warrant for either customs officials or this court to sit in review of the decisions of scholars as to the bypaths of learning upon which they shall tread. The question is solely whether, as to those persons who will see the material, there is a reasonable probability that it will appeal to their prurient interest . . . that material whose use will be restricted to those in whose hands it will not have a prurient appeal is not to be judged by its appeal to the populace at large.

In the other decision in 1971 the U.S. Supreme Court upheld the right of the Postal Service to refuse transport and delivery of obscene materials. [12] In that case Norman George Reidel had advertised in the newspaper the sale to persons over 21 years of age a booklet titled "The True Facts About Imported Pornography"; and he was indicted for mailing copies of the booklet in violation of Section 1461, Title 18 of the United States Code, which prohibits the knowing use of the mails for delivery of obscene matter. After U.S. District Court for the Central District of California dismissed the indictment, the prosecution appealed to the Supreme Court. There the Court held that the federal obscenity statute which prohibits the mailing of obscene material was not unconstitutional as applied to the distribution of such material to willing recipients who state that they are adults. In the majority opinion Justice Byron R. White stated in part:

■ . . . the trial judge reasoned that if a person has a right to receive and possess this material, then someone must have the right to bring it to him . . .
The District Court gave Stanley too wide a sweep . . . The personal constitutional rights of those like Stanley to possess and read obscenity in their homes and their freedom of mind and thought do not depend on whether

---

12. United States v. Norman George Reidel, 402 U.S. 351 (May 3, 1971).

the materials are obscene or whether obscenity is constitutionally protected. Their rights to have and to view that
material in private are independently saved by the Constitution.

Reidel is in a wholly different position. He . . . stands
squarely on a First Amendment right to do business in
obscenity and use the mails in the process. But Roth has
squarely placed obscenity and its distribution outside the
reach of the First Amendment and they remain there
today.

Three years later on June 24, 1974, the U.S. Supreme
Court upheld the conviction of William L. Hamling for
conspiring to mail advertisements that promoted the sale of a
book titled *The Illustrated Presidential Report on Obscenity
and Pornography.* The advertising matter contained explicit
photographs and thus were deemed to be obscene. The
majority opinion of the Court, presented by Justice Rehnquist,
stated that "the federal obscenity statute need not be interpreted as requiring proof of a national standard."[13]

The kinds of items unacceptable by the Postal Service and
prohibited from entry into U.S. territory by the Customs
Service today are fairly similar in nature and have not changed
materially in more than a hundred years. The Federal Code
of Regulations contains lists of prohibited articles and regulations governing their disposal, with those of the Customs
Service under Title 19 and those of the Postal Service under
Title 39.

Over the years, Postal and Customs procedures moved from
arbitrary seizure and destruction of prohibited matter to greater
due process of law, with the courts having final authority for
determining what is obscene and thus may be denied entry into
the country or use of the mails. In 1958 the position of

---

13. William L. Hamling et al v. United States, 418 U.S. 87 (June 24,
    1974).

Solicitor in the Post Office Department was replaced by a General Counsel and a method for hearings was established, thus divorcing the judging function from those who initiate action. Vigilance against subversive and seditious communication has diminished. In the main, however, what was prohibited is still prohibited, with the Comstock Act of 1873 and the Tariff Act of 1930, although amended, still in force.

The United States mail today is well protected against arbitrary seizure, and the privacy of sealed matter is guaranteed. Regulations governing mailability are published in the Postal Manual, which is revised periodically with copies for employees and available for public inspection at all post offices. Section 123.33 states:

■ Postmasters are not authorized to decide whether written, printed, or graphic matter is, because of its content, nonmailable. Postmasters are not permitted to deny entry to such matter or exclude it from the mail.

Regulations prohibit any postal employee from detaining mail, except dead letters. Anything written, printed, or graphic that appears to be nonmailable must be reported in writing to the Inspection Service, and "it may not be withheld from dispatch or delivery except where the Inspection Service acting in accordance with postal regulations specifically instructs such withholding."

Sealed mail may not be opened without a search warrant, but an inspector may order suspicious mail detained for a reasonable time for assembling "evidence to satisfy requirements for a search warrant" and for applying and obtaining a warrant.

Postal employees are not permitted to grant a request from a federal, state, or local law enforcement agency or intelligence or other government agency for access to or information about mail matter. Instead, such requests must be referred to the Inspection Service, which is responsible for liaison with government agencies for requests of that kind.

U.S. Customs Service personnel are restricted in a manner similar to those of the Postal Service in regard to the protection of mail. No customs personnel without a search warrant may open, read, or allow any other person to read, or transfer to any other person the correspondence in sealed mail. Without a search warrant, however, designated personnel of the U.S. Customs Service may open or inspect mail that has originated outside the United States and is addressed to delivery within the country provided they have reasonable cause to suspect that the mail contains dutiable or prohibited items.

Briefly, articles prohibited from importation by Section 305 of the Tariff Act of 1930 are (1) Obscene matter; (2) Articles for causing unlawful abortion; (3) Matter advocating treason or insurrection against the United States or forcible resistance to any law of the United States; (4) Matter containing any threat to take the life or inflict bodily harm upon any person in the United States, and (5) Lottery matter.

Among matter prohibited by the Postal Service —

■ Mail by means of which a person obtains or attempts to obtain remittances of money or property of any kind through the mail for an obscene, lewd, lascivious, indecent, filthy, or vile thing, or deposits in the mail or causes to be deposited in the U.S. mail information as to where, how, or from whom such a thing may be obtained.

■ Sexually oriented advertisement meaning any advertisement that depicts, in actual or simulated form, or explicitly describes, in a predominately sexual context, human genitalia, any act of natural or unnatural sexual intercourse, any act of sadism or masochism, or any other erotic subject directly related to the foregoing.

■ Any pandering advertisements which offer for sale matter which the addressee in his sole discretion believes to be erotically arousing or sexually provocative.

■ Any matter (including advertisements) which is unsolicited by the addressee and which is designed, adapted, or intended for preventing conception (except unsolicited samples thereof mailed to a manufacturer thereof, a dealer therein, a licensed physician or surgeon, or a nurse, pharmacist, druggist, hospital, or clinic).

■ Literature and advertisements concerning unlawful abortions and devices for producing such abortions.

Postal regulations also prohibit the mailing of —

■ Chain letters involving money but not those offering prayers and good luck.

■ Fictitious names and addresses as a means of carrying on activity in violation of postal regulations.

■ Matter which is in the form of, or reasonably could be interpreted or construed as, a bill, invoice, or statement of account due, but constitutes, in fact, a solicitation for an order by the addressee of goods or services, or both.

■ Vehicle master keys or any pattern, impression, or mold from which a motor vehicle master key may be made, or any advertisement for the sale of any such key pattern, impression, or mold.

■ By special permit only: alcoholic beverages, narcotics, explosives, firearms.

Procedures for seizing and disposing of prohibited matter are fairly detailed for both the Customs Service and the Postal Service. They, too, have not changed materially in more than a century except that senders/shippers and addressees/recipients have more legal rights than was once granted.

Postal officials anywhere, in Washington or elsewhere, may still seize any mail believed to be obscene or fraudulent or in violation of postal regulations. If the local postmaster is upheld by the office of the Postmaster General in Washington, the sender is notified that his mail is being held and will be destroyed unless a written petition is received by certified mail within 14 days, addressed to the Recorder, Judicial Officer Department., U.S. Postal Service, Washington, D.C.

Once the petition is received, the Recorder schedules a hearing, which must be held within 28 days, with an Administrative Law Judge presiding. The hearing may not necessarily be held in Washington, but may be in another large city somewhere in the country. The Postal Service does not pay expenses for witnesses and depositions. A decision in writing is handed down; and there are provisions for the sender to appeal in a Federal District Court, which is a costly and time-consuming process.

Both Customs and Postal regulations prohibit the transport of matter pertaining to lotteries, which is somewhat anomalous. For almost a hundred years lotteries of any kind were strictly illegal anywhere in the United States. On July 27, 1868, Congress enacted a law making it illegal to mail anything relating to lotteries. The law stated that it was a criminal offense to deposit in the mail or send or deliver by mail —

■ Any letter, package, postcard, or circular concerning any lottery, gift enterprise, or similar scheme offering prizes dependent in whole or in part upon lot or chance;

■ Any lottery ticket or part thereof ... Any check, draft, bill, money, postal note, or money order for the purchase of any ticket or part thereof ...

■ Any newspaper, circular, pamphlet, or publication of any kind containing any advertisement of any lottery ...

The law regarding Customs states:

■ Whoever brings into the United States ... any paper, certificate, or instrument purporting to be or to represent a ticket, chance, or interest in or dependent upon the event of a lottery, gift enterprise, or similar scheme ... shall be fined not more than $1,000 or imprisoned not more than 2 years, or both.

The law didn't stop lotteries, however. In fact, beginning the next year the Louisiana Lottery ran for eleven years and became the most successful lottery the country had ever known. It held a monopoly on betting numbers in the state and hired the Civil War hero P.T. Beauregard as its spokesman. In 1890, however, Congress enacted another law, one that prohibited all forms of interstate commerce in lottery tickets and materials. That killed privately operated lotteries and kept the mail closed to information and materials related to all forms of lotteries, including charity raffles. The Louisiana Lottery was forced to close, as it had sold most of its tickets by mail throughout the United States. Its operation was then transferred to Honduras, but the Company eventually faded away.

Then, 73 years later in 1963, the State of New Hampshire instituted a state lottery; and since that time 34 more states as well as the District of Columbia, Puerto Rico, and the U.S. Virgin Islands have established government-operated lotteries.

Under the original law a newspaper or a magazine could lose its second-class mailing permit by publishing information and advertising about lotteries; so when states began instituting lotteries, Congress amended the law. It now reads in part:

■ Prohibited: Use of the mail for obtaining money or property by means of false representations or in conducting a lottery, gift enterprise, or scheme for the distribution of money or of real or personal property, by lottery, chance, or drawing of any kind.

Not prohibited: the mailing of (1) a newspaper of general circulation containing advertisements, lists of prizes, or information concerning a lottery conducted by a State acting under authority of State law, published in that State, or in an adjacent State which conducts such a lottery, or (2) tickets or other materials concerning such a lottery within that State to addressees within that State.

That means that lottery tickets may be mailed within states

that have state lotteries but not to any address in another state. In other words, it is legal for example to mail a Florida lottery ticket from Tampa to Jacksonville, but not from Florida to someone in Maryland or anywhere else outside Florida.

It also means that a newspaper published in a state that conducts a state lottery may publish advertisements of or information concerning the lottery in that state and of lotteries conducted in any adjacent states. For example, a newspaper in the State of New York, which conducts a state lottery, could legally publish advertisements of and information about state lotteries in Massachusetts, Connecticut, New Jersey, and Pennsylvania as those states are adjacent to New York and also conduct state lotteries. A newspaper published in New York State could not legally publish advertisements for or information about state lotteries in Maine or Michigan because those states are not adjacent to New York State. A newspaper published in Virginia could not legally publish advertisements for or information about the lottery in Maryland, even though Maryland is adjacent to Virginia because Virginia does not conduct a state lottery.[14]

Newspapers and other periodicals were unable to publicize or advertise such forms of lotteries as raffles and bingo conducted for charity without jeopardizing their second-class mailing permits until the Charity Games Advertising Clarification Act became effective in 1990. Accounts of unusual events connected with lotteries, bingo, and raffles have always been publishable, however, as the publication of news cannot be outlawed.

---

14. The restrictions apply also to radio and television.

CHAPTER
32

❀

OBSCENITY IS UNPROTECTED SPEECH

OBSCENITY IS UNPROTECTED SPEECH

❀

Obscenity is illegal. Both the federal government and the states have laws prohibiting its publication and circulation. The courts have held that obscenity is not protected by the First Amendment guarantee of free speech.

The reasons are that obscenity is offensive, it violates standards of morality, it is blasphemous, and it may cause wrongdoing.

Any speech, whether spoken or symbolic, and any publication or action is illegal and not within the realm of free speech and press guaranteed by the U.S. Constitution if it tends to lead to misconduct, causes people to break the law, incites people to riot, or endangers life and property. Obscenity falls within that class of speech because it appeals to prurient interests. Prurient means "arousing unusual sexual desires," which can cause some people to commit unlawful and immoral acts.

The words "obscenity" and "pornography" are used interchangeably in this book although they have different dictionary definitions. Opinions of the U.S. Supreme Court seem to center on obscenity as a term that includes pornography.

The word "obscene," which has been in use since 1593, comes from the Latin word *obscenus*, which means disgusting. Obscene today means repulsive, disgusting, and abhorrent to morality or virtue. The word pornography, which entered the language in 1864, is from the Greek *porne*, which means harlot, and the Greek word *graphein*, which means to write. The literal meaning of pornography is thus "the writing of harlots." The word now means pictures, drawings, and words intended to cause sexual excitement. The word "indecent," which also appears in some court decisions, means offensive to morals and manners.

As obscenity and pornography are believed to destroy morality and blasphemy is believed to weaken faith, both church and state for centuries have been trying to protect people from those immoral and ungodly influences. Laws have been enacted, books have been banned and burned, printing and pictures have been censored, and writers and booksellers have been fined and imprisoned.

The overriding problem in such control lies in deciding precisely what constitutes obscenity, in deciding when a word, sentence, book, or picture is obscene and when it is only offensive and indecent, which may be unpleasant but not illegal. The question is answered readily enough when the decision is made by an ecclesiastical authority or a magistrate or a censorship board, but not so readily in a society such as that of the United States where free speech is a cherished and legal right of the people. Legislators have found that writing laws to cover the infinite variety of forms that obscenity, pornography, and erotica may take is virtually impossible. Jurists have been equally perplexed in trying to decide what is obscene and what is not.

The present interpretation of what constitutes obscenity in the U.S. developed through a series of court cases over more than a century, starting with common law in England. There cases of obscenity were once handled by church authorities through ecclesiastical courts; but gradually they became the concern of government. By 1725 pornographers were being tried in government courts under English common law rather than being punished by the church, a change indicating that obscenity was being classed as a crime, as it continues to be, rather than as a sin and an outrage against religion.

One of the first such common law cases was tried in 1727 in the Court of the King's Bench. In that case a publication of little if any literary merit titled *Venus in the Cloister or The Nun in Her Smock* was judged obscene on the grounds that it was a menace to general morality.

It would be more than a hundred years later, however, before a court would attempt a definition of obscenity. In 1857 Lord John Campbell introduced a bill in Parliament which when enacted made the sale and distribution of obscene material a crime in England. The law, known as Lord Campbell's Act of 1857, applied only to "words written for the purpose of corrupting the morals of youth and were of a nature to shock the common feelings of decency in any well-regulated mind."

The Act was tested in 1868 when a case concerning a pamphlet titled "The Confessional Unmasked" came before Benjamin Hicklin, the Recorder of London. Judge Hicklin held that although the pamphlet was undoubtedly obscene, its publication did not violate the Campbell Act because it had been published to expose what purportedly happens in the confessional and not for the purpose "of corrupting the morals of youth." Upon appeal the case went before Chief Justice Sir Alexander Cockburn who reversed the decision. In so doing, he said:

> ■ I think the test of obscenity is this, whether the tendency of the matter charged as obscenity is to deprave and corrupt those whose minds are open to such immoral influences and into whose hands a publication of this sort may fall.

That has since been known as the Hicklin test for obscenity, although the decision was the opposite of what Judge Hicklin ruled. Two aspects of the test are significant: One is that the publication was judged obscene on the basis of isolated passages, not on the publication as a whole. The other is the influence the publication would have on susceptible persons, not on the public generally.

More than forty years passed before the Hicklin test was challenged in this country, and then inconclusively. The challenge was by Mitchell Kennerly, a publisher, in 1913.[1] The case arose when a clerk was arrested, tried, and convicted in a New York State court for selling a copy of *Hagar Revelly* by Daniel Carson Goodman, which had been published by Kennerly. The book was declared to be obscene, although it would not be considered so by today's standards.

Kennerly took the case to a federal court where Judge Learned Hand upheld the conviction. In ruling on the case, he interpreted obscenity as " the present critical point in the compromise between candor and shame at which the community may have arrived here and now." A federal court of appeals later decided that the book was not obscene.

The Hicklin test that a book or other publication can be judged as obscene on the basis of isolated words or sentences began to crumble in the United States in 1920 in a case that arose when a bookstore clerk named Raymond D. Halsey, on November 17, 1917, sold a copy of the English translation of *Mademoiselle de Maupin* to John S. Summer, who was an agent for the New York Society for the Suppression of Vice.

The book, published in France in 1836, was written by Theophile Gautier, one of the leading French authors of the 19th century, and had become part of French literature. In the introduction Gautier stated that he wrote the novel "to make light of fornication, adultery, and homosexuality." Thus it is not surprising that the Society for the Suppression of Vice considered the book to be obscene.

Halsey was tried in the Court of Special Sessions for violating the New York State obscenity law and was acquitted. The case was appealed, and the Court Appeals voted 4 to

---

1. United States v. Kennerly, 209 F. 119 121 (D.N.Y., 1913).

2 in favor of Halsey, which meant that the majority of the judges ruled that the book was not obscene. In the majority opinion of the Court of Appeals, handed down in 1920, the Court ruled that the book must be judged as a whole, not on the basis of isolated passages.[2] Judge Andrews, in the opinion, stated in part:

■ The book contains many paragraphs . . . which taken by themselves are undoubtedly vulgar and indecent. No work may be judged from a selection of such paragraphs alone. Printed by themselves they might, as a matter of law, come within the prohibition of the statute. So might a similar selection from Aristophanes or Chaucer or Bocaccio or even the Bible. The book . . . must be considered broadly as a whole.

The beginning of attempts to reach a satisfactory definition of obscenity came ten years later in 1930 when a U.S. Court of Appeals set aside the conviction of Mary Ware Dennett for selling copies of her pamphlet, the *Sex Side of Life*, which she had written primarily for her two boys. When they reached the age of 11 and 14 in 1919, she decided that she ought to teach them about the sex side of life. After examining about sixty publications on the subject and believing them to be inadequate and unsatisfactory, she wrote a manuscript which she titled *Sex Side of Life*. She allowed some of her friends to read it; and when the owner of the *Medical Review of Reviews* learned about the manuscript, he asked permission to publish it.

About a year later, the manuscript was published as a pamphlet, which Mrs. Dennett priced at 25¢ a copy, with a discount for quantity purchases; and she distributed about 25,000 copies in that way.

---

2. Halsey v. New York Society for the Suppression of Vice, 191 App. Div. 245, 180 N.Y.S. 836 (1920).

In 1926 Mrs. Carl A. Miles, who lived in Virginia and was an entrapper for the Post Office Department, received a copy from the author through the mail. This led to an indictment of Mrs. Dennett by a grand jury for violating the Comstock law, which prohibits sending obscene matter by mail. She was tried in a federal court in Brooklyn where the jury found her guilty, and the judge fined her $300.

The conviction was reversed on March 5, 1930, by the Federal Circuit Court of Appeals.[3] In the opinion in this reversal, Judge Augustus N. Hand, cousin of Judge Learned Hand who presided in the Kennerly case, stated:

■ We hold that an accurate exposition of the relevant facts of the sex side of life in decent language and in manifestly serious and disinterested spirit cannot ordinarily be regarded as obscene . . . The direct aim and the net result is to promote understanding and self-control. Mrs. Dennett is acquitted.

In the jury trial Mrs. Dennett sought to prove the cost of the publication in order to show that there could have been no motive of gain on her part. She also offered to prove that she had received orders from the Union Theological Seminary, Young Men's Christian Association, the Young Women's Christian Association, the public health departments of various states, and from no less than four hundred welfare and religious organizations, as well as from clergymen, college professors, and doctors, and that the pamphlet had been in use in the public schools at Bronxville, N.Y.

The trial court refused her offer on the ground that the defendant's motive in distributing the pamphlet was irrelevant and that the only issues were whether she caused the pamphlet to be mailed and whether it was obscene.

---

3. U.S. v. Dennett, 39 F. 2d. 564 (2d Civ. N.Y. 1930).

In acquitting Mrs. Dennett, the panel of judges in the Appeals Court did not find the jury in the lower court incorrect in judging her guilty; rather, they agreed unanimously that the case should never have been presented to a jury because as a matter of law the pamphlet on sex education was not obscene.

In every court case there are two questions to be answered. One is "What is the law?" The other is "What are the facts?" A general rule is that the court (the judge) decides the law; the jury decides the facts. In the case of Mrs. Dennett, the jury had no choice but to decide that it was a fact that she did mail a copy of the pamphlet to Mrs. Miles. That would be a violation of law, however, only if the pamphlet were obscene. When the judges decided that it was not obscene, then the jury decision was irrelevant because the defendant had not broken the law.

The Hicklin test finally passed into history with the court decisions in 1933 in the Ulysses case,[4] discussed in Chapter 31.

The decisions in the trial court and the appeals court in that case were significant in that they established the principle that obscenity must be judged on the basis of the dominant effect of the entire book, not just passages, on a person with "average sexual instincts" rather than on the "most susceptible" person, as had been ruled in the Hicklin decision in England years before. The judges also ruled in the Ulysses case that an evaluation of the author's intent in writing the book should be considered as well as the relevance of the theme to the passages considered indecent or obscene.

The first major case on obscenity to come before the U.S. Supreme Court arose when a bookseller was convicted under a New York State law for selling what had been declared an obscene publication. In that case, decided in 1948, the Court

---

4. United States v. One Book Called "Ulysses," 5 F. Supp. 182 (S.D.N.Y., 1933).

ruled that the law was unconstitutional because it was too vague and indefinite.[5] The Court held that a person should not have to guess at the meaning of a law to know what is legal or illegal.

The next quarter century saw a whole series of Supreme Court decisions that liberalized and attempted to clarify the meaning of obscenity. Especially active was the Warren Court, so-called because of its chief justice, Earl Warren, who served in that capacity for 16 years from 1953 to 1969. Obscenity cases continued into the years to the Burger Court, of which Warren E. Burger was chief justice for 17 years from 1969 to 1986.

The Warren Court handed down 17 major decisions related to pornography and obscenity, one of the most significant of which was *Roth v. United States* in 1957 as it marked the first time the Supreme Court attempted to define obscenity.

Actually, the Court heard two cases together, but the decision is commonly known as the Roth case.[6] The defendants were Samuel Roth and David Alberts, both of whom were dealers in what could be called "smut."

Roth conducted a business in New York in the publication and sale of books, photographs, and magazines. He was convicted by a jury in the District Court for the Southern District of New York on four counts of a 26-count indictment charging him with mailing obscene circulars and advertisements and an obscene book in violation of the federal obscenity statute.

Alberts conducted a sex-oriented mail order business from Los Angeles. He was found guilty by the judge of the Municipal Court of the Beverly Hills Judicial District, having

---

5. Winters v. New York 333 U.S. 507 (1948).
6. Roth v. United States and Alberts v. California, 354 U.S. 476 (1957).

waived a jury trial, of the misdemeanor of "lewdly keeping for sale obscene and indecent books, and with writing, composing, and publishing an obscene advertisement of them, in violation of the California penal code."

Both convictions were upheld in appeals; and the cases then went to the U.S. Supreme Court which by a 5-to-4 vote also upheld the convictions. In doing so, however, the Court wrestled with the problem of defining obscenity in such manner that it could be clearly distinguished from the kind of speech and printing that is protected by the First Amendment. In the majority opinion of the Court, Justice William J. Brennan Jr. stated, "We hold that obscenity is not within the area of constitutionality protected speech or press . . ." In support of that statement, he wrote:

■　The dispositive question is whether obscenity is utterance within the area of protected speech and press. Although this is the first time the question has been squarely presented to this Court, either under the First Amendment or under the Fourteenth Amendment, expressions found in numerous opinions indicate that this Court has always assumed that obscenity is not protected by the freedoms of speech and press . . .

The protection given speech and the press was fashioned to assure unfettered interchange of ideas for the bringing about of political and social changes desired by the people.

. . . All ideas having even the slightest redeeming social importance — unorthodox ideas, controversial ideas, even ideas hateful to the prevailing climate of opinion — have the full protection of the guarantees, unless excludable because they encroach upon the limited area of more important interests. But implicit in the history of the First Amendment is the rejection of obscenity as utterly without redeeming social importance.

This rejection for that reason is mirrored in the universal judgment that obscenity should be restrained, reflected in the international agreement of over 50 nations, in the obscenity laws of all the 48 states, and in the 20 obscenity laws enacted by the Congress from 1842 to 1956.

Another point made by Justice Brennan is that obscenity is not sex per se, but rather how sex is portrayed. He said that sex and obscenity are not synonymous. "Obscene material is material which deals with sex in a manner appealing to prurient interest. The portrayal of sex, for example, in art, literature and scientific works, is not itself sufficient reason to deny material the constitutional protection of freedom of speech and press . . . It is therefore vital that the standards for judging obscenity safeguard the protection of freedom of speech and press for material which does not treat sex in a manner appealing to prurient interest."

The Supreme Court decision stated further: "The early leading standard of obscenity allowed material to be judged merely by the effect of an isolated excerpt upon particularly susceptible persons. Some American courts adopted this standard but later decisions have rejected it and substituted this test: whether to the average person, applying contemporary community standards, the dominant theme of the material taken as a whole appeals to prurient interest."

In summary, therefore, the Roth decision provided this test for obscenity:

- Does the material taken as a whole appeal to the prurient interest in sex?

- Is the material patently offensive because it affronts contemporary community standards relating to the description or representation of sexual matters?

- Is the matter utterly without redeeming social value?

Among the four justices who dissented from the majority decision, William O. Douglas said in part:

■ The tests . . . require only the arousing of sexual thoughts. Yet the arousing of sexual thoughts and desires happens every day in normal life in dozens of ways . . . The absence of dependable information on the effect of obscene literature on human conduct should make us wary . . .

■ This issue cannot be avoided by saying that obscenity is not protected by the First Amendment. The question remains, what is the constitutional test for obscenity?

A question raised but not answered in the Roth decision was what is meant by "contemporary community standards"? Are those standards national in scope, or do they differ among communities throughout the country? That point was clarified seven years later in 1964 in a case that arose when Nico Jacobellis, manager of a motion picture theater in Cleveland Heights, Ohio, was convicted on two counts of possessing and exhibiting an obscene film titled *Les Amants* (The Lovers) which contained an explicit love scene.[7]

Upon appeal, the case reached the U.S. Supreme Court which viewed the film and decided 6 to 3 that it was not obscene in terms of the Roth test. In making that decision, the majority of the justices held that applying local community standards was unconstitutional. In that connection, Justice Brennan stated in the majority opinion:

■ It has been suggested that the "contemporary community standards" aspects of the Roth test implies a determination of the constitutional question of obscenity in each case by the standards of the particular local community from which the case arises . . . We affirm . . . that the constitutional status of an allegedly obscene work must be determined on the basis of a national standard. It is, after all, a national constitution we are expounding.

---

7. Jacobellis v. Ohio, 378 U.S. 184 (1964).

In concurring with the decision, Justice Potter Stewart said, "I shall not today attempt further to define the kind of material I understand to be embraced within that shorthand description (of hard-core pornography), but I know it when I see it."

The principle of a "national standard" for judging obscenity, as stated in that case, remained in effect for only nine years. In the decision in the case of *Miller v. California* in 1973, the Supreme Court held that a "standard" by which to judge the entire country was impossible.[8] "To require a State to structure obscenity proceedings around evidence of a *national* community standard would be an exercise in futility," Chief Justice Burger stated in the majority opinion. He continued:

> ■ It is neither realistic nor constitutionally sound to read the First Amendment as requiring that the people of Maine or Mississippi accept public depiction of conduct found tolerable in Las Vegas, or New York City . . . our nation is simply too big and too diverse for this Court to reasonably expect that such standards could be articulated for all 50 States in a single formulation . . .

A different perspective on "standards" was presented by Justice William O. Douglas, three years after his retirement from the U.S. Supreme Court, in which he pointed to an inherent danger in an adoption of community standards for judging obscenity. He stated:[9]

> ■ "The justification used for banning 'obscene' publications is that they are 'offensive' to many people ...

---

8. Miller v. California, 413 U.S. 15 (1973). Also discussed in Chapter 33.

9. William O. Douglas, "The First Amendment: Introduction," *The Quill*, September 1976, pages 17-20. The justification mentioned in his first sentence refers to Court decisions in the cases of Miller v. California, 413 U.S. 15 (1973) and Paris Adult Theatre I v. Slaton, 413 U.S. 49 (1973).

What if the community's standards, not the national standards, determined whether a speaker or publisher or merchant is sent to prison for an 'obscene' publication? If a community can make criminal one 'offensive' idea, what bars it from making criminal another 'offensive' idea?"

On the same day of the Roth decision in 1957, the Supreme Court handed down another significant decision in the case of *Kingsley Books, Inc., v. Brown.*[10] The question here was not whether a particular publication was obscene but rather whether a state obscenity law could be constitutional.

The law being challenged was passed by the New York State Legislature in 1954 to control obscene publications. In writing the law the legislators took a cue from the Tariff Act of 1930, which allows either civil action against a publication deemed obscene or criminal action against the person who tries to import an obscene publication. That procedure was used in the Ulysses case in which the book itself, not the importer, was on trial. So under the New York law authorities could obtain a court injunction against anything printed that was "of a filthy, indecent, or immoral nature." With this procedure they could seize and destroy such copies without going through the formality of grand jury action or issuing an indictment.

The law did not prohibit the publication of anything obscene as that would be prior restraint and thus unconstitutional, but such material could be seized immediately after publication. When a judge issued an injunction against a particular publication, it could be seized and destroyed anywhere in the State of New York, not just in the jurisdiction in which the injunction was issued. The law provided that a person whose publication was seized had a right to a trial

---

10. Kingsley Books, Inc. v. Brown, 354 U.S. 436 (1957).

within one day and a judge's decision within two days after the trial.

This case arose when a complaint was filed against Kingsley Books, Inc., on September 10, 1954, charging the company with displaying a series of 14 paperback obscene books under the general title of "Nights of Horror." The publishers waived a jury trial and admitted that the books were obscene, but argued that the law under which they were seized was unconstitutional. Judge Matthew Levy upheld the law, defining obscenity as "dirt for dirt's sake." His decision was upheld by the Court of Appeals of New York; and the case then went to the U.S. Supreme Court which decided by the narrow margin of 5 to 4 that the law was constitutional.

In the majority opinion upholding the law, Justice Felix Frankfurter said:

■ In an unbroken series of cases extending over a long stretch of this Court's history, it has been accepted as a postulate that "the primary requirements of decency may be enforced against obscene publications."

In dissenting, Chief Justice Earl Warren said, "The New York law places the *book* on trial. There is totally lacking any standard in the statute for judging the book in context . . . It is the conduct of the individual that should be judged, not the quality of art or literature."

A third obscenity case of significance decided by the U.S. Supreme Court in 1957 besides Roth and Kingsley Books was *Butler v. Michigan* in which the Court ruled unanimously that the same test for obscenity cannot be applied to adult literature as it is for children's literature, because if it were, then adults would be limited to reading only what is considered appropriate for children.[11]

---

11. Butler v. Michigan, 352 U.S. 380 (1957).

The case arose when Alfred Butler was charged with selling to a Detroit policeman a book the judge at his trial described as "containing obscene, immoral, lewd language tending to incite minors to violent or immoral acts and to corrupt the morals of youth." Selling such a book was in violation of a Michigan law designed to protect children from obscene literature. Butler was found guilty, and the case was appealed to the Supreme Court where Justice Felix Frankfurter, in the majority opinion, stated in part:

■ ... the appellant was convicted because Michigan, by Sec. 343 (of the Michigan Penal Code), made it an offense for him to make available to the general reading public ... a book that the trial judge found to have a potentially deleterious influence upon youth.

The State insists that, by thus quarantining the general reading public against books not too rugged for grown men and women in order to shield juvenile innocence, it is exercising its power to promote the general welfare. Surely, this is to burn the house to roast the pig.

... The incidence of this enactment is to reduce the adult population of Michigan to reading only what is fit for children. It thereby arbitrarily curtails one of those liberties of the individual now enshrined in the Due Process Clause of the Fourteenth Amendment, that history has attested as the indispensable condition for the maintenance and progress of a free society. We are constrained to reverse this decision ...

More recently, the U.S. Supreme Court decided a case that can serve as a warning to dealers in pornography.[12]

What made it different was an indictment for violation of the Racketeer Influenced and Corrupt Organization Act

---

12. Ferris J. Alexander, Sr. v. United States, 509 U.S. 125 L Ed 2d 441, 113 S Ct (June 28, 1993), (1957).

(RICO). The Act contains a provision that allows the government to seize money and property acquired through racketeering,

The protagonist in this case was Ferris J. Alexander, Sr., owner of more than a dozen stores and theatres dealing in sexually explicit materials. He was convicted after a criminal trial in the U.S. District Court for the District of Minnesota on 17 counts of committing substantive federal obscenity offenses and 3 counts of violating the RICO Act.

The sentence was staggering: Six years in prison, a fine of $600,000, and the cost of all prosecution, incarceration, and supervised release. Plus the forfeiture of almost $9 million which he was found to have acquired through racketeering. Plus the forfeiture of his wholesale and retail businesses which were found to have been used to conduct his racketeering enterprise.

In carrying out the sentence, the government seized and destroyed the inventory of books and video tapes in the stores, including hundreds of original titles and thousands of copies, whether they had been judged to be obscene or not. In fact, some of the materials destroyed were the very ones the jury had determined not to be obscene.

The defendant argued that the forfeiture under the RICO Act constituted prior restraint and thus violated his right of free speech under the first Amendment; but the Supreme Court ruled in a 5-to-4 decision that the forfeiture provision as applied in this case did not violate the First Amendment. In its decision, however, the Court remanded the case for the Court of Appeals to consider Alexander's claim that the forfeiture atop his prison term and fine was excessive as prohibited by the Eighth Amendment, which states, "Excessive bail shall not be required, nor excessive fines imposed, nor cruel and unusual punishment inflicted."

In the opinion of the Court, as delivered by Chief Justice William H. Rehnquist, "The petitioner's assets were forfeited because they were directly related to past racketeering violations, and thus they differ from material seized or restrained on suspicion of being obscene without a prior judicial determination."

He stated further, "Where RICO forfeiture stems from a previous speech offense, the punishment served not only the government's interest in purging organized crime taint, but also its interest in deterring the activities of the speech-related business itself."

In a strong dissent, which he read aloud, Justice Anthony Kennedy said that "under the principle the Court adopts, any bookstore or press enterprise could be forfeited as punishment for even a single obscenity conviction."

"Until now," he said, "I thought one could browse through any book or film store in the United States without fear that the proprietor had chosen each item to avoid risk to the whole inventory and indeed to the business itself. This ominous, onerous threat undermines free speech and press principles essential to our personal freedom."

A decision by the U.S. Supreme Court in 1959 had the effect of increasing availability of books to the public and further limiting antiobscenity law.[13] The case arose when Eleazer Smith, proprietor of a bookstore, was convicted under a Los Angeles ordinance that made it unlawful "for any person to have in his possession any obscene or indecent writing (or) book . . . in any place of business where . . . books . . . are sold or kept for sale."

Justice Brennan, in the opinion of the U.S. Supreme Court, explained the background:

■ The offense was defined by the Municipal Court, and by the Appellate Department of the Superior Court, which affirmed the Municipal Court judgment imposing a jail sentence on appellant, as consisting solely of the posses-

---

13. Smith v. California, 361 U.S. 147 (1959).

sion, in the appellant's bookstore, of a certain book found upon judicial investigation to be obscene. The definition included no element of sciential-knowledge by appellant of the contents of the book — thus the ordinance was construed as imposing a "strict" or "absolute" criminal liability.

The appellant made timely objection below that if the ordinance were so construed it would be in conflict with the Constitution of the United States.

The majority of the justices voted to reverse the conviction on the grounds that requiring a bookseller to know the contents of all the books he has on hand for sale would have the effect to restricting the public's access to books that are not obscene. Justice Brennan said:

■ ... the ordinance tends to impose a severe limitation on the public's access to constitutionally protected matter. For if a bookseller is criminally liable without knowledge of the contents, and the ordinance fulfills its purpose, he will tend to restrict the books he sells to those he has inspected; and thus the State will have imposed a restriction upon the distribution of constitutionally protected as well as obscene literature... And the bookseller's burden would become the public's burden, for by restricting him the public access to reading matter would be restricted.

CHAPTER
33

BUT WHAT IS IT?

BUT WHAT IS IT?

❀

The first recorded obscenity case in the United States was in 1821 when a Massachusetts court ruled the book, *Memoirs of a Woman of Pleasure*, to be obscene. The book, better known as *Fanny Hill*, was written by John Cleland in England about 1750. It tells the story of a 15-year-old girl who went to London to find work as a housemaid but instead joined a bordello. The book describes her experiences as a prostitute and various sex acts in the brothel.

More than a century after the book had been banned in Massachusetts, the attorney general brought suit to have the book declared legally obscene. The case eventually reached the U.S. Supreme Court which ruled 6-to-3 in 1966, nine years after the Roth case, that *Fanny Hill* was not obscene.[1]

In making the decision, the U.S. Supreme Court held that three elements "must coalesce" for a work to be obscene. In the majority opinion, Justice Brennan stated:

■   The sole question before the state courts was whether *Memoirs* satisfies the test of obscenity established in the Roth decision . . . Under this definition, as elaborated in subsequent cases, three elements must coalesce: it must

---

1. A Book Named "John Cleland's Memoirs of a Woman of Pleasure" v. Attorney General of the Commonwealth of Massachusetts, 383 U.S. 413 (1966); 345 Mass. II; 184 N.E. 2d 328.

be established that (a) the dominant theme of the material taken as a whole appeals to a prurient interest in sex; (b). the material is patently offensive because it affronts contemporary community standards relating to the description or representation of sexual matters; and (c) the material is utterly without redeeming social value.

The (Massachusetts) Supreme Judicial Court erred in holding that a book need not be "unqualifiedly worthless before it can be deemed obscene." A book cannot be proscribed unless it is found to be *utterly* without redeeming social value. This is so even though the book is found to possess the requisite prurient appeal and to be patently offensive. Each of the three federal constitutional criteria is to be applied independently; the social value of the book can neither be weighed against nor canceled by its prurient appeal or patent offensiveness.

One of the most litigated books was *Tropic of Cancer* by Henry Miller, indicted as obscene in more than 60 criminal suits in at least nine states. In some trials the book was found to be obscene, in others it was not.

The book is a novel about an American man who visits Paris intending to become a writer, but much of the story describes numerous sex episodes in minute detail. An appeal from a conviction in Florida reached the U. S. Supreme Court, which in 1964 by a vote of 5-to-4 reversed the decision without writing an opinion, thus ruling that the book was not obscene. The same decision had been reached by a majority in the Supreme Judicial Court of Massachusetts two years earlier in the case titled *Attorney General v. The Book Named "Tropic of Cancer."*

The intractable obscenity problem, as Justice John Marshall Harlan once called it, continued to plague the Court. A major aspect of the problem was the lack of agreement among the justices on what constituted obscenity in the various cases. That was illustrated by 14 separate opinions by seven justices in decisions handed down on March 31, 1966, in three cases — *Mishkin v. New York, Memoirs v. Massachusetts,* and

Ginzburg v. United States which is discussed in Chapter 34. Although the Court has consistently held that obscenity is not protected by the First Amendment and that laws may be enacted against obscenity, drafting laws with sufficient precision to avoid conflict with the constitutional guarantee of free speech and press appeared virtually impossible — and it still does.

In a dozen cases the Supreme Court has defined obscenity or modified previous decisions, yet most of its decisions have upheld the right of free speech and press. In a period of six years, for example, beginning with *Redrup v. New York* in 1967[2] and continuing to 1973, the Court reversed 31 convictions for obscenity per curium (meaning "by the Court" as a whole) without opinions. The cases are known as the Redrup reversals. It was a time of permissiveness in contrast to strict enforcement of obscenity laws earlier in the century.

The Supreme Court has not ruled in favor of all defendants, however. Among such cases, it upheld the conviction of Ralph Ginzburg in 1966 for "pandering" (See Chapter 34) and those of Samuel Roth and David Alberts in 1967 for violation of the federal obscenity statute. Also in 1966 it upheld the conviction of Edward Mishkin in the case of *Mishkin v. New York.*[3] Mishkin, who operated a bookstore near Times Square in New York City, had been sentenced to three years in prison and fined $12,500 for publishing more than 50 books portraying and describing sadism and masochism. He argued that his books did not appeal to the prurient interests of the average person, but the Court did not accept that argument and upheld his conviction by a vote of 6 to 3.

The Court also upheld the conviction of a man named Marvin Miller in 1973 in a decision that was significant in that

---

2. Redrup v. New York, 386 U.S. 767 (1967).
3. Mishkin v. New York, 383 U.S. 502 (1966).

it rejected two tests for obscenity that had been enunciated in previous decisions.[4]

The case arose when Miller began a mass mailing campaign to advertise some books euphemistically called "adult" material. The brochures offered four books for sale titled *Intercourse, Man-Woman, Sex Orgies Illustrated,* and *An Illustrated History of Pornography.* Although the books contained some printed descriptions, they consisted mostly of pictures and drawings of men and women engaging in a variety of sexual activities, some with genitals prominently displayed.

When a brochure arrived by mail at a restaurant in Newport Beach, California, the manager and his mother complained to the police. Miller was arrested, and in a jury trial he was found guilty of violating the California Penal Code by knowingly distributing obscene matter. The conviction was upheld by the Appellate Court, and it finally reached the U.S. Supreme Court. There in the majority opinion by Chief Justice Warren E. Burger, the Court revised and restated the Roth test for obscenity. The opinion reads in part:

■ The basic guidelines . . . must be:

(a) whether "the average person, applying contemporary community standards," would find the work, taken as a whole, appeals to the prurient interest,

(b) whether the work depicts or describes, in a patently offensive way, sexual conduct specifically defined by the applicable state law, and

(c) whether the work, taken as a whole, lacks serious literary, artistic, political, or social value.

We do not adopt as a constitutional standard the "*utterly* without redeeming social value" test: that con-

---

4. Miller v. California, 413 U.S. 15 (1973).

cept has never commanded the adherence of more than three Justices at one time.

We emphasize that it is not our function to propose regulatory schemes for the States. That must await their concrete legislative efforts. It is possible, however, to give a few plain examples of what a state statute could define for regulation under the second part (b) of the standard announced in this opinion:

(a) Patently offensive representations or descriptions of ultimate sexual acts, normal or perverted, actual or simulated.

(b) Patently offensive representations or descriptions of masturbation, excretory functions, and lewd exhibition of the genitals.

Sex and nudity may not be exploited without limit by films or pictures exhibited or sold in places of public accommodation any more than live sex and nudity can be exhibited or sold without limit in such public places.

At a minimum, prurient, patently offensive depiction or description of sexual conduct must have serious literary, artistic, political, or scientific value to meet First Amendment protection.

The Court voted 5-to-4 for upholding the conviction in this case, the divided opinion typical as very few decisions by the Supreme Court in obscenity cases have been unanimous. Differences in opinion have been common. In 13 obscenity cases adjudicated between 1957 and 1967, there were 55 different opinions by the justices.

The difficulty in arriving at a satisfactory definition of obscenity was recognized by Chief Justice Burger in the majority opinion in *Miller v. California.* In that regard he said:

■ Apart from the initial formulation in the Roth case, no majority of the Court has at any given time been able to agree on a standard to determine what constitutes obscene, pornographic material subject to regulation under the States' police powers . . .

This much has been categorically settled by the Court, that obscene material is unprotected by the First Amendment . . . We acknowledge, however, the inherent dangers of undertaking to regulate any form of expression. State statutes designed to regulate obscene materials must be carefully limited. As a result, we now confine the permissible scope of such regulation to works which depict or describe sexual conduct. That conduct must be specifically defined by the applicable state law, as written or authoritatively construed . . .

The difficulty in formulating an acceptable test for obscenity is further illustrated by Chief Justice Burger's ruling in the *Miller v. California* case that obscenity is to be determined by applying "contemporary community standards," not "national standards." That ruling is indeed logical as it is improbable that every community in the country would have identical standards, yet it poses a dilemma for publishers. How is one to know in which communities a book would meet standards of acceptability and in which it would be declared obscene.

By the time *Miller v. California* arose in 1973, the Supreme Court was obviously weary and frustrated after 25 years of trying to solve the problem of obscenity. Justice Douglas, in dissent in the case of *Miller v. California*, said, "Obscenity — which we cannot define with precision — is a hodge-podge."

Justice Brennan in dissent in another decision handed down on the same day as *Miller v. California*, wrote: "No other aspect of the First Amendment has, in recent years, demanded so substantial a commitment of our time, generated such disharmony of views, and remained so resistant to the formulation of stable and manageable standards."

Dissent also arose in the case of *Paris Adult Theater I v. Slaton* in which the Court upheld the constitutionality of a

Georgia law by a vote of 5-to-4, the same as it had done in *Miller v. California.*[5] In dissent in that case, Justice Brennan stated further:

■ The problem is . . . that one cannot say with certainty that material is obscene until at least five members of this Court, applying inevitably obscure standards, have pronounced it so . . . I am forced to conclude that the concept of "obscenity" cannot be defined with sufficient specificity and clarity to provide fair notice to persons who create and distribute sexually oriented materials, to prevent substantial erosion of protected speech as a by-product of the attempt to suppress unprotected speech . . .

Despite the many laws and ordinances, arrests and trials, and civic and governmental efforts to control or abolish obscenity-pornography,[6] it continues to persist. It persists because there is a market for it, evidently one that is very lucrative. Out of this welter, however, some trends are discernible:

---

5. Paris Adult Theatre I v. Slaton, U.S. 49 (1973).
6. Among national organizations:
   Americans for Decency, Staten Island, N. Y., Founded 1975. Loosely formed group of individuals whose goal is to "promote decency in America."
   American Family Association, Tupelo, Miss. Founded 1977. Donald E. Wildmon, Ex. Secy. Compiles statistics on television broadcasts of scenes involving sex, profanity, and violence. Urges viewers to write letters to networks and sponsors protesting shows that promote violence, profanity, and vulgarity.
   Citizens Against Pornography, Falls Church, Va. Founded 1982. Fights the proliferation and sale of magazines such as *Penthouse* and *Playboy*, seeks to stop production and distribution of adult videos and the opening of adult book stores.
   Citizens for Media Responsibility Without Law, Rancho Cordova, Calif. Founded 1984. Individuals united to demand

(1) The Supreme Court continues to be highly protective of the constitutional guarantees of the rights of free speech and press, of privacy, and of due process of law. At the same time, the Court seems increasingly reluctant to review cases involving pornography, preferring to leave their adjudication to the trial courts and local juries.

(2) Greater permissiveness exists today than earlier in the century, with the result that obscenity-pornography, except for unwilling adults and for children, is being increasingly tolerated.

Decreasing attempts to control *adult* pornography was reflected in a recommendation of the President's Commission on Obscenity and Pornography in 1970, which reads in part:

> ■ The Commission recommends that federal, state, and local legislation should not seek to interfere with the right of adults who wish to do so to read, obtain, or view explicit sexual materials.
>
> Public opinion in America does not support the imposition of legal prohibitions upon the rights of adults to read

---

social responsibility of corporations and the media for the marketing and distribution of violent pornography.

Children's Legal Foundation, Phoenix, Ariz. Founded 1957. Assists law enforcement agencies and legislatures in enacting and enforcing Constitutional statutes, ordinances, and regulations controlling "obscenity and pornography and materials harmful to juveniles."

Feminists Fighting Pornography, New York, N.Y. Founded 1962. Operates the National Obscenity Law Center, a clearinghouse of legal information on obscenity cases.

National Coalition Against Pornography, Cincinnati, Ohio. Founded 1983. Seeks to assist religious and civic groups who wish to eliminate what the group considers obscenity and pornography.

Women Against Pornography, New York, N.Y. Founded in 1979 by Susan Brownmiller and others who seek to change public opinion about pornography so that Americans no longer view it as socially acceptable or sexually liberating.

465

or see explicitly sexual materials. Society's attempts to legislate for adults in the area of obscenity have not been successful. Present laws prohibiting the consensual sale or distribution of explicitly sexual materials to adults are extremely unsatisfactory in their practical application.

Although those recommendations may be valid, many city and county governments are opposed to the sleaze that adult bookstores, adult movie houses, and nude dancing in bars bring to the areas in which they operate. Success in banning them, however, has been spotty because laws and ordinances prohibiting their operation often seem to infringe on freedom of expression. Involved in that "freedom" are movies, plays, photographs, paintings, music, silent picketing, and flag burning as symbolic speech.

Among court decisions in that area was one in 1968 in which the California Supreme Court ruled that topless dancing by Kelly Iser in a San Pablo nightclub was entitled to protection under the First Amendment.

Four years later in 1972 the U.S. Supreme Court in a 6-to-3 decision upheld regulations in California that prohibited "bottomless" dancing and erotic shows in bars and nightclubs.[7] The case began when various holders of liquor licenses and dancers instituted court action, challenging the constitutionality of statewide rules adopted by the Department of Alcoholic Beverage Control that prohibited explicitly sexual live entertainment and films at bars and other establishments that dispense liquor by the drink.

The U.S. District Court for the Central District of California held certain of the regulations invalid, thus finding for the plaintiffs; but the U.S. Supreme Court reversed that decision. In the majority opinion Justice William H. Rehnquist said that "the California Department of Beverage Control has wide

---

7. California et al v. Robert LaRue et al, 409 U.S. 109 (December 5, 1972).

latitude under the Twenty-first Amendment to control the manner and circumstances under which liquor might be dispensed, and the conclusion that the sale of liquor by the drink and lewd or naked entertainment should not take place simultaneously in licensed establishments is not irrational or unreasonable."

Although the Twenty-first Amendment repealed the Eighteenth Amendment which prohibited the manufacture, sale, or transportation of intoxicating liquor in the United States, Section 2 of the Twenty-first Amendment still authorizes legal control of the sale and use of liquor.

In 1975 the Supreme Court ruled that an ordinance in North Hempstead, New York, prohibiting topless dancing was overly broad and thus was not enforceable.[8] Six years later in 1981 the Court struck down a zoning ordinance in the Borough of Mount Ephraim, Camden County, New Jersey, that banned live entertainment entirely. On January 9, 1990, it struck down key provisions of an ordinance in Dallas, Texas, that was designed to rid the city of adult bookstores and adult theaters. The Court, in nullifying those provisions, ruled that the ordinance gave too much unfettered power to city officials and inadequate protection to the right of free speech to the owners of bookstores and theaters.

In 1989 in a unanimous decision the U.S. Supreme Court held that the First Amendment bars police from seizing the inventory of adult book stores before any of the publications have been found at trial to be obscene.[9]

In contrast the Court two years later upheld an Indiana law that bans nude dancing in night clubs and barrooms. In the case of *Barnes v. Glen Theater* the Court in a 5-to-4 decision on June 21, 1991, ruled as constitutional a state law that makes the display of male or female genitals and buttocks and female

---

8. Doran v. Salem Inn, 422 U.S. 922 (1975).
9. Fort Wayne Books v. Indiana, 489 U.S. 46 (1989).

nipples in public a misdemeanor.[10] Attorneys for Indiana argued that nude barroom dancing in JR's Kitty Kat Lounge in South Bend and in similar clubs violated the state's public decency law. The Court agreed, stating that to comply with the law dancers must wear at least pasties and a G-string.

In 1988 Congress enacted a law to prohibit indecent and obscene speech by telephone and on radio and television, primarily to protect children. The law would have put "dial-a-porn" out of business as it would have made it a crime to offer both indecent and obscene telephone messages commercially. The law was not enforced because of a court challenge by Sable Communications of California, Inc., a company that provides sexually explicit recorded messages available by dialing 900 telephone numbers.

On June 23 the next year, the U.S. Supreme Court unanimously struck down that portion of the law that banned indecent speech by telephone, holding that it is protected by the First Amendment; but by a vote of 6 to 3 it upheld that part of the law banning obscene language. Federal District Judge A. Wallace Tashima of Los Angeles ruled that the law was valid in prohibiting obscenity, but its prohibition against indecent speech violated the First Amendment. The U.S. Supreme Court affirmed that decision.[11]

In the opinion of the Court, Justice Byron R. White said, "We have repeatedly held that the protection of the First Amendment does not extend to obscene speech." He said that while the goal of the law to prevent children from being exposed to indecent telephone messages is valid, "the law has the invalid effect of limiting the content of adult telephone

---

10. Barnes v. Glen Theater, 115 L Ed. 2d 504, 111 S. Ct. 2456 (June 21, 1991).
11. Sable Communications of California, Inc. v. Federal Communications Commission, 109 S. Ct. 2829, 106 L. Ed. 93 (June 23, 1989).

conversations to that which is suitable for children. It is another case of burning up the house to roast the pig."

Within a year Congress had enacted a similar law that prohibits obscenity but allows those over age 18 to hear indecent messages on the telephone provided they subscribe for the service in writing.

Audio Enterprises Inc., agreed in November 1988 to pay a fine of $50,000 imposed by the FCC and stop making obscene messages available on interstate telephone lines. It was one of the first dial-a-porn fines ever imposed by the Federal Communications Commission. The FCC had investigated the company after receiving a letter from a mother in California who reported that her 13-year-old son and his friends had run up a telephone bill of $74 by dialing a pay-to-listen 900-number and listening for 211 minutes.

The FCC imposed the fine because the company did not keep such material inaccessible to children.

Two years later, on June 15, 1990, the FCC adopted rules to keep minors from listening to pornographic telephone recordings, rules based on a new law sponsored by Senator Jesse Helms that prohibits obscene messages but permits anyone over 18 years of age to send or hear such messages after they subscribe for such service in writing.

In October 1992, the FCC imposed a fine of $105,000 on Radio Station KLSX-FM in Los Angeles for raunchy morning broadcasts by Howard Stern, who is reputed to regale audiences with talk of sexual practices and bathroom habits.

In support of local control of obscenity, the U.S. Supreme Court, with one dissenting vote, handed down a decision on October 15, 1990, that let stand the seizure of three adult bookstores and nine video rental shops in Virginia, seizures carried out under a provision of the Federal Racketeer Influenced and Corrupt Organization Act (RICO). The provision aimed at obscenity was added to the RICO Act by Congress in 1984.

As the war on obscenity continued, obscenity took new forms. A rap music group, "2 Live Crew," in Miami, Florida, was indicted in 1990 on obscenity charges arising from a performance of songs from its recording, *As Nasty As They Wanna Be*, which a federal judge had ruled as obscene. It was the first musical recording ever banned by a court. Also, a record store owner in Fort Lauderdale was convicted on obscenity charges for selling a copy of a "Live Crew" recording to an undercover police officer.

The first trial of an art center for obscenity took place in Cincinnati, Ohio, the same year. There the Contemporary Art Center and its director, Dennis Barrie, were tried for pandering obscenity by displaying five photographs depicting sadomasochistic homosexual acts and two of children with their genitals exposed. The photographs were among 175 by Robert Mapplethorpe on exhibit. The show opened on April 7, 1990, and the trial was held in the fall with the jury acquitting the Center and its director on October 5. A few days later a jury in Florida acquitted the rap group "2 Live Crew" on obscenity charges. In each case the jury relied on the testimony of experts to find some artistic merit in the material, although few magazines and newspapers would be willing to print the offending Mapplethorpe pictures or the words of the song from the album, *As Nasty As They Wanna Be*.

The major emphasis today in pornography control is centered on the protection of children and unwilling adults rather than on total suppression. That was suggested back in 1954 by Justice Brennan who, in considering the legal problems posed by obscenity, wrote in the majority opinion in the Jacobellis case:

■   State and local authorities might well consider whether their objectives in this area would be better served by laws aimed specifically at preventing distribution of objectionable material to children, rather than at totally prohibiting its dissemination.

New York State enacted a statute the next year that spells out in detail matter that may not be sold to persons under 17 years of age, and other states have similar laws. Regarding children, the President's Commission in 1970 recommended "legislative regulations upon the sale of sexual materials to young persons who do not have the consent of their parents." Most states and municipalities have such laws, with the age in juvenile obscenity statutes fixed at under 17 or under 18 years.

The Child Protection Act passed by Congress in 1984 defines jurisdiction in regard to pornography, giving authority to the Customs Service to prevent entry of pornography into U.S. territory, to the FBI to seize pornography in interstate transportation, and to the Postal Service to monitor domestic mail. Under the Omnibus Drug Initiative Act of 1988 Congress expanded the language of the Child Pornography and Obscenity sections of the statute to forbid the use of computers as a means of transmitting and distributing pornographic materials.

After the passage of the Child Protection Act, the Customs Service with its authority clearly defined established a Child Pornography and Protection Unit in Washington, D.C., and appointed special agents in its larger offices to conduct child pornography investigations. Child pornography (kiddie porn) is defined by Customs as "a visual description of anyone under the age of 18 engaged in explicit sexual conduct, real or simulated, or the lewd exhibition of the genitals."

The Customs Service and the Postal Service must necessarily work together in pornography control, as pornography imported into the United States typically arrives by mail, with approximately half of the seizures of obscene material involving some form of child pornography. Domestic or homemade materials are often sent abroad, primarily to Asian and North European countries, for processing of films and worldwide distribution.

Now engaged in the battle against child pornography at the federal level are the National Obscenity Enforcement Unit of the Department of Justice, the National Center for Missing and Exploited Children, the U.S. Postal Service Inspection Service, the Federal Bureau of Investigation, and the Child Pornography and Protection Unit of the Customs Service. All but the last named remain active, with the Child Pornography and Protection Unit having been disbanded in February 1991 for budgetary reasons. The Customs Service insists that despite discontinuance of the Unit, the protective work is still being carried on. In support of that contention, government statistics show that agents spent more than 27,000 hours in 1992 investigating child pornography.

Agents and officials in that work deal with the distribution of pornographic materials, which is a crime and results in the tragic sexual abuse of innocent children. Evidence indicates that child pornography is consumed primarily by persons who are child molesters.

Both federal and state laws support the battle against child pornography. The Child Protection Act of 1984 as amended authorizes the seizure by federal officers of child pornography, even if it is not intended for sale. Receiving child pornography by mail or other shipping method is a federal crime, punishable by up to 10 years in prison and up to $250,000 in fines. On April 18, 1990, the U.S. Supreme Court upheld an Ohio law that makes it a crime to possess pornographic pictures of children, which is similar to laws in 18 other states.

That case arose when police in Columbus, acting on information provided by a postal official, obtained a warrant to search the home of Clyde Osborne where they found four sexually explicit photographs of a 14-year-old boy.[12] The Supreme Court upheld Osborne's conviction by a vote of 6 to 3.

Twenty-one years earlier in 1969, the Court had ruled in the case of *Stanley v. Georgia* that it was not illegal to have

---

12. Osborne v. Ohio, 109 L. Ed. 2d 98 (April 18, 1990).

pornographic materials in one's home.[13]   In the majority opinion in that case, Justice Thurgood Marshall said: "Whatever may be the justification for other statutes regulating obscenity, we do not think they reach into the privacy of one's home. If the First Amendment means anything, it means that a state has no business telling a man, sitting alone in his own house, what books he may read or what films he may watch."

Justice Byron R. White, however, in the majority opinion in the Ohio case stated that the case was not governed by the decision in the Georgia case. He said that the purpose of the Ohio law is "to protect victims of child pornography" while the Georgia law which the Court ruled as unconstitutional sought to proscribe the private possession of obscenity because the legislators were concerned that "obscenity would poison the minds of its viewers." The law in Ohio, on the other hand, "hopes to destroy a market for the exploitative use of children."

Additional protection was given children by the Supreme Court in its decision in 1968 upholding a New York state law that prohibits the sale to minors under the age of 17 of material defined as obscene on the basis of its appeal to minors whether or not such material would be obscene to adults.[14]

In that case the defendants were Mr. and Mrs. Ginzberg who operated Sam's Stationery and Luncheonette in Bellmore, Long Island. They were tried and found guilty of selling two "girlie" magazines to a 16-year-old boy in violation of the New York law that did not prohibit the stocking and selling of such magazines to adults but did to minors.

The case was appealed to the U.S. Supreme Court with Ginzberg arguing that "the scope of the constitutional freedom of expression secured to a citizen to read or see material concerned with sex cannot be made to depend upon whether the citizen is an adult or a minor."

---

13. Stanley v. Georgia, 394 U.S. 557 (1969).
14. Ginzberg v. New York, 390 U.S. 629 (1968).

In the majority opinion upholding the law, Justice Brennan said in part: "The well-being of its children is of course a subject within the State's constitutional power to regulate, and in our view . . . justifies the limitations . . . upon the availability of sex material to minors under 17. The prohibition against sales to minors does not bar parents who so desire from purchasing the magazines for their children."

That decision differed from the one in the case of *Butler v. Michigan* in 1957 in that the Michigan law prohibited selling anything that might "corrupt the morals of youth," even to adults, whereas in the Ginzberg case the New York law only prohibited selling "girlie" magazines to juveniles, not to adults.[15]

In 1963, the Supreme Court struck down a system of censorship being used in Rhode Island designed to protect juveniles from obscenity. This case had its origin in 1956 when the Rhode Island State Legislature created the Rhode Island Commission to Encourage Morality in Youth. One activity of the Commission was advising distributors which books and magazines were obscene. The advisory notices informed distributors that any publication designated by the Commission as obscene would need to be removed from circulation; otherwise, the matter would be referred to authorities for criminal prosecution.

Four New York publishers brought suit, and the case finally reached the U.S. Supreme Court, where by a vote of 8 to 1 the Court invalidated that system of censorship.[16] In the majority opinion, Justice Brennan explained the background of the case as follows:

■ Max Silverstein is the exclusive wholesale distributor of the appellants' publications (the four New York pub-

---

15. Butler v. Michigan, 352 U.S. 380 (1957). See Chapter 32.
16. Bantam Books v. Sullivan 372 U.S. 58 (1963).

lishers) throughout most of the State (of Rhode Island). The Commission's practice has been to notify a distributor on official Commission stationery that certain designated books or magazines distributed by him had been reviewed by the Commission and had been declared by a majority of its members to be objectionable for sale, distribution or display to youths under 18 years of age.

Silverstein had received at least 35 such notices at the time this suit was brought. Among the paperback books listed by the Commission as "objectionable" was one published by appellant Dell Publishing Company, Inc., and another published by appellant Bantam Books, Inc.

The typical notice to Silverstein either solicited or thanked Silverstein, in advance, for his "cooperation" with the Commission, usually reminding Silverstein of the Commission's duty to recommend to the Attorney General prosecution of purveyors of obscenity. Copies of the lists of "objectionable" publications were circulated to local police departments, and Silverstein was so informed in the notices.

Silverstein's reaction on receipt of a notice was to take steps to stop further circulation of copies of the listed publications. He would not fill orders for such publications and would refuse new orders. He instructed his field men to visit his retailers and to pick up all unsold copies, and would then promptly return them to the publishers.

A local police officer usually visited Silverstein shortly after Silverstein's receipt of a notice to learn what action had been taken. Silverstein was usually able to inform the officer that a specified number of the total of copies received from a publisher had been returned.

According to the testimony, Silverstein acted as he did on receipt of the notice, "rather than face the possibility of some sort of court action against ourselves, as well as the people we supply." His "cooperation" was given to avoid becoming involved in a "court proceeding" with a "duly authorized organization."

Justice Brennan called the procedure "a scheme of state censorship effectuated by extralegal sanctions," saying that the Commission members "acted as an agency not to advise but to suppress."

"What Rhode Island has done," Justice Brennan continued, "has been to subject the distribution of publications to a system of prior administrative restraints, since the Commission is not a judicial body and its decisions to list particular publications as objectionable do not follow judicial determinations that such publications may lawfully be banned." He stated further:

■ We have tolerated such a system only where it is operated under judicial superintendence and assured an almost immediate judicial determination of the validity of the restraint. The system at bar (in Rhode Island) includes no such saving features. On the contrary, its capacity for suppression of constitutionally protected publications is far in excess of that of the typical licensing scheme held constitutionally invalid by this Court.

There is no provision whatever for judicial superintendence before notices issue or even for a judicial review of the Commission's determination of objectionableness . . . although the Commission's supposed concern is limited to youthful readers, the "cooperation" it seeks from distributors invariably entails the complete suppression of the listed publications; adult readers are equally deprived of the opportunity to purchase the publications in the State.

Protection of children from "unsuitable material," which the U.S. Supreme Court has held that the states can constitutionally regulate, has been extended to warning labels on records. In 1985 record companies agreed to label potentially objectionable records after a publicity campaign by the Parents' Music Resource Center placed pressure on them; and in March 1990 the Recording Industry Association of America, a 55-member trade organization, agreed to place warning labels on recordings that contain lyrics that may offend some people. The National Association of Independent Record Distributors and Manufacturers also encouraged its members to label such records.

The wording of labels vary. Some may read, "Parental Advisory: May Contain Language Not Suitable for Minors," or "These Songs Contain Explicit Lyrics; Parental Guidance Suggested."

Record manufacturers and distributors adopted voluntary labeling to forestall government action, as bills were introduced in the late 1980s in several state legislatures to require such labeling. A major reason for opposing such laws is that labeling requirements could, and most likely would, vary from state to state, resulting in enormous marketing problems.

Numerous attempts have been made to define pornography and obscenity, without complete success. Among them is this: "Pornography is the representation of directly and indirectly erotic acts with an intrusive vividness which offends decency without aesthetic justification."[17]

The Bible states, "I know, and am persuaded . . . that there is nothing unclean of itself; but to him that esteemeth any thing to be unclean, to him it is unclean."[18] Despite its source, this principle has not generally been accepted in the United States as a satisfactory definition of obscenity and pornography, nor has any satisfactory definition yet been devised, and likely never will be. The chief reason is that they are intangible offenses against society, unlike such offenses as murder, robbery, arson, and rape, where there is tangible evidence.

The effects of obscenity and pornography are intangible. According to the Report of the Commission on Obscenity and

---

17. George P. Elliot, *Harper's*, March 1965.
18. Romans 14:14

Pornography in 1970, "Exposure to explicitly sexual materials doesn't cause social or individual harms . . . nor does it affect character or moral attitudes." That conclusion has been hotly disputed. Poet-Librarian Felix Pollak has argued, "If one denies the power of the word to do evil, one denies the power of the word to do good. In effect, one denies the power of the word."[19] In the same vein, Professor Irving Kristol stated, "If you believe that no one was ever corrupted by a book, you have also to believe that no one was ever improved by a book (or a play or a movie).[20] In agreement that reading and seeing affect behavior, the Foundation to Improve Television has found that numerous studies show a definite link between street violence and violence on television.

All human activity must be subject to some restraint. Society must have the right to declare some actions beyond the realm of acceptable behavior. Otherwise, the result is chaos and nihilism. The problem lies in drawing the line between freedom and restraint equitably and intelligently in each case. As Mr. Kristol puts it: "I'll put it bluntly; if you care for the quality of life in our American democracy, then you have to be for censorship."

19. Quoted by Ruth Brine, "Pornography Revisited: Where To Draw the Line" *Time*, April 5, 1971, pages 64-65.
20. Irving Kristol, "Pornography, Obscenity and the Case for Censor ship" *The New York Times Magazine*, March 28, 1971, pages 24-25, 112-116. See also, *Where Do You Draw the Line? An Exploration Into Media Violence, Pornography, and Censorship*, by Irving Kristol, Brigham University Press, 1971.

CHAPTER
34

❋

PANDERING IS A NO-NO

PANDERING IS A NO-NO

❀

In a decision in 1966 upholding an obscenity conviction, the U.S. Supreme Court used a standard it had never used before, that of use of the mail to pander erotic material. The case was widely discussed at the time, and the Court itself split 5 to 4 in its decision. The case began in December 1962 when Ralph Ginzburg was served with a federal indictment for violating 28 counts of the Comstock law. Ginzburg was publisher of *Eros*, a hardcover magazine of expensive format; *Liaison*, a biweekly newsletter; and a short book titled *The Housewife's Handbook on Selective Promiscuity*, all containing sexually oriented material.

He applied for mailing privileges at the post office in Blue Ball and Intercourse, Pennsylvania, which were denied because those offices were too small to handle the volume. However, he was able to obtain a second-class mailing permit at Middlesex, N.J., where he mailed several million circulars soliciting subscriptions to *Eros* and *Liaison*. For that mailing he was indicted, tried, found guilty on all 28 counts, and sentenced to three years.

The U.S. Supreme Court handed down a decision in this case on March 21, 1966,[1] upholding the conviction, not on the

---

1. Ginzburg v. U.S., 383 U.S. 463 (1966).

basis that the publications were necessarily obscene but rather because of the method used to sell them. In the majority opinion, stated by Justice William J. Brennan, Jr., the Court said:

■ We view the publications against a background of commercial exploitation of erotica solely for the sake of their prurient appeal . . . there was abundant evidence to show that each of the accused publications was originated or sold as stock in trade of the sordid business of pandering . . . Where the purveyor's sole emphasis is on the sexually provocative aspects of his publications, that fact may be decisive in the determination of obscenity.

Although the Ginzburg decision favored the Post Office Department, other court decisions had hobbled its censorship powers so much that during the 1960s pornographers began to flood the mail with their literature and advertisements, sending them to large numbers of people who found them highly offensive because of their "lewd and salacious character." Especially objectionable was the use of mailing lists of youth organizations by pornographers to send such materials to juveniles. The problem became so acute that at Congressional hearings on the subject postal officials reported that complaints had increased from 50,000 to 250,000 annually.

Congress attempted to alleviate the problem by including a special provision in the Postal Revenue and Federal Salary Act of 1967. Title III of the Act gives anyone who receives unsolicited mail that he considers to be "pandering advertising" the right to request the Postal Service to have his name removed from the mailing list of the firm sending the advertisements. When so requested, the Postal Service must notify the sender to stop mailing any such material to the person making the request.

Under this law, called the Federal Anti-Pandering Act, the person receiving the mail and not the Postal Service becomes the judge of what he receives is "erotically arousing or sexually provocative." In other words, each individual becomes his own censor.[2]

Title III of the Act is entitled "Prohibition of pandering advertisements in the mails." After it became effective in 1968, a group of distributors, owners, and operators of mail order houses, mailing list brokers, and owners and operators of mail service organizations brought suit against the Postal Service, claiming that the law infringed upon their freedom of speech, press and distribution. In 1970, the U.S. Supreme Court unanimously upheld the law.

The opinion of the Court, delivered by Chief Justice Warren Burger, states in part:[3]

■ It (the law) provides a procedure whereby any householder may insulate himself from advertisements that offer for sale "matter which the addressee in his sole

---

2. Anyone who receives mail he considers to be pandering advertising that offers for sale erotically or sexually provocative matter and wants it stopped should obtain from the post office a copy of Form 2150, "Notice for Prohibitory Order Against Sender of Pandering Advertisement in the Mails," fill in the form, and return it to the post office. The Postal Service will order the publisher to remove that name from the mailing list within 30 days. If the unwanted mail continues, the post office should be notified. The publisher is liable to both civil and criminal legal action for disobeying the Postal Service order.

    If a person wants his name and address taken off mailing lists for "junk" mail, he should send a request to Mail Preference Service, Direct Mail Marketing Association, 6 East 43rd Street, New York, N. Y. 10017. That will greatly reduce the number of catalogues and other sales and promotional materials that arrive mostly as third class mail, but it is not effective permanently. The Service is a goodwill action on the part of the Marketing Association, not mandated by law, and does not involve action by the Postal Service. It is not related to the matter of obscenity or pornography.

3. Rowan v. Post Office, 397 U.S. 728 (1970).

discretion believes to be erotically arousing or sexually provocative."

(The law) was a response to public and congressional concern with the use of mail facilities to distribute advertisements that recipients found to be offensive . . . A declared objective of Congress was to protect minors and the privacy of homes from such material . . .

Weighing the highly important right to communicate . . . against the very basic right to be free from sights, sounds, and tangible matter we do not want, it seems to us that a mailer's right to communicate must stop at the mailbox of an unreceptive addressee . . .

Nothing in the Constitution compels us to listen to or view any unwanted communication, whatever its merit; we see no basis for according the printed word or picture a different or more preferred status because they are sent by mail. The ancient concept that "a man's home is his castle" into which "not even the king may enter" has lost none of its vitality, and none of the recognized exceptions includes any right to communicate offensively with another . . . The asserted right of a mailer . . . stops at the outer boundary of every person's domain . . .

CHAPTER
35

❀

MOTION PICTURES ARE A FORM OF SPEECH

MOTION PICTURES ARE A
FORM OF SPEECH

❀

Motion pictures don't actually move, they stand still. Not for long, just a fraction of a second.

Motion picture film is made up of individual pictures called "frames." Most motion pictures shown in commercial theaters are on 35mm film with 16 frames per foot. When a motion picture is being photographed, each frame stops completely, the camera shutter opens for an exposure then it snaps shut, and a claw mechanism pulls the next frame into position for exposure.

The same process operates when the film is shown on a screen. Each frame stops momentarily for a light to shine through to project it on the screen. Both of those operations are rapid, with 24 frames being exposed per second at normal speed when the pictures are being photographed and 24 frames per second running through the projector when they are being shown on a screen. Motion pictures are thus a series of still pictures shown at a rapid rate.

This process gives the illusion of continuous movement because of a characteristic of human sight known as persistence of vision. Because we see something for about a tenth of a second after it has moved on or disappeared, a series of related pictures shown in rapid succession looks like uninterrupted motion. It is a phenomenon that has been known for centuries. The ancient Greeks, for example, asked why a flaming brand whirled over one's head seems to form a continuous circle when in reality at any given instant it can be in only one place.

The development of photography including motion pictures covered many years and involved inventors in several countries. Among the best-known names are the Lumiere brothers of Lyon, France; Louis Daguerre of France, inventor of a successful method of photography; George Eastman, of the Eastman Dry Plate and Film Company, later renamed the Eastman Kodak Company, Rochester, New York; and Thomas A. Edison, in whose laboratory in West Orange, New Jersey, the motion picture projector was developed.

It was Edison who hit upon the idea of placing small holes or slots along each edge of film so the film could be moved on a sprocket wheel, thus making starting and stopping for a fraction of a second possible while pictures were being projected on the screen.

By 1894 Kinetoscope machines from the Edison laboratory had been installed in parlors on Broadway in New York, where one could drop a penny in a slot and watch a motion picture peep show. The next year, on December 28, 1895, Auguste and Louis Lumiere of France began showing motion pictures for paying audiences in the basement of the Grand Cafe at 14 Boulevard des Capucines in Paris with the Cinematographe which they had developed. The word cinema, meaning motion picture or motion picture theater, derives from Cinematographe.

In April 1896 the Edison Vitascope caused a sensation when it was used for the first time in the Koster and Bial Music Hall, a vaudeville theater in New York City. Images that had been seen as tiny in peep shows were now life-size.

The Great Train Robbery, created by Edwin S. Porter, who had begun motion picture work with Edison in 1896, was first shown in 1903 and was the first major film to tell a story. The nickelodeon, so named because admission was a nickel, came into being about 1905 and quickly spread across the country as films became longer, more narrative, and more plentiful. Many of the early theaters were in converted store fronts, often with makeshift seating; but the motion picture industry, born in the 1890s, grew with astonishing rapidity. By 1915 there were an estimated 28,000 movie theaters of all kinds in the country.

The Birth of a Nation by David Wark Griffith in 1915 revolutionized filmmaking. It cost $110,000 to produce, five times more than any previous film; and it ran three hours, longer than any other film made up to that time. The movie opened in Los Angeles as *The Clansman* and then in New York as *The Birth of a Nation*, becoming a smash hit, a top money maker, estimated to have grossed $50 million. Tickets cost as much as $2 in New York, high by any standards in those days. It was a time when a nickel would buy a loaf of bread and 1¢ would buy a copy of *The New York Times*.

The Birth of a Nation portrays a critical epoch in American history, with Part I telling about the North and the South before and during the Civil War and Part II the South during the Reconstruction period. A silent film, as were all films until synchronized sound became a part of motion pictures in 1927, it contains scenes of the first slaves landing in Virginia, Abraham Lincoln brooding in the White House, Civil War battles, and Grant and Lee at Appomattox. Through a family in the North and one in the South, plus a large cast, the film pictures social conditions and customs of the times. Although an enormous success, *The Birth of a Nation* was severely criticized by some for its racial biases, its portrayal of black-white relationships, and was actually banned in the Capri Theater in Boston.

With that film, however, motion pictures came of age in America. Further, *The Birth of a Nation* proved conclusively that money could be made in the movie industry; and throughout its history the number one criterion of success has been and continues to be the making of films that make lots of money.

Because of its fascination, novelty, and popularity, many persons believed that this new medium had potential for evil as well as for good and therefore should be controlled.[1] As a result movie censorship began early. The first ordinance to control the showing of motion pictures was enacted by the Chicago city council in 1907, giving the chief of police authority to stop any movie being shown. Other cities and states soon introduced their own censorship ordinances and laws. New York City established a board of censorship in 1909, and within a few years similar boards were established in Ohio, Pennsylvania, and Kansas. State censorship laws were enacted in New York, Maryland, Florida, Louisiana, Virginia, and Massachusetts, and more than 150 cities had movie censorship ordinances.

As an example of such control, the New York State statute stated that "a film would not receive a license to be shown to the public if such film or part thereof is obscene, indecent, immoral, inhuman, sacrilegious, or is of such character that its exhibition would tend to corrupt morals or incite crime."

In Ohio, a board within the State Industrial Commission was established to view films in advance of their showing and approve only those it found to be "moral or educational, amusing, and harmless." In drawing up the law establishing the board, the Ohio General Assembly provided no guidelines for determining which films should be approved and which should be disapproved for showing.

The Mutual Film Corporation, a major distributor of motion pictures in Ohio, filed suit in protest of the law, contending that submitting 2,500 reels or more each year to

---

1. They had reason for seeing potential for evil, not only because of the powerful influence the medium can exert on audiences but also because both still and motion picture photography from their beginnings have been used for pornographic purposes.

the board for review would take so much time that the delay would ruin its business. When the Corporation lost the case in Ohio, it appealed to the U.S. Supreme Court, which in 1915 affirmed the right of the State of Ohio to censor films.

The majority opinion in this case was written by Justice Joseph McKenna, who held in effect that moving pictures are not a form of communication protected by the First Amendment guarantee of free speech. Rather, he saw them as a form of entertainment being shown in penny arcades and vaudeville theaters and at carnivals, which they were; and he said that states may legally censor or even precensor films as they choose without any limits except those limits contained in their constitutions. His opinion reads in part:[2]

■ It cannot be put out of view that the exhibition of motion pictures is a business pure and simple, originated and conducted for profit, like other spectacles, not to be regarded, nor intended to be regarded by the Ohio Constitution, we think, as part of the press of the country or as organs of public opinion.

They are mere representations of events, of ideas and sentiments published and known, vivid, useful and entertaining no doubt, but, as we have said, capable of evil, having power for it, the greater because of their attractiveness and manner of exhibition.

It was this capability and power, and it may be in experience of them, that induced the State of Ohio, in addition to prescribing penalties for immoral exhibitions, as it does in its Criminal Code, to require censorship before exhibition, as it does under the act under review. We cannot regard this as beyond the power of government.

That such censorship might be in violation of the First Amendment guarantee of free speech apparently did not enter

2. Mutual Film Corp. v. Ohio, 371 U.S. 230 (1915).

the deliberations in this case. That is not surprising as the movies in those days were simply a novelty, that is a form of entertainment and not regarded at all as a method of communication.

But entertainment they became! By 1920, only five years after Judge McKenna's decision, the movies had grown to be the nation's fifth largest industry; and in less than a decade later after the advent of talking pictures they were the nation's fourth largest industry. Hollywood had developed into a glamour city and a mecca for men and women anxious to achieve success in motion pictures. Actors and actresses became highly publicized "stars" whose careers and activities were followed avidly by the public and whose dress styles were widely imitated. Yet there was the negative side — stories of unconventional behavior and wild parties in the bohemian movie colony, and even scandals. Most publicized was the case in 1921 of Roscoe "Fatty" Arbuckle, a prominent comedian accused of murder.

On Labor Day weekend that year Arbuckle rented a suite in the St. Francis Hotel in San Francisco, and during a drinking party there he disappeared into the bedroom with a model named Virginia Rappe. A few hours later she became ill, was hospitalized, and died, after which the district attorney indicted Arbuckle for rape and murder. The case was front page news for weeks.[3]

Although the Arbuckle case was the most notorious, there were so many reports of other scandalous affairs that Hollywood rapidly acquired a reputation that reflected directly and negatively on the movies. As a result, legislators across the country began advocating censorship of "an industry out of control." Almost a hundred censorship bills were introduced

---

3. That ended Arbuckle's acting career; but later using the name William Goodrich he directed a few motion pictures. He died in 1933 at the age of 46.

in the legislatures of 37 states in 1921 alone.

State and local censorship placed an enormous burden on distributors and exhibitors, a major reason being that censorship rules and regulations were not uniform. For example, in the 1920's women could not be seen smoking in motion pictures in Kansas but could be in Ohio. A pregnant woman could not be seen on the screen in Pennsylvania, but she could in New York. Such variations meant cutting films and adjusting content when pictures were sent across state lines or to different communities.

Cutting and splicing a silent film to satisfy a censor was not particularly difficult, but that changed with talking pictures. The first feature film with synchronized speech as well as music was *The Jazz Singer* starring Al Jolson. First shown on October 6, 1927, in New York City, it revolutionized the movies.[4] In this film, and others to follow for some time, the sound was recorded on disks, which were then mechanically synchronized with the film by means of the Vitaphone system which Warner Brothers had acquired. Making a change in any part of the film might be relatively easy, but not so with the sound track on a disk. Later that system was discarded in favor of a sound track that is a strip of the motion picture film itself, using magnetic tape or varying light to reproduce the sound.

---

4. As with other aspects to motion picture development, synchronized sound and pictures did not appear suddenly. Experimentation had been going on for years; and as early as 1900 three competing systems were on exhibition at the Paris Exposition that year. *The Jazz Singer* starring Al Jolson in 1927 was not the first film with synchronized sound but it sparked a revolution in the movies.

CHAPTER
36

❀

THE PRODUCTION CODE WAS SELF-CENSORSHIP

THE PRODUCTION CODE
WAS
SELF CENSORSHIP

❧

As a means of lobbying against censorship legislation and of speaking with a unified voice, motion picture company executives organized a trade association in 1922 titled Motion Picture Producers and Distributors of America. They persuaded Will H. Hays, former national chairman of the Republican Party and at the time Postmaster General, to become president of the Association at a salary of $100,000 a year. Because of the scandals, what was needed and what Hays was able to provide was assurance that the industry was stable so that investors would continue with the necessary capital and a public relations program that would dampen the growing trend in censorship by state and local governments.

Hays set up a public relations committee to advise the Association on "public demands and moral standards," including in the membership a number of prominent citizens, some of whom were critical of the movie industry. Later he created a formula which directed members of the Association "to exercise every possible care that only books or plays which are of the right type be used for screen presentation."

Those actions marked the beginning of a form of motion picture self-regulation that continued for almost forty years but proved to be unsatisfactory and as stifling to creativity as was censorship by state and local governments.

Restraints imposed by the Hays office on motion picture content were tolerated, often reluctantly, and avoided if possible by the motion picture industry producers who believed that movies that were a bit risqué, that were spiced with a touch of sex, usually attracted larger attendance and consequently were more profitable than bland pictures. With only the Association Formula as a caution, studios began turning out titillating movies, not particularly obscene but with more nudity and sex than the country was accustomed to. It was a time of Clara Bow, the "It Girl,"[1] with a series of motion pictures crossing boundaries of decency set by censors as well as by what church and civic groups would tolerate without protest.

By 1927 the Hays office was in a dilemma, its member producers objecting to the "clean movies" policy because they believed that it was causing them to lose business. On the other hand, church and civic protesters were calling for federal censorship legislation, and state and local censorship boards were becoming increasingly heavy handed.

Something needed to be done, so in an effort to bolster self-regulation as a means of reducing the censorship problem, Hays established a Studio Relations Office and appointed Colonel Jason Joy, who had been assigned to public relations in the War Department, to read scripts and advise producers of potential censorship.

After a study of rules of various censorship boards around the country, Joy prepared a list of "Don'ts" and "Be Carefuls" for movie companies, which was approved by the Association in October 1927. The list included warnings against profanity, nudity, drug trafficking, sex perversion, white slavery, miscegenation, sex hygiene and venereal disease, scenes of childbirth, children's sex organs, ridicule of the clergy, and offenses against a nation, a race, or a creed.

Producers were not unanimously impressed, however, and before long they were submitting only about a fifth of their scenarios for Joy to review. Their continued production

---

1. Clara Bow's movie career ran from 1922 to 1933.

of movies with levels of sex and violence unacceptable to church organizations brought more protests; and in early 1929 a bill was introduced in the U.S. Senate to place the movie industry under the direct control of the Federal Trade Commission. Local and state censorship boards were requiring thousands of deletions, and Australian and Canadian governments were banning scores of American pictures.

That summer Martin Quigley, publisher of *Motion Picture Herald* and consequently a man with a deep interest in the industry, developed an idea for a motion picture code, one that would be binding on all producers. He obtained approval of the Catholic Church for Father Daniel Lord, S.J., professor of dramatics at St. Louis University, to draft a code. In January 1930 the code was presented to Hays, who was delighted with it. In February it was adopted by the Association of Motion Picture Producers, an organization that included West Coast producers; and in March it was adopted by the Motion Picture Producers and Distributors of America.

Although amended a number of times, that Motion Picture Production Code remained in effect until 1968 when it was supplanted by a rating system to regulate attendance instead of a code to control motion picture content.

The Production Code "to govern the making of talking synchronized and silent motion pictures" listed three general principles:

1. No picture shall be produced which will lower the moral standards of those who see it. Hence the sympathy of the audience should never be thrown to the side of crime, wrongdoing, evil or sin.

2. Correct standards of life, subject only to the requirements of drama and entertainment, shall be presented.

3. Law, natural or human, shall not be ridiculed, nor shall sympathy be created for its violation.

In a dozen sections the Code listed in considerable detail what is forbidden in regard to criminal behavior, sex, vulgarity, obscenity, profanity, costumes, dances, religion, national feelings, titles, location, and repellent subjects.

Under Profanity, for example, the Code stated, "Pointed profanity (this includes the words God, Lord. Jesus, Christ — unless used reverently — Hell, S.O.B., damn, Gawd), or every other profane or vulgar expression, however used, is forbidden."

Appended to the Code was a Resolution for Uniform Interpretation which explained the procedure for film approval, method for making an appeal, and reasons for supporting the Code.

Although motion picture producers who signed the Code agreed to conform faithfully to its provisions, very little changed. Because they generally looked upon the Code as a public relations device rather than a guide, virtually the same incidence of sex and violence continued in the movies, arousing renewed protests. Jason Joy, as head of the Studio Relations office, issued suggestions and warnings; but since he laid down no requirements for changes in scenarios, he was largely ignored by the producers. After his resignation in 1932, he was succeeded by James Wingate, a former school administrator who had been director of the New York board of censors for the past five years; but Wingate was no more effective than Joy had been in enforcing the provisions of the Production Code.

Disturbing portents indicating a need for change were obvious. In 1932 a resolution was introduced in the U.S. Senate calling for an investigation of the motion picture industry. In January 1933 widespread attention was centered on the content of movies through publication in *McCall's* magazine of an abbreviated version of a scientific study of the effects of motion pictures on social attitudes and the behavior of audiences. The complete study on the effects of all the mass media, sponsored by the Payne Fund, was published later in nine volumes.

In 1934, displeased with the failure of the Production Code to clean up the movies, the Catholic Church formed the Legion of Decency, which condemned motion pictures not meeting certain moral criteria. Titles were announced from the pulpit and published in printed form, warning members not to attend. The Legion claimed that in the first year seven to nine million members pledged not to see any movie listed with a scarlet C, which meant it had been condemned by the Legion rating board.

Because this was during the Depression when attendance had dropped off sharply, with a third of the nation's movie houses closed by 1933, the threat of boycott was taken seriously by producers as was the threat of federal control of the industry. At the same time, censors were cracking down, requiring expensive cuts in films.

Movie producers were caught in a bind because motion picture companies, like most other companies in that time of Depression, were in a financial squeeze. They believed that the more sensational a motion picture was, the more profitable it would be; but opposition by the Catholic Church and other religious and civic groups was daunting. Reformers were finding all sorts of arguments in the Payne Report to support their demands that Washington regulate the industry.

The denouement came in the spring of 1933 when Hays laid the matter squarely before the motion picture producers, warning them that they must adopt strict self-discipline or face the consequences. The producers capitulated.

When Justice McKenna wrote in the Supreme Court decision in 1915 that "the exhibition of motion pictures is a business pure and simple, originated and conducted for profit," he was indeed correct in one very important respect. Motion picture moguls agreed to the demands laid down by Will Hays, not because they were primarily interested in producing clean movies and in moral uplift, but rather because doing so would be financially beneficial through forestalling attendance boycotts and further government censorship and control of the industry. Movies may have been a form of art and an influence on social behavior, but the bottom line came first.

Hays stipulated that beginning in 1934 all scripts must be submitted for approval by the Production Code Administration, an office that had replaced the Studio Relations Office; that a fine of $25,000 would be imposed for any film produced, distributed, or exhibited without the Production Code Seal; that motion picture companies were to refuse to show any picture in their theaters that did not bear the Seal. That last stipulation was important because the major motion picture companies at that time owned and controlled the best and most profitable theaters in the country.

Another change was made in regard to appeals of Production Code Administration rulings on film content. The Hollywood Jury, which had operated like "an old boy network," was abolished with appeals now to be made to the Motion Picture Association Board in New York.

Joseph Ignatius Breen, who had been employed in 1930 to manage public relations for the Production Code, was appointed director of Production Code Administration. He was a Catholic with close relationship with the hierarchical leadership in Chicago, had prior experience as a reporter and foreign correspondent, had managed press relations for the Eucharistic Congress in Chicago in 1926 and for the Chicago World's Fair, and most recently had been public relations officer for the Peabody Coal Company.

Through a combination of firmness and diplomacy, Breen was able to enforce the Production Code; and with the major studios in complete control of the industry by producing motion pictures and exhibiting them in their own theaters, no important feature film was released without the Production Code Seal during the next 16 years.

Those were years of contention between freedom and control, however. An example of this conflict is in the use of the word "damn." When Selznick International/Metro-Goldwyn-Mayer made a motion picture of Margaret Mitchell's best-selling novel, *Gone With the Wind*, in 1939, it ran into numerous Code problems, including the use of the word "nigger" and picturing the can-can dance. Near the end of the film, Scarlett pleads with Rhett not to leave her, saying, "Oh, my darling, what shall I do?" Rhett replies, "Frankly, my dear, I don't give a damn."

That swearword was permitted to remain only after it was debated in two sessions of the Association Board of Directors and then followed by a written understanding that henceforth the words "damn" and "hell" would not be used in any film except when they were essential to the story and "no such use shall be permitted which is intrinsically objectionable or offends good taste."

Sex was not totally eliminated by the Code, as producers were able to enliven many of their films with hints and suggestions, although nothing like those in films today. Among motion pictures with such scenes were *Ecstasy*, 1933, showing Hedy Lamar baring her breasts; *Gone With the Wind*, 1939, with Clark Gable carrying Vivien Leigh up the stairs "to do it"; *The Outlaw*, 1943, with focus on Jane Russell's breasts; and *Some Like It Hot*, 1959, with Marilyn Monroe's skirt being blown up her body, revealing her legs and panties.

A combination of factors led to the eventual discontinuance of the Production Code and the institution of a Classification System:

■ Opposition by a substantial segment of the public to restrictions imposed by the Code, considering them a form of censorship that stifled creativity and obstructed realism in motion pictures. Not only individuals but also such organizations as the National Council on Freedom From Censorship and the American Civil Liberties Union opposed much of the industry's self-censorship as did most if not all authors, directors, and actors engaged in movie making.

■ Public perception of morality, which gradually became more liberal and tolerant, especially during and after the trauma and dislocation resulting from World War II; the civil rights marches of the early 1960s; and the sexual revolution, campus sit-ins, the counterculture movement, and the Vietnam War protests of the late 1960s and early 1970s.

■ Pressure to go beyond Code requirements by motion picture producers themselves who believed that too strict compliance with the Code lowered profits and at times interfered with art.

■ Loss of monopoly by the major studios when they were forced to divest themselves of their theater chains following the decision of the U.S. Supreme Court in 1948 upholding a Justice Department ruling that under the Sherman Act such vertical control of production, distribution, and exhibition was in restraint of trade and therefore unlawful.[2]

■ Growing number of independent producers, the influx of foreign films, the increasing number of American films made abroad, and the development of network television.

■ Decisions by the U.S. Supreme Court defining obscenity, which had the effect of loosening both civil and governmental controls on film content.

Provisions of the Production Code were never easy to enforce, although the public was largely unaware of the

---

2. United States v. Paramount Pictures, Inc. 334 U.S. 131 (1948). In recent years movie producers have begun buying theaters and now own about a third of all movie screens in the United States.

bargaining, the discussions, and the compromises involved as the Hays office censored hundreds of films.[3] Among the many over which there was extended discussion and appeals were such well-known motion pictures as *The Outlaw*, 1943; *The Postman Always Rings Twice*, 1946; *A Streetcar Named Desire*, 1951; *The French Line*, 1954; *Lolita*, 1962; and *Who's Afraid of Virginia Woolf*, 1966.

The first real crack in the Production Code came in 1950 when three of the five Association's major theater chains announced plans to show *The Bicycle Thief* without the Production Code Seal. This was a foreign film by Produzioni Di Sica that had won high acclaim in Europe after its release there in 1948 and was attracting record-breaking crowds at the World Theater in New York after it premiered there on December 12, 1949.

After much discussion, the Production Code Seal was denied, although the film was praised by critics, not condemned by the Legion of Decency, and was awarded an Oscar as the Best Foreign Film of the Year. Its success in independent theaters promised such hefty financial returns that breaking an agreement and running the film without the Code Seal was irresistible to executives of three theater chains. It was the first time since 1934 that a major movie company had booked a movie that did not bear the Production Code Seal.

Three years later in July 1953 the crack in the Code widened when Otto Preminger released *The Moon Is Blue* after it had been denied the Production Code Seal. Three major theater companies controlling more than 2,400 theaters agreed to run the movie, and it was a box office success — without the Code.

Times were changing. Movie production companies no

---

3. The story of the American motion-picture industry's self-censorship is told in the book, *The Dame in the Kimono*, by Leonard J. Leff and Jerold L. Smoons, Weidenfeld & Nicholson, 1990.

longer owned the chains of theaters and thus no longer had a monopoly on which films could be shown in the most profitable theaters. Television was seriously eroding movie attendance, with the audience declining by almost half in the decade between 1946, which marked the advent of television, and 1956.

A decision by the U.S. Supreme Court in 1952 had a far-reaching effect on the movie industry by ruling that motion pictures are protected by the First Amendment.[4] That was a reversal of the decision in the case of *Mutual Film Corporation v. Ohio* in 1915; and it was the first time the Court had so ruled, although in the case of *United States v. Paramount Pictures* in 1948, Justice Douglas had said, "We have no doubt that motion pictures, like newspapers and radio, are included in the press whose freedom is guaranteed by the First Amendment."

The case arose after Joseph Burstyn, Inc., imported the Italian-made film, *The Miracle*, starring Anna Magnani, which had been critically acclaimed at the film festival in Venice in 1948. On November 30, 1950, after having examined the film, the motion picture division of the New York Education Department issued a license authorizing its showing. The film with English subtitles, one part of a trilogy titled *Ways of Love*, opened on December 12 in a New York theater and ran for about eight weeks.

During that time the New York State Board of Regents, under which the education department operates, received "hundreds of letters, telegrams, post cards, affidavits and other communications" both protesting against and defending the showing of *The Miracle*. The theater was picketed and there were bomb threats.

As a result, the Chancellor of the Board of Regents requested three members of the Board to view the picture and

---

4. Joseph Burstyn, Inc. v. Wilson, 343 U.S. 495 (1952).

make a report to the entire Board. The committee's opinion was that there was basis for the claim that the picture was "sacrilegious." On February 16, 1951, the Regents, after viewing the film, decided that it was sacrilegious and ordered the Commissioner of Education to rescind the license for its being exhibited.

The Miracle tells of a girl who, while tending her goats, mistakes a bearded stranger for Saint Joseph and begs him to take her to heaven. Falling asleep after their conversation, she is not sure upon awaking that it was not a dream. A priest tells her it is possible that she really did see a saint. Her pregnancy, revealed later, subjects her to such cruel mockery from old and young alike that she takes refuge in a lonely cave. Finally, she stumbles out and manages to reach an empty church where she gives birth. The film closes with a baby crying in the background and the exalted girl exclaiming, "My son! My love! My life!"

The case eventually reached the U.S. Supreme Court which ruled unanimously in 1952 that the film was not sacrilegious. The majority opinion by Justice Tom C. Clark placed motion pictures under protection by the First Amendment, but did not entirely proscribe film censorship. The opinion reads in part:

■ The present case is the first to present squarely to (the Court) the question whether motion pictures are within the ambit of protection which the First Amendment, through the Fourteenth, secures to any form of "speech" or "the press."

It cannot be doubted that motion pictures are a significant medium for the communication of ideas. They may affect public attitudes and behavior in a variety of ways . . . The importance of motion pictures as an organ of public opinion is not lessened by the fact that they are designed to entertain as well as to inform . . .

It is urged that motion pictures do not fall within the First Amendment's aegis because their production, distribution, and exhibition is a large-scale business conducted for profit. We cannot agree. That books, newspapers, and magazines are published and sold for profit does not prevent them from being a form of expression whose liberty is guarded by the First Amendment. We fail to see why operation for profit should have any different effect in the case of motion pictures.

It is further urged that motion pictures possess a greater capacity for evil, particularly among the youth of the community, than other modes of expression. Even if one were to accept this hypothesis, it does not follow that motion pictures should be disqualified from First Amendment protection. If there be capacity for evil it may be relevant in determining the permissible scope of community control, but it does not authorize the substantially unbridled censorship such as we have here.

For the foregoing reasons, we conclude that expression by means of motion pictures is included within the free speech and free press guarantee of the First and Fourteenth Amendments. . .

(That), however, is not the end of our problem. It does not follow that the Constitution requires absolute freedom to exhibit every motion picture of every kind at all times and all places . . . Nor does it follow that motion pictures are necessarily subject to the precise rules governing any other particular method of expression . . . But the basic principles of freedom of speech and the press . . . do not vary . . .

Application of the "sacrilegious" test, in these or other respects, might raise substantial questions under the First Amendment's guarantee of separate church and state with freedom of worship for all. However, from the standpoint of freedom of speech and the press, it is enough to point out that the state has no legitimate interest in protecting any or all religions from views distasteful to them which is sufficient to justify prior restraints upon the expression of those views.

It is not the business of government in our nation to suppress real or imagined attacks upon a particular religious doctrine, whether they appear in publications, speeches, or motion pictures . . . We hold only that under the First and Fourteenth Amendments a state may not ban a film on the basis of a censor's conclusion that it is "sacrilegious."

Seven years later in 1959 the Supreme Court was asked to consider the constitutionality of the New York law that required all motion pictures to be passed by a censor before being shown. The law stated that a license would be granted "unless such film or part thereof is obscene, indecent, immoral, inhuman, sacrilegious, or is of such character that its exhibition would tend to corrupt morals or incite to crime."

The case centered on a French movie based on the book, *Lady Chatterley's Lover* by D. H. Lawrence, a book discussed in Chapter 31. The censorship board refused to approve the film for exhibition because it "attractively portrays a relationship contrary to the moral standards, the religious precepts, and the legal code of the State's citizenry."

The Supreme Court in a unanimous decision ruled that the ban violated the First Amendment guarantee of freedom to advocate ideas. In the Court opinion, Justice Potter Stewart said in part:[5]

■ What New York has done . . . is to prevent the exhibition of a motion picture because that picture advocates an idea — that adultery under certain circumstances may be proper behavior. Yet the First Amendment's basic guarantee is of freedom to advocate ideas. The State, quite simply, has struck at the very heart of constitutionally protected liberty.

Although that Supreme Court decision placed motion pictures under protection of the First Amendment, it did not

---

5. Kingsley International Pictures Corporation v. Regents of the University of the State of New York, 360 U.S. 684 (1959).

unequivocally rule censorship as being unconstitutional. The New York statute that authorized the licensing of films before they were shown provided that every motion picture film was to be submitted for examination, be promptly examined, and "unless such film or part thereof is obscene, sacrilegious, indecent, immoral, inhuman, or is of such a character that its exhibition would tend to corrupt morals or incite to crime, be issued a license therefor."

Movie censorship by both the Hays office and state and local governments boards was based on isolated scenes, occasionally on words, rather than on the motion picture as a whole. Censorship of books was also based on excerpts until the U.S. Supreme Court ruled in the *Ulysses* case in 1933 "obscenity must be judged on the basis of the dominant effect of the entire book, not just passages."[6]

After ruling in 1952 that motion pictures are protected by the First Amendment, the Supreme Court in subsequent cases ruled various censorship laws containing such words as "sacrilegious," "immoral," and "harmful" as unconstitutional because such words are imprecise and thus capable of varied interpretation. With laws of that kind, film makers could not know exactly what was permitted, and censors had wide discretion in deciding which films could legally be exhibited, the Court held.

It was not until 1961 that the Supreme Court was asked to decide whether government censorship of motion pictures was per se unconstitutional, and the Court decided by the narrow margin of 5-to-4 that such censorship is not unconstitutional.[7]

The City of Chicago had an ordinance requiring that all motion pictures be issued a permit by the censorship board

---

6. United States v. One Book Called "Ulysses," 5 F. Supp 182 (S. D. N. Y. 1933).
7. Times Film Corporation v. Chicago, 365 U.S. 43 (1961).

before being exhibited. The ordinance read in part: "Such permit shall be granted only after the motion picture film for which said permit is requested has been produced at the office of the commissioner of police for examination or censorship."

The Times Film Corporation, an independent distributor, decided to test the constitutionality of the ordinance by refusing to submit for examination an inoffensive film titled *Don Juan*, which is a version of the Mozart opera, *Don Giovanni*. The case eventually reached the U.S. Supreme Court which upheld the right of the City of Chicago to censor films. In the majority opinion Justice Tom C. Clark said in part:

■ The movie company would have us hold that the public exhibition of motion pictures must be allowed under any circumstances ... Chicago emphasizes here its duty to protect its people against the dangers of obscenity in the public exhibition of motion pictures. To this argument the movie company's only answer is that regardless of the capacity for, or extent of, such an evil, previous restraint cannot be justified. With this we cannot agree.

In a strong dissent, Chief Justice Earl Warren said that "the extent to which censorship has recently been used in this country is indeed astonishing," and he then proceeded to list numerous examples of the pettiness and unpredictability of motion picture censors. Among them:

■ Memphis: *Curley* banned because it contained scenes of white and Negro children in school together.

■ Atlanta: *Lost Boundaries*, the story of a Negro physician and his family who "passed" for white, barred on the ground that the exhibition of the picture "will adversely affect the peace, morals and good order" of the city.

■ New York: *Damaged Lives*, a film dealing with venereal disease, banned even though it treated a difficult subject with dignity and had the sponsorship of the American Social Hygiene Society.

■ Chicago: Scene in *Street With No Name* excised in which a girl was slapped because this was thought to be a "too violent" episode.

■ Ohio: *Professor Mamlock*, produced in Russia and portraying the persecution of the Jews by the Nazis, condemned as "harmful" and calculated to "stir up hatred and ill will and gain nothing."

■ Providence, Rhode Island: Police refused showing of *Professor Mamlock* on the ground that it was communistic propaganda.

■ Pennsylvania: *Spanish Earth*, a pro-Loyalist documentary film, was banned.

■ Kansas: A speech by Senator Wheeler opposing the bill for enlarging the Supreme Court was ordered cut from the *March of Time* because it was "partisan and biased."

■ Maryland: A Polish documentary film was restricted because "it failed to present a true picture of modern Poland."

■ Chicago: Charlie Chaplin's satire on Hitler, *The Great Dictator*, was banned, apparently out of deference to the large German population in the city.

■ Other examples included Memphis censors' banning *The Southerner*, which deals with poverty among tenant farmers, because "it reflects on the South" and the film *Brewster's Millions* because a radio and film character named Rochester, a Negro, was deemed "too familiar"; Chicago refused a permit for the showing of *Anatomy of a Murder* because it contains the words "rape" and "contraceptive"; and an Ohio censor objected to an early version of *Carmen* because it shows cigarette-girls smoking cigarettes in public.

Chief Justice Warren's objection to the system of film censorship being used at that time lay in its arbitrary use of authority. The censors decided what films could or could not be shown, what scenes must be excised to make a film acceptable for showing. Their decisions were final, except, of course, a film distributor could take the matter to court, which was expensive and generally so time-consuming as to make scheduling impossible.

Regarding the case before the Court, Warren in his dissent pointed out that all procedural safeguards afforded litigants in courts of law were absent in the kinds of censorship being conducted in Chicago at that time. "The likelihood of a fair and impartial trial disappears," he said, "when the censor is both prosecutor and judge." He continued:

■ To me, this case clearly presents the question of our approval of unlimited censorship of motion pictures *before* exhibition through a system of administrative licensing . . .

The inquiry stated by the Court, but never resolved, is whether this form of prohibition results in "unreasonable strictures on individual liberty," whether licensing, as a prerequisite to exhibition, is barred by the First and Fourteenth Amendments.

I am aware of no constitutional principle which permits us to hold that the communication of ideas through one medium may be censored while other media are immune. Of course each medium presents its own peculiar problems, but they are not of the kind which would authorize the censorship of one form of communication and not the others. . .

(The Court's decision in this case) gives official license to the censor, approving a grant of power to city officials to prevent the showing of any motion picture these officials deem unworthy of a license. It thus gives formal sanction to censorship in its purest and most far-reaching form . . .

(This decision) officially unleashes the censor and permits him to roam at will, limited only by an ordinance which contains some standards that . . . are patently imprecise . . .

510

Moreover, more likely than not, the exhibitor will not pursue judicial remedies. His inclination may well be simply to capitulate rather than initiate a lengthy and costly litigation . . . The standards of proof, the judicial safeguards (do not) hinder the quick judgment of the censor . . .

Four years later in 1965 the Supreme Court, while not declaring all film censorship unconstitutional, did place curbs on it. In a unanimous decision delivered by Justice Brennan, the Court ruled that "a noncriminal process which requires the prior submission of a film to a censor avoids constitutional infirmity only if it takes place under procedural safeguards designed to obviate the dangers of a censorship system," and then stated these two requirements:[8]

■ First, the burden of proving that the film is unprotected expression must rest on the censor.

■ Second, the exhibitor must be assured . . . that the censor will, within a specified brief period, either issue a license or go to court to restrain showing of the film.

These two restrictions on censorship met the major objection raised by Chief Justice Warren in 1961 that censorship procedures do not provide judicial safeguards.

The case arose when Ronald Freedman exhibited the film, *Revenge at Daybreak,* in his Baltimore theater without first submitting the picture to the Maryland Board of Censors as required by law. He did so contending that the law in its entirety impaired freedom of expression and was therefore unconstitutional. He was found guilty and appealed the case all the way to the U.S. Supreme Court which unanimously ruled in his favor.

8. Freedman v. Maryland, 380 U.S. 51 (1965).

The Court opinion reads in part in regard to the Maryland law:

■   There is no statutory provision for judicial participation in the procedure which bars a film, not even assurance of prompt judicial review . . .

The administration of a censorship system for motion pictures presents peculiar dangers to constitutionally protected speech.   Unlike a prosecution for obscenity, a censorship proceeding puts the initial burden on the exhibitor or distributor.

Because the censor's business is to censor, there inheres the danger that he may well be less responsive than a court . . . to the constitutionally protected interests in free expression.   And if it is made unduly onerous, by reason of delay or otherwise, to seek judicial review, the censor's determination may in practice be final.

With this decision of the Supreme Court, followed by other court decisions in 1973 and 1974 hobbling their authority, censorship boards withered away across the country.   In 1981 the last in the U.S. ceased functioning in Maryland when the state legislature stopped funding it.

Also events gradually moved the motion picture industry closer to abandonment of the Production Code and adoption of the Rating System in effect today.   They included changes in leadership of the Association and liberalizing the Code several times.

Will Hays stepped down as president of the Motion Picture Producers and Distributors of America in September 1945 but was retained as an advisor for the next five years at $100,000 a year.[9]   Eric Allen Johnson, president of the U.S.

---

9. Will Hays died in 1954, and in that same year Joseph Breen was succeeded by Geoffrey M. Shurlock as Production Code Administrator.   Breen died in December 1965 and Shurlock in April 1976.

Chamber of Commerce, was named president; and one of his first acts was to change the name of the organization to Motion Picture Association of America (MPAA), which it remains today.[10]

Eric Johnson died in August 1963, and the position was filled temporarily by Ralph Hetzel, Association executive secretary. In 1966 Jack Valenti, special assistant to President Lyndon B. Johnson, was appointed president and chief operating officer at a salary of $170,000-plus annually.

---

10. Headquarters of MPAA is at 1133 Avenue of the Americas, New York, N.Y. 10036.

CHAPTER
37

✿

MOVIE CLASSIFICATION REPLACED THE CODE

MOVIE CLASSIFICATION REPLACED THE CODE

❊

The first sign of classification of motion pictures with a system of rating rather than self-censorship of content with a Code came in June 1966 when the movie *Lolita* was released bearing the Production Code Seal followed by the words, "Adults Only," which meant "suitable for persons over 18 years of age." The film, based on a novel by Vladimir Nabokov, tells about an older man's obsession with a 13-year-old nymphet who seduced him. It could not have come close to meeting Code restrictions years before; but now after much haggling it was assigned the Seal with the Adults Only tag.

When the movie opened at Loew's State Theater, a guard was posted to prevent anyone under 19 years from entering. Among those turned away was Sue Lyon who had played the role of "Lolita" in the film and was only 15 years of age. Eventually she was permitted to enter.

Although the Code had been amended to allow greater liberties in content of motion pictures, the Board faced an enormous problem in 1966 in its consideration of *Who's Afraid of Virginia Woolf?* starring Elizabeth Taylor, Richard Burton, Sandy Dennis, and George Segal. The film, faithful to the stage play by Edward Albee, is laced with profanity and obscenity that challenged even a relaxed Code.

Here was a film based on a play that had earned a Tony Award, a citation by the New York Drama Critics Circle, and was nominated for a Pulitzer Prize. It had a serious theme, starred noted actors and actresses, was produced at a cost of $7.5 million, and could possibly win an Academy Award as the best of the year. While it did not, both Elizabeth Taylor and Sandy Dennis did win Oscars for their roles.

Granting a Production Code Seal to a film with that kind of language would virtually destroy the Code; so would refusal to grant the Seal to a film of that caliber. After much discussion, the Board granted *Virginia Woolf* an exception to the Code.

That decision signaled the approaching end. The Code was rewritten to allow more freedom, particularly in regard to sex, and then abandoned in less than two years and replaced by the Code and Rating Administration. Although the Hays office was often vilified during the more than 30 years in which the Code held sway as arbiter of what Americans would see in motion pictures, the fact is that customer satisfaction with the movies has never been higher than it was during the decades of the 1930s and 1940s before television. In the best years of that time of censored movies, Hollywood made as many as 600 feature films annually; and, although attendance dropped off sharply in the early years of the Depression, 80 to 90 million admissions a week was common in the later years of the 1930s and in the 1940s.

The United States was one of the last Western nations to adopt a rating system for motion pictures, and it is one of the very few in the world in which the rating system is voluntary and not administered by government. Also this country is one of the few that has no Federal law governing motion picture content and exhibition.

In a booklet titled *The Voluntary Movie Rating System,* published by MPAA in 1987, Jack Valenti explained the adoption of the rating system:

■ When I became president of the Motion Picture Association of America in May 1966, the slippage of Hollywood studio authority over the content of films collided

517

with an avalanching revision of American mores and customs.

The national scene was marked by insurrection on the campus, riots in the streets, rise in women's liberation, protest of the young, questioning of church dogma, doubts about the institution of marriage, abandonment of old guiding slogans, and the crumbling of social traditions. It would have been foolish to believe that movies, that most creative of art forms, could have remained unaffected by the change and torment in our society.

The result of all this was the emergence of a "new kind" of American movie — frank and open, and made by filmmakers subject to very few self-imposed restraints.

Almost within weeks of my new duties I was confronted with controversy, neither amiable nor fixable. The first issue was the film, *Who's Afraid of Virginia Woolf?*, in which, for the first time on the screen the word "screw" and the phrase "hump the hostess" were heard. In company with the MPAA's general counsel, Louis Nizer, I met with Jack Warner, the legendary chieftain of Warner Bros., and his top aide, Ben Kalmenson. We talked for three hours, and the result was the deletion of those words.

The second issue surfaced only a few months later. This time it was Metro-Goldwyn-Mayer and the Antonioni film, *Blow-Up*. I met with the company head, Bob O'Brien, for this movie also represented a first — the first time a major distributor was marketing a film with nudity in it. The Production Code Administration in California had denied the Seal. I backed the decision, whereupon MGM distributed the film through a subsidiary company, thereby flouting the voluntary agreement of MPAA member companies that none would distribute a film without a Code Seal.

Finally, in April 1968, the U.S. Supreme Court upheld the constitutional power of states and cities to prevent the exposure of children to books and films that could not be denied to adults. (*Ginzberg v. New York*)

It was plain that the old system of self-regulation, begun with the formulation of the MPAA in 1922, had broken down. What few threads holding the structure created by Will H. Hays had now snapped.

I knew that the mix of new social currents, the irresistible forces of creators determined to make "their" films (full of wild candor, groused some social critics), and the possible intrusion of government into the movie arena demanded my immediate action.

Within weeks, discussions of my plan for a movie rating system began with the presidents of the National Association of Theatre Owners (NATO), and with the governing committee of the International Film Importers & Distributors of America (IFIDA), an assembly of independent producers and distributors.

Over the next five months I held more than 100 hours of meetings with these two organizations as well as with guilds of actors, writers, directors and producers, with craft unions, with critics, with religious organizations, and with the heads of MPAA member companies.

By early fall the rating plan had been designed and approved, with three organizations, NATO, IFIDA, and MPAA as partners in the enterprise. It was announced by the MPAA on October 7, 1968, and became effective for all motion pictures released on or after November 1. Eugene D. Dougherty, Production Code Administrator at the time, was placed in charge; and a rating board consisting entirely of persons who were parents was appointed.

The Rating Board, first located in California but now in New York City, is composed of seven persons headed by a chairman. There are no special qualifications for Board membership except that a member must have a shared parenthood experience and must love movies, must possess an intelligent maturity of judgment, and have the capacity, according to Mr. Valenti, to put himself or herself in the role of most parents and view a film as most parents might — parents trying to decide whether their children ought to see a specific film.

The purpose of the rating system, states the MPAA, is to provide advance information to enable parents to make judgments on movies they want their children to see or not to see. The system is not meant to be a surrogate parent. Rather, the responsibility of the parent to make the decision is basic.

Because the Rating Board does not approve or disapprove of films but only classifies them, it does not consider its actions as censorship. Any producer dissatisfied with a rating can appeal to the Rating Appeal Board comprised of 22 members from the movie industry organizations that govern the rating system. Overseeing the Rating Board is a Policy Review Committee consisting of officials of the MPAA and the NATO, who set guidelines and monitor the work of the Rating Board.

The system began with four rating categories: G, for general audiences, with all ages admitted; M, for adults and mature audiences; R, for restricted, with anyone under 16 to be accompanied by a parent or guardian; and X, for adults with no one under 16 admitted. That age was later raised to 17, although it varied among cities and states.

Like the Code, the Rating System was amended more than once. M became GP. PG-13, "not recommended for children under age 13," was added in 1984.[1] Some theaters post PG-13 films with the warning, "Parents strongly cautioned as some material may be inappropriate for teenagers."

The most far-reaching change in the Rating System was made in September 1990 by instituting category NC-17 and abolishing the X rating, with NC-17 meaning "no children

---

1. The PG-13 rating, incidentally, has been picked up for use by at least one public library. The trustees of the Memorial Library in Oak Lawn, Illinois, adopted the use of a PG 13 library card in 1990 as an option for children under age 14. Children whose parents request the special card for them are restricted to the children's room, unable to have the run of the library where they can read anything available.

admitted."

The ratings today are G, PG-13, R, and NC-17. A motion picture listed with NR means that it has not been rated by the MPAA. Some theaters will not run NR movies; others will not permit children to attend them. The great bulk of movies being shown in commercial theaters today are rated PG, PG-13, and R, with only a thin sprinkling of G and NC-17 films. Some theaters have adopted in-house ratings provided by the MPAA to give further guidance to parents on R-rated films. They are Rv, excessive violence; Rs, excessive sex or nudity, R1, excessive profanity; and Rd, glorification of drugs.

The prime reason for abolishing the X-rating was that it had become synonymous with pornography, although that had not been intended. The MPAA stated that the X-rating was for films that the Rating Board considered unsuitable for youth under age 17. When the Rating System was instituted, the MPAA registered all ratings as trademarks except X, an omission which meant that X could be used legally by anyone. As a result, "adult" theaters began to advertise their films as X or as XXX or even XXXX. The X-rating thus came to mean pornographic to the general public regardless of what the MPAA intended.

It was a rating that became a blight that producers wanted to avoid because most regular theaters and movie chains would not book X-rated pictures, thus limiting their showing to the relatively small number of "adult" theaters. Also, television and radio would not accept advertising for X-rated movies, and few newspapers would list, advertise, or review them, so the potential for income for X-rated movies was limited.

The Rating System thus placed producers in a bind at times. An X-rating was practically the kiss of death for a film. A producer could accept the rating assigned by the MPAA Board, or could edit the film to get a better rating, or could appeal. Producers generally preferred to submit to that kind of "censorship" for two reasons. One was that many theaters were reluctant to show unrated films. The other more compelling reason is their belief that industry self-government as represented by the Rating System is preferable to government regulation. Additional regulation is seen as possible, even probable, if production were allowed to go unbridled, especially in view of pressure for such legislation by numerous civic and religious organizations concerned with the content of motion pictures.

As with the Production Code, so has the Rating System been criticized for various reasons ever since it was instituted. Producers themselves expressed frustration and dissatisfaction, some even threatening to drop membership in the MPAA. As the X-rating was the chief problem, various recommendations were made for added ratings, especially for one between R and X for "challenging adult films that do not deserve the stigma of an X-rating." A number of writers, directors, and critics believed that there should be a new rating, perhaps A (for adult) or M (for mature) to indicate that the film contains a strong adult theme or image that is not suitable for minors.

The MPAA was hesitant to make any change, but pressure mounted as time went by; and in July 1990 more than thirty leading movie producers signed a letter to Jack Valenti stating that "the artistic freedom and integrity of American filmmakers are being compromised by an outdated and unfair rating system," and called for a "new adult rating in place of the X." The abolition of the X came a couple of months later, accompanied by the NC-17 rating "to give parents more useful information," Mr. Valenti said, "so they can decide which films their children can see."

Adoption of the NC-17 rating was applauded by producers, who saw the change as giving them freedom to make films as they wished, films that could be shown uncut. The rating was first used in October 1990, about a month after its adoption, with the release of *Henry & June*, a film based on the autobiography of Anais Nin which describes her sexual, emotional, and literary relationship with writer Henry Miller and his wife June in Paris in the 1930s. The movie was described by one critic as "marvelously funny, insightful and erotic." By the end of the following January, 23 films had been assigned the NC-17 rating.

The new rating did not meet with universal approval, however, not even in the movie industry which soon discovered that the new rating shut out the profitable teenage market, that many theaters would not show NC-17-rated movies, and some newspapers refused to run advertisements or publish reviews of them.

Numerous protests arose outside the industry in the belief that "changing the name of the X category would not change the nature of the films." Both the U.S. Catholic Conference and the National Council of Churches condemned the new rating, protesting that the change is neither in the public interest nor in the best interest of the motion picture industry. The editor of *The Christian Century* said, "The new rating gives movie makers a respectable category for their excesses," and the *Catholic Messenger*, Davenport, Iowa, stated, "The marketplace now has more freedom to disturb children's growth."[2] Two daily newspapers, the *Birmingham News* in Alabama and the *Sacramento Union* in California, promptly announced that they would not accept advertising for NC-17 rated films.

In January 1991, less than four months after the adoption of the NC-17 rating by the MPAA, Blockbuster Video announced that it would no longer handle those film videos for sale or rental. The company, largest in the United States with more than 1,800 outlets across the country, made the decision to maintain a family image, a spokesperson said. The company now applies the same criteria to NC-17 rated films as it

---

2. George W. Cornell, "Churches Assail New Movie Rating," *Sarasota Herald-Tribune*, November 10, 1990, page 4E.

did to X-rated films, which it never stocked.

Others have been critical of the basis for rating. One critic wrote that while the stated purpose of the system is "to help parents decide what they want their children to see," the rating board considers a "a four-letter word or the sight of a bare breast to be dynamite, but slaughter and carnage are acceptable fare for children." He continued, saying that "sex goes only for adults, but violence is for any age." Another called the system a joke, saying, "There isn't a teenager in America who can't get someone over 18 to take him or her to an R-rated movie."

Both the Film Commission of the National Council of Churches and the National Catholic Office for Motion Pictures withdrew their support of the Rating System in 1971 because they found the ratings to be unreliable. Some adjustments have been made over the years, and the rating of motion pictures has become generally accepted by the public. The Code and Rating Administration of the MPAA became the Classification and Rating Administration in 1977. The National Catholic Office for Motion Pictures closed in 1980.

Abandonment of the Production Code no doubt has been a factor in loosening restraints on the movie industry. Finding a motion picture in theaters classified "G," for general audience, is indeed rare as almost all contain one or more scenes of sex, violence, vulgarity, ugliness, or depravity. "The dream factory has become a poison factory, assaulting our most cherished values and corrupting our children," states movie critic Michael Medved in his book, *Hollywood v. America.*[3] As a result, great numbers of Americans are disenchanted with today's movies.

Jack Valenti, who continues as president of the MPAA, can rightly be given major credit for the rating system in its present form. He is quoted as saying that its purpose is "to

---

3. Michael Medved, *Hollywood v. America: Popular Culture and the War on Traditional Values*, Harper Collins Publishers, 1992.

encourage artistic expression by expanding creative freedom and insuring that the freedom which encourages the artist remains responsible and sensitive to the standards of a larger society." The fact is that either the motion picture industry had to set up its own voluntary, self-rating system or submit to rating by government. Supreme Court decisions had made that a distinct possibility — even probability. Although the Supreme Court had ruled that motion pictures are protected by the First Amendment, it did not rule out all forms of state and local control; and therein lay the threat.

In 1968, before the MPAA had adopted the rating system, the U.S. Supreme Court had ruled in the case of *Ginzberg v. New York*, discussed in Chapter 33, that "The well-being of its children is well within the State's constitutional power to regulate." In the same year the Court by a vote of 8-to-1 approved the principle of movie classification relating to minors, but ruled that the Dallas municipal licensing ordinance was too vague to be constitutional.[4] The ordinance read in part:

■ A film shall be considered likely to incite or encourage crime, delinquency or sexual promiscuity on the part of young persons, if, in the judgment of the Board, there is a substantial probability that it will create the impression on young persons that such conduct is profitable, desirable, acceptable, respectable, praiseworthy or commonly accepted.

A film shall be considered as appealing to "prurient interest" of young persons if in the judgment of the Board, its calculated or dominant effect on young persons is substantially to arouse sexual desire.

Justice Thurgood Marshall in the majority opinion stated, "We have indicated . . . that because of its strong and abiding interest in youth, a state may regulate the dissemination to

---

4. Interstate Circuit, Inc. v. City of Dallas, 390 U.S. 676 (1968).

juveniles of, and their access to, material objectionable as to them, but which a state clearly could not regulate as to adults."

As a result of those decisions, educators and church groups began calling for a classification system. Bills were introduced in several state legislatures to make classification mandatory, and Senator Margaret Chase Smith of Maine proposed a federal classification system. Action by the MPAA in October that year forestalled legislative action and assured the country of a voluntary, self-policing system of motion picture rating.

Five years later in 1973 the U.S. Supreme Court handed down a major decision in the *Paris Adult Theatre I v. Slaton* case regarding the showing of obscene movies (discussed in Chapter 33). In previous decisions, the Court had ruled that states and cities may constitutionally protect minors and unconsenting adults from obscenity. This decision confirmed the authority of a state to ban the showing of obscene films entirely.

The case began December 28, 1970, when a complaint was filed alleging that two "adult" films being shown in Paris Adult Theatres I and II in Atlanta were obscene and thus in violation of Section 2.6 — 21101 of the Georgia Code. The films were titled *Magic Mirror* and *It All Comes Out in the End.* The theaters were advertised as "Atlanta's Finest Mature Feature Films." At the entrance was a notice, "Adult Theatre — You must be 21 and able to prove it. If viewing the nude body offends you, Please Do Not Enter."

The district attorney contended that the films depicted sexual behavior that was hard-core pornography and "left little to the imagination." At the trial the judge conceded that the films were obscene, but he ruled that because the proper notices had been posted and minors were not admitted, the theaters had a constitutional right to show the films.

The Georgia Supreme Court reversed that ruling, holding that the films were hard-core pornography and thus their exhibition was not protected by the First Amendment. The case was appealed to the U.S. Supreme Court which by a vote of 5-to-4 affirmed that decision.[5] In the majority opinion Chief Justice Warren Burger stated:

■ . . . we do not undertake to tell the States what they must do, but rather to define the area in which they may chart their own course in dealing with obscene material. This Court has consistently held that obscene material is not protected by the First Amendment as a limitation on the state police power by virtue of the Fourteenth Amendment . . . The States have a long-recognized legitimate interest in regulating the use of obscene material in local commerce and in all places of public.

The sum of experience, including that of the past two decades, affords an ample basis for legislatures to conclude that a sensitive, key relationship of human existence, central to family life, community welfare, and the development of human personality, can be debased and distorted by crass commercial exploitation of sex. Nothing in the Constitution prohibits a State from reaching such a conclusion and acting on it legislatively . . .

Although state and local governments may limit the showing of pornographic films by law, restriction of attendance to adults and refusal of admittance of youth to some kinds of movies is not based on state statutes or city ordinances. Rather, the movie rating system is enforced by theater management, not by police or government officials. Authority to limit attendance is based on the common law right of proprietors of businesses and services open to the public to establish reasonable, nondiscriminatory rules governing the use of their facilities. An example is the right of restaurants to refuse service to customers who do not comply with a dress code.

---

5. Paris Adult Theatre I v. Slaton, 413 U.S. 49 (1973).

CHAPTER

38

❀

ADVERTISING IS COMMERCIAL SPEECH

ADVERTISING IS COMMERCIAL
SPEECH

❦

Suppose in your newspaper you see a shirt advertised for $25. When you go to the store to buy one, you are told that the price has been raised to $27.50.

Did the store act illegally in advertising an item at one price and then requiring a higher price? Can it be forced in a court of law to sell at the advertised price?

The answer is No. An advertisement is not a contract; it is only a public notice, an offer to negotiate. If the store had signed a contract to sell you a particular item at a certain price, then legally it would have to do so; but neither you nor the store was party to a contract in regard to the advertisement.

Not only is a person or a company free to change the price without notice, but also it has the right to refuse to sell at all. Suppose you go into a drugstore where you see a toothbrush marked 99¢. You take it to the cash register, where the clerk tells you that those brushes have been withdrawn from sale. Or suppose you are driving along a country road and see a sign at a farm offering cattle for sale. You stop, look over the herd, and tell the farmer which one you want to buy. He says, "That one is not for sale."

Can the drugstore owner or the farmer be forced legally to sell what he has advertised? Again the answer is No. No one has to sell any property he owns, even though he has advertised it for sale. Everyone has a right to change his mind about selling something he owns. He may raise the price, or lower the price, or withdraw it from sale — even though he has advertised it, but not after a sales contract has been signed.

An exception to the right of refusal to sell lies in the condemnation of property by the government for public use. The government can require the owner of a property to sell the property under the right of eminent domain. An example would be condemnation of a piece of land for use as a highway right of way. The government must pay for the property, but the owner does not have to accept the amount of compensation offered. He can take the case to court where a jury will decide what amount the owner should receive.

Another exception to the right of refusal to sell lies in the matter of discrimination. Anyone who has a business or a service open to the public cannot legally refuse to sell or to provide service because of a customer's or a client's race, religion, or national origin, and also in some cases because of gender, age, and physical handicap. That applies also to advertising. There are federal, state, and local laws that prohibit discriminatory advertising. An example is the Federal Fair Housing Act, which prohibits discrimination in the advertising, rental, and sale of homes and living quarters.

Periodicals and broadcast stations have the right to decide what kinds of advertising they will accept, if any, what kinds they will refuse, and what they will charge for the space or the time they sell. They are, however, prohibited from refusing to sell advertising because of a customer's race, religion, or national origin, the same as any other business; and they are limited in the right to refuse in another respect.

They cannot discriminate among classes of businesses. For example, a newspaper or radio or television station cannot sell advertising to all department stores that wish to advertise except one and refuse to sell to that one. The reason is that this would constitute restraint of trade, which is prohibited. If an advertising medium accepts advertising from a lawn mower repair shop, or an auto dealer, or an "adult" movie theater, it must accept advertising from all lawn mower shops, auto dealers, and "adult" movie theaters that want to buy advertising time or space. In other words, it is all of a kind or none.

Within those limitations a newspaper or a radio or television station has the same right to refuse advertising as does the farmer have the right to refuse to sell his cow. The courts have repeatedly upheld that principle. In a decision in 1933, for example, a court ruled, "A newspaper is strictly a private enterprise; the publishers therefore have a right to publish whatever advertisements they desire and to refuse to publish whatever advertisements they do not desire to publish."[1] Also Section 3(h) of the Communications Act of 1934 states that a broadcaster shall not be deemed a common carrier and therefore is not required to accept all matter which may be offered to him for broadcast.

On May 29, 1973, the U.S. Supreme Court ruled that radio and television stations have an absolute right to refuse to sell time for advertisements dealing with political campaigns and controversial public issues. The case involved the Democratic National Committee and the Business Executives' Move for Vietnam Peace which claimed that they had been denied the right of free speech when the broadcasters refused to sell them time to present their views.[2]

That right of refusal differs from that of a business conducted as a public utility, such as a gas company, an electric company, a bus company, or a telephone company. Utilities

---

1. Shuck v. Carroll Daily Herald, 247 U.S. 813 (1933).
2. Business Executives Move for Vietnam Peace v. FCC, 412 U.S. 94, (1973).

are monopolies granted by government and are required to provide service to all who apply and meet certain requirements. The courts have held that the mass media — newspapers, magazines, radio, and television stations — are not public utilities and thus may deal with whom they please.

Advertising is the major source of revenue for both print and broadcast media, so that readers and viewers/listeners pay little or nothing for access to these media. Only about 25 percent of the cost of producing a newspaper is derived from circulation, which means that without advertising subscription prices would be four times what they are now. In other words, without advertising, a newspaper that now costs a quarter would cost a dollar.[3]

Radio listeners and television viewers pay nothing for the programs they receive. Their only cost is buying a radio or television receiver and paying cable fees if their television sets are on cable.

Advertising is sold in terms of time on radio and television, in terms of space in print publications. On radio and television, commercials are sold in blocks of seconds and minutes, in magazines by the page or fraction of a page, and in newspapers display advertising is sold by the column inch and classified advertising by the line or by the word.

In general, the larger the circulation of a printed publication or the greater the number of viewers of a television program or listeners to a radio program, the higher the price of advertising. Another variation in prices for advertising on broadcast media is time of day, because the number of listeners or viewers varies. For example, since more people watch television in the evening than at any other time of day,

---

3. Newspaper advertising in the U.S. amounted to $30.575 billion in 1991; all forms of broadcast advertising, $35.775 billion and all advertising $126.680 billion.

those hours are called Prime Time. In general, commercials broadcast during Prime Time are priced higher than those broadcast at other times during the day.

The price of advertising in newspapers is based largely on circulation. As examples, *The New York Times* with a circulation of 1,108,447 weekdays and 1,686,974 Sundays has an open rate of $358 for a column inch of advertising, while the *Sentinel-Tribune* in Bowling Green, Ohio, with a circulation of 14,244 charges $7.75 per column inch.[4]

It is generally held that a newspaper or a magazine with a paid subscription is a better advertising medium than one that is unpaid or free. The theory is that a person will take more interest in a publication he has paid for than in one that costs him nothing. On that basis, advertisers and advertising agencies want to know the actual number of paid subscriptions of a periodical in which they place or may place advertisements.

Since a larger number of paid subscriptions means a higher price for advertising space, some publishers may overstate their circulation figures. Years ago that was especially true, with the result that advertisers seldom knew what or whom to believe.

To remedy that condition, an independent non-profit organization named Audit Bureau of Circulations (ABC) was established in 1914 to report accurate circulation figures for publications that wished to use its service. Membership is voluntary, but most leading newspapers and magazines published in the U.S. and Canada are members, as are many advertisers and advertising agencies. The organization is supported by membership dues, with about 5,000 members in the U.S. and Canada. The mastheads of many periodicals that are members contain a line which reads, Member, Audit Bureau of Circulations.[5]

---

4. Figures are as of September 30, 1990.
5. The ABC headquarters is at 900 Meecham Road, Schaumburg, Illinois 60173.

The content of advertising is controlled by advertisers themselves, by the media that publish or broadcast it, and to some extent by government.

Advertisers present their messages in ways they believe will not only increase sales but also promote a favorable reputation for themselves and will retain the goodwill of the public and especially of their customers.

Most periodicals and broadcast stations maintain standards for acceptance that mark the kinds of advertising they will or will not accept. Some will not accept advertising for liquor, tobacco, sale of guns and ammunition by mail, contraceptives, abortion clinics, fortune tellers, massage parlors, escort services, "adult" theaters and bookstores, tip sheets for giving odds on betting, or for any advertising that is offensive or in poor taste or may be fraudulent or libelous or that would invade privacy.

The federal government has some control over advertising content through various agencies. These include the Federal Trade Commission (FTC), organized in 1914; the Federal Communications Commission and the Securities and Exchange Commission, both organized in 1934; and the U.S. Postal Service.

Under Title 18, USCS 1304, radio and television stations are forbidden to broadcast advertising for a lottery. However, Section 1307 allows broadcasters to advertise state-run lotteries if the broadcast station is licensed in the state that runs a lottery.

Those limitations on advertising were upheld by the U.S. Supreme Court in a decision handed down on June 25, 1993, a decision that in effect affirms that broadcast stations in states that do not operate lotteries may not carry advertising for lotteries, nor advertising for lotteries in adjoining states.

The decision came in a case in which a radio station in North Carolina brought suit against the United States and the Federal Communications Commission in the U.S. District

Court for the Eastern District of Virginia.[6] Seeking declaratory and injunctive relief, the broadcaster alleged, among other things, that Sections 1304 and 1307 violated the First Amendment of the U.S. Constitution.

The station that brought suit is located in North Carolina, a state that does not conduct a lottery. It is located near the border of Virginia, which does conduct a lottery — so near that more than 90 per cent of the station's listening audience live in Virginia.

The District Court entered a decree holding that the statutes as they applied to the broadcaster are constitutionally invalid as to commercial speech. The U.S. Court of Appeals for the Fourth Circuit affirmed; but on certiorari, the U.S. Supreme Court reversed. In a 7-to-2 decision, the court held among other things, that the restriction imposed by the statutes regulate commercial speech in a manner that does not violate the First Amendment.

In dissent, Justice John Paul Stevens, joined by Justice Harry A. Blackmun, expressed the view that the restriction imposed by Title 18, USCS, sections 1304 and 1307 could not withstand scrutiny under the First Amendment, since the state's interest in discouraging its citizens from participating in state-run lotteries was not so substantial as to outweigh the broadcaster's right to distribute and the public's right to receive, truthful and nonmisleading information about a neighboring state's lottery.

The FCC has authority to limit the amount of time broadcast stations may use for commercials as well as to establish other rules governing broadcast advertising. Much of the restraint in advertising, however, is exercised by the broadcasters themselves rather than being imposed by the FCC or

---

6. United States and Federal Communications Commission v. Edge Broadcasting Company, 509 U.S., 125 L Ed. 2d 345, 113 S. Ct (June 25, 1993).

Congress. Although no federal law prohibits the advertising of "hard" liquor on radio and television, a number of states have such laws. As many broadcast signals cross state lines, broadcasters avoid risk by not using such commercials. That television commercials do not show anyone drinking beer or wine is a holdover from the former NAB Code. One reason for its retention is the possibility of public protests arising from commercials showing people drinking beer and wine.

The FCC has authority to decide whether acknowledgments by noncommercial stations of sponsorship of programs are only that, or whether they constitute commercials. That has become especially important because of the growing tendency for nonprofit stations not only to name sponsors but also under "enhanced credit" announcements tolerated by the FCC to describe in some detail the products and services of the sponsors.

The FCC requires that when a broadcast station transmits any matter for which money, service, or other valuable consideration is either directly or indirectly paid or promised ... the station at the time of the broadcast announce that such matter is sponsored, paid for, or furnished either in whole or in part and by whom.

Cigarette advertising is in a class by itself. Although the manufacture, possession, and use of cigarettes is legal, advertising them on radio and television has been prohibited by law since January 1, 1971, which is the date on which the Public Health Cigarette Smoking Act of 1969 became effective. Health warnings on cigarette packs and in all printed display advertisements of cigarettes have been required since 1965 by the Cigarette Labeling and Advertising Act. Example:

SURGEON GENERAL'S WARNING:
Smoking Causes Lung Cancer,
Heart Disease, Emphysema, And
May Complicate Pregnancy.

The act of Congress was followed by another in 1986

537

which requires this warning in all advertisements for snuff and chewing tobacco: "This product may cause mouth cancer."

It is quite possible that similar warning labels will be required for alcoholic beverages at some future time. Bills have already been introduced in both the U.S. Senate and House of Representatives calling for a series of rotating warnings for both print and broadcast advertisements similar to those now required in tobacco advertising, but none have yet become law. The purpose, sponsors of the bills state, is not to restrict the use of alcohol but to warn of the danger of alcohol abuse.[7]

Another instance of Federal control was the enactment by Congress of an anticrime law in 1991 that makes advertising of marijuana illegal.

Requiring a warning or a statement to accompany a news story or editorial comment would be unconstitutional. That it is permissible in printed advertising clearly indicates a legal distinction between commercial speech (advertising) and noncommercial speech.

The SEC exercises control over the content of the advertising of new issues of securities as well as of the release of certain kinds of data which if delayed or announced prematurely would be advantageous to sellers and buyers. Buying and selling stock based on information unavailable to everyone is called "insider trading" and is considered fraudulent under SEC regulations.

SEC control can be detected, for example, in advertisements announcing new issues of securities. Such advertisements list the dollar amount of the issue, state the price of each, and give the name of the company issuing the securities. In addition, it contains a statement similar to this:

---

7. *Editor & Publisher*, May 22, 1993, p. 28.

■ This announcement does not constitute an offer to sell or the solicitation of any offer to buy nor shall there be any sale by any person in any jurisdiction in which such an offer, solicitation, or sale would be unlawful. The offer is made solely by the prospectus.

The purpose of the prospectus is to provide potential buyers with more complete information than that provided by newspaper advertisement.

The Securities and Exchange Commission has authority to define fraudulent and deceptive practices in the sale of securities and to prosecute dealers who violate SEC regulations. To protect buyers, any person or company planning to issue a block of new stock or bonds is required to register them with the SEC along with a complete financial statement, as it is illegal to sell unregistered stock interstate or by mail.

The Federal Trade Commission through its Advertising Practice Division promotes truth in advertising by watching for deceptive statements and by requiring proof of claims for consumer products. Examples of violations:[8]

■ A false claim that a product is original or first in the field.

■ A false claim of approval by a government agency.

■ A false claim that a product was patented.

■ A false claim of a product's life or effectiveness.

■ A false reference to the product developed in a research laboratory that did not exist.

■ A false claim of protein, Vitamin C, or other nutritional content.

---

8. *Public Relations Journal*, July 1971.

The Division requires copies of tests that prove what advertisements say about products is true. Here are examples of the kinds of statements the FTC has questioned and for which it requested proof in the year or so after it began its substantiation program in 1971:[9]

■ Volvos are more economical to own and operate than competing makes of automobiles.

■ Fedders air conditioners have greater reserve cooling capacity than competing makes.

■ The Chevrolet Vega is the best handling car ever built in the U.S.

■ The Buick Opel has a chassis that never needs lubrication.

As another example, the FTC entered complaints against a strip mining company in Kentucky that advertised that "every acre of land surface mined is promptly and effectively restored — often to more beneficial use than before it was mined." It also accused the Coca Cola Company of making false claims in regard to the nutritional value of its Hi-C fruit drink; and it questioned the truth in advertising that touted the nutritional superiority of Wonder Bread which said that it "helps build strong bodies 12 ways."

Such FTC surveillance is not uncommon. More recent examples were complaints filed in 1992 against Dollar Rent-A-Car Systems, Inc. of Los Angeles and Value Rent-A-Car Inc. of Boca Raton for misleading rates quoted in their advertisements through failure to mention such extra costs as surcharges, geographic driving restrictions, and mandatory fuel charges.

---

9. *Wall Street Journal*, August 8, 1971; October 13, 1972; November 6, 1973.

The U.S. Postal Service has control over advertising primarily through the second class mailing permit, discussed in Chapter 30. The permit, vital for virtually all periodicals that circulate totally or partially by mail, can be revoked for carrying advertising that is in violation of law or postal regulations.

Some federal laws contain provisions that affect advertising. The Fair Housing Act, mentioned earlier, prohibits advertising that indicates any limitation or preference based on race, color, religion, sex, handicap, national origin, or family status. The Airline Deregulation Act of 1978 (ADA) is another example as it prohibits states from enforcing laws regulating rates, rules, and services. In 1988 attorney generals in five states notified TWA, Continental, and British Airways that some of their advertising violated guidelines established under the ADA.

After the attorney general of Texas issued an intent to sue in 1988 under its consumer protection law to enforce guidelines regarding allegedly deceptive airline advertising in that state, TWA and British Airways contended that he could not do so because the federal law preempted state law. They were upheld by the court which issued an order enjoining any state enforcement against the advertising, an order that was affirmed by the Court of Appeals and in a 5-to-3 decision by the U.S. Supreme Court.[10]

In dissent, Justice John Paul Stevens said in part: "Because Congress did not eliminate federal regulation of unfair or deceptive practices, and because state and federal prohibitions of unfair or deceptive practices had coexisted during the period of federal regulation, there is no reason to believe that Congress intended . . . to immunize the airlines from state liability for engaging in deceptive or misleading advertising."

---

10. Dan Morales, Attorney General of Texas v. Trans World Airlines, 112 S. Ct. 2031, (June 1, 1992).

The Truth in Savings Act, passed by Congress in December 1991 and effective June 21, 1993, requires that advertising by banks and savings institutions be clear and complete. For example, checking advertised as free must not carry any hidden charges or conditions.

Besides federal control, various state agencies exercise some control over the content of advertising. As an example, the Department of Consumer Affairs in New York City brought suit against Sears Roebuck & Co. in 1988 for violating city ordinances in its advertising. The Department charged that Sears had advertised that a carpet-cleaning special was about to end when actually it was not, publicized a tire sale by emphasizing the cost of lower-priced tires but not the higher-costing ones, and promoted a discount price on clothing without listing the usual price.

In its suit, the Department asked the court to impose a fine of $500 for each violation and to issue an injunction against deceptive advertising. Sears entered a counter suit in which it contended that the advertisements were accurate and also that they were protected by the First Amendment.[11]

As another example, Florida requires all child care centers and family day-care centers to list their license numbers in advertising their services. It also requires advertising of all kinds for mobile home parks to be filed with the Division of Florida Land Sales, Condominiums, and Mobile Home Parks for approval at least ten days prior to use. Upon approval, the advertisement is given an identification number, which must appear in the printed advertisement when it is published.

The Florida Department of Insurance requires prior approval, that is, review, of brochures and advertising in newspapers and on radio and television on long-term health care insurance. The material must be submitted for approval at least 30 days in advance of its use, and the Department has 15

---

11. *Sarasota Herald-Tribune,* August 2, 1988.

days in which to notify the company, newspaper, or broadcast station of any objections it has to the contents.

Advertising by lawyers was for many years limited mostly to "hanging out a shingle" and hoping clients would appear, but restrictions have been loosened considerably. One factor has been a degree of permissiveness by the U.S. Supreme Court. In 1985, for example, the Court ruled that "an attorney may not be disciplined for soliciting legal business through printed advertising containing truthful and nondeceptive information and advice regarding legal rights of potential clients."[12]

The door is far from wide open, however. Restrictions on advertising by lawyers in Florida, as an example, are stringent. A revision of regulations that became effective on January 1, 1991, after being recommended by the Florida Bar Association and approved by the Florida Supreme Court, prohibit the use of testimonials, statements that are merely self-laudatory, and comparisons that cannot be substantiated. Forbidden in radio and television commercials are dramatizations such as those of celebrity voiceovers.

The regulations also prevent attorneys who handle injury and wrongful death cases from sending brochures and printed advertisements to prospective clients until more than 30 days after the accident or disaster has occurred. A U.S. District judge ruled in 1992, however, that that prohibition is unconstitutional as it violates the right of free speech and press as well as due process and equal protection under the law. That ruling was upheld by the Supreme Court (1995). Besides the limit on time for sending advertisements, the rule also states that the first sentence of the communication shall be, "If you have already retained a lawyer in this matter, please disregard this letter." It also states that each page of advertising material shall be plainly marked "advertisement" in red ink.

---

12. Philip Q. Zauderer v. Office of Disciplinary Counsel of the Supreme Court of Ohio, 471 U.S. 626 (May 28, 1985).

The Consumer Fraud Act in Arizona prohibits such misleading advertising as "bait and switch," that announces bankruptcy and going-out-of-business sales for businesses that are not actually closing, that contain "endorsements" by models rather than by actual consumers, and that contain false statements and claims that cannot be verified.

In some states, discrimination in help-wanted advertisements is illegal. An advertiser can be fined or sued over advertisements that reflect bias in regard to race, color, religion, sex and national origin. Discrimination in regard to gender is commonly prohibited. In such case it is better to advertise for "a sales person" rather than for "a salesman."

Such control of advertising is generally considered permissible under the regulatory powers of the states. Since the authority of the states to regulate various kinds of commercial activities within their boundaries is not preempted by federal regulatory agencies, the states may legally impose such requirements on advertising. In that respect, prior approval of advertising content by a state government agency is not considered censorship.

The rationale for government control is that consumer protection is needed because the mass of individuals who are buyers and users are no match for the sophistication and ingenuity of large companies, advertising agencies, and product manufacturers. Misleading packaging, guarantees that ignore the common-law rights of buyers, and the small print on insurance policies and in sales contracts that are unfair to individual buyers should be prohibited. Some puffery is allowed in advertising but not to the extent that it becomes untruthful or deceptive.

That government exercises some control over advertising is somewhat surprising in that as a highly important social and economic form of communication advertising would seem to fall under the First Amendment guarantee of free speech and press. Congress and state legislatures, however, view advertising as a function of trade and commerce, not in the same category as news and editorial comment; and on that basis they have enacted laws to protect the public from deceptive and fraudulent advertising. It appears to be somewhat inconsistent, however, that a state government agency can require prior approval of an advertisement but not prior approval of a newspaper or magazine article or a broadcast on the same subject included in an advertisement.

The First Amendment makes no distinction between commercial speech (advertising) and noncommercial speech (news, editorials, feature stories, etc.). In three cases the U.S. Supreme Court has ruled that commercial speech (advertising) is protected by the First Amendment guarantee of free speech and press, but its rulings were not unanimous and not definitive in regard to the extent to which commercial speech is protected. In general the Court has held that "what has come to be known as 'commercial speech' is entitled to protection of the First Amendment, albeit to protection somewhat less extensive than that afforded 'noncommercial speech'."

At first the Court was hesitant about placing commercial speech under protection of the First Amendment, as indicated in a decision in 1939.[13] In that case the Court ruled that although the First Amendment prohibited a city from requiring a person to obtain a permit before soliciting for a religious case, it cautioned that it did not hold that "commercial solicitation and canvassing may not be subjected to such regulations as this ordinance requires."

In a case three years later, the Court continued to place commercial speech in a restricted category separate from other speech. At that time it ruled that a city ordinance regulating the distribution of handbills was not unconstitutional, even if one side of the handbill contained a protest against the ordinance. The Court stated that while streets are proper places for the exercise of freedom of communicating

---

13. Schneider v. Irvington, 308 U.S. 147 (1939).

information and disseminating opinion and that states and municipalities may not burden or proscribe such activities in public thoroughfares, "we are equally clear that the Constitution imposes no such restraint on government as respects purely commercial advertising.[14]

More than thirty years later the Supreme Court reversed its thinking by deciding in two cases a year apart that commercial speech is protected by the First Amendment. Both cases concerned laws in Virginia. The first of the two, decided in 1975, originated when the editor of a weekly newspaper was convicted in the circuit court of Albemarle County, Virginia, of violating a Virginia statute that made it a misdemeanor, by sale or circulation of any publication, to encourage or prompt the procuring of an abortion. The editor had violated the law by publishing an advertisement from another state offering services related to obtaining legal abortions.

Upon appeal, the Supreme Court of Virginia affirmed the verdict, holding that "as the advertisement was a commercial one which could be constitutionally prohibited by the state, it lacked a legitimate First Amendment interest." The U.S. Supreme Court reversed that decision, ruling that "speech is not stripped of its First Amendment protection merely because it appears in the form of a paid commercial announcement" and holding that "the statute as applied to the editor infringed constitutionally protected speech.[15]

The vote was 7-to-2, with a dissent by Justice William H. Rehnquist, joined by Justice Byron R. White, who expressed the view that "an advertisement is a commercial proposition toward the exchange of services rather than the exchange of ideas and thus is entitled to little constitutional protection."

A year later in 1976 the Court, although still divided on the question, placed commercial speech firmly under First Amend-

---

14. Valentine v. Christensen, 316 U.S. 52 (1942).
15. Jeffrey Cole Bigelow v. Commonwealth of Virginia, 421 U.S. 809 (June 16, 1975).

ment protection. The case centered on another Virginia law, this one making it unprofessional conduct for a pharmacist licensed in Virginia to advertise any price for drugs dispensed by prescription. A Virginia resident and two nonprofit organizations brought suit in the U.S. District Court for the Eastern District of Virginia to challenge that portion of the law that they believed violated consumers' rights.

The District Court declared the challenged portion of the law void and enjoined its enforcement; and on direct appeal, the U.S. Supreme Court affirmed that ruling by a vote of 7-to-1, with one justice not participating.[16]

In the majority opinion, Justice Harry A. Blackmun, who had written the opinion in the Virginia law case the year before, stated that "since 'commercial speech' was protected under the First Amendment, the advertisement of prescription drug prices was protected under the First Amendment, notwithstanding its commercial character."

In his dissent, joined by Justice Byron R. White, Justice Rehnquist stated, "Balancing the interest of individual free speech against public welfare . . . the rights of the plaintiff were marginal at best while societal interest . . . was extremely strong, not warranting a First Amendment open door policy toward such commercial advertising."

In 1980 the Supreme Court considered a case in which the Public Service Commission of the State of New York had ordered public utilities to cease promoting the use of electricity because of fuel shortages. Three years later after the fuel shortage had eased the Commission proposed a continuation of the ban on advertising. In response the Central Hudson Gas & Electric Company challenged the order, claiming that the Commission was restraining commercial speech in violation of the First and Fourteenth Amendments. The Court of Appeals upheld the Commission order, ruling that "the gov-

---

16. Virginia State Board of Pharmacy v. Virginia Citizens Consumer Council, Inc., 425 U.S. 748 (May 24, 1976).

ernment interests outweighed the limited constitutional value of the commercial speech at issue."

That ruling was reversed by the U.S. Supreme Court in a 5-to-4 decision, in which Justice Lewis F. Powell Jr. stated in the majority opinion that "the ban on promotional advertising by electric utilities imposed by the Commission violated the First Amendment as applied to the states through the Fourteenth Amendment, since despite the substantial nature of the state's asserted interests in prohibiting such advertising — which advertising was concededly neither inaccurate nor related to unlawful activity, and which was a species of commercial speech protected by the First Amendment —the link between the advertising prohibition and the state's interest in ensuring fair and efficient rates was too tenuous and speculative to justify the ban . . ."[17]

Again in dissent, as he had in the two Virginia statute cases, Justice Rehnquist said, "The monopoly power conferred by the state upon a utility justifies a state's wide-ranging supervision and control under the First Amendment, and the restriction on 'commercial speech' in this case was not a violation of the First Amendment, the ban on advertising falling within the scope of permissible state regulations."

Another case arose over a law in Puerto Rico that prohibited gambling casinos from advertising their facilities to residents of Puerto Rico, although residents were not permitted to gamble in the casinos. The law permitted casinos to advertise to visitors and to people not living in Puerto Rico but not to residents. The operator of a casino filed suit, contending that the statute and the regulations restricting such advertising violated its commercial free speech under the Constitution.

The case eventually reached the U.S. Supreme Court

---

17. Central Hudson Gas & Electric Co. v. Public Service Commission of New York, 447 U.S. 557 (June 20, 1980).

which in a decision handed down on July 1, 1986, upheld the law by a vote of 5 to 4. In the majority opinion Justice William H. Rehnquist (later appointed Chief Justice) ruled that the statute and the regulations do not violate the First Amendment guarantee of freedom of speech and the press. In the opinion. He stated:[18]

■ Commercial speech receives a limited form of First Amendment protection so long as it concerns a lawful activity and is not misleading or fraudulent; once it is determined that the First Amendment applies to the particular kind of commercial speech at issue, then such speech may be restricted only if the Government's interest in doing so is substantial, the restrictions directly advance the Government's asserted interest, and the restrictions are no more extensive than necessary to serve that interest.

Justice Rehnquist's opinion in that case was consistent with his previous thinking, having expressed similar views in previous cases and quoted as having written in 1977:

■ The First Amendment speech provision, long regarded by the Court as a sanctuary for expressions of public importance or intellectual interest, is demeaned by invocation to protect advertisements of goods and services.

Apparently under the impression that the U.S. Supreme Court considered advertising (commercial speech) less deserving of First Amendment protection than noncommercial speech, the City of Cincinnati became involved in litigation over the use of vending machines on city streets for distribution of free advertising material.

The case had its origin in a decision by the city council in February 1989 to permit Discovery Center of Cincinnati, a

---

18. Posadas de Puerto Rico Associates v. Tourism Company of Puerto Rico, 478 U.S. 328 (July 1, 1986).

subsidiary of Discovery Network, Inc., of Chicago, to place vending machines on city streets for distribution of free advertising materials on adult education courses and social activities. At the same time it gave permission to Harmon Publishing Co. of New York to distribute free materials advertising new homes.

A month later the city council changed its mind and asked the Department of Public Works to enforce an ordinance banning the distribution of commercial handbills in a public right-of-way. The action required discontinuing the use of 62 machines by Discovery Center and Harmon Publishing. As a result, Discovery Center joined by Harmon Publishing filed suit in June against the City of Cincinnati to regain the right to use those vending machines for their advertising brochures. The crux of the matter was whether the city could legally exclude printed advertising material and still permit machines on public property to be used for newspapers. In other words, should advertising material have the same right of distribution as newspapers?

Both the U.S. District Court and the U.S. Court of Appeals said *yes*, it should, thus upholding the right of both Discovery Center and Harmon Publishing to use the vending machines on public property. In his opinion for the Appeals Court in 1991, Judge Danny J. Boggs said commercial speech should be presumed to enjoy full First Amendment protection unless it is shown to be false, deceptive, or liable to create some distinctively harmful effect.

The U.S. Supreme Court agreed with those lower court decisions by a vote of 6-to-3 in a decision handed down on March 24, 1993, ruling that the city may not deny the distribution of advertising material while permitting distribution of newspapers and other noncommercial material.[19]

---

19. City of Cincinnati v. Discovery Network, Docket No. 91-1200 (March 24, 1993).

The decision, however, did little to clarify the extent of protection provided by the First Amendment guarantee of free speech and press. Justice John Paul Stevens, who wrote the majority opinion, said that while Cincinnati's stated goals of reducing clutter and obstructions on city streets were legitimate, its chosen means were not.

He said that the Court's precedents required a "reasonable fit" between a government regulation of commercial speech and the goal that the regulation was supposed to accomplish. In this case, he continued, removing 62 of 2,000 vending machines could not make a dent in the city's sidewalk clutter; and Cincinnati's distinction between advertising and newspapers "has absolutely no bearing" on the problem.

Chief Justice William H. Rehnquist in dissent said that the city's regulation being "underinclusive" did not make it unconstitutional. "Because commercial speech has a lower level of constitutional protection than political and other noncommercial speech, government agencies are free to single it out for regulation as long as the regulation is related to the 'overall problem' the agency is trying to solve."

In this case, he said, although the advertisers' 62 machines were only a small part of the problem, singling them out for removal was permissible because "every news rack that is removed from the city's sidewalks marginally enhances the safety of its streets and esthetics of its cityscape."

CHAPTER
39

✤

STUDENTS' RIGHT OF FREE SPEECH IS TENUOUS

STUDENTS' RIGHT OF FREE
SPEECH IS TENUOUS

❖

A principal reads the copy for the next issue of the school newspaper, then calls in the student editor and tells him, "You can't print this article."

Is that an example of prior censorship, prohibited by the First Amendment guarantee of a free press? Does that guarantee extend to the student press? The answer may be Yes or No, depending upon the conditions under which the decision occurs.

Among the unnumbered instances in which student publications have been censored by teachers and school authorities, decisions in the relatively few cases that have reached the courts have at times supported student rights while balancing those rights with rights and responsibilities of school administrators to maintain order and control the educational process.

One such case occurred in Alabama where during the 1966-67 school year Dr. Frank Rose, president of the University of Alabama in Tuscaloosa, was criticized by some state legislators for not cracking down on a student publication at the university for publishing excerpts from speeches by a Communist and by a radical student leader.

A student named Gary Clinton Dickey at Troy State College in the southeast part of the state wrote an editorial in support of Dr. Rose for publication in *The Tropolitan*, the college student newspaper of which he was editor. Both the faculty adviser and the president of the college warned him against publishing the editorial, reminding him that the college had a rule that prohibited editorials in the student newspaper critical of the governor or of the state legislature. Dickey then left the space for the editorial blank except for the word "censored."

For that action, Dickey was charged with "willful insubordination" and was not permitted to register for classes that fall. The case was taken to court where the judge decided in favor of the student, ruling that "a state cannot force a college student to forfeit his constitutionally protected right of freedom of expression as a condition for his attending a state-supported institution."[1] The judge held that a school could censor a student publication only when it could show that that was necessary to avoid material and substantial interference with the requirements of adequate discipline. Upon appeal, the case was dismissed on procedural grounds.

Another case arose at Fitchburg State College in Massachusetts when a printer refused to set the type for an article for the student newspaper, *The Cycle,* because it contained what he considered obscene words. He called the president of the College, who agreed that the article should not be printed. The student editors filed suit in the U.S. District Court in Boston where in February 1970 Judge W. Arthur Garrity Jr. ruled in favor of the students. He stated that "in order for a college to be able to restrict speech, it must show that the publication is incompatible with the school's obligation to maintain order and discipline necessary for the success of the educational process."[2]

Another case decided in favor of student press freedom was one in which Judge George Beamer of the U.S. District Court in South Bend, Indiana, ruled, "The School Corpora-

---

1. Dickey v. Alabama State Board of Education, 273 F. Supp. 613 (M.D. Ala. 1967), disssmissed as moot, 402 F 2d. 515 (5th Cir. 1968).
2. Antonelli v. Hammond, 308 F. Supp 1329 (D. Mass 1970).

tion shall not prohibit publication of articles in official school newspapers on the basis of the subject matter or terminology unless the article or terminology used is obscene, libelous, or disrupts school activities."[3]

The case arose ironically in Liberty City, Indiana, when the student editor of the *Liberty Link*, the high school newspaper, wrote an article on planned parenthood which both the journalism adviser and the principal forbade her to publish.

In California in November 1990 the First Appellate District Court dismissed a libel suit brought by a teacher against the student newspaper *Flight* in Foothill High School in the San Francisco East Bay area. A story in the newspaper called the teacher "a babbler" and "the worst teacher in FHS."

Although decisions in those cases upheld students' rights of expression, not all have resulted in the same outcome. In one case, the U.S. District Court in the Southern District of Ohio ruled on December 13, 1973, that the principal has the responsibility of maintaining order and the right to control the contents of the school newspaper.[4] That decision was reversed in the next year upon appeal. The case arose after the principal of the Reynoldsburg High School in Ohio had confiscated copies of the school newspaper, *Doubloon*, in October 1971, because he objected to the contents.

A more far-reaching decision was handed down by the U.S. Supreme Court on January 13, 1988. In the majority opinion, written by Justice Byron White, the Court ruled that the principal has the legal right to censor a school newspaper.[5] The rationale was that the school newspaper as a device for

3. Wesolek v. South Bend Community School District, Cov. Act. No. 73-2-101 (N.D. Ind., Oct. 2, 1973) (unreported).
4. Hannahs v. Endry, CA No. 72-306 (S.D. Ohio, Dec. 13, 1973), reversed CA No. 74-1196, (6th Cir., June 17, 1974).
5. Hazelwood School District v. Kuhlmeier, 107 S. Ct. 926, 93 L Ed. 2d 978, (January 13, 1988).

learning is essentially a part of the curriculum and thus under the control of the school.

The case arose in East High School in Hazelwood, Missouri, where the principal ordered two of the six pages of an issue deleted after he had read the proofs. Since the principal did not tell the student editors what he had done, they were dismayed when the printed copies of the newspaper, *The Spectrum*, arrived — the date was May 13, 1983 — with only four pages. Missing were feature stories they had written on teenage pregnancy and the effects of divorce on youth. The principal, according to reports, offered the student staff members no explanation for censoring the articles except that he considered them inappropriate.

The students filed suit, and in 1986 the Eighth Circuit Court of Appeals ruled that the principal had violated the First Amendment rights of the students. The U.S. Supreme Court reversed the Appeals Court decision, ruling in favor of the principal. In effect, the Court held that prior restraint is constitutional when applied to most high school publications.

After the Hazelwood decision, the incidence of censorship of high school publications skyrocketed across the country. Among them was one the next year in New Jersey in which school officials in Gloucester County, acting in the belief that the Hazelwood decision gave them the authority, refused to allow a review of two R-rated movies to be published in *The Pioneer Press*, student newspaper of Clearview Regional Junior High School in Mullica Hill. The reviews were of the movies *Rain Man* and *Mississippi Burning*, written by Brian Desilets and scheduled for publication in February 1989. School officials felt that the reviews were unsuitable for a junior high school newspaper.

The American Civil Liberties Union brought suit, the first of its kind in New Jersey, to challenge the extent to which school administrators could control the editorial content of student newspapers. On May 7, 1991, Superior Court Judge Robert E. Francis ruled that censoring the movie reviews had violated the students rights under the State Constitution.[6] While agreeing that under the Hazelwood decision officials had the right to censor school newspapers, Judge Francis decided in favor of the students in this case on the basis that the New Jersey State Constitution provides broader protection for freedom of speech than does the First Amendment of the U.S. Constitution.[7]

"Too often the constitution is reserved for just adults," he said. "Students don't realize they have rights." In deciding for the plaintiff, the judge ordered the school district to allow Brian Desilets to publish a statement about the court case in the next edition of the school newspaper.

As the case in New Jersey illustrates, the constitution or laws of some states protect student press freedom. In fact, five states have enacted such legislation and a score of others have considered it. Kansas, one of the five, adopted a law in 1992 that protects student expression except when it is libelous, slanderous, obscene, or would incite student to actions that are criminal or would result in a student's suspension or expulsion from school. Similar laws are on the books in California, Colorado, Iowa, and Massachusetts.

At the same time, relying on the Hazelwood decision to control the content of student publications can be tempting when the publications contain material that administrators and parents consider "unsuitable." An example is action taken by the Board of Trustees of the Independent School District of Austin, Texas, on September 23, 1991. There the Board voted five to two to authorize principals to review all material for high school student newspapers in the District before publication. The action was in response to protests by

---

6. Desilets v. Clearview Regional Board of Education, No. c-23 90 (N.J. Super Ct. Law Div. May 7, 1991).
7. That is in keeping with the legal principle that a State cannot provide less protection for individual rights than the U.S. Constitution provides, but it can provide more.

angry parents and other residents to articles on teenage sexuality, AIDS, and safe sex that were published in April that year in the *Lone Star Dispatch*, student newspaper of Bowie High School.

Establishing legal guidelines for the student press is complex. The major reason for the complexity is that the student press has characteristics not found in the commercial or professional press. For one thing, school administrators in general look upon publications written and edited by students as educational activities, as part of the curriculum. Viewed in that manner, the student press comes under the same supervision and control as any other subject or educational activity, a view supported by the U.S. Supreme Court in 1988 in the Hazelwood case. In that decision the Court ruled that (a) a school has the authority to operate a school newspaper for the purpose of a supervised learning experience and (b) censorship is not a violation of free speech when it has a valid purpose — and a teaching method constitutes a valid purpose.

Another significant difference between the student press and the commercial or professional press lies in the age of the editorial staffs. Few students, at least among those below college level, have reached legal age, a condition that places them in a separate class from adults both legally and socially. Although everyone, regardless of age, has the same protection under the U.S. Constitution, juveniles are subject to a number of laws and restrictions that do not affect adults. Among them are statutes that limit hours and control conditions of work for pay, prohibit the publication of names of juvenile offenders, and govern adoption and guardianship. Youth may legally drive an automobile at age 16; may vote, join the Armed Forces, and buy cigarettes and lottery tickets at age 18; but they must be 21 to buy alcoholic beverages, enter gambling casinos and bingo parlors, attend race tracks with pari-mutuel betting, and have title in their own name to certain kinds of property. The legal age for marriage varies from 16 to 18 among the states.

In school, students are governed by rules established by the board of education, the superintendent, the principal, and other officials — rules students must obey to remain in school, obtain an education, and eventually graduate. As schools have a legal and moral responsibility for students, they act *in loco parentis* in several respects. As students lack maturity, teachers and administrators have a responsibility to provide supervision and guidance in their formative years and to maintain an orderly atmosphere in the school, both of which can translate in certain situations into control of virtually all student activities including the publication of school newspapers.

Many school administrators look upon the student newspaper as a kind of "house organ," with its reporting limited to what is positive and complimentary to the school and its faculty and administration. Subject to censorship are criticisms of and unfavorable articles about teachers, administrators, and policies. As a medium for projecting a favorable image of the school, the student newspaper must limit its coverage to school activities and publish nothing controversial or anything that affects the lives of students away from the school, such as teenage pregnancy, use of drugs, racism, and divorce.

Administrators bolster their claim to the right of control of student newspapers on the basis that the school, not the students, is the publisher. The question arises as to whether school officials or the student editorial staff are responsible for any transgressions student publications may make, whether it be libel, invasion of privacy, contempt of court, violation of pornography and obscenity laws, or good taste. The courts have ruled in cases involving college newspapers that administrative officials that do not precensor the publications are not liable. Still, student publications emanate from the school, with the school providing office space, supplies, and printing costs. Although funds may come from student fees, plus advertising, the school has some responsibility in regard to collecting and disbursing funds. Because of those conditions, a school principal may assume that he or she has a legal and administrative obligation to decide what may and what may not be published.

In summary, administrators, particularly those in schools below college level in general maintain that —

■ As the publisher, the school has a legal obligation to approve the content of student publications.

■ The student press is part of the curriculum and is thus under the control of the school as are other parts of the curriculum.

■ The student newspaper functions as "a house organ" and as such should present a positive image of the school, with its contents restricted to school activities and devoid of criticism of school policies and controversial topics.

■ In regard to all forms of student expression, school officials maintain that students are immature and thus require guidance and supervision, which include control necessary for the orderly operation of the school program.

A more liberal view interprets the function of the student newspaper not as a house organ to enhance the image of the school but rather as an important medium of communication for the school community. As such students would enjoy greater freedom of expression, publishing the newspaper would provide a much better educational experience, and a much improved publication.

That view sees close supervision and arbitrary censorship as having negative effects. They hinder the development of a sense of responsibility on the part of student publication staff members, and they have a deleterious effect on the quality of reporting and editing. A study by the Commission on Enquiry into High School Journalism, published in 1974 under the title *Captive Voices,* states, "Censorship is the fundamental cause of the triviality, innocuousness and uniformity that characterize the high school press."

Under the watchful eye of the principal, students are

discouraged from reporting on issues that affect them as citizens and students. In effect, they practice self-censorship because they know what school officials will object to. "Fear of reprisals and unpleasantness, as well as the lack of a tradition of an independent high school press, remain basic forces behind self-censorship," states *Captive Voices* .

Students are taught in history and government classes that the Constitution guarantees everyone the right to speak, write, and publish freely without government restraint, even on unpopular topics; but in face of frequent denial of that right by school officials, including censorship of the student newspapers, students see rights of expression stopping at the schoolhouse door.

The production of the school newspaper is generally an activity of considerably less importance than are such activities as football, basketball, and the marching band. As a result, the person appointed as journalism teacher/student-newspaper adviser may be someone with little or no training or experience in reporting and editing. Often, as a kind of afterthought, an English teacher is assigned those duties because journalism is related to her major studies, or the business education teacher gets the job because of knowing how to type.

"Surveys indicate that a majority of teachers and advisers not only have little or no journalism background, but have relatively little interest in taking the job in the first place," states *Captive Voices*. Few teachers want the job because of the sensitiveness of school officials regarding what is published, because of the low priority given journalism and the student newspaper, because of their lack of training and experience, and because in general English teachers look on journalism as an inferior kind of literature. Relatively few high schools accept journalism courses as English requirements. As a result, the turnover is high, with about a third of the teacher/advisers changing jobs annually and as many as two thirds in some states.

In one important respect, the position of journalism adviser in many high schools is largely unacceptable. In schools where the principal insists on reading all copy or seeing all proofs of the student newspaper before it goes to press, and arrogates to himself the right to approve the contents, he indicates in the strongest terms that he does not trust the faculty adviser or the student staff to use good judgment, to know right from wrong, or to be intelligent enough to avoid such legal offenses as libel, obscenity, and invasion of privacy. No other faculty member is accorded such treatment.

The act of censorship, an affront to both the faculty adviser and the students, is largely avoided in some schools by the adoption of a statement of policy and procedures for student publications. The statement is in the form of an operating manual, prepared jointly by the principal, the faculty adviser, and the student editors, and approved by the superintendent and the board of education.

The manual contains a statement of the purpose or purposes of the school newspaper, and of any other student publications if others are being published; procedures for financing and publishing specific publications; standards for acceptance of advertising; the role of the faculty adviser; and qualifications, method of selection, and duties of the various student staff members. The manual is revised every year or so as experience indicates the need for revision.

Advantageous, also, is the appointment of a student faculty publications committee to adjudicate disputes and to mediate conflicts that arise. A committee of that kind is sometimes vested with the title of publisher and as such functions either as an advisory or a governing body in establishing policy. A student-faculty publications committee gives support to the journalism adviser in time of crisis, so that the adviser is not standing alone when difficult decisions are necessary.

In the same vein, a student handbook developed cooperatively with the Student Council minimizes difficulties that may arise in regard to other kinds of student expression, such as distribution of leaflets or off-campus publications on the school grounds, posting notices of non-school activities on bulletin boards, and so forth.

In keeping with the spirit of the First Amendment guarantee of freedom of the press, the student publications manual states that "the school newspaper is free to comment on national, state, local, and school political, social, cultural, and economic issues, and may criticize policies and procedures of the school administration." A school newspaper that functions as an effective medium of communication for the school community it serves cannot be limited in content only to what pleases the school administrators. As Justice Fortas stated in the majority opinion in the case of *Tinker v. Des Moines Independent School District* in 1969, "In our system, students may not be regarded as closed-circuit recipients of only that which the state chooses to communicate. They may not be confined to the expression of those sentiments that are officially approved."

To be complete, the manual lists the responsibilities that accompany freedoms, such as requiring fairness as a guiding principle in presenting various points of view on controversial matters and using good taste in the selection and presentation of news and comment.

Such manuals clearly state that there will be no prior censorship except that the adviser has the right to prohibit the publication of any stories or articles that he or she believes to be libelous, violates law, or might result in litigation if published.

Neither the adoption of a student publications manual nor the establishment of a student-faculty publications committee diminishes the responsibilities of the principal but rather provides methods for the principal's governing cooperatively rather than arbitrarily.

Student rights aside from press freedom, primarily those pertaining to symbolic speech and the distribution of literature on campus, have generally been supported by the courts. Among decisions is one handed down by the U.S. Supreme Court on February 24, 1969, upholding the right of students in the Des Moines public schools to wear black arm bands in protest to America's involvement in Vietnam at that time.[8]

In that decision, the Court stated, "Students and teachers do not shed their constitutional rights to freedom of speech or expression at the schoolhouse gate."

The case began in December 1965, when seven students decided to express opposition to the war by wearing arm bands in the days before the Christmas holidays. When the school principals learned of the plan, they decided to forbid wearing of the arm bands and to suspend any student who persisted in doing so. A high school student named Christopher Eckhardt and five Tinker children disobeyed the ban and were suspended until they would return to school without the arm bands. The fathers of the students filed for an injunction to stop that action by the principals.

The U.S. Supreme Court in that case ruled 7 to 2 that "the act of wearing an arm band is closely akin to 'pure speech' and the school administration could not ban an act of 'pure speech' simply because it might cause some discomfort or unpleasantness."

Judge Abe Fortas, who wrote the majority opinion, stated that "students in school as well as out of school are persons under the Constitution," and said that "personal intercommunication among students is an important part of the educational process."

"A student's rights therefore do not embrace merely the classroom hours," Justice Fortas said. "Whenever a student is at school no matter what the hour or the activity, that student is free to express his or her views as long as they do not

---

8. Tinker v. Des Moines Independent School District, 393 U.S. 503 (1969); 37 U.S. L.W. 4121 (February 24, 1969).

materially and substantially interfere with the operation of the school."

The wearing of an arm band was thus judged to be a form of symbolic speech and therefore permitted under the First Amendment, provided, as Justice Fortas expressed it, that the student do so "without materially interfering with appropriate discipline of the school and without colliding with the rights of others."

There are numerous methods of communication, some of which may be in conflict with school regulations. For example, handing out printed material at school without permission might get students in trouble. A court case arose over that very activity in Rippowan High School in Connecticut.

The Board of Education of Stamford, Connecticut, adopted this rule on November 18, 1969:

■   No person shall distribute any printed or written matter on the grounds of any school or in any school building unless the distribution of such material has been approved by the school administration.

When some students in the high school were denied permission to distribute copies of a mimeographed newspaper and some printed literature they had prepared, they filed suit against the Board of Education. In that case the Court decided that the rule was unconstitutional and that the School Board could not legally enforce it.[9]

The court held that the rule prohibiting the distribution of printed or written material without prior approval was too vague, that it provided no procedures for submitting material for approval, no time limit for the making of decisions, and no review procedure when permission was denied. In other

---

9. Eisner v. Stamford Board of Education, 440 F 2d 803 (2d Civ. Conn. 1971).

words, the court did not deny the Board of Education the right to establish rules governing the distribution of printed materials in the schools; rather it implied that such rules cannot be so general as to permit any kind of censorship or prohibition school authorities might choose to adopt.

In making that decision, the U.S. District Court judge stated, "The risk taken if a few students abuse their First Amendment rights of free speech and press is outweighed by the far greater risk run by suppressing free speech and press among the young."

In another case the Court also decided that a similar rule by the Chicago Board of Education imposed prior restraint in violation of the First Amendment and therefore was unconstitutional.[10] The rule required that "no person shall be permitted . . . to distribute on the school premises any books, tracts, or other publications . . . unless the same shall have been approved by the General Superintendent of Schools."

The case arose when two seniors at Lane Technical High School, Burt Fujishima and Richard Peluso, were suspended for distributing about 350 copies of an underground newspaper titled *The Cosmic Frog* free of charge between classes and during lunch breaks, and a sophomore named Robert Balanoff was suspended for giving another student an unsigned petition calling for "teach-ins" regarding the war in Vietnam. The three students filed suit against the Board of Education.

The court, in its decision in 1972, declared that the rule on distribution of materials in the school without permission was unconstitutional.[10] It indicated, however, that the Board of Education could establish reasonable regulations that stated specifically when, how, and where students could distribute literature; and it added that the Board could include a provision for punishing students who publish and disseminate any obscene or libelous material on the school grounds.

---

10. Fujishima v. Chicago Board of Education, 460 F 2d 1355 (7th Cir. 1972).

In a decision in 1940, the U.S. Supreme Court said students may be required to pledge allegiance to the flag.[11] Then three years later the Court reversed itself and decided that schools may not require students to pledge allegiance to the flag.

The first case arose after the Board of Education in Minersville, Pennsylvania, adopted a requirement that teachers and pupils repeat the pledge as part of a daily ritual. Among the pupils were William Gobitis, aged 12, and his sister Lillian Gobitis, aged 10. As Jehovah's Witnesses, the Gobitis family considered saluting the flag an act of idolatry and thus forbidden by their religion. After the two children refused to pledge allegiance to the flag, they were expelled from school.

The father filed suit; and when the U.S. Supreme Court heard the case, it balanced liberty of conscience against authority of the school board and decided by a vote of 8 to 1 in favor of the Board. In the majority opinion, Justice Felix Frankfurter stated that "flag salutes are indisputably within the exclusive province of the states. Any interference with educational officials on this score would make the Supreme Court the nation's school board."

In line with that decision, the West Virginia Board of Education adopted a regulation on January 9, 1942, requiring that the flag salute be a regular part of the program of activities in the public schools of that state. Here, again, a group of Jehovah's Witnesses objected and filed suit. The case went all the way to the U.S. Supreme Court where on June 14, 1943, the Court decided in favor of the Jehovah's Witnesses, setting aside mandatory flag salutes and reversing a decision made only three years earlier.[12]

---

11. Minersville School District v. Gobitis, 310 U.S. 586 (1940).
12. West Virginia v. Barnette, 319 U.S. 624 (June 14, 1943 — a decision handed down appropriately on Flag Day).

In the majority opinion, written by Justice Robert Jackson, the Court stated that freedom of mind is preferable to officially disciplined uniformity; that, although boards of education have vital functions, none may be performed in violation of the rights guaranteed by the Constitution, and that the right of free speech and the press and the right to worship are not subject to political or public vote. While the Court did not question the right of school officials to instill a sense of national unity through the schools, it questioned whether compulsory exercises such as saluting the flag are appropriate means for doing so. The opinion reads in part:

■ We think the action of the local authorities in compelling the flag salute and pledge transcends constitutional limitations on their power and invades the sphere of intellect and spirit which it is the purpose of the First Amendment of our Constitution to control . . .

If there is any fixed star in our constitutional constellation, it is that no official, high or petty, can prescribe what shall be orthodox in politics, nationalism, religion, or other matter of opinion, or force citizens to confess by word or act their faith therein.

Delicate problems can arise over student privacy. The Family Education Rights and Privacy Act gives some protection in regard to release of information; but the question may arise as to whether school officials may search student lockers for such articles as drugs, guns, and knives without violating students' rights under the Fourth Amendment. The courts have generally upheld the right of school officials to make such searches without court orders, provided that searches are reasonable. In a landmark decision in 1985,[13] the U.S. Supreme Court held that the Fourth Amendment does apply to searches of students by public officials, but the decision

---

13. New Jersey v. T. L. O., 105 S. Ct. 733 (1985).

supported school administrators who have a substantial interest in maintaining order and discipline in the schools.

In another case, a circuit court of appeals ruled in 1980 that using a dog to sniff lockers is legal, but strip searches are unreasonable, unconstitutional, and contrary to common decency.

Students have rights that do not stop at the schoolhouse door, but court decisions indicate that those rights are not absolute, that they are tempered by the authority and responsibility of school officials to direct an orderly and effective educational process without placing undue and unconstitutional restrictions on the rights of students.

CHAPTER
40

❀

COPYRIGHT PROTECTS
OWNERSHIP

COPYRIGHT PROTECTS OWNERSHIP

❋

As copyright gives its owner exclusive rights to reproduce, publish, and sell literary and artistic work, it can be regarded as a legal limitation on the right to read and to enjoy artistic expression. On the other hand, as copyright makes financial reward possible, it encourages the production of literary and artistic work.

Copyright is available for written material, whether it is printed or not, as well as for photographs, motion pictures, radio and television programs, music, song lyrics, poems, plays including pantomimes and choreography, sound recordings of all kinds, computer programs, maps, drawings, cartoons, sculpture, paintings, and similar art.[1]

The Copyright Law, which became effective on January 1, 1978, superseding the Copyright Law of 1909, gives legal protection to original literary, artistic, and musical work for the life of the author, artist, or composer plus 50 years. After that time the work is considered to be in the public domain, which means that anyone may use or reproduce it without permission. Plays by Shakespeare, essays by Montaigne, and

---

1. Copyright registrations are issued by the Registrar of Copyrights, Library of Congress, Washington, D. C. 20559. The fee is $10. Application forms may be obtained by writing to the Information Section LM-455. The Public Information Office telephone number is 202/707-3000.

poems by Robert Browning, authors who died many years ago, are examples of works in the public domain.

The copyright law applies to creative work by individuals, companies, and organizations but not to the government. Publications by the U.S. Government cannot be copyrighted. For example, the court decisions reproduced in this book are not copyrighted and were included without permission.

Public records have always been available to interested persons without cost and for use without permission, but that may change because government, especially some local and state governments, are discovering that public records and especially computerized records can be sold to data base firms that in turn sell the information to subscribers. Data base is a collection of information organized for rapid retrieval by computers.

To protect ownership, local governments may attempt to copyright their public records. In fact, the State Legislature of Colorado recently passed a law enabling the state to copyright all public information, according to an article in *Editor and Publisher* subtitled "the government trend to charge more and more for its electronic records is hampering the public's ability to acquire them."[2]

Among items that cannot be copyrighted are facts. That Mt. Everest is 29,028 feet high and is located on the border between Nepal and Tibet in Asia is not copyrightable, but a description of the mountain would be. The fact that the Mississippi River is 2,348 miles long cannot be copyrighted, but a story of one's trip on the River can be.

Ideas and beliefs cannot be copyrighted; the way they are expressed can be copyrighted. As one writer has explained, "Copyright laws protect the expression of ideas, not the ideas themselves."

---

2. *Editor and Publisher*, May 15, 1993, page 9.

News cannot be copyrighted. Such facts as when, where, and how of an accident, for example, the number of persons injured, and extent of damage, are facts available to everyone; but a newspaper can copyright its account of the accident. When it does so, it does not copyright the facts but rather its style of presentation.

Titles cannot be copyrighted, so a person is free to use the same title for a book, an article, or a song that someone else has already used without incurring legal liability.

Copyright registration gives the copyright owner greater legal protection in any litigation that may arise. An application for copyright registration is merely asking a government agency to note that a claim is being made to a particular piece of intellectual property. The copyright office does not make a search to determine whether the material is a duplication or is similar to other material that has been copyrighted. Also it does not set a standard of quality or excellence that a work must meet in order to receive copyright registration. What is submitted may be excellent or it may be inferior, but either receives the same copyright protection.

Fair use of copyrighted material is provided by law. An example of fair use would be a quotation from a copyrighted book to use in a review of that book, or it could be a quotation with proper acknowledgment in an article. The law also allows making one copy of copyrighted material, provided the purpose is educational and not commercial. In other words, it is illegal to reproduce anything that is copyrighted and then offer the reproductions for sale. That is known as copyright infringement.

In past years a number of books published and copyrighted in the United States have been reproduced in other countries, notably in the Orient, and then offered for sale at reduced prices. More recently numerous first-run movies, cassettes, and computer software, as well as books copyrighted in the U.S. have been copied in large numbers in Latin American countries south of the Rio Grande, and sold at cheap prices. The appropriation of such property without permission from or payment to the owners is known as literary piracy.

Patents for inventions and trademarks for products, although creative works, are different from copyrightable material. They are regulated by the U.S. Patent Office, an agency of the Department of Commerce.

INDEXES

❀

CASE INDEX
INDEX

579